Justice and the Human Good

William A. Galston
Justice and the Human Good

The University of Chicago Press

Chicago and London

WILLIAM A. GALSTON is an associate professor
in the Department of Government at the
University of Texas at Austin and is the author
of *Kant and the Problem of History*.

The University of Chicago Press, Chicago 60637
The University of Chicago Press, Ltd., London

©1980 by The University of Chicago
All rights reserved. Published 1980
Printed in the United States of America
84 83 82 81 80   9 8 7 6 5 4 3 2 1

Library of Congress Cataloging in Publication Data

Galston, William A.   1946—
  Justice and the human good.

  Includes index.
  1. Justice. 2. Worth. I. Title.
JC578.G34   340.1'1   79-25945
ISBN 0-226-27963-4

To my teachers, with gratitude and respect

Still pleased to teach, and yet not proud to know.
ALEXANDER POPE

Contents

Contents

Preface

In the past decade it has become evident that the obituary of political theory current in the 1950s was promulgated prematurely. Political theory, it seems, can be practiced without any sacrifice of philosophical integrity, and it must be practiced if the muddled but pressing political controversies of our time are to be clarified. But as the fog of all-embracing doubt has lifted, other difficulties have come into view.

First, there is the risk that in their enthusiasm to reoccupy the forbidden territory of substantive moral inquiry, theorists will go to the other extreme, forgetting the sensible caveats embedded in the excessive skepticism of the previous generation. The sophisticated appeal to shared moral consciousness that Rawls has made popular must be carried out with adequate awareness not only of cultural diversity but also of discordant voices within our own tradition. If not, moral consensus becomes thinly disguised ideology or a rhetorically effective exposition of individual prejudice. Second, a very considerable gap still exists between "Anglo–American" and "Continental" theorists. Attempts to develop a common vocabulary and agenda are not very far advanced, in spite of the Hegel revival in the Anglo–American world and the partial assimilation of ordinary language philosophy and empirical political inquiry in Europe. Characteristically, European theory views the domain of politics as a *historical totality*, while the dominant Anglo–American stance is *ahistorical individualism*. European theorists typically take Hegel and Marx as their points of departure, Anglo–Americans, the social contract tradition, Hume, Kant, and John Stuart Mill. Third, within the Anglo–American academic world, the subject matter of political inquiry is divided among separated, frequently warring "disciplines" whose differences are primarily generated by methodological predilections and accidents of intellectual history. To talk sensibly about politics, one is forced to touch on topics now parceled out among departments of economics, sociology, psychology, history, and philosophy, as well as political science.

In the course of this study I have tried to remain constantly aware of these problems, which have both a substantive and a rhetorical side. I do not flatter myself that I have overcome them. No doubt my effort to develop a coherent way of talking about moral questions by critically working through past doubts and present proposals will be found incomplete in important respects. My quasi-Aristotelian approach to political inquiry, which finds a place for individuality and totality, for temporal particularity and atemporal generality, will not convert determined partisans of established views. And in my attempt to deal comprehensively with the problem of justice, I have been forced to deal summarily with an enormous range of questions and body of literature. I strongly suspect that, all too frequently, I have stumbled on concepts and arguments already worked out with much greater sophistication in sectors of literature of which I am wholly unaware. I can only hope that I have rediscovered the wheel more often than phlogiston.

As will quickly become obvious to the reader, not only my stance but also my method of argument is somewhat Aristotelian. I examine the views of others, not as a display of erudition, but rather to discover the dimensions of the problems that interest me. I make extensive use of what seems to me true in these views. My originality, if any, lies in the arrangement and emphasis given to familiar concepts.

In addition, my procedure is dialectical. After advancing my own views, I state and respond to as many criticisms of them as I can find or devise. In criticizing the views of others, I frequently try to imagine how they would respond to my objections and in turn to reply to these new arguments. Every author must decide the extent to which the presentation of his argument will mirror the original process of discovery. If I have erred, it is in the direction of fidelity; it usually seemed to me that the process of discovery furnished an essential context of significance, in the absence of which my conclusions appeared dry and deracinated.

Finally, whether defending my own claims or criticizing those of others, I use a multiplicity of independent considerations that cannot be reduced to a single focal point. Philosophical reflection is, I believe, a kind of comprehensive structural description. When confronted with a problem, it is best to circumnavigate it, reporting everything of significance one sees along the way. Like physical objects, philosophical problems have different qualities and dimensions, each describable in different terms, the totality of which constitutes their truth insofar as it can be known. To stop short, to be incomplete, is to risk being seduced into a false reduction determined largely by the initial subjective direction of one's particular interests. It is, I suspect, the reductionist impulse, a necessary ingredient of the theoretical enterprise, that leads to serious error, if unchecked, by inducing us to distort some facts while overlooking others entirely. To counteract this, we must remain as open as we can to the objects of our inquiry as they present themselves. We can avoid dangerous folly, establish the context and limit of significance, only through the patient accumulation of the obvious. In part, this is what George Orwell meant when he remarked that "the restatement of the obvious is the first duty of intelligent men."

The substantive strategy of this book is simple. Drawing on the recent revival of ethical naturalism, I have combined a quasi-Aristotelian view of the human good with Aristotle's formal analysis of justice as proportionality and have applied the resulting material principles to the different categories of distributional questions that arise in the course of everyday political controversies. In comparison with other recent theorists, this orientation places me at a grave disadvantage. To the best of my knowledge, there is no Aristotelian regime, party, or movement in need of intellectual refurbishing that will hail me as its spokesman. My anachronistic choice of mentors must, it appears, condemn my efforts to irrelevance, however interesting they may be as an intellectual exercise.

For reasons stemming from my sense of political theory and of our current situation, I am not sure matters will turn out that way. This book is not a slavish transcription of Aristotle; it is not even, strictly speaking, updated Aristotelianism. Rather, it is an attempt, inspired by Aristotle, to think about contemporary problems from a perspective that differs from both contemporary orthodoxies and heterodoxies. I hope to be able to show that although our ruling *ideas* are anything but Aristotelian, many of our *experiences* and *intuitions* are. Making this tension explicit may highlight the sources of the dissatisfaction many feel with inherited political ideas and point toward a more satisfactory resolution of some of the vexing conundrums of modern political life.

Composing the first draft of this book was a painfully solitary act, but in revising it for publication I have been blessed with a number of patient and perspicacious critics. Charles Beitz, Alan Gewirth, and Patrick Riley provided searching prepublication reviews that led me to recast and clarify much of my argument. Their willingness to consider, and to suggest improvements in, theses with which they fundamentally disagreed reflected a scrupulous fairness for which I shall always be grateful. Joe Oppenheimer called my attention to the contradiction between Aristotelian proportionality and Pareto-optimality and acutely identified a number of logical gaps in my argument. Susan Meld Shell induced me to reconsider the extent to which the full development of each individual within a community is compatible with the development of all the others and correctly suggested that I had allowed intuitive judgments to play an unnecessarily large role as I applied my general theory to specific cases.

The Department of Government of the University of Texas at Austin provides its members with a diverse and stimulating group of colleagues, many of whom have materially contributed to the development of my thoughts, in ways of which they may not be fully aware. I am indebted to James Miller, James Schmidt, and Thomas Schwartz for taking the time to read the initial draft of this manuscript, wholly or in part, and for making innumerable useful suggestions. I am especially indebted to Harrison Wagner for his careful reading and generous willingness to spend hour after hour discussing it with me, in the process providing me with what must be described as an education.

Finally, I would like to thank the University of Texas Conference on Social Thought and the political theorists at Boston College for affording me the opportunity to present pieces of various drafts to them. The friendly but vigorous criticism I received on both occasions helped me recognize that many of my assumptions urgently required a more adequate defense, which I have subsequently endeavored to supply.

1
Introduction

The susceptibility of intellectual life to fads is a perennial scandal. It would be unwise, however, to dismiss the recent explosion of interest in the question of justice as merely the latest of them. Unlike many problems debated heatedly but fleetingly, justice is both theoretically meaningful and practically important. Its thematic reemergence is, moreover, linked to recent fundamental political changes that are likely to constitute our situation for some time to come. The crumbling of ideological certainty all along the political spectrum has revived demands for public, practical philosophy that offers intelligible judgments about political means and ends. Regimes based on liberal principles tolerate vast inequalities of wealth and income and neglect the welfare of large numbers of their citizens; Marxist regimes with varying orientations restrict political participation, repress dissent, and surreptitiously reintroduce class divisions. Concerned thinkers everywhere are seeking standards for evaluating these and related phenomena. Equally important, the long-standing belief in untrammeled growth has been overlaid by the fear that we are running up against limits. Accordingly, politics, national and international, is increasingly regarded as revolving around classic distributional questions.

Since the Greeks, justice has been linked to the "common good": a conception of justice identifies a generally advantageous mode of cooperative collective existence. But the common good, so conceived, is doubly ambiguous. First, although cooperation—the willingness to share a common fate with others—frequently leaves all parties better off than they would have been without cooperation, sometimes it does not. In the name of the common good or of justice, some individuals, groups, or nations are called on to make sacrifices for the sake of others. This gives rise to the skepticism and cynicism depicted at the beginning of the *Republic*, and the problem recurs in every subsequent serious discussion. Rawls has no trouble showing that the "least advantaged" will gladly embrace the Difference Principle, but (as he admits) it is more difficult to convince those with superior natural gifts or socioeconomic positions that they have no cause to resist it.[1] Second, in the happy situations in which cooperation can make everyone better off, the criterion of the common good does not tell us how the benefits of cooperation are to be divided.

Hobbes's theory seeks to abolish these ambiguities. Justice is political cooperation, which always leaves everyone better off in the decisive respect; quarrels over the division of benefits from cooperation lack rational foundation and, when pressed forcefully, reduce or annihilate the benefits. The individual who denies justice in the name of self-interest is a fool and, if reckless, a dangerous fool. The difficulty, of course, is that to achieve this clarification Hobbes's theory is compelled to offer a questionable, protoemotivist account of moral discourse and to advance a radically simplified theory of value that subordinates the quality of existence to the fact of existence and denies that there is any rational trade-off between them. Clearly this lexical ordering does not describe human behavior, and one may well doubt its adequacy as a standard of behavior.

Human beings advance and seek to further their claims to what they think to be good. The conflict among these claims, typically reflecting agreement about what is good, is the perennial experience that gives rise to the concern about justice. There is, of course, no guarantee that philosophy can requite this concern. In varying proportions, force, rhetoric, and habit have prevailed whenever philosophy offered no answers or could not contrive to put them into effect.

Within political communities, individuals advance claims both against other individuals and against the collectivity. The evaluation of these claims presupposes a theoretical examination of the relation between the individual and the community. Historically, two implausibly extreme characterizations of this relation have been advanced. *Hyperorganicism* devalues individual subjectivity and particularity, hypostatizing the community as a unified entity. This is the focus of Aristotle's critique of the *Republic,* summed up in the remark that, while an even number may be the sum of odd numbers, it makes no sense to talk of the well-being of the community apart from the well-being of its members. Not only do we retain separate pleasures and pains, benefits and harms, but also a guiding purpose of the political community is the preservation and improvement of the individuals who comprise it. The way of life enjoyed by individuals is a crucial measure of the quality of the community. The same issue figures in the existentialist critique of Hegel and of orthodox Marxism, amusingly exemplified in a story told by Simone de Beauvoir.

Toward the end of the afternoon, sitting on the grass next to Queneau, I had a discussion with him about the "end of history." It was a frequent subject of conversation at the time. We had discovered the reality and weight of history, now we were wondering about its meaning. Queneau, who had been initiated into Hegelianism by Kojève, thought that one day all individuals would be reconciled in the triumphant unity of Spirit. "But what if I have a pain in my foot?" I said. "*We* shall have a pain in your foot," Queneau replied.[2]

A similar intention motivates Rawls's charge that utilitarianism does not take seriously the separateness of individual existences.

The other extreme, *hyperindividualism*, overemphasizes the separateness of individuals, focusing on the claims or "rights" they can assert without considering their effects on other individuals or on the nature and very possibility of the political community. This orientation leads to self-refuting excesses like Nozick's concept of rights as absolute "side-constraints" blocking legitimate coercion of particular individuals, whatever the consequences of this prohibition for the collective welfare, even when welfare is defined as maximizing the extent to which individuals in the collectivity enjoy immunity from coercion.

Rights-based hyperindividualism comes to grief when it is forced to confront the fact that, in a broad sense, every political community is a welfare state and that welfare is an aggregate function sensitive to, though not determined by, the level of well-being enjoyed by the members of the community. Disputes arise both about the definition of human welfare and about the most appropriate or efficacious ways of obtaining it. In practice, a surprising degree of agreement about ends prevails; most political disputes center on means. It makes no sense, then, to consider principles of justice in isolation from the interests of those whose lives they regulate. This injunction need not commit us to a simple teleological view of justice, but it does mean that strict deontology is almost sure to go astray. *Fiat iustitia, pereat mundus* cannot be correct, for no principle that would cause the world to perish could possibly be just.

In recent thought, two different kinds of strategies have been employed in the attempt to give moral weight to, and to reconcile, the competing claims of individuals and the collectivity. The first is *monistic*. Taking their cue from Mill's discussion of justice, utilitarians have attempted to derive individual rights from long-run considerations of collective welfare. In the same spirit, but with opposite intent, theorists such as Ronald Dworkin have sought to derive collective welfare from an analysis of the conditions necessary to maximize rights and to render them effective and enforceable. The second strategy is *pluralistic*, taking individual and collective considerations as mutually irreducible. One kind of pluralism is intuitionism: the rights of the individual are balanced against the welfare of the community on a case-by-case basis.

1. Introduction

There is no general principle under which the cases can be subsumed, but at most an intuition about the appropriate shape of the indifference curve. Another kind of pluralism is offered by Rawls: Individual rights constrain the criterion of collective welfare but are themselves constrained by the requirements of collective agreement and by the rational decision to consider natural abilities of individuals as "collective assets" rather than as bases for individual claims.

In many ways Rawls's approach appears to be the most promising. The competing monisms are clever but unpersuasive and artificial, while intuitionistic pluralism seems at best an elegant restatement of the problem, at worst a confession of philosophic defeat. I believe, however, that Rawls, like all contract theorists, has a defective understanding of the relation between the individual and the political community. Contract theories see free, independent, fully formed individuals deliberating about the kinds of mutual connections and limitations to which they should severally agree. Each individual, considering personal interest in the context of a general understanding of the empirical requirements of physical and material security, comes to regard as advantageous the sort of association we call *political*. But if these empirical requirements happen to be different, there is no reason to agree to enter into the political community.

This understanding of the political community crucially affects the way Rawls poses the question of justice. He distinguishes between obligations, all of which "are accounted for by the principle of fairness," and natural duties: "In contrast with obligations, it is characteristic of natural duties that they apply to us without regard to our voluntary acts."[3]

Justice is not composed of natural duties, because the content of principles of justice is defined by a specific kind of voluntary act: "A group of persons must decide once and for all what is to count among them as just and unjust. The choice which rational men would make in [a] hypothetical situation of equal liberty . . . determines the principles of justice."[4]

This characterization of justice is questionable, for two reasons. First, I would argue, it rests on a mistaken view of the political community. Political life has an important "natural" component. We are, as Aristotle suggested, beings so constituted that we can achieve development and satisfaction only within a political community. For this reason, it is misleading to see the political community as entirely produced by choice or agreement, in the manner of a business contract. The error is in no way mitigated if the contract is viewed as a theoretical reconstruction rather than as a historical actuality or practical requirement. As human beings, our separate existences are linked in important ways prior to our application of reason and will to the construction of a common life. If this is so, then it is necessary to explore the ways in which justice, the chief virtue of communities, expresses these links—that is, the extent to which justice must be conceived of as consisting of natural duties. I shall argue that the basic principles of justice can be adequately understood in this manner.

Second, Rawls's approach rests on a dubious epistemological claim about principles of justice. We do not seek answers to mathematical puzzles by asking what various individuals would assent to. Rather, the independently determined answer serves as the criterion of rational assent. Of course, if the answer is correct we usually assume that a rational individual with the requisite background knowledge can be led to agree. Similarly, if a proposed principle is just, we may believe that a rational individual would assent to it, but there is no a priori reason to assume that the assent is the source of justification for the principle. As David Lyons observes, to the extent that Rawls's argument is contractarian, it seems to assume that no alternate mode of argument leading to an independent criterion of justice is possible.[5] But there is no reason to believe that this is the case, especially in light of Rawls's assertion that many kinds of moral principles rest on noncontractarian grounds.

Let me now sketch the analysis of justice I present and defend in this book.

In its primary meaning, justice characterizes states of affairs, *situations*. Just acts and just human beings are those that tend to bring just situations into being. The situation with which justice is concerned consists in an ensemble of possessive relations. In a possessive relation, the individual is treated as at least analytically distinct from the object or mode of treatment that he controls, appropriates, or enjoys. Justice, then, may be defined as *rightful possession*. To possess something rightfully is to hold it in accordance with one's entitlement or valid claims. A claim is a basis or reason for having something that stands in a rational relation to that thing. A valid claim is any claim not dominated by others in the context in which it is advanced.

There are two fundamental kinds of valid claims— need and desert. *Need* is defined as lack of the ensemble of means needed to realize the human goods of preservation and development. *Desert* rests on the possession of some quality that places an individual in a preferred position relative to some good. Need contains an important universal element, while the content of desert is highly dependent on context.

Rights, considered by some as an independent kind of valid claim, are at most a kind of shorthand for other sorts of moral and prudential reasons.

1. Introduction

The theory of justice contains, as an indispensable element, an independent theory of the individual human good. General distributional principles are vacuous without some determinate concept of what benefits and what harms individuals; such principles and the theory of individual good are mutually irreducible, neither being entailed by the other. Since there are relational goods—relations of fitness or appropriateness—as well as individual goods, justice does not stand in any simple teleological relation to the individual good. Since there are no means that are good in all situations and quantities or for all purposes, individual good is an ensemble of ends in light of which different possible means are seen as desirable in varying circumstances.

Valid claims differ quantitatively as well as qualitatively. Usually each claimant will have a valid claim to some extent. Thus, distribution in accordance with claims implies distribution in proportion to claims. This conclusion, the Aristotelian principle of proportional justice, can be shown to be entailed by a small number of weak postulates.

The content of proportional justice is affected by three kinds of variables. First, allocable goods are divided into different categories: economic goods—income, property, productive tasks; opportunities for development; political goods—citizenship and positions of leadership or authority; and recognition goods—honor, status, prestige. Each of these categories brings into play a distinctive ensemble of claims.

Second, distributive principles are affected in important ways by the overall level of allocable goods, that is, by scarcity and abundance. This is the case because some claims—in particular, those based on needs—are expressed in absolute rather than relative terms. The arguments of Hume and Rawls that the problem of justice would altogether disappear in circumstances of abundance are incorrect, since it may be unjust for an individual to possess some good even if no one else is thereby deprived of the opportunity to possess the same or equivalent good. Even if Hume and Rawls were correct, the problem of justice will not disappear even under the most favorable circumstances, since some "positional" goods—leadership, public honor—are intrinsically scarce.

Third, it is customary to conceive of distributive principles as applicable within particular human communities. As Aristotle put it, "The just in political matters is found among men who share a common life in order that their association bring them self-sufficiency . . . the just exists only among men whose mutual relationship is regulated by law."[6] But this conception is subject to three qualifications. There are relations of justice, economic and political, among different political communities whose interactions are not regulated by law at all, or regulated only imperfectly. There are relations of justice between present and future generations, even though future generations cannot articulate their claims against us and cannot press them through political and legal mechanisms binding on us. Finally, there are relations of justice between human beings and nonhuman animals, even though animals cannot participate in the political community or apprehend the law as a system backed by moral authority as well as by force and habit.

Having sketched my argument, let me now briefly indicate how the parts of this book fit together and contribute to it. Chapter 2 opens with a description of the "utopian" component of political theory and proceeds to defend utopian theory against various types of objections. The most serious of these rest, I argue, on skepticism about the possibility of moral theory as a rational enterprise. Eschewing further methodological debate, I offer an analysis of some contemporary attempts to renovate moral theory. The purpose of this analysis is to uncover various points of departure that seem correct or suggestive, as a foundation for my own argument.

Chapter 3 begins by sketching the role of a theory of the good in an overall theory of justice and indicating some general features that all elements of the human good must share. I argue that when we examine the intuitive view of the human good that comes into play whenever justice is substantively discussed, four distinct elements emerge: the worth of self-preservation; the worth of developed existence; the worth of happiness (viewed as subjective satisfaction); and the worth of rational action. While exploring these elements and trying to provide a foundation for them, I examine the arguments of Plato, Aristotle, Hobbes, Kant, and Sartre. In a final section, the elements of the good are brought together, revealing both tensions among them and some basis for rank-ordering them. I argue that the judgments we make reflect the interaction of two very different ordering principles—intrinsic worth and urgency. In a brief appendix I explore and reject the contention that freedom, however defined, constitutes an autonomous element of the human good.

Chapter 4 seeks to describe the domain of justice. It characterizes the kinds of goods and problems with which justice deals and argues that the benchmark or measure of justice is the way of life enjoyed by the individuals affected by allocative decisions or by events with allocative consequences. To accomplish this, the concept of *distribution* is explored in considerable detail. Next I examine the relation between scarcity and justice, looking first at the problem of defining scarcity, then at the suggestions of Hume, Rawls, and Rescher. I then discuss the issue of how to specify what Brian Barry calls *reference groups*. The existence of separate political communities raises the very general question of whether individuals within a particular community are morally justified in treating themselves preferentially. The existence of nonhuman living creatures raises the question of whether we are free to use them as pure instruments. I argue that restrictions on the human use of animals flow from the fact that animals have interests that we cannot consistently ignore. Finally, I explore and reject recent attempts to renovate the concept of rights as the basis for a theory of justice, and I discuss the implications of this negative finding for the possibility of defending nonutilitarian theories.

Chapter 5 brings together the results of the preceding chapters to define formal and material principles of justice. The formal principle of justice, Aristotle's principle of allocation in proportion to claims, is defended both deductively and from the standpoint of moral intuition. Next I examine critically some recent egalitarian arguments, focusing on Vlastos's view of the equality of individual worth and proposals, advanced by Rawls and Gewirth, in favor of quantitative thresholds for key qualities, above which differences are morally irrelevant. Rejecting these, I propose and defend two principles: equality of consideration of all interests, which turns out to be little more than the requirement of impartiality; and the equal worth of the full development of each individual. I then turn to the material principles that form the basis of my theory—need and desert. Need is advanced as the claim on the totality of means required to realize the human goods of self-preservation and development, and the plausibility and utility of this view is defended against various criticisms. After defining desert in general terms and indicating its dependence on context, I trace the relation between desert and the principle of equality of opportunity. I defend equality of opportunity, understood in a restricted sense, against the vehement objections of Michael Young, John Schaar, and Robert Nozick.

Chapter 6 applies the principle of proportionality, combined with the substantive claims of need and desert and the general view of the human good, to the four major kinds of allocable goods: economic goods, opportunities for development, political goods, and honor. In each case a complex combination of claims emerges as relevant. Running through the discussion are problems stemming from the simple fact that every human act has two dimensions—effects on the agent, and effects on the external world of nature and other human beings. Justice requires that we keep both dimensions constantly in view. In our concern for the individual, we cannot forget that the individual is embedded in a system of production, collective decisionmaking institutions, and an ensemble of social relations. At the same time, we cannot forget that collective arrangements are primarily instrumental and that the ultimate measure of policies and institutions is their effect on the totality of individual lives.

Chapter 7 briefly explores some of the implications of this analysis for

three very general areas: the relation between justice and democracy; the worth of justice—our motive for choosing justice rather than injustice; and the incompleteness of any theory of justice, embedded as it is, implicitly or explicitly, in a more comprehensive view of a desirable human existence.

Robert Nozick has remarked that the eminence of John Rawls's theory is such that "political philosophers now must either work within [it] or explain why not."[7] As a description of a rhetorical situation Nozick is surely correct; Rawls's theory is widely known and admired and for many has come to serve as a point of reference. I offer the following brief remarks, therefore, in the hope that the essential features of my position will become clearer if I identify some of the major points at which it diverges from that of Rawls.

First, as Ronald Dworkin has persuasively argued, the Rawlsian contractual situation, the original position, appeals to and gains its moral force from an underlying assumption of "a natural right of all men and women to equality of concern and respect."[8] However congenial this principle may be to contemporary tastes, it cannot, I shall later argue, be accepted without qualifications that would significantly alter Rawls's conclusions.

Second, Rawls correctly maintains that a theory of justice requires an independent theory of the "good." But his interpretation of the good as "primary goods," universal means, is inadequate and untenable. Rawlsian primary goods are not neutral among life plans, and, as Rawls eventually concedes, it is *not* rational to choose to increase one's supply of them regardless of what one already possesses. Further, the primary goods thesis makes it theoretically impossible to consider the varying effects that the identical means may have on different individuals. But these effects are crucial. The sick need more than the healthy, the threatened more than the secure, in order to achieve the end-states that all desire. In my own theory, therefore, need is a crucial category, and it is defined relative to a substantive interpretation of the human good as an ensemble of end-states rather than means. Rawls's rejection of this as "perfectionism" rests on a caricature of the perfectionist position and on the unproved contention that no substantive theory of the human good can be defended.[9]

Third, I argue systematically against Rawls's contention that desert plays no independent role in a theory of economic and political distribution. It may be useful to enumerate some implications of my reliance on need and desert as the two basic categories of claims.

1. It is widely felt that neither strict equality nor unbridled inequality is acceptable as the outcome of proposed principles of justice. Rawls's theory gains much of its intuitive force by limiting inequality without

delegitimating it. Taken together, need and desert point in the same direction. "Need" expresses what we have in common with others, while "desert" gives weight to what distinguishes us from others. Need points toward equality (of end-states, not holdings), while desert allows for, though does not require, inequality. The interplay of these two kinds of claims permits us to synthesize the competing experiences of human similarity and difference to which Aristotle traces the most intractable political controversies.[10]

2. Nozick's distinction between end-state and historical principles has struck a responsive chord, as has his insistence that our moral intuitions do not allow us to overlook the latter. But Nozick's demand that we altogether abandon end-state considerations is warranted by neither intuition nor argument. In my theory, need expresses the force of end-state considerations, while desert, suitably interpreted, gives content to historical principles. A community that can but does not satisfy the needs of all its members is unjust, no matter how this situation has come about. But equally unjust is a community that overlooks specific acts of acquisition or differences of contribution and effort. "To each according to need" is a necessary but not sufficient condition of justice.

3. Justice is frequently distinguished from humanitarian principles. We are, it is said, morally required to rescue a drowning child and, by extension, to avert starvation in poor countries, but it is not justice that requires us to do so. Justice is an obligation that links specific individuals to one another, while humanity or beneficence are generalized duties. We do wrong to ignore the dictates of beneficence, but no particular potential beneficiary can claim our aid as a right.

In my view, this distinction is of limited importance and will not bear much weight. In many situations—for example, the drowning child—there is only one relevant potential beneficiary. You wrong *that* child by not going to its aid; that child's situation makes certain claims on you, directly. Further, the existence of multiple potential beneficiaries does not imply that you may behave just as you like to any one of them in particular. Beneficence is regulated by distributive considerations. If you encounter two starving men and could provide each of them with enough nourishment to avert death but instead, using the same resources, treat one to a banquet while leaving the other to die, you have wronged the one you ignored.

In my theory, justice encompasses all the considerations that exert a moral influence on distribution, including those usually treated under the rubric of beneficence. Need is a claim-engendering feature of individuals. To leave needs unsatisfied through choice or neglect is to ignore specific claims we ought to honor and is thus to behave unjustly.[11]

4. Need and desert are the bases of entitlements. But it does not follow that holdings are necessarily unjust if they do not correspond to entitlements. To be entitled to *x* is to have a valid claim to use *x*. But you may decide for some reason not to press your claim or to transfer it to someone else through exchange or donation. Nozick is partly right. Within limits (to be discussed later) the transformation of entitlements through voluntary acts preserves the justice that initially prevailed. If we encounter a very able and hardworking but unusually poor individual, it makes a difference whether he is a farmworker or a member of some monastic order. Justice requires us to focus on entitlements and to inquire into the causes of divergences between entitlements and holdings. Some divergences signal the existence of unjust states of affairs; others do not. Thus, in Nozick's terms, while my conception of valid claims or entitlements is wholly "patterned," my conception of appropriate holdings is not.

I conclude this introduction by noting an unresolved difficulty in my undertaking. Reflecting on the recent neo-Aristotelian revival in practical philosophy, Jürgen Habermas remarks that "the ethics and politics of Aristotle are unthinkable without the connection to physics and metaphysics, in which the basic concepts of form, substance, act, potency, final cause, and so forth are developed." But, he continues, "today it is no longer easy to render the approach of this metaphysical mode of thought plausible."[12] Leo Strauss, whom Habermas identifies as a major figure in this revival, points to the same difficulty:

> Natural right in its classic form is connected with a teleological view of the universe. All natural beings have a natural end, a natural destiny, which determines what kind of operation is good for them. In the case of man, reason is required for discerning these operations: reason determines what is by nature right with ultimate regard to man's natural end. The teleological view of the universe, of which the teleological view of man forms a part, would seem to have been destroyed by modern natural science.[13]

There are two possible responses to this difficulty. The first is to sever practical philosophy from theoretical philosophy, restricting the former to a self-contained exploration of consciousness, opinions, decisions, or acts. This strategy, the most popular in our time, is hardly confined to neo-Aristotelians. Rawls begins by characterizing his analysis of justice as "a theory of the moral sentiments" that must be consistent with a "definite if limited class of facts"—our "considered judgments."[14] But he unhesitatingly appropriates Kant's conviction that a person chooses moral principles as " the most adequate possible expression of his nature as a free and equal rational being"—without, however, finding it necessary either to endorse or to reconstruct the theoretical arguments Kant used to make plausible this characterization of human nature.[15] Rawls's procedure is symptomatic of the necessary failure of the severing strategy. No investigation of the practical sphere can move beyond description to normative conclusions without appealing to some notion of human nature (or of human existence), which must then be supported by theoretical arguments.

It seems, then, that those who find Aristotle's practical philosophy an appealing point of departure must recognize the need for some theoretical commitments. Whether these must be an endorsement of Aristotelian physics and metaphysics is uncertain, in part because the logical relations between Aristotle's theoretical and practical philosophy have not been definitively clarified. One may, for example, grant that they are mutually consistent while wondering whether his theoretical philosophy is the only possible foundation for his ethics. The former may be sufficient for the latter without being necessary.

In the discussion that follows, this problem will not be resolved. Much of what I say is influenced by Kant's distinction between intrinsic and extrinsic teleology. Briefly, intrinsic teleology characterizes the internal relations among the various parts and processes of an organized entity, while extrinsic teleology characterizes functional/ hierarchical relations among different (kinds of) entities. My analysis of the human good views human beings as specific kinds of intrinsically teleological entities, but I find it neither necessary nor useful to introduce the extrinsic teleological contentions that figure so prominently in the opening arguments of the *Politics*.

I do not prove that the concept of intrinsic teleology is either internally coherent or compatible with the methods and results of scientific inquiry. I hope to have more to say about these matters at a later date.[16] For now, I can argue only that this order of inquiry is not question-begging; it makes sense to begin by establishing a fact before seeking to explain it. Kant exhibited what he took to be examples of synthetic a priori propositions before investigating the grounds of their possibility. Similarly, to the extent that the theory I offer in these pages is appealing, regressing to the theoretical ground of its possibility becomes interesting and unavoidable.

2
Utopian Thought and Moral Philosophy

One of the main virtues of Rawls's *Theory of Justice* is his reliance on a concept of "ideal theory." Ideal theory has a special object: a human association, all of whose members are just, that enjoys favorable material circumstances. Ideal theory in Rawls's sense is, to employ the traditional term, *utopian:* its object is a vision of the comprehensively good human association. It has, further, a particular epistemological status. It is presumed to be impartial, atemporal, and general, conceived in abstraction from specific social circumstances. The theory of justice in the full sense is the set of distributive principles appropriate to the association that forms the object of ideal theory, although it is intended to serve as a standard for judgment and action in nonideal circumstances as well, those of material scarcity or individual injustice.[1]

Its advantages notwithstanding, Rawls's presentation of ideal theory suffers from two defects. First, it tends to suggest that the distributive principles appropriate to nonideal circumstances are somehow less *just* than those suited to the ideal. This is surely a mistake. To be just is to behave appropriately within given circumstances, whatever their character. The punishment of wrongdoers is not less just than the blissful repose of the judge with no defendants in the docket; the abandonment of the "priority of liberty" in conditions of scarcity is as just as adhering to it in the midst of material sufficiency. Of course, justice becomes less attractive as its circumstances deteriorate; punishment is a disagreeable necessity. Only in ideal circumstances is justice unqualifiedly choiceworthy. Justice is good, but it is hardly the whole of the political or human good.

Second, Rawls is insufficiently explicit about the nature of ideal or utopian theory, in part because he is so confident of its possibility and utility. Although his confidence is, I shall argue, ultimately warranted, his presentation suffers from his failure to recognize, let alone respond to, the various objections that have been leveled against the entire tradition of utopian theory and especially against the epistemological status it claims.

In this chapter I shall begin by defending utopian theory as the most appropriate procedure for political philosophy, by cataloguing and responding to the most important objections. I shall then examine some recent attempts to renovate moral philosophy as a basis for utopian theory. This conception of the role of moral philosophy can be traced back to Aristotle and is, I shall argue, essentially correct. Thus, the purpose of my critical examination is to identify what usable contributions recent thinkers have made to an enterprise whose validity I endorse and whose character determines the theoretical structure of this book.

2.1. The Problem of Utopian Thought

Most human action is both conscious and purposive. These two elements do not coexist harmoniously; consciousness dissolves our immediate, unreflective purposive certainty, leaving doubt and irresolution. Moral philosophy is the vector sum of the destruction of immediate purposes and our enduring need for grounds of action. It seeks to provide reflective grounds capable of withstanding skeptical corrosion. Utopian thought is the political branch of moral philosophy, so conceived.

Utopias are images of ideal communities; utopian thought tries to make explicit and to justify the principles on the basis of which such communities are held to be ideal. For example, the *Republic* contains both the image of a class-divided community and a defense of the principles of specialization and meritocracy that underlie that division. In my view, the philosophic importance of utopias rests on utopian thought, although the practical effect of a utopia may be quite independent of its philosophic merits.

Utopian thought performs three related political functions. First, it guides our deliberation, whether in devising courses of action or in choosing among exogenously defined alternatives with which we are confronted. Second, it justifies our actions; the grounds of action are reasons that others ought to accept and—given openness and the freedom to reflect—can be led to accept. Third, it serves as the basis for the evaluation of existing institutions and practices. The *locus classicus* is the *Republic*, in which the completed ideal is deployed in Plato's memorable critique of imperfect regimes.

Until the end of the eighteenth century nearly all political theory contained an overtly utopian element. In the aftermath of the French Revolution, utopian thought came under attack from powerful forces, revolutionary and conservative. Burke's redefinition of the theory/practice relation led him to view all utopian theories as dangerous falsifications. Hegel's attack on the Kantian "ought" or "bad infinity" in the name of "actuality," understood teleologically, was ratified and popularized in the classical Marxist distinction between utopian and scientific socialism. The shattering events that followed Stalin and Hitler's accession to power produced another wave of antiutopian thinking, including Popper, Niebuhr, and the celebrants of the "end of ideology." The brief spasm of utopian thought and action in the 1960s seems, as its most enduring legacy, to have resuscitated Burke's opposition to the political influence of general ideas and their purveyors: whence neoconservatism and such cautionary tracts as Moynihan's *Maximum Feasible Misunderstanding*.

Many commentators have greeted the decline of utopian thought with equanimity if not satisfaction. I cannot, because I am convinced that no political theory that seeks to be practical can dispense with it. Thus, utopian thought comes to lead a covert existence in antiutopian theories that preserve a practical intention. Marx assumed the validity of many "bourgeois" principles as the basis of his critique of bourgeois politics and society.[2] In all such cases, the critique of utopian thought cannot abolish it but rather replaces explicit, systematic reflection on its characteristic themes with tacit and ungrounded assumptions.

The contention that utopian thought is a necessary condition of practical theory is hardly an adequate defense; there is no a priori guarantee that practical theory is possible. We must, then, directly confront the critique of utopian thought. In the following remarks I shall sketch what I take to be the most plausible account of utopian thought, the main features of which are Aristotelian, and then consider the major arguments against it. I conclude that these arguments are unpersuasive. Some are incoherent; some, though valid in themselves, are directed against a caricature of utopian thought; some raise important doubts but are far from proving their case.

2.2. The Elements of Utopian Thought

Utopian thought attempts to specify and justify the principles of a comprehensively good political order. Typically, the goodness of that order rests on the desirability of the way of life enjoyed by the individuals within it; less frequently, its merits rely on organic features that cannot be reduced to individuals. Whatever their basis, the principles of the political good share certain general features.

First, utopian principles are in their intention universally valid, temporally and geographically.

Second, the idea of the good order arises out of our experience but does not mirror it in any simple way and is not circumscribed by it. Imagination may combine elements of experience into a new totality that has never existed; reason, seeking to reconcile the contradictions of experience, may transmute its elements.

Third, utopias exist in speech; they are "cities of words." This does not mean that they cannot exist but only that they need not ever. This "counterfactuality" of utopia in no way impedes its evaluative function.

Fourth, utopian principles may come to be realized in history, and it may be possible to point to real forces pushing in that direction. But our approval of a utopia is not logically linked to the claim that history is bringing us closer to it or that we can identify an existing basis for the transformative actions that would bring it into being. Conversely, history cannot by itself validate principles. The movement of history (if it is a meaningful totality in any sense at all) may be from the more desirable to the less; the proverbial dustbin may contain much of enduring worth.

Fifth, although not confined to actual existence, the practical intention of utopia requires that it be constrained by possibility. Utopia is realistic in that it assumes human and material preconditions that are neither logically nor empirically impossible, even though their simultaneous copresence may be both unlikely and largely beyond human control to effect.

Sixth, although utopia is a *guide for* action, it is not in any simple sense a *program of* action. In nearly all cases, important human or material preconditions for good politics will be lacking. Political practice consists in striving for the best results achievable in particular circumstances. The relation between the ideal and the best achievable is not deductive. The ideal order is, like all political orders, multidimensional. In pursuing two or more of these dimensions most practical situations will require some trade-off among them, the most appropriate terms of which cannot in any simple way be derived from our idea of perfection. Further, the complexity and constant novelty of problems precludes any attempt to use this idea as the basis for a comprehensive and infallible manual of technical procedures. This is not to say that some generalizations may not be well entrenched. Thus, the incompleteness of utopia, far from constituting a criticism of it, is inherent in precisely the features that give it evaluative force. As has been recognized at least since Aristotle, the gap between utopian principles and specific strategic/tactical programs can be bridged only through an inquiry different in kind and content from that leading to the principles themselves. If so, the demand that utopian thought contain within itself the conditions of its actualization leads to a sterile hybrid that is neither an adequate basis for rational evaluation nor an accurate analysis of existing conditions.[3]

2.3. Objections to Utopian Thought
2.3.a. First class of objections: "Transcendence" is impossible
The external determination of thought

Utopian thought presupposes that reason is transcendent in the sense that it has a distinctive activity and telos that it pursues without being determined by (though of course always under the influence of) external forces. But, it is argued, we know that reason is so determined. This familiar thesis has taken many forms, corresponding to the variety of conditioning forces: linguistic categories; the invisible horizon of the historical situation; the psychological impulses—passion, desire, interest, the unconscious—that dominate reason.

No one can doubt that all thought begins by being situated. The question is whether these original limits can be breached. Plato's *Symposium* offers the classic vision of transcendence, but that dialogue, and perhaps every Platonic dialogue, is a comedy of the conditioned. Each participant begins with unexamined beliefs and erotic desires that structure the thesis he defends. The conversion of these conditions into speech creates the possibility of overcoming them.

The conditionality of all thought cannot be maintained as a universal thesis because its self-referential character is incompatible with the claim it makes for truth. The thesis tacitly assumes as its ground a transcendent standpoint beyond conditions.[4] Let us then reformulate the thesis as, "All thought is conditioned except the proposition that all thought is conditioned." I can see only two ways in which the truth of this can be established. It might be claimed that the exempted proposition differs from all others in precisely those respects that make transcendence possible. We can enumerate the necessary and sufficient bases of transcendence and show that only the exempted proposition possesses them. But this strategy patently fails; it presupposes the existence of unconditioned knowledge—for example, the bases of transcendence, the general features of all propositions save one—in addition to the exempted proposition. Left without a general argument, we have no strategy other than exhaustive induction. But that is ridiculous. Thought is not a finite, denumerable totality, and even if it were, the inductive procedure assumes that our process of inquiry is unconditioned in the same sense as the exempted proposition.

This style of argument may seem sophistical to some, so let me argue from experience. It is possible to be compelled by the force of an argument that runs athwart one's beliefs and interests; if you prefer, there is an "interest of reason" that can occasionally compete successfully with the other determinants of our judgment. There are certain kinds of propositions, for example, the mathematical, the rational force of which is especially powerful because they contradict our other interests to such a limited degree. And there are important thematic continuities, stretching across situations, that render certain arguments immediately intelligible and powerful. In the *Gorgias,* for example, Socrates examined the relation between pleasure and morality and demonstrated, against Callicles, that a thoroughgoing hedonism is incompatible with devotion to the aristocratic virtues.[5] This dialectical argument is, I claim, both intelligible and determinative for us. To avoid the contradiction into which Callicles falls, Nietzsche must reject hedonic utilitarianism as he embraces the aristocratic virtues.

The disappearance of the object of thought

The possibility of transcendence may be questioned in another manner, by focusing on the implied goal of rational inquiry rather than the environment of its activity. Like all rational inquiry, utopian thought proceeds through language; its telos is an experience of the good or value pointed to by, but beyond, language, discovered rather than constituted. But, it is argued, the ground of this experience, the "transcendental signified," does not exist in the moral sphere or, indeed, in any other. As Jacques Derrida puts it,

> Peirce goes very far in the direction that I have called the deconstruction of the transcendental signified, which, at one time or another, would place a reassuring end to the reference from sign to sign. . . . But *what broaches the movement of signification is what makes its interruption impossible. The thing itself is a sign. . . . The so-called "thing itself" is always already a representamen* shielded from the simplicity of intuitive evidence. The *representamen* functions only by giving rise to an *interpretant* that itself becomes a sign and so on to infinity. The self-identifying of the signified conceals itself unceasingly and is always on the move. The property of the *representamen* is to be itself and another, to be produced as a structure of reference, to be separated from itself.[6]

This argument seems less than self-evidently true to me. In the first place, at least some chains of signs do come to an end. Some of the questions children ask can be answered with ostensive definitions. Wittgenstein correctly pointed out that not all language has ostensive meaning and that the act of ostensively defining presupposes a horizon within which the significance of pointing is understood by the child.[7] But this is not to deny the distinction between signs and things signified.

Second: we encounter things, experience them. As finite beings, encountering the other, the nonself, is the fundamental characteristic of our existence. For this reason, we must think of experience as presence, presentation; *presence* signifies the inescapable epistemic relation between self and other. This is not to say that seeing is necessarily the preferred mode of presentation. God is as much present to Jeremiah as voice as the Good is present to Socrates as vision. Aristotle articulated this concept of experience: "Words are the symbols of mental experience ... all men have not the same speech ..., but the mental experiences, which these directly symbolize, are the same for all, as also are those things of which our experiences are the images."[8] What allows man to move from experience to the experienced? Just this: "Man's soul is, in a certain way, [all] beings."[9] Aquinas supplied the meaning of this by describing the soul as that "which is suited to come together with [that is, conform itself to] all beings."[10]

I am not concerned to argue here for the adequacy of classical realism; I am not persuaded of its truth. But it does not seem to me to be obviously false either. In a decisive moment of modern philosophy, Kant abandoned realism because it cannot produce substantive certainty.[11] Perhaps the quest for certainty is the mother of illusion; perhaps categorial as well as particular knowledge arises through induction. At any rate, Kant's move was not a dialectical necessity dictated by self-contradictions of realism. In the absence of a comprehensive internal critique (to reject Husserl, for example, is not to refute realism as such), some version of classical realism remains a live possibility.

2.3.b. Second class of objections: Utopian thought is unnecessary
The devaluation of politics

According to some early Christians, utopian thought tacitly ascribes to the political realm an importance it does not possess. What really matters is beyond politics; utopias err in trying to mix the transcendent and mundane. We should willingly render unto Caesar because only what we owe God is a worthy object of concern. Utopian thought denies this separation; it rests on the principle that politics matters. This is not necessarily to say that politics is the highest realm, or the only realm, of human activity, but only that it affects us in ways that do not permit us to be indifferent.

To this early Christian objection may be added an Augustinian gloss: the earthly city, the outcome of self-love, is the unredeemable realm of fallen man; utopian thought embodies the illusion not only of significance but also of efficacy. This charge is correct. Utopian thought rests on the claim that the political community is in part a human contrivance the character of which is significantly affected by the skill and vision of its contrivers. Utopias are conceived in hope and wither in the face of necessity.

2. Utopian Thought and Moral Philosophy

Conventionalism

It is also possible to argue that utopian thought is unnecessary because there is no reason to object to everyday institutions and practices. The first maxim of Descartes's provisional morality is the resolve "to obey the laws and customs of my country."[12] But he linked exercise of this rule to expediency: his philosophic inquiries were to be facilitated by conformity. Obviously, conformity does not have this happy result in all instances. (Consider the cases of Socrates and Heidegger.) In general, every reason for going along with prevailing practices contains the ground of a possible critique. On one level, for example, Hobbes tried to eliminate all bases for external judgments of justice and injustice directed against existing institutions. But because he saw political community as brought into being through collective action to serve a shared goal, he could not avoid distinguishing between wise and unwise governance and thus justifying disobedience in the name of that goal.

Some contemporary moral philosophers deeply impressed by Wittgenstein's view of language have contended that an appropriate understanding of the role of moral discourse within human communities enables us to avoid the shoals of "conventionalism" without being forced to invent nonexistent utopian standards. Perhaps the most thoroughgoing of these philosophers is R. W. Beardsmore, who begins by endorsing the crucial passage in the *Philosophical Investigations:*

> "So you are saying that human agreement decides what is true and what is false?"—It is what human beings *say* that is true and false, and they agree in the *language* they use. That is not agreement in opinion but in a form of life. (241, p. 88e)
>
> If language is to be a means of communication there must be agreement, not only in definitions, but also (queer as this may sound) in judgments. (242, p. 88e)

He proceeds to develop the thesis that the meaning and boundary of moral discourse is established by the "social context" or tradition to which the speaker belongs. This does not mean that a tradition contains a precise detailed set of moral propositions to which every member assents, but rather that each tradition contains some view of what counts as a "moral reason." A moral reason is an "ultimate justification," in the sense that no further reason can be furnished or ought to be requested. Examples of moral reasons are integrity, greed, adultery, suicide, honesty, and murder. Members of a community can understand or feel the force of a claim as a *moral* claim only insofar as it can be linked to a previously accepted reason.[13]

This thesis can be questioned from many different standpoints. First, Beardsmore recognizes that his position can be identified with the "conventionalism" of Bradley and Hegel, with the claim that "to be moral is to live in accordance with the moral tradition of one's country."[14] He tries to defend himself by identifying this conventionalism with manipulative surface compliance—going along with the group for personal advantage, without genuine moral feeling—and distinguishing this compliance from "moral sincerity," for which a moral reason is a *sufficient* reason for judgment and action.[15] But we may grant the force of the distinction between compliance and sincerity without conceding that Beardsmore has disposed of the underlying difficulty. In the first place, Bradley and Hegel were speaking of moral sincerity, not manipulative compliance. Further, conventionalism is a problem because it suggests that there are many different moral systems, each embedded in a different cultural or historical community, and that no *reason* for a system or for any of its components beyond agreement can be furnished. Thus, the only alternative to unthinking conformity is paralyzing moral skepticism. Beardsmore barely seems to recognize this problem, and he offers no means to cope with it.

Second, Beardsmore's claim that a moral reason is an "ultimate" justification is questionable, since, as he is well aware, such reasons can come into conflict. When we confront a choice between, for example, lying and allowing the death of an innocent person, we come to realize the limited and prima facie character of at least one of the purportedly ultimate reasons.

Third, Beardsmore's thesis commits him to the claim that when a "rebel" questions one part of his moral tradition, it can only be on the basis of another part of that same tradition. But consider the case of someone raised to respect the claim of justice as a moral reason who nevertheless comes to ask, "Why should I act justly when it is not to my advantage to do so?" This question can arise (one is tempted to say that it *naturally* arises) even in a tradition no element of which gives any aid and comfort to the proposition that "personal advantage is good (or a moral justification)."

Fourth, Beardsmore's view of moral reasons as "ultimate" leads him to an incomplete view of moral argument that emphasizes the probability of disagreement or breakdown. He describes a disagreement between a scientist and an antivivisectionist over the use of live animals in research, a clash between the value of scientific work and of avoidance of suffering as "overriding considerations." "There is no neutral standard, no 'common evidence,' by which the dispute can be resolved."[16] His conclusion is unwarranted, however, for each party may continue the discussion by putting additional questions to the

2. Utopian Thought and Moral Philosophy

other. For example, the antivivisectionist may ask about the scientist's willingness to conduct comparable experiments on human beings and—if the answer is negative, as it usually is—to provide a reasoned argument distinguishing the two cases. Obviously (and here Beardsmore's opposition to more extreme claims is justified) there is no guarantee that agreement will result. But because most reasons are proximate rather than ultimate and because, as Beardsmore himself emphasizes in another connection, participants in a moral discussion almost always share *some* concepts and judgments, many disagreements can be resolved.

Fifth, Beardsmore's thesis rests on a partial view of what it means to question a tradition from within. He supposes that a tradition consists in a set of moral ultimates, some of which contradict others. The rebel, or moral skeptic, simply rejects the ultimates to which his community or culture ascribes the greatest worth and puts others from the approved list in their place. This can of course occur. But it is also possible that the questioner, observing the conflict internal to a tradition, will be led into a dialectical inquiry in which the opposing elements are modified. An example of this occurs in the *Republic*, in which Socrates closed the breach between justice and advantage that Glaucon opened by progressively modifying the prevailing understanding of both justice and advantage.

Sixth, Beardsmore seems to hesitate between a formal and a substantive account of moral reasons. On the one hand, as we have seen, they are constitutive elements of communities whose moral beliefs vary widely. On the other hand, he claims that "there is a range of concepts . . . which are in some sense constitutive of a morality";[17] if a proposition does not employ a concept from this range, it cannot be said to make a moral claim at all. This serves as a criterion for any way of life, not merely for our tradition.

This thesis has the attraction of seeming to find a middle way between the "relativist" claim that any concept or characteristic can be invested with moral weight and the "absolutist" claim that moral concepts have fixed empirical referents and that the truth or falsity of propositions in which they appear can be determined with as much certainty as any scientific or factual question. The difficulty is that Beardsmore's account of the source of our moral belief makes it difficult to see how a range of concepts valid *across* cultural boundaries could be constructed. We know what constitutes a moral reason within our tradition; we can understand assertions in other traditions as making moral claims if they can be brought into some relation to *our* moral reasons. Thus, the movement from our moral understanding to a transcultural canon of moral concepts must be mediated by one of two propositions: either every way of life makes use of roughly the same catalogue of reasons, though with different rank-orderings and weights; or our own moral heritage is so broad and diverse as to contain within it every significant moral possibility. Neither of these propositions can be defended within the bounds of Beardsmore's argument.[18]

Immanent critique

It may be argued that the practical import of utopian thought can be preserved through the *immanent critique* of existing institutions. But, I would respond, immanent critique either appeals to transcendent standards or lacks critical force. Immanent critique is a kind of dialectical argument that reveals contradictions between ideals and practices or between the presuppositions underlying different practices within a collectivity. But, first, revealing a contradiction cannot tell us which of its poles to reject. Indeed, on this basis we do not even know whether one or both cannot be maintained. The civil rights movement of the 1950s confronted the United States with the gap between professed ideals and discriminatory practices, and public policy moved gradually to abolish these practices. A century earlier, the Abolitionists' attack on slavery led some Southern thinkers to abandon their belief in universal rights. We approve of the former and deplore the latter on the basis of our *external* adherence to certain principles. Second, contradiction has practical force in arguments because the telos of theoretical speech is truth, and it is impossible for all components of a contradiction to be true simultaneously. But the telos of a political community may be compatible with practices the justifications of which contradict one another. Machiavelli traced the strength and glory of Rome to the enduring struggle between patricians and plebeians. Practices may be opposed to one another or mutually limiting, but it is a mistake to say that they contradict one another. Underlying the faith in immanent critique is the preference for a harmonious, rational community, the component practices of which can be justified in a mutually consistent manner—an admirable goal, perhaps, but one the justification of which lies outside the process of the critique.

History

Classical Marxism claims that utopia can be replaced by history; hence it distinguishes between utopian and scientific socialism. As Engels recognized, the Hegelian view of *actuality* underlies this claim. Hegel's argument runs roughly as follows: Ultimately, thought and its object are identical; the rational is the actual. Actuality is not equivalent to factic-

23

ity as such, but rather to its essence or underlying structure. As essence, actuality is not static but rather contains an internal principle of motion; it is self-moving. Its movement is development, a progressive unfolding of what is implicit in the origin. Actuality is, in addition, the principle of unity. Every being possessing actuality is a totality whose elements are related to one another and intelligible in light of its actuality. All utopian thought errs in distinguishing between the real and the ideal; what we are accustomed to thinking of as ideal is in fact actuality, being or the real in its fullest sense. But this does not mean that utopian thought can be replaced by a purely contemplative metaphysics; the actuality of human existence is revealed in its temporal unfolding, its history.[19]

Hegel equated his interpretation of actuality with Aristotle's concept of *energeia*. For Aristotle, energeia meant: activity as opposed to potentiality; the characteristic activity of an entity, not just a logical possibility; the telos of that entity, its fully developed manifestation. Thus, the energeia of man is actual in Hegel's sense in that it is the full unfolding of what man is immanently. Human perfection is not an ought, externally imposed.

The difficulty is that the identification of actuality and energeia is incomplete, in the crucial respects that block any simple movement from Aristotle's teleology to Hegel's historical orientation.

First, Aristotle distinguished between energeia and physis (nature). Nature is the set of entities possessing an internal principle of motion. The question then arises: Is the full development of each entity achieved naturally, through its self-motion? For many entities, the answer is affirmative; for man, negative. For example, virtue is part of man's perfection, but, as Aristotle stressed, there is no immanent impulse toward virtue.[20] This fact creates the need for will, convention, *paideia*—indeed, for politics. And neither the initiation nor the perfection of the political association is achieved on the basis of immanent impulse alone.[21]

Second, the energeia of an entity cannot be equated with its temporal end, although it involves temporal change.[22] The need thus arises for nontemporal specifications. In a characteristic discussion in the *Ethics*, Aristotle tried to define the human telos in a general way through philosophical anthropology.[23] The resulting priority of reason is immanent in the sense that various aspects of our experience are said to point toward the appropriate ordering of reason and desire, but not in the sense that we naturally tend to achieve this ordering as our lives progress.[24]

Third, history is not the kind of totality that can have an internal principle of motion or an energeia that could serve as a practical standard. History is not really an organized entity at all, but rather a set of particulars with at most local connections. Further, what we call history is in part the product of human decision—convention as opposed to nature. There is no reason to believe that these decisions constitute a patterned totality. Moreover, there is no necessary connection between historical temporality and teleological development, although all development presupposes temporality. Finally, teleological knowledge is not a priori but rests on observation of the fully developed form of the entity in question.[25] It is difficult to conceive how we could recognize a completed cycle of historical development, let alone give sense to that concept.

If history is merely temporality, it lacks normative force, even if it were both patterned and predictable. It might be argued, in the manner of the Stoics or Spinoza, that virtue is the recognition of necessity. But even if valid, this claim is "utopian" in the sense that it is brought to rather than implicit in the fact of temporal necessity, for it is possible to maintain the greater nobility of opposing an irresistible fate, even at the cost of self-destruction.

2.3.c. Third class of objections: Utopian thought contradicts politics understood as practical activity
Oakeshott

Michael Oakeshott attacks "rationalism," which he characterizes as the attempt to devise generally valid principles for judging and directing human practices. Utopian thought is the most influential form of rationalism. His critique may be summarized in the following propositions.

First, to be understood accurately, each form of human activity requires an appropriate method and a correct characterization of the feasible goal of inquiry. But rationalism advocates a universal method that aims at a kind of certainty unattainable in moral or political inquiry. Second, political communities are held together by shared habits, beliefs, and traditions. Rationalism disparages these sentimental bonds as unreasonable and reactionary, seeks to dissolve them and to replace them with universally apprehended knowledge. Third, political activity properly takes its bearings from variations of circumstance in accordance with which appropriate goals and practices will vary. Rationalism seeks uniform solutions, applicable without regard to time or place. Fourth, political activity aims at the best possible in given circumstances. Rationalism holds out the possibility of, and aims at, perfection. Fifth, political activity pursues the "intimations" of a particular tradition, that is, the possibilities it contains, and it proceeds through the rectification of anomalies. Thus, particular practical decisions can be made contextually, without regard to transcendent theory. For example, an appropriate criminal punishment can be determined only by examining how the legal system has treated similar acts committed in comparable circumstances. Rationalism's attempt to distinguish between the just and the legal and to use the former as a criterion is unnecessary and fruitless. And, sixth, rationalism claims that all rational activity stems from, and is guided by, an "independently premeditated end." But this is impossible. Reason is capable only of reflecting on already existing practices, each of which is characterized by intrinsic ends and procedures. Posterior reflection at most generates a partial abstract of the activity, in the form of technical rules.[26]

Oakeshott's critique fails. All his valid claims are directed against the excesses rather than against the essence of utopian thinking, and all his arguments directed against utopian thought, properly understood, are false. We can see this most clearly by constructing an Aristotelian response to his charges.

Aristotle granted, indeed insisted upon, the political role of particular instances that cannot be reduced to general rules; witness his discussion of equity and grounding of deliberation on the direct perception of individual facts. He argued that different subjects could be expected to be understood with different degrees of precision and through different modes of investigation. He emphasized the role of habit in both moral activity and the observance of law, criticizing contemporary theorists who overlooked the function of habitual behavior. He insisted that political practice must respond to variations of circumstance and be limited by what is achievable in given circumstances.

But in spite of these important practical agreements with Oakeshott, Aristotle insisted on the relevance and necessity of transcendent theory. First, it is correct to say that most political practice pursues possibilities inherent in a tradition. But it is far from clear which of the many contradictory intimations one ought to pursue. A judgment about the highest potentialities of a tradition cannot be made within that tradition but requires an external standpoint. Further, in some rare but important situations, traditions must be *founded* on the basis of at least partly nontraditional considerations. Second, some practical questions can be resolved contextually, but many cannot. Are we really content to say that justice means hanging the man who steals a loaf of bread if that is the prevailing punishment and is not a moral anomaly in that community? We may begin by identifying the just with the legal, but we cannot stop there. Third, it is in large measure correct to assert that practical philosophy begins by reflecting on existing activities. When

Aristotle stated that politics comes into being for the sake of life and persists for the sake of the good life, he sought neither to bring a novel activity into being nor to impose a premeditated end on existing politics. Rather, he tried to describe politics in a way that will command immediate assent. But politics propounds a question without being able to supply an answer, since the content of the "good life" is constantly disputed. Thus, philosophic reflection on politics can produce a transformation of political self-understanding, arising dialectically from political activity itself. The practical application of this new understanding is neither inconceivable nor necessarily destructive.

Arendt

Hannah Arendt's critique of utopian thought begins from the Aristotelian distinction between making and acting. *Making* aims at the production of a product or end, separable from the process of production, that provides both the justification and standard of judgment of that act. *Acting* does not produce a separable product; the end of acting is the act itself. Through action human beings achieve their fullest development, and each individual is revealed as unique. The great deeds and speeches through which self-revelation occurs presuppose, as other forms of human behavior do not, the presence of others. Politics is the totality of self-revealing activity; the political community provides both the space within which this activity occurs and the remembrance that ministers to the actor's dread of oblivion and desire for immortality. The elaboration of utopias is thus a perversion of politics. Action is deprived of its uniqueness. Indeed, uniqueness is deprived of value, since everything human is examined in the cold light of a universal standard. Further, utopia is a blueprint for action and constitutes a goal separable from the action. Politics is thus falsely reinterpreted as a form of making, and the worth and meaning of the activity is now determined in reference to its end.[27]

Arendt's analysis is at best a partial truth. It seems much more reasonable to say that political activity is both an end in itself and the means to an end that transcends it. Consider political actors grappling with a grave crisis. They find themselves taxed to the limits of their capacities, and they feel more fully alive than when in repose, unchallenged. The activity is an energizing pleasure, an end in itself. But at the same time, those involved are seeking to respond prudently to the crisis. This goal furnishes external criteria by which their efforts will subsequently be judged.

Further, the analysis of political action as self-revealing appearance leads to profoundly dangerous irresponsibility, since greatness lies neither in the motivation nor in the achievement of action, but "only in the performance itself." The criteria of performance are the "extraordinary" and the "radiant"—aesthetic rather than moral categories.[28] Arendt's position amounts to an unqualified endorsement of the Periclean interpretation of Athenian greatness, ignoring its weaknesses. The apparent rejection of external criteria for political action in fact represents an endorsement of courage, boldness, and imagination (the hubristic virtues) at the expense of moderation and justice.

Finally, Arendt's claim that the fateful utopian substitution of making for acting was motivated by impatience with the frustrations and uncertainties of political action is profoundly misleading. Both Plato and Aristotle, the alleged perpetrators, examined the *content* of the phenomenon that so deeply impressed Arendt—political speech—and discovered that it consists largely of conflicting claims and justifications. Fully articulated, each of these implies some utopia. Utopias are not imposed on political action but rather are immanent in it. Plato and Aristotle merely asked whether any rational grounds exist for choosing among or balancing conflicting claims. But even this question is in a real sense immanent, since in practice every political community must somehow deal with such conflicts. Arendt's understanding of political speech as individual revelation obscures its central functions— persuasion, coordination of action through securing shared premises, justification by relating the controversial particular to the uncontroversial generalization—and thereby obscures the intrinsic relation between politics and utopian thought.

Ends and means

Machiavelli's rejection of "imagined republics and principalities" as leading to the self-destruction of the political actor who pays attention to them also misses the mark.[29] In its Aristotelian form, at least, utopian thought is compatible with political prudence. Aristotle was perfectly willing to countenance limited employment of the nasty means Machiavelli recommended. Public-spirited political leadership must maintain its authority to accomplish its objectives, and significant improvements sometimes require a measure of harshness. But maintaining power is not, as Machiavelli seemed to assume, an end in itself.

Machiavelli's critique is really directly against individualistic morality seen as commandments—prohibitions on certain means *per se* without regard to the consequences of forbidding their use. Christians can turn the other cheek only by devaluing the things of this world; Kant's moralized statecraft culminates in *fiat justitia, pereat mundus.*

Machiavelli's critique is decisive in these cases to the extent that we attach moral significance to the political consequences as well as intrinsic characteristics of possible means.

In defending utopian thought against Machiavelli's charge of excessive fastidiousness, it may seem that the other flank has been exposed. It is frequently argued that utopian theory is not merely incomplete but rather radically and dangerously defective because it does not reflect seriously enough on the conditions of its actualization. Utopian theorists presuppose favorable circumstances through acts of imagination; but confronted with the recalcitrance of the world, they tend to argue that the worth of the ends they seek legitimates the use of any and all possible means. Utopianism in thought means brutality in action.

As a psychological generalization, this charge has some merit. But, I would argue, thoughtful utopians acknowledge the force of the "reformer's paradox": the principles that provide foundations for their ends place limits on the means that can be employed to realize them.[30]

Suppose we know that a possible situation, B, is more nearly just than the prevailing situation, A, and that a complex of means, M, will enable us to move from A to B. There can, it seems, be three kinds of objections to the use of M.

First, it may be argued that the use of M is from a moral standpoint *absolutely* forbidden, however salutary the consequences may be. Against this I would argue that the concept of absolute prohibition makes no sense, morally or politically, and can be defended only on theological grounds. There are means the intrinsic characteristics of which are so bad that their use can be legitimated only in extreme circumstances. To judge M, then, we must consider both how unjust A is and how much of an improvement B constitutes. There are no firm rules to guide our judgment. Some extreme cases are clear. In a community divided between oligarchs and starving peasants, the use of force to procure the means of survival and a minimally dignified existence can hardly be criticized. At the other end of the spectrum, the wholesale disruption and extinction of an urban bourgeoisie to eliminate barriers to the forging of a "new revolutionary consciousness" is indefensible; it is hardly accidental that the Pol Pot regime was reduced to claiming that its policies were undertaken to avert a severe agricultural crisis. In general, the problem is fairly straightforward if the harm inflicted on a few is necessary to avert an equal or greater harm for many others. Harming a few severely to procure marginal gains for many others is very questionable, even in cases in which a sensible application of the classic utilitarian calculus seems to legitimate it.

Second, it may be argued that the distinction between ends and means is artificial. M is not a magic wand producing an instantaneous transition from A to B. Rather, it produces a sequence of intermediate situations that must be given the same weight as A and B.[31]

As we shall see in our discussion of justice between generations, this objection is, within limits, well taken. There are analogues on the level of individual experience. Even if the goal of victory is taken to be highly valuable, there is something distasteful about the regimen even the very youngest swimmers are forced to undergo. One wants to say that the extended training is not a means to a kind of existence but rather a part of that existence. Similarly, concentrating on the attainment of some long-deferred material goal can lead to the false view of the process of acquisition as pure means rather than what it is, a way of existing with its own intrinsic characteristics. But this kind of objection does not undermine M altogether. At most, it forces us to recall what should always have been an integral part of our moral calculation—the temporal dimension of political action. A revolution that requires for its success a brief burst of terror is very different from one that must institutionalize the use of terror over many generations to move haltingly toward its goals.

Third, it may be argued that it is incorrect from a moral point of view to place actuality and possibility on the same footing. The brute fact that within A specific individuals possess or enjoy specific objects and opportunities must be given considerable moral weight. There is a difference between choosing to transform A into B and preferring B to A in a context in which neither exists. Three arguments may be offered in support of this view. One: there is a widespread tendency to believe that extended physical or legal possession generates a kind of moral entitlement; two: collective existence requires stable expectations, without which planning and striving are impossible—interrupting expectations is intrinsically harmful and cannot be equated with *ex nihilo* creation; three: even if A is unjust, individuals within A have made life plans and have undertaken long-term commitments based on the distribution that prevails. Altering this distribution not only changes patterns of possession but uproots lives; there is no way of disentangling the unjust foundations from the lives that rest on them.

From a prudential standpoint, these classic conservative arguments have considerable merit. As Aristotle argued, political changes cannot simply be equated with changes in the arts and sciences. The efficacy of law rests on custom as well as reason. We cannot simply compare snapshots of A and B; reflection on the conditions of actualizing B may incline us in favor of A even when B is abstractly better.[32]

But the force of these prudential arguments, as well as their more specifically moral weight, depends on circumstances. If a community is organized along manifestly unjust lines, there is little reason to believe that possession implies entitlement or that the disruption of the expectations and lives of the privileged is a bad thing. Not only are disruptions likely to produce a better life for the dispossessed in such circumstances, but also it is difficult to feel that the privileged have been treated unfairly. They should have recognized that their lives were built on foundations of injustice, on the denial of the valid claims of others. The stability and security of their plans rested on self-regarding cynicism, willful blindness, or culpable ignorance.

We may suggest, then, that the same principles are used to evaluate ends and means and that limits on acceptable means are imposed in the name of justice. That is, sound political action seeks to maximize justice within the constraints of circumstances, but maximization itself may compel us to forgo efforts to actualize what we would create if we had a magic wand or divine power.

2.3.d. Fourth class of objections: Utopian thought rests on a vacuous concept of "possibility"

Possibility is a limiting condition of utopian thought, for two reasons. First, if an imagined state of affairs is in no way possible, it cannot serve as a ground of criticism. It would be absurd to dream of a world in which we no longer needed to eat and on that basis to criticize human beings for manifesting dependence and destruction in their relations to food. This criterion emerges in moral theory in the principle that *ought* implies *can*. Obligation ceases in the face of impossibility, and praise and blame are not applicable to acts or events over which the agent can have no control. Second, an impossible state of affairs is not an appropriate object of endeavor and, therefore, is not a suitable guide for practice. As Aristotle pointed out, we may long for the impossible, but we choose and act in the belief that our goal is possible. Action guided by longing leads either to despair or to a frenzy of destructive rage at the world's permanent resistance. Utopian seriousness is the mean between abstract negation and the cynical or unthinking acceptance of facticity.

The difficulty is to determine the limits of possibility, a concept that has many different meanings. Something is *logically possible* when it can be conceived without contradiction. But, as Kant observed, a logically possible concept "may none the less be an empty concept, unless the objective reality of the synthesis through which the concept is generated has been specifically proved; and such proof . . . rests on principles of possible experience, and not on the principle of analysis (the law of contradiction). This is a warning against arguing directly from the logical possibility of concepts to the real possibility of things."[33] We may call an object of possible experience *categorially possible*. But, further, not everything categorially possible is *nomologically possible*. It is categorially possible that, for example, the constants in well-entrenched laws of nature could be other than they are, but from a scientific standpoint these constants are brute facts, limiting the range of causal events and human interventions. Finally, not everything nomologically possible is *practically possible*. Relative to a given set of facts, a state of affairs may be impossible to attain, even though a nomologically possible alteration of these facts would render it possible. The concept of practical possibility has both technological and political application. Given present knowledge and techniques, it is impossible to fly to Sirius; given present challenges, real or perceived, it is impossible to persuade Congress to make a 90 percent cut in the defense budget.

We may now say: A political state of affairs is a fantasy when it is logically or categorially but not nomologically possible. It is a utopia when nomologically possible, whether or not it is practically possible. The gap between nomological and practical possibility is the sphere of serious political action.

But can the notion of nomological possibility be applied to utopian thought with any determinate results? We may distinguish between external and internal necessities. External necessities are those regularities or brute facts that constrain the translation of intentions into actions. Internal necessities constrain the formation of intention or character. The former are relatively uncontroversial. No one would take very seriously a political proposal that depended on perpetual motion machines busily working to improve the human estate. And Aristotle's critique of the *Republic* has at least hypothetical force: if, as he alleged, Plato propounded the transformation of human particularity into an organic entity for which the sensations of one part are felt equally by all, then no institution resting on this foundation need be given serious consideration.

The core of the controversy, then, concerns internal necessity: is there a general structure, "human nature," that constrains character or intention, limiting the possibilities of political *Bildung?* The first theorist to offer an unequivocally negative answer was Kant:

> For whereas, so far as nature is concerned, experience supplies the
> rules and is the source of truth, in respect of the moral laws it is,
> alas, the mother of illusion! Nothing is more reprehensible than to
> derive the laws prescribing *what ought to be done* from what *is
> done*, or to impose upon them the limits by which the latter is
> circumscribed. . . . For what the highest degree may be at which

mankind may have to come to a stand, and how great a gulf may still have to be left between the idea and its realization, are questions which no one can, or ought to, answer. For the issue depends upon freedom; and it is in the power of freedom to pass beyond any and every specified limit.[34]

Marx extended this idea of freedom in the *Grundrisse:*

When the narrow bourgeois form has been peeled away, what is wealth, if not the universality of needs, capacities, enjoyments, productive powers, etc. of individuals, produced in universal exchange? What, if not the full development of human control over the forces of nature—those of his own nature as well as those of so-called "nature"? What, if not the absolute elaboration of his creative dispositions, without any preconditions other than the antecedent historical evolution which makes the totality of this evolution—i.e., the evolution of all human powers as such unmeasured by any *previously established* yardstick—an end in itself? What is this, if not a situation where man does not reproduce himself in any determined form, but produces his totality?[35]

At the other extreme stand some of the more deterministically inclined proponents of sociobiology.[36]

My own view is that neither of these extremes is tenable; there is a wide but not unlimited range within which character and intention may be transformed. Let me give one important example. Aristotle was, I believe, correct in asserting that "self-love" is the primary source of action.[37] The task of education is not to promote a universalized altruism or concern for others, but rather to achieve an ennobling broadening of the self we love. If successful, education so conceived will allow us to obtain some of the hypothetical benefits of altruism by moderating our desire for those objects whose scarcity engenders destructive competition, by broadening the range of individuals whose well-being is felt to affect our own, and by increasing the efficacy of reason in determining action.

Self-love takes on any number of forms, each of which constrains politics to some degree. Desires for material goods suggest that no economic system can wholly dispense with material incentives. Self-expression requires some physical objects that individuals are free to select and arrange. Socially, self-love is expressed in the desire for human relations—of family and friendship—that are "one's own," set apart from a more general web of relations, and in the desire for recognition and respect.

Two kinds of objections to the concept of "human nature" are commonly advanced. The first is empirical: individual and cultural diversity makes it impossible to assign any determinate content to the

33

concept, which is, therefore, philosophically and politically useless.

Given a teleological interpretation of nature, the simple fact of diversity is not decisive. The contention that it makes sense to specify a fully developed human being is compatible with diversity; different ways of life may be said to actualize different aspects of human potentiality, to varying degrees.

But we need not embrace teleology, with all its attendant difficulties. Our experience of diversity is compatible with an actually existing, underlying unity. Wherever we observe human beings, certain patterns emerge. Let me list the most obvious and important: a distinctive kind of consciousness, self-awareness, that produces both introspection and the knowledge of mortality; a distinctive kind of comprehension, rationality; a distinctive kind of communicative competence; complex and differentiated passions; the interpenetration of reason, passion, and desire that constitutes the moral realm; unique kinds of activities, such as artistic expression; a distinctive form of association that we call "political," containing enormously complex conventions; and, finally, what we may with Rousseau think of as instinctual underdetermination. It seems reasonable to assert that something like this ensemble of fundamental characteristics is what we mean by human nature and that they constitute some very general limits of possibility.

The second kind of objection is moral and political. Critics charge that talk about human nature as setting limits is nothing but an ideological cloak for the conservative defense of the status quo. Social Darwinism and the obiter dicta of modern sociobiologists are the most frequently cited examples.

In the first place, it is important not to conflate human nature as a general concept with specific assertions about it. To speak of human nature is *not* necessarily to assimilate man to nonhuman species. Indeed, *human* nature is most plausibly interpreted as an ensemble of defining characteristics that are distinctive, either singly or taken as a whole. Thus, one may resist any simple attempt to make inferences about human behavior on the basis of nonhuman species or to conflate the shared characteristics of the human and the nonhuman with the totality of the human while defending some concept of the human. This is hardly a new point. Socrates was most unimpressed with Callicles' claim that tyranny is natural and legitimate because strong animals dominate weaker ones. In its place he offered a very different understanding of what is natural for *human beings*.

Second, the practical consequences of rejecting human nature are far from unambiguous. We may be led to extol man's untrammeled freedom, but we will also be tempted to emphasize human malleability, achievable through manipulations of the natural and social environment. As Chomsky and others have pointed out, there are enormous dangers inherent in the political engineering that is likely to be conducted on this basis.

A determinate concept of human nature may deprive us of some of our dreams, restricting the absolute freedom of our fantasy life, but it also stands as a bulwark against the worst forms of tyranny. The limits it asks us to recognize are the limits of humanity; to disregard them is quite literally to deprive others (and oneself) of humanity.[38]

2.3.e. Fifth class of objections: Utopian thought is wrecked on the shoals of moral relativism

Ultimately, the most serious objection to utopian political thought is the contention that it is impossible because moral theory, of which it is a branch, cannot achieve its goal. There is no general good or right, knowable through reason, that can serve as a standard for endeavor.

For many reasons the relativist position is less popular now than it was a generation ago. Within Anglo–American philosophy, the brand of positivism that impugned the rational significance of moral discourse is moribund; conventionalism, Oakeshottian or Wittgensteinian, has manifestly failed to fulfill the promise it held out of replacing moral theory; the much-heralded distinction between ethics and metaethics begs the most important questions and probably cannot be maintained.[39] Within Marxism, the conflation of morality with historical process has been called into question for both theoretical and practical reasons, and efforts are under way to furnish it with a new moral foundation, through either philosophical anthropology or an autonomous theory of value. The growing historical pessimism of the Frankfurt School induced its principal members to move toward explicitly moral utopian conceptions, culminating in Habermas's willingness to employ "counterfactual" judgments derived from imagining a situation that has never existed and may never exist to evaluate existing political conditions.[40]

One may wonder whether the reaction against relativism has not proceeded too hastily. R. S. Peters has perceptively remarked that many moral philosophers simply became bored with "minute questions of meaning."[41] He might well have added that the pleasures of indulging the perennial impulse to break the shackles of a reigning orthodoxy may tempt us to propound substantive judgments insufficiently distinguished from private sentiments. Our urgent need for moral theory must not lead us to mistake the wish for the fact.

In the following discussion I shall examine what I consider to be the most important of the recent attempts to renovate moral theory. Though my tone will be largely critical, my purpose is to identify the most plausible claims and promising strategies of argument.

Ethical formalism

R. M. Hare has attempted to isolate the major formal features of moral discourse and to show how they may be used to clarify, and in some cases to resolve, moral disputes. There has, I believe, been a general disposition to accept Hare's contention that genuine moral propositions share many characteristics of rational discourse: they contain descriptive criteria that constitute sufficient conditions for application to specific cases; they must satisfy the demand for consistency; and they are universalizable. It is clear, moreover, that Hare's criteria are a powerful weapon against individuals who exempt themselves from moral principles the general validity of which they acknowledge, and which they seek to enforce against others. His formalism is a barrier against selfishness and hypocrisy.[42]

The difficulty in Hare's position, much discussed in recent literature, is that his criteria cannot weed out many moral contentions that seem distasteful and implausible. The fanatic who is willing to accept the possibility of being harmed by the racist principles he advances and who unflinchingly endorses the factual and conceptual propositions to which his position commits him cannot be subjected to any further philosophic scrutiny, although we may continue to believe that he is dangerously mistaken. Ethical formalism, then, leaves the problem of relativism unresolved, although it does reduce the number of positions that we may maintain.

Hare's formalism rests squarely on his acceptance of the Humean dichotomy between facts and moral judgments or decisions. It is noteworthy that Hare, while continuing to insist that the relation between factual and moral propositions cannot be one of logical entailment, has in his more recent writings been disposed to say that there is a nonarbitrary consistency to what we call good, that our judgments are for the most part relative to certain ends—sometimes called fundamental human needs—that flow from the kinds of beings we are and serve as springs of action.[43] I shall discuss this "naturalistic" move later. For present purposes it suffices to remark that Hare's admission coexists very uneasily with his Humean inclinations; at the least, the acknowledgment of empirical considerations decisively weakens the force of the "logical" contention that facts cannot entail moral propositions.

Coherence arguments

Recently, moral philosophers have begun to explore the possibility that the appropriate model of moral truth is not correspondence but rather coherence. Moral philosophy is the attempt to become aware of the full range of considerations that bear on disputed questions and to fit these considerations together into a coherent whole. In the process, we find ourselves inclined in some direction rather than others, although none of the various considerations taken by itself entails the conclusion we eventually come to favor. Painstaking moral craftsmanship reveals that some orientation is richer, less artificial, more encompassing than its competitors.

One of the most self-conscious proposals for the reconstruction of moral philosophy along these lines is Rawls's method of *reflective equilibrium*. We must begin, he contends, from particular moral intuitions or opinions and seek both to harmonize them and to make explicit the general judgments of which they are instances. In the course of our inquiry we move back and forth from the general to the particular until we reach a coherent set of judgments. Our resting place is necessarily provisional; we cannot ascribe any final truth to our judgments, for we know only that they have survived all the scrutiny to which we have so far been able to subject them.[44]

Rawls wavers between two significantly different versions of his thesis. According to the first, the procedure is completely dialectical: particular examples may force revisions in general principles, and principles may force us to abandon our original particular opinions. Nothing is exempt from inquiry; our unexamined opinions serve only to initiate discussion. According to the second, our initial opinions are divided into two groups—those of which we are (somewhat) unsure, and the "fixed points," which we will not abandon and to which, therefore, all proposed general principles must be accommodated.[45]

Rawls's hesitation is surely understandable. The first version deprives moral theory of any polestar and would have the effect not only of reopening questions, such as slavery and religious intolerance, that Rawls is sure are closed but also of opening the door to historical and geographical relativism, since different starting points are likely to lead to different equilibria.[46] The second version commits him to a kind of intuitionism for which he does not provide any foundation, which arbitrarily forecloses discussion (you do not ask *whether* a fixed point is valid, but only *why*), and which renders moral theory dependent, not just on eventual agreement, but on initial agreement as well. For example, no one who believes that interesting arguments exist for limitations on religious tolerance can participate in the discussion as anything but a bemused observer.

This impasse exemplifies a very general difficulty. Coherence theories cannot move beyond formalism without incorporating some fixed points that perform the same function as basic statements in scientific inquiry. But if these fixed points are derived from what "we" think, then relativism returns through the back door, for the empirical diversity of "considered judgments," especially across rational and religious boundaries, is established beyond question. Substantive moral philosophy, then, is compelled to search for fixed points that do not rest entirely on consensus.[47] At present three alternatives are being explored: the renovation of Kant's claim that rational being must be viewed as an end in itself; the elucidation of moral premises immanent in rational discourse or rational action; and the return to a quasi-Aristotelian naturalism. Let me briefly consider each of these.

Kant: rational being as moral end

In recent years many political theorists with substantive commitments nearly spanning the political spectrum have appealed to the Kantian principle of rational or autonomous being as an end in itself. They have done so almost without argument, suggesting either that the principle does not require any justification or that Kant's justification is both well understood and decisive. Neither of these contentions is valid. Let me briefly and tendentiously summarize a long debate.

As is well known, Kant initiated his discussion of morality in the *Foundations* by arguing for a formal criterion: No action can be moral if one is unable to will its maxim as a universal law. Shortly thereafter, he spoke of persons (all rational beings) as objective ends-in-themselves and derived from this concept another criterion of morality, which states, "Never treat humanity, in your own person or in the person of any other, merely as a means." He went on to insist that the two criteria are "at bottom one and the same." If Kant was right about this, we have a substantive end entailed by or implicit in the bare form of moral rationality—a gratifyingly powerful result.

In nearly two centuries of debate, three major positions have emerged. The first, advanced in different forms by Hegel and Mill, is that Kant was indeed correct to identify the two criteria, but that he deceived himself in thinking that the second added anything to the formality of the first *unless* other principles were smuggled in. Hegel argued that Kant relied, without being fully aware of it, on practices and concepts of the self that prevailed in his historical epoch; Mill contended that Kant was forced into a naked and wholly inconsistent appeal to the principle of utility.

The second position is that the two criteria are not the same and that Kant, aware of this, was led to propound independent teleological arguments in support of the second criterion. On this reading, substantive moral theory as Kant understood it has two distinct components: a formal characterization of genuinely moral judgments, and the general end that it is rationally necessary for all rational beings to affirm and promote.[48]

The third position is that Kant's identity-claim is sustainable *and* that the second criterion goes beyond simple formalism. This has been urged concisely and cogently by John Atwell.[49] The defects of his argument reveal precisely why this position cannot be maintained.

Atwell observes correctly that Kant deployed the doctrine of objective ends in the third and fourth examples in the *Foundations*, which respectively enjoin us to "perfect ourselves (by developing our natural talents and by striving for moral virtue) and to promote the happiness of others as far as possible." Atwell dismisses self-perfection on the grounds that the duty to pursue it "is not a teleological duty." But his argument deals only with *moral* perfection, leaving untouched the problem of "natural talents," which is a teleological concept if anything is.[50] This difficulty is more than verbal, since it is clear that Kant did not integrate the development of natural capacities into the conception of moral virtue in the way that a certain kind of Aristotelian might.

Atwell devotes more attention to Kant's attempt to establish the duty to help others on a nonteleological basis. He summarizes Kant's argument as follows:

First, human beings are beings of needs, and one of their most important needs is the love and sympathy of others. Hence, by their very nature, human beings have the desire to be aided by others especially when they find themselves placed in dire circumstances. Second, human beings are beings of ends, i.e., they are constantly in pursuit of this or that end; and though the end the person actually pursues varies from moment to moment, it will always be regarded as contributing to or constituting personal happiness (cf. *Gr.* 415). Thus, since he "who wills the end, wills (so far as reason has decisive influence on his actions) also the means which are indispensably necessary and in his power" (*Gr.* 417), we can justifiably infer that everyone must also will that he be assisted in attaining his end if assistance is necessary for such attainment. And it is simply a fact of life that certain ends are not attainable unless others assist in attaining them, so to will those ends entails willing assistance of others in attaining them. Never

to will the assistance of others in achieving one's ends is, in consequence, never to will any ends at all—a human impossibility. If
Kant's reasoning is sound (and it is surely plausible) then he who
acted on a maxim never to help others under any condition would
contradict his own will, were his maxim to be a universal law
governing the conduct of all men.[51]

I do not think this succeeds, either as a logical argument or as a Kantian
argument, for three reasons.

First, in appealing to special features of human agency, Kant surely
went beyond the nonempirical formality of the universality criterion.

Second, in basing his argument on man as a being of needs, he
employed features of human existence that man does not share with all
rational beings *as such*. (This is conceptually true, whether or not there
are any nonhuman rational beings.) But the point of morality for Kant,
the source of its special obligatory force, was that it is valid for all
rational beings by virtue of their rationality.

Third, even if the foregoing objections are waived, Kant's argument
is not convincing, for reasons rooted in its most salient structural
feature—universalized prudential selfishness. An example will make
this clear. Suppose I am driving down the road and spy a man on the
shoulder with a flat tire. As I zip by, I muse, "What if no one stops to
help me when *I* have a flat?" My answer may well be: "I am willing to
accept that, for I see people with flats much more often than I have one
myself." The point is that if, as Atwell suggests, we are thinking pru-
dentially, then we must take into account the fact that helping others
interferes with the attainment of our purposes just as surely as not
being helped by others when we are in need. It is then an empirical—
and to a certain extent psychological—question whether we knowingly
choose actions the maxim of which excludes mutual assistance.

If, as I suggest, the gaps in Atwell's argument show why the third
position cannot be maintained, then we are driven back to the first two.
We have already discussed the shortcomings of ethical formalism as a
substantive position; it is, besides, implausible as a reading of Kant,
who was surely a self-conscious, substantive moral philosopher. I conclude, then, that the most sensible and sympathetic reading is the second. If so, we are led to consider the kinds of strategies by which a
substantive principle such as Kant's might be independently
established. Setting aside direct appeals to moral intuition, which
Kant's language occasionally suggests, there are, it seems to me, two
related possibilities: principles that are immanent in some very general features of human practice; and principles suggested by facts that
are very generally characteristic of the human species. Principles of the

latter kind are frequently called "naturalistic"; of these, teleological propositions are a subset.

Morality as immanent

Habermas: The presuppositions of speech.—In recent years Jürgen Habermas has attempted to develop a new foundation for political evaluation through an examination of the presuppositions and implications of speech. His basic hypothesis is that

> the human interest in autonomy and responsibility . . . is not mere fancy, for it can be apprehended a priori. What raises us out of nature is the only thing whose nature we can know: *language.* Through its structure autonomy and responsibility are posited for us. Our first sentence expresses unequivocally the intention of universal and unconstrained consensus.[52]

Thomas McCarthy lucidly sketches the outline of Habermas's argument for this connection as follows:

> The argument for the connection is meant to be analytic. The analysis of speech shows it to be oriented toward the idea of truth. The analysis of "truth" leads to the notion of a discursively achieved consensus. . . . The analysis of the notion of a grounded consensus ties it to a speech situation which is free from all external and internal constraints, that is, in which the resulting consensus is due simply to the force of the better argument. Finally, the analysis of the ideal speech situation shows it to involve assumptions about the context of interaction in which speech is located. The end result of this chain of argument is that the very structure of speech involves the anticipation of a form of life in which autonomy and responsibility are possible.[53]

Habermas goes on to characterize the relation between this ideal and empirical reality in the following terms:

> No matter how the intersubjectivity of mutual understanding may be deformed, the *design* of an ideal speech situation is necessarily implied in the structure of potential speech, since all speech, even of intentional deception, is oriented toward the idea of truth. This idea can only be analyzed with regard to a consensus achieved in unrestrained and universal discourse. In so far as we master the means for the construction of the ideal speech situation, we can conceive the ideas of truth, freedom, and justice, which interpret each other—although of course only as ideas. On the strength of communicative competence alone, however, and independent of

the empirical structures of the social system to which we belong, we are quite unable to realize the ideal speech situation; we can only anticipate it.[54]

This proposal presents a number of difficulties. First, it is far from self-evident that all speech is oriented toward the idea of truth; indeed, it is not clear in what sense this proposition is to be understood. Certainly deceptive speech makes an external claim to be true, only succeeds if its hearers take it as true, and must take what is true about the audience and the situation into account in devising an effective distortion. But the deceiver cares about the promotion of a particular personal or collective interest, not about seeking the truth. The deceiver worries about lying only insofar as others value truth or integrity or to the extent that a reputation for mendacity makes it more difficult to secure one's objectives.[55] For the committed deceiver, language is a tool or weapon and does not contain any *immanent* restrictions on its employment.

Plato took up this problem in the *Gorgias*, focusing on the relation between instrumental speech (rhetoric) and justificatory speech (philosophy). The basic question is whether rhetoric can be shown to contain an internal contradiction that forces it to move toward philosophy. The answer is negative. Socrates succeeded in refuting one of his interlocuters, Gorgias, by exposing him to the public consequences of a too-frank avowal of instrumentalism. He silenced another, Callicles, by showing him that the neutrality of his instrumentalism conflicted with his own deeply held moral convictions. In general, Socrates succeeded in showing that, if arraigned before the bar of philosophy, rhetoric can defend itself only by radicalizing its instrumentalism, that is, by accepting a thoroughgoing moral relativism. This is a powerful conclusion, but it falls short of the initial task, for two reasons: the movement from rhetoric to philosophy is achieved, not on the basis of immanent tendencies, but rather through *ad hominem* arguments; the issue is to a certain extent prejudged by forcing rhetoric to offer a *philosophical* justification. As Callicles came to realize, it is quite possible to refuse to play the "justification game." If the rhetorical understanding of speech is true to itself, it realizes that a willed silence is sometimes necessary and appropriate. Even if it is granted that making claims involves some commitment to supplying justifications if challenged, the rhetorician recognizes that the claim is in no way the *basis* of the deed it defends and that in certain situations silence is the deed's best defense.

Thus (to return), Habermas's proposed relation between speech and truth rests on a philosophical conception of the relation between speech and deed, and this presupposes the prior rejection of competing conceptions. This rejection is unavoidably a moral choice. Habermas in effect concedes this when he says that the counterfactual assumption that all speakers are equally committed to the process of justification is the "basis of the humanity of intercourse among men who are still men."[56] But either this is a normative definition of being human or, if it purports to be empirical/anthropological, then the question posed by a line of argument stretching from Callicles through Machiavelli to Nietzsche cannot be avoided: Why not (wholly or partly) be an animal?

The second of the difficulties presented by Habermas's proposal is that there is a serious ambiguity in the claim that rational discourse presupposes the possibility of coming to an agreement or consensus. Interpreted in the strong sense, the claim would be that rational discourse presupposes the existence of some locus of agreement toward which discussion will move. Interpreted in the weak sense, the claim would be that discussion cannot occur or be meaningful if it is known that agreement is impossible. The weaker claim is sensible. Surely it is futile to argue, for example, about differing preferences for flavors of ice cream, because it is in the nature of such tastes not to be open to discussion. If disagreement on such matters is succeeded by agreement, the change cannot be motivated solely by argument. But the stronger claim cannot be supported. The real possibility of agreement cannot be validly inferred from the proposition that agreement cannot be *known* to be impossible. Further, it is existentially and psychologically false to assert that participants in a discussion are convinced that agreement is possible. As long as clarification of issues can be achieved, discussion makes sense. The failure to reach agreement says nothing about the eventual achievement of agreement. Most Socratic dialogues break off inconclusively; the participants do not know whether they can ever get where they want to go, only that they have not gotten there yet and that some hope of progress still exists.

This seemingly abstract point has considerable practical significance. Habermas wants to employ philosophical discourse to evaluate and reconstruct politics. But there is an important difference between the two activities. The participants in an inconclusive philosophical discussion can terminate it, with or without a commitment to return to it later; there is no compulsion to reach agreement (ever). But in politics, it is frequently necessary to make a collective decision, to embark on a course of action, whether or not a rational consensus has been or can be reached. An inconclusive dispute cannot just be dropped. However incomplete the evidence, however uncompelling the arguments, something must be done. If it were the case that participants in a free and unfettered political discussion could be sure that rational agreement were possible, they would have an incentive to persevere; if they know only that they do not know that such agreement is impossible, their incentive is, to say the least, considerably reduced. Thus, deliberative bodies are not simply debating societies; they devise institutions and adopt procedures to produce decisions, even in the absence of substantive consensus. Whether or not a particular deliberative body has achieved an appropriate balance between discussion and decision is always open to question; the need for such balance is not. Thus, even in very desirable circumstances it cannot be the case that in politics the only justified constraint is the force of argument. The force of circumstances and the imperatives of action must be given their due.

The third of these difficulties is that the preceding considerations suggest a broader question: To what extent can Socratic philosophical discourse serve as the model for political decisionmaking? The first response is that Socratic discussion takes place between two interlocutors or at most among a very small number. To have any hope of reaching agreement or understanding, individuals must confront one another directly and in depth. Increasing the number of participants transforms the activity; arguments constantly interrupted and deflected cannot be pursued to their conclusion, and the awareness of others to whom one is appearing as one speaks tends to introduce sub-philosophical motives. For this reason, the Greeks identified rhetoric as the mode of discussion appropriate for large groups. Habermas assumes without any argument that numbers make no significant difference. Our every day experience contradicts this. The second response is that the aim of philosophical discourse is the acquisition of clarity and truth. Political activity aims at benefiting the individuals who make up the community and sometimes others as well. It does not seem at all obvious that unclarity, concealment, and lying are always politically wrong, are always in the service of repression and injustice. In some cases telling the truth about the past poisons the future. In some cases replacing ambiguity with clarity eliminates the possibility of joint action by exposing divisions. In some cases myths may be salutary.

Habermas seems to believe that if all the external factors that distort speech were eliminated, most serious differences among human beings would disappear and collective action would be wholly compatible with truth. This is the pure faith of the Enlightenment; Habermas offers us nothing to support it. There are two considerations that argue strongly against it. First: since, as we saw earlier, there is nothing about rational discourse that guarantees that knowledge is available or agreement possible, the unshielded exposure of political opinion to rational examination may lead, not toward a rational society, but to skepticism and disintegration. The destruction of tradition by reason may leave communities with no basis for a common life. Habermas assumes that if a tradition, a system of beliefs and practices, cannot be rationally justified, it is an ideology that serves only to conceal and legitimate domination. He does not consider the possibility that shared belief may satisfy the need for order and provide the ground for collective life, essential tasks to which unaided reason may not be equal. Second: Habermas defines the ideal speech situation as symmetry of opportunities to participate, coupled with the absence of coercion, external or internal. But, as McCarthy points out, formal symmetry is not sufficient to ensure the rationality of discourse or the acceptability of answers. The "reflective capacities of the participants" must be considered as well.[57] Habermas must assume, if his argument is to make any sense, that all human beings are *fully* and *equally* rational—that all have the inclination and ability to participate in complex argument and, therefore, that the worth of the assent of every party to the discussion is the same. There is no reason to believe that this would be true, even in a community in which from birth each individual had the unfettered opportunity to develop fully. In creating a new basis for political evaluation, Habermas wishes to combine the freedom and elevation of Greek philosophical discussion with modern egalitarianism. The two elements of his synthesis are incompatible. It can be held together only by counterfactually denying both human inequality and the distinction between philosophical and political agreement.

The fourth difficulty raised by Habermas is that it is plausible to contend, as he does, that unconstrained discourse is made possible by certain modes of economic/political organization and hindered or even precluded by others. But the empirical implications of such discourse cannot be spelled out on the basis of a purely formal description. Suppose, for example, that human beings suffer not only from external (socially derived) constraint but also from internal constraint and that this can be counteracted only through a rigorous, hierarchically organized moral training and philosophical education. The *Republic* sketches the political implications of this hypothesis. At the beginning of the *Metaphysics* Aristotle noted a connection between free inquiry and the emergence of a leisure class, a link reformulated more recently by Rousseau and Arendt. I do not mean to suggest that either of these arguments is obviously correct or decisive, but only that the problem they point to is unavoidable: Free discourse must be understood not only formally but also substantively if its political implications are to be grasped adequately.

Nevertheless, Habermas's suggestion is important, for two reasons. First: even if political and philosophical discourse are not entirely congruent, they are not disjoint either. It is reasonable and revealing to ask: to what extent and in which respects can philosophy serve as a model for political activity; what is the relation between politics and truth; in what ways are the possibility and substance of philosophical activity conditioned by politics? Second: as McCarthy points out, on one level there is a clear connection between truth and freedom. To assert the truth of a proposition is to claim that one has come to accept it on the basis of argument and evidence rather than out of internal compulsion (passion, desire) or external compulsion (fear, force). Of course, a proposition put forward under compulsion may be true. But the speaker will not know that it is true and probably will not even believe that it is true. The truth of a forced proposition can be established only by an external judge on the basis of free consideration.[58] The question then arises: What is the relation between freedom of the mind and political freedom?[59]

Winch: The presuppositions of community.—Peter Winch's intention is to argue for an intrinsic relation between the fact of language and certain moral norms, such as truth telling, and then to generalize his conclusion to cover a wider range of social practices. He proceeds as follows:

> The notion of a society in which there is a language but in which truth-telling is not regarded as the norm is a self-contradictory one. The conception of a distinction between true and false statements . . . could not *precede* a general adherence to the norm of truth-telling. The relation between these is totally unlike that, say, between a conception of the distinction between the left hand and the right hand side of the road and an adherence to the norm of driving on the left hand side; for here we could first contemplate the two alternatives and *then* decide which one to adopt. But adherence to the norm of truthfulness *goes along with* the distinction between true and false statements; without the one there could not be the other.[60]

Winch considers a possible counterexample: a Hobbesian card game in which the players are all known to one another to cheat when they think they can get away with it. Here, although the game is in a sense constituted by the rules, it is not contradictory to play the game in the full knowledge that you and everybody else will be constantly calculating whether to obey the rules. Even if language is linked to certain rules, why cannot those rules be generally regarded in the same light? Winch replies by denying that this is

> a possible microcosm of a whole society. That would mean that a man's expectation that others will, in general, tell the truth would have to be of a similar kind, as would his own attitude to the alternatives of speaking truthfully and lying. Speaking could only

be regarded as a means of attaining some advantage by manipulating the reactions of other people in a desired way.... Of course an individual can, at least sometimes, regard his utterances in that way, but not all, or even most, uses of language in a society could be generally so regarded. For one can only use words to manipulate the reactions of other men in so far as those others at least think they *understand* what one is saying.[61]

We can begin to evaluate this claim by thinking of it as analogous to the much-discussed "free rider" problem. From the fact that a given practice would, if generally followed, benefit every member of a group it does *not* follow that each member, calculating in isolation, will conclude that everyone ought to comply with that practice. The benefits of noncompliance may well appear greater, provided that most other members of the group do comply. But if most, or even many, individuals reach this conclusion and act on it, the practice will collapse, and they and everyone else will be worse off. Recognizing the dynamic of this development, the individuals in question learn to establish institutions that will enforce compliance on all by imposing penalties on noncompliers. Now, it is certainly the case that the success of the liar rests on generalized expectations about truth telling. Further, the general inculcation of a strong condemnation of lying serves to create an institution that imposes penalties on deviants. But let us suppose, as frequently happens, that the institution fails to accomplish its objective and the practice collapses. Does this mean that "language" has collapsed? I think not. Instead, its character changes. It can be used to conceal what one is doing, to influence others' perceptions, and to inflict pain, even when the speaker is not believed.

Winch's deeper point, although he would certainly not want to state it this way, is that if truth telling collapses, so does language as the framework of human community or sociality. But since language is "essentially social in character," it cannot collapse into an instrument for the pursuit of individual aims. Winch develops this argument in explicit opposition to Hobbes's theory of language, but in at least one respect Hobbes's view seems more sensible. After sketching the uses of speech, Hobbes went on to speak of its abuses. Abuses are catalogued and judged with reference to the standards of use, but abused speech remains speech. With the exception of self-contradictory affirmations, it is not absurd, contradictory, or unintelligible but, rather, wrong to commit an abuse.[62] Winch tries to undermine this position by claiming that it entails Hobbes's contention that society is not natural but, rather, the product of agreement; since this contention is untenable, so is the theory of language.[63] This move is unconvincing. Let us grant, against Hobbes, that society is in some sense natural and language and society go together, language both constituting and reflecting the form of life of the community. Even so, it is perfectly possible that on occasion the form of life will disintegrate because of internal conflicts and that the contending parties, while continuing to speak the same language, cease to use it primarily to communicate and to reach agreement but, instead, redirect it to the attainment of private advantage.

Nevertheless, the core of Winch's position is plausible: The relation between language and truth telling does not seem to be conventional in the same manner as, for example, rules of driving or systems of measurement. The problem is to account for this intuition convincingly. Although I shall not try to prove my case here, I strongly suspect that an examination of the uses or purposes of language will turn out to be the most illuminating point of departure. If, for example, we note the way in which the child's developing language makes possible an increasingly precise description of need and discomfort, we can see how truth telling contributes to timely and beneficial parental acts. And it is in view of the purposes of language that we can understand how exceptions to the norm of truth telling can sometimes be justified. Winch does not deny the validity of exceptions. But because he roots truth telling so deeply in the formal characteristics of language, he is unable to give a satisfying account of the process of justifying exceptions.[64]

Finally, it should be noted that Winch is more of a Hobbesian than he thinks. To say, as he does, that what is nonarbitrary in morality arises out of man's social condition or the common life between men is to assert in effect that all discourse about individual perfection is conventional and that morality, at least as a matter of philosophical as opposed to sociological interest, deals with the regulation of those activities or transactions among men that "concern their living together in peace and unity."[65] This becomes clear when Winch tries to generalize his argument:

> *Integrity* . . . is to human institutions generally what truthfulness is
> to the institution of language. . . . To lack integrity is to act with
> the appearance of fulfilling a certain role but without the intention
> of shouldering the responsibilities to which the role commits one.
> If that, *per absurdum*, were to become the rule, the whole concept
> of a social role would thereby collapse.[66]

Note that integrity is understood, not in relation to the good or worth of the individual who possesses or lacks it, but as necessary, logically and empirically, for the maintenance of a collective activity. This hardly constitutes a defense of integrity as a moral conception unless the collapse of social roles, as Winch conceives of them, is either bad or logically impossible. The latter, unfortunately, is false. For example, a Chicago newspaper recently opened a bar to investigate the enforcement of building and operating codes, only to discover that nearly every city inspector was willing to overlook code violations in exchange for bribes. The city continues to exist and flourish; indeed, its own boosters (and many outsiders) frequently cite it as the preeminent American example of a "city that works." But clearly it does not work on the basis of integrity. In Winch's terms, we would have to say that the concept of a social role has collapsed. But so what? Clearly, if Winch's argument is to be salvaged, his understanding of the "social role" must be viewed neither as logical nor empirical but rather as *moral:* Integrity is good because it is essential for a desirable way of life in which individuals can by and large count on each other to act sincerely and to take their commitments seriously.

Winch provides no argument in favor of this proposition and in fact adduces one against it: If a role (for example, concentration camp commandant) is substantively evil, carrying it out in a committed manner is commonly thought to make it worse, both practically and morally. It may well be that "the propensity of people to act like that was nonetheless an essential factor in the continued existence of such institutions."[67] But that judgment simply goes to show that integrity cannot be an independent virtue because its value is relative to the worth of the institutions it serves to sustain. One can hardly maintain that the continued existence of every institution, or political regime, or form of life is preferable to its collapse. Hobbes tried to do something like that; would Winch really be willing to follow him and to accept the obvious consequences of that position?

Gewirth: The presuppositions of action.—In a painstaking and impressive argument, Alan Gewirth attempts to derive a supreme principle of morality, the Principle of Generic Consistency, through an analysis of the immanent presuppositions of human action. He summarizes his argument as follows:

> An agent is a person who initiates or controls his behavior
> through his unforced, informed choice with a view to achieving
> various purposes; since he wants to fulfill his purposes he regards
> his freedom and well-being, the necessary conditions of his suc-
> cessful pursuit of purposes, as necessary goods; hence he holds
> that he has rights to freedom and well-being; to avoid self-
> contradiction he must hold that he has these generic rights insofar
> as he is a prospective purposive agent; hence he must admit that
> all prospective purposive agents have the generic rights; hence he

must acknowledge that he ought at least to refrain from interfering with his recipients' freedom and well-being, so that he ought to act in accord with their generic rights as well as his own.[68]

Gewirth makes the strong claim that this argument is "dialectically necessary" in that it rests only on assumptions that human beings must accept, implicitly if not explicitly.[69] This is questionable. First, the movement from individual action to the general principle is mediated by the criterion of noncontradiction, but Gewirth does not and cannot show that reason is more than a fundamental commitment that flows from a specific vision of what makes us human or perfects our existence.[70] I shall later argue that this commitment is not a mistake. But the strength of our commitment should not lead us to forget that it is not in the strict sense necessary. Even if, as Gewirth asserts, reason is the only path to objectivity and truth, we must still face Nietzschean skepticism about the worth of truth. Second, Gewirth assumes that we are all agents, pursuing ends that we believe to be good. This assumption overlooks the possibility of skeptical despair—the belief that all goals are equally valueless and unjustifiable. Nietzsche went so far as to assert that self-conscious rationality leads us to the situation of the "logical disciple of Heraclitus" who could no longer act at all.

For the sake of argument, let me grant Gewirth his point of departure, a world of rational agents. The Principle of Generic Consistency cannot be derived from analysis of rational agency, for two reasons.

First, the worth of the ends of action does not imply the worth of the categorial features of action. We may in some cases recognize in ourselves a propensity to abuse our freedom in ways that prevent us from attaining the ends we value. We may, for example, suffer from weakness of will, inadequacies of evaluative skill, or irresolution. It may then be perfectly rational to surrender a portion of our freedom, perhaps permanently. Gewirth dismisses such cases as "pathological," but this cannot be done on conceptual grounds, and his empirical evidence is not persuasive.[71] Nor is it adequate to dismiss suicide—the deliberate annihilation of agency—as an "extreme, untypical case" that does not affect "what holds true in the standard conditions and generic features of action."[72]

Second, even if the categorial features of action are instrumentally necessary to the attainment of our purposes, it does not follow that we necessarily claim that we have rights to them. On the one hand, Gewirth advances a traditional analysis of individual rights as entailing strict obligations for others:

The actions and, more usually, the omissions on which they are predicated are regarded by the agent not merely as preferable or fitting, but rather as required or mandatory, so that he holds that he is entitled to redress and his respondents are subject to severe censure and other appropriate countermeasures . . . if the required conduct is not forthcoming.[73]

On the other hand, the basis of the right-claim is, as Gewirth emphasizes, "prudential": *you* ought to refrain from interfering with x because I need x to be an agent, and I need to be an agent to fulfill my purposes.[74] But I need not regard my purposes as generating claims that others are obliged to honor. First, I recognize that my purposes are not likely by themselves to persuade others that they are obligated to me. Second, I realize that other individuals have purposes that conflict with mine and that I may not be justified in claiming a preferred position for my own. Third, claims based on my purposes are at most provisional. As I shall later argue, there can be no right to do what is wrong, although in some circumstances it may be useless or counterproductive to attempt to prevent such actions. Thus, if someone were to persuade me that my action was morally wrong, I would cease to affirm any right to perform it.

Gewirth might contend that this final objection rests on a misconception. The point of his argument is to establish a criterion of morality by showing that the rational agent is forced to universalize, hence limit, his right-claims. Thus, it makes no sense to apply a moral criterion to the individual agent prior to the stage of universalization, for no such criterion exists.

This reply would be mistaken. I am arguing that the moral limitation on right-claims is built into the concept of the right to act, at least insofar as it imposes obligations on others. Prior to moral reflection the rational agent cannot know that the contemplated act is permissible and thus cannot move directly from the conditions of personal action to right-claims.

Summary: Advantages and disadvantages of immanent arguments.— Immanent arguments are attractive in many ways. By anchoring morality in general features of human existence, they clarify the origin of moral precepts and show why they constitute a distinctively human sphere. By suggesting that these general features involve assertions expressed as norms or claims, they bypass the pitfalls of moving from specific facts (that is, states of affairs) to moral propositions. By arguing that these general features are "necessary" and that their implications may be implicit as well as conscious, they hold out the hope of avoiding both infinite regress and the difficulties inherent in any appeal to an actually existing consensus.

The foregoing analysis has, however, exposed some problems as well. First, the choice of basic features is somewhat arbitrary. Habermas focuses on speech, Winch on community, Gewirth on agency. Each is a plausible point of departure; none is obviously superior. It might well be argued that any fully adequate analysis would have to take all three into account: man is the political, speaking, acting animal, and capable of rationality in all these spheres.

Second, the definition of basic features is by no means simple or obvious. For example, Habermas's characterization of speech turns out to have a normative component; it gives interpretive preference to a particular kind of speech that aims at uncoerced agreement. Similarly, Winch's notion of community rests on a debatable concept of social roles.

Finally, it is questionable whether the proposed basic features are necessary general facts about human beings. We need not speak, at least not in Habermas's sense; we need not exercise rational agency; and we may act for private gain in ways that, if generalized, would undermine the possibility of community.

Immanent arguments do not, then, eliminate all elements of choice or commitment from our moral life. If cogent, they identify the points at which commitments are unavoidable and show that these choices involve the most fundamental issues of how and in what respects we are to be human.

Morality and human needs

In the past two decades a group of thinkers has developed a moral theory that can be labeled *neonaturalist* or *neo-Aristotelian*.[75] The relation of this theory to others, in particular the prescriptivism of Hare, has been much discussed.[76] I do not wish to add to this discussion but rather to examine, more or less in isolation and with no pretense of scholarly completeness, the neonaturalist theses that are most relevant for my purposes.

In a series of articles, a leading member of this group, Philippa Foot, has argued somewhat as follows:

1. Moral language has an intrinsic relation to factual language.
2. This relation is not only formal but also substantive. Not all facts are morally relevant or can be used as bases of moral evaluation.
3. The range of morally relevant facts is delimited on the basis of certain fundamental characteristics of human existence—our wants, needs, or interests.
4. There are some needs that all or nearly all human beings have in common.

5. "Moral virtues" are activities valued because their habitual practice benefits the individual, that is, furthers each individual's pursuit of fundamental needs.

In support of her second argument, Foot offers the example of a man
who clasps his hands three times an hour. She asks how this could
possibly be described as a "good action." The answer, she suggests,
involves the creation of an interpretive background within which this
action takes on significance. Further, to bring this action into the moral
sphere, the action "must be connected with human good and harm,
and . . . it is quite impossible to call anything you like good or harm."[77]
The first half of this claim is granted by many antinaturalists; Hare, for
example, not only concedes it but goes on to link our attitudes about
good and bad to certain ends or needs, in effect affirming the third
argument as well.[78]

The battleground thus shifts to Foot's fourth argument: Are there any
limits, derived from the specifics of human need, to what can be called
good or harm? Foot offers as an example loss of eyesight or of
hands, which "play a part in so many operations that a man could only
be said not to need them if he had no wants at all."[79]

An anecdote concerning the philosopher Brentano has been cited as a
counterexample. When friends expressed sorrow that Brentano had lost
his eyesight, Brentano is said to have replied that he viewed this loss as
a benefit: previously he had not been able to concentrate on the activities that mattered most because his attention was constantly being
captured, willy-nilly, by events around him.[80] But this counterexample
does not seem to me to be decisive. First, Brentano's blindness rendered him more dependent on the eyesight of others; it did not abolish
his need but only transferred the means of satisfying it. This points up
the difference between "possessing" something and "having the use"
of it. Second, Foot's case is strong if, as seems certain, it is very generally the case that sight is desired and prized; the infrequent counterexample may reveal interesting issues without affecting the basic
contention. Third, as Foot emphasizes, to say that all have *a* strong
reason to want something is not to say that reason will *always* be overriding.[81] In fact, to argue as she does that something is instrumentally
necessary is to leave open the possibility that in certain circumstances
the usual relation between means and ends will be disrupted. When
Aristotle argued at the beginning of the *Metaphysics* that all human
beings desire to know, he offered as evidence the intensity with which
we prize sight, which is thought to make an essential contribution to
knowing. The Brentano anecdote merely shows that under some very
special circumstances someone can come to believe that sight no longer

promotes but rather hinders the acquisition of knowledge. The goal that provides the basis for the rule also explains exceptions to it.

For the sake of argument, let us grant that there are some needs that are generally shared and that these needs comprise not only bare survival but also the development of certain abilities or capacities. Even if this were true, the final step in Foot's argument—the identification of moral virtues with those habits that conduce to the attainment of our needs—is open to objection. First, there are some such habits that no one would want to call "virtues." Thus, Foot has at most identified a necessary condition of virtue without laying bare its distinctiveness. Second, the instrumental view of virtue obscures our intuitive belief that virtue is choiceworthy for itself as well as for its fruits—in Aristotle's terms, that it is "noble" as well as "useful." Foot shades over this distinction by talking on the one hand of "needing" the virtues and on the other of virtue as "a quality by which a man [comes] to act well." [82] This ambiguity is displaced once again when the virtues are said to "benefit the man who has them," [83] for benefit can be seen either as intrinsic or as instrumental or both. Third, however one interprets benefit, Foot's insistence that the virtues must benefit each individual who possesses them leads her straight to the problem of the *Republic:* Courage, wisdom, and moderation are usually beneficial, while justice all too frequently is not. She faces the question squarely, but her underlying instrumentalism forces her to offer what is in effect the Hobbesian answer: In the long run the unjust man cannot fool all of those on whom his well-being depends and therefore runs an unreasonable risk of achieving the worst outcome. [84] But alas, this assertion is contrary to our experience; it is either flatly untrue as a generalization, or if true in the long run, only the Keynesian long run in which we are all dead anyway. [85]

Foot's quandary points toward a deeper question. It seems reasonable to assume that morality is somehow related to what benefits individuals. But even if benefit can be given a determinate content, this can at most be a partial understanding. Morality has two other general features that cannot be overlooked: it is concerned with ways in which individuals benefit and harm one another, not only themselves; and it is thought to conform to the dictates of reason. These features figure centrally in any attempt to define and defend justice, though they are not wholly irrelevant to the other virtues. To put the same point more simply: Any account of morality comprehensive enough to deal with justice must contain two elements—an account of what benefits and harms individuals, and a principle or principles according to which these benefits and harms are to be distributed. Neither element can be reduced to or derived from the other; they are independent and must be independently established.

3
Elements of the Human Good

3.1. The Role of a Theory of the Good

It is evident that every theory of justice rests on some view of the good. *Justice* is a term of approval or commendation; we assume that justice is good, or at least preferable to injustice. Without this assumption, the quest for the knowledge of justice on the basis of which we may act justly would make no sense.

The origins of this assumption are revealed in our prereflective opinions about the nature of justice. If we believe that justice is a subset of rational action, its value is a corollary of the value we attach to rationality. If we believe that justice is beneficial or, with Socrates, that the just man harms no one, then the value of justice stems from the worth of the benefits it confers.[1] If we believe that the just is the appropriate or fitting treatment of individuals, we presuppose a dual view of the good: goodness of treatment, and valuable qualities or acts that generate entitlements to good treatment.

Characteristically, though not invariably, justice becomes explicit or thematic during disputes over practices or courses of action. There are two kinds of practical disputes. In disputes over ideals, for example, sincere wars of religion, the nature of the good is itself controversial. In disputes over interests, all parties agree about the nature of the good. The difficulty is to determine who is to receive it, in what amounts, on what basis. Opposed claims in the name of justice arise during the latter kind of dispute. The participants are generally agreed that, for example, increased wealth, educational opportunities, or political influence are valuable, but they disagree about allocative procedures and criteria. It is not farfetched to assert that most political disputes take place in the context of widespread agreement about what is desirable, valuable, or good, and that a greater variety of opinions would decrease competition and increase tranquillity.

There is, I suggest, very considerable agreement about what it means to "benefit" an individual or for an individual to receive "good treatment." The partial theory of the human good that I shall sketch in this chapter will attempt to make the fundamental elements of this agreement explicit and to justify them to the extent that justification is possible. These elements turn out to be *ends:* states, qualities, and activities that human beings value for their own sake. Questions of justice arise, then, in two ways: when these ends are to be allocated directly, and when means to them are to be allocated.

This kind of theory of the good implies the rejection of two other kinds. First, it is incompatible with the theory of the good as universal means. As I shall try to show in my discussion of Rawls's theory of primary goods (pp. 113–15), there are no means that it is rational to value, whatever one's plan of life may be. In my view, appropriate means will vary with circumstances, but the worth of means and of varying quantities of means is determined by their instrumental relation to *determinate* ends that delimit without completely specifying the human good. Second, it is incompatible with any simple and direct equating of individual benefit and individual preference. Although I shall argue that the content of desire points decisively toward the human good, we are nevertheless capable of preferring, and of striving for, proximate goods that do not benefit us. Thus, any "social welfare function" defined in terms of subjective preferences is unlikely to be an adequate measure of human welfare. Conversely, institutions and practices that thwart our subjective preferences may nevertheless promote our welfare. (The theoretical truth of this proposition does not imply that it would be beneficial to create thwarting institutions in many practical situations.)[2]

3.2. Principles of the Human Good: General Features

Before entering into a substantive discussion of the basic principles of the human good, it may be helpful to offer some brief general remarks about their character and purpose.

First, these principles are intended to provide an adequate basis for judgments about justice and other related questions concerning public policy. I do not claim that they can resolve all the moral issues that arise in politics, nor do I claim that morality as a whole can be traced back to them. At the very least, if they are accepted as correct, any additional principles must be compatible with them; this requirement may serve as a useful criterion. In addition, it may well come to seem plausible that other apparently ultimate and irreducible principles can better be understood as derived from and limited by the ones I designate as *basic*.

I do not, for example, deal systematically with the moral virtues other than justice. This may seem to some to be a strange and dangerous omission, especially on the part of a theorist who claims to be inspired by Aristotle. There are three reasons for this seeming omission. First, I understand Aristotle to be arguing against the Platonic thesis of the

unity of the virtues. Each virtue embodies a distinctive set of supporting considerations and applies to a special range of activities. To consider one virtue in isolation from the others is not necessarily to distort
it. Second, I believe that the virtues as traditionally understood can be
largely though not entirely interpreted as excellences—that is, as the
appropriately developed forms of basic human capacities or as the
means by which our capacities can be well exercised. If this is so, then
my discussion of the *worth of development* as a principle of the human
good covers a significant portion of the issue I might appear to have
neglected. Finally, although distinguishing characteristics of individuals play a large role in my view of justice, I shall argue that the kinds of
characteristics relevant to justice are for the most part excellences that
are in the broadest sense *skills:* the demonstrated ability to act successfully in various spheres. The virtues enter the sphere of justice only
insofar as they enable us to perform activities that give rise to claims
that others are rationally compelled to honor. If this is so, then those
aspects of the virtues left untouched by the discussion of development
do not affect the question of justice, although they are of great human
significance for other reasons.

My second general remark is that these principles are not intended as
an arbitrary axiomatization, justified only by clarity and simplicity.
Rather, they have descriptive, experiential force, in two senses. They
are widely acknowledged by those engaged in practical reasoning; more
precisely, normal deeds and judgments presuppose them, and most of
us can be led to acknowledge them through discussion. Further, they
seem to be presupposed by a wide variety of existing moral theories.

My third remark is that these principles are intended to be recognized
as *ultimate.* This is not to say that one cannot appeal beyond them to
some higher or more general principle, but only that such an appeal
seems neither necessary nor productive. One possible explanation is
that these principles provide the horizon for, or are constitutive of, the
moral sphere. It is only in light of them that particular moral questions
arise and have any possibility of being answered.

Fourth, if these principles are subjected to a fundamental challenge,
no compelling defense is available. They are neither synthetic-
necessary nor analytic truths, and it is not clear that any evidence can
influence the beliefs of those who really reject them. To put it another
way: I shall argue that there is a peculiarly close relation between the
moral sphere and belief, so that the content of our belief, after due
reflection, is the most powerful kind of evidence in moral argument. An
appeal to what is generally believed, even if factually correct, will not
persuade someone who begins by rejecting either the content of this
belief or its evidentiary force.

Fifth, despite these arguments, the fact of agreement is not accidental nor its content arbitrary. Both are rooted in widely shared features of human existence. If basic characteristics of human beings were different, or if our circumstances were radically transformed, the content of our moral beliefs would be different. Thus, if Kant is interpreted as proposing a substantive moral theory valid for "all rational beings," it is very doubtful that such a theory could be wide enough to ground more than a small fraction of our judgments.[3]

Sixth, the fact that I am proposing a multiplicity of basic principles, mutually irreducible, means that conflicts and problems of priority will emerge in practice. *Ex hypothesi,* these difficulties cannot be resolved by appealing to some "higher" principle. If intuitionism (in Rawls's sense) is to be avoided, then the ordering and harmonization of principles must be based on considerations internal to the principles themselves.

3.3. The Worth of Existence

Aristotle put the case for the worth of existence in the following terms:

> Life is in itself good and pleasant. We can see that from the very fact that everyone desires it.... Moreover, when a person sees, he perceives that he sees; when he hears, he perceives that he hears; when he walks, he perceives that he walks; and similarly in all other activities there is something that perceives that we are active. This means that, in perception, we perceive that we perceive, and in thinking we perceive that we think. But to perceive that we are perceiving or thinking means that we exist, since, as we saw, existence is perceiving or thinking. Now, to perceive that we are living is something pleasant in itself, for existence is by nature good, and to perceive that that good thing is inherent in us is pleasant.[4]

Note that the good of life and the pleasure of life are distinguished and that the pleasure we take in existence is rendered dependent on its goodness. But the most important point is that the general *desire* for life is a criterion of its worth. This makes sense only if we supply a premise something like: Anything that is generally desired is good.

That good and pleasure are distinguished does not mean that they are unrelated. Aristotle recognized that extreme physical pain can lead to a negative judgment about the worth of existence.[5] Moreover, he acknowledged the fact of suicide, tracing it to psychological–moral as well as physiological causes.[6] These are not inconsistencies. To say that life is good is not to assert that it is *the* good but rather *a* good. Thus, it can be at once desired and rejected.

Does the argument from general desire make sense? First, to assert that anything generally desired is good is not to claim that anything good is generally desired. General desire is a sufficient but not necessary condition of goodness. Second, Aristotle noted that it is logically possible to reject this argument but that this move undercuts substantive moral reasoning altogether.[7] If morality does not reflect fundamental facts about human existence, in what else can it consist? It expresses, orders, clarifies, and, when necessary, supplements them; it can neither contradict nor ignore them. More generally, human existence sets the problem for which morality is the purported solution. The "good" in moral discourse is relative to this problem. Moral discussion begins with the decision to take the problem seriously, to give weight to the fact and content of existence.

It is of course possible to reject this internal or "humanist" characterization of morality in the name of morality itself. Existence, one may insist, cannot be said to have worth unless it is grounded in something the worth of which cannot be disputed. In some form this premise underlies most theological claims concerning human existence. This premise is open to three kinds of objections. First, the (probably necessary) failure of philosophical theology means that the source of absolute worth becomes manifest only through faith. It is, to say the least, not clear that replacing the assumptions of humanism with the demands of faith renders morality any more secure or less disputable. Second, while the rejection of humanism leaves open other ways of accounting for morality, including the theological, the theological argument is an all-or-nothing proposition: either faith or despair. This is more than an abstract problem. Contemporary nihilism, so pervasive and dangerous, comes into existence by combining the theological premise about the source of meaning or worth with a denial of the existence or intelligibility of that source.[8] Third, it is not clear that the demand for certainty at the heart of the theological argument is either proper or necessary. If moral claims are intrinsically deniable and arguments supporting them at most probable and suggestive, the quest for certainty may pervert rather than defend the moral sphere. If this assertion seems somehow mystical and evasive, consider the problem of proving the existence of the external world. Is it not clear, after centuries of effort, that the quest for a proof is misguided and that this provides us with insight into the kind of relation we have to the world rather than with a reason for skeptically denying it? Perhaps the beginning of wisdom is the realization that we ought not to doubt everything we can doubt.[9]

The plausibility of Aristotle's premise emerges clearly when the problem of suicide is considered. If someone has ceased to desire life, and his death will not have a significant negative impact on anyone to whom he is responsible, what arguments can or ought to dissuade him from killing himself? Perhaps his circumstances or his self-perception will change so that existence will again come to seem desirable; by killing himself he is depriving himself of this favorable opportunity. Fair enough; but this is to concede the validity of the major premise.

The argument that suicide is a form of murder, subject to the same prohibitions, works no better. First, the negative judgment of murder itself presupposes the worth of existence. To see this, imagine a world in which individuals generally perceive their lives as burdensome and welcome death, but in which for complex psychological reasons most individuals cannot kill either themselves or others. In such a world murder would be seen as beneficial and would therefore be encouraged, and the ability to commit it would be a sign of unusual virtue. Second, we resist the assimilation of suicide to murder. Intuitively we feel that murder is more horrible than suicide and that killing someone is less horrible if that person asks to be killed. Indeed, under some circumstances, complying with that request may be a duty of friendship and a refusal, the result of squeamishness and self-regard (consider the ending of *Julius Caesar*, or the mercy killing of someone paralyzed and racked by pain).

These intuitions reflect our belief that we stand in a special relation to our own lives; we are at liberty to deal with ourselves in ways that would not be appropriate to impose on others. Also, taking someone else's life ceases to be reprehensible if that person wishes to die. Of course it is our duty to examine the reasons carefully. If despair is based on false information, or short-range considerations, or an inadequate view of what is possible, or intrinsically unrealistic hopes, or incorrect self-perception, we must do everything in our power to make the other person aware of this. But if none of these is the case, what can we say? Moreover, at some point subjective sense becomes decisive. Even if someone's unalterable weariness with existence is based on a mistake, the absence of desire to live means that his existence has been deprived of worth *for him*. The views of others on this matter are not of equal weight.

If the formal connection Aristotle wished to establish between the desire for life and its worth is granted, the rest of the argument flows easily. It seems clear that this desire, though not universal, is very widespread and that it serves as one of the fixed points for the evaluation of moral claims and public policy. For example, linking a proposed course of action to the public safety is ordinarily a powerful though not decisive argument. There is little disagreement about the provision of subsistence and medical care as goals. Even those who recently called for deliberate starvation and neglect as instruments of population planning invariably based their proposals on the claim (the factual merits of which are contestable) that the failure to take distasteful steps now would only lead to more deaths through war and starvation later.

3.4. The Worth of Developed Existence

We exist as beings of a certain kind, endowed with organs of sense, practical abilities, and intellectual capacities. These facts carry with them an evaluative force: in general we believe that it is preferable to develop and exercise these powers and that their full development constitutes the norm through which partial realizations are judged. This belief is not merely imposed on our existence. Children have a natural impulse to develop themselves by sharpening their senses, gaining physical dexterity, and satisfying their curiosity. Good childrearing fosters and, when necessary, regulates this impulse; the bad represses it.

As further evidence, consider the following facts. We seek to reduce the incidence of birth defects, among the most serious of which are impairment of senses and retardation. We view with particular horror the severe childhood malnutrition that permanently stunts innate capacities. Very few of us would consent to operations or drugs that we knew would permanently impair our capacities, even if we were promised inner tranquillity or prolonged physical existence in return.

Three sorts of objections are commonly raised against the worth of developed existence. First, there are circumstances in which the abandonment of senses seems reasonable, even good. Second, some innate abilities ought not to be developed. Third, the development of the intellect contradicts the requirements of human well-being.

There is nothing odd about choosing to be anesthetized before an operation or about wanting to faint when witnessing the murder of one's children. Even the story that Brentano welcomed the loss of his sight as an aid to philosophical concentration makes sense. But such examples are not decisive. As soon as one grants, as one must, that the possession of senses is not the sole good, then it becomes very likely that circumstances will arise in which other—contradictory—goods are judged to be more important. In addition, such circumstances seem to be relatively rare. It is not unreasonable to take one's bearings from what is usual. Also, there is a crucial difference between voluntary and involuntary loss of senses, between permanent and temporary loss, and between losing a sense and never having it. Brentano did not contend that he would have been a better philosopher had he been born blind. Presumably, those who believe that Beethoven's growing deafness was causally linked to the increased reflectiveness, depth, originality, and power of his later music would not argue that being deaf from birth would have been preferable.

There are indeed some innate abilities that should not be developed. Once again this reflects the fact that basic principles limit one another in ways that we later shall try to make more precise. For example, the killer can usually exercise his art only by depriving others of what is rightfully theirs, and irreplaceable. The question becomes more complex when what is good for others is not an issue. If someone develops the ability to lie in ways that conduce to the attainment of selfish ends without harming anyone else, we could oppose this only by arguing that it conflicts with other goals that the actor will ultimately judge to be more important. Perhaps the habit of lying will make it difficult to sustain friendships or will reduce the felt value of achieved ends; perhaps it will lead to self-contempt if one comes to believe that it reflects a lack of courage. This question is further complicated by the fact that one's own good and the good of others can diverge. In wartime it may be necessary to swallow one's distaste and develop a wide range of innate but ordinarily suppressed abilities. A stock literary theme is the difficulty many experience in controlling the exercise of these abilities once peace returns; we cannot simply be wiped clean like slates. But these sad facts suggest a further difficulty: it is impossible to specify abilities that should under no circumstances be developed. At this point in the discussion we can say only that the principle of developing one's abilities has prima facie force; the alternatives seem to imply frustration, tension, or mediocrity. But this principle must be restricted by considerations of one's own good (broadly conceived), the good of others, and special circumstances.

The case against the worth of intellectual development has become familiar since Rousseau. Such development, it is charged, leads to the destruction of the horizon of belief needed for individual and collective existence, leaving in its place a debilitating and dangerous skepticism. It undercuts the basis for passionate commitment to courses of action, without which nothing great can be accomplished. It destroys the active, creative powers, replacing them with the merely passive and critical. In destroying the natural bonds and sympathies that unite us, it promotes alienation from others, a calculating selfishness; at the same time we become alienated from ourselves. The worth of the sensual is denigrated. Worse, the sense of worth of our individual existence ceases to be internal and self-generated; it becomes fatally dependent on the approbation of others, who are equally concerned with self-affirmation. In principle, then, external validation can never replace internal. Thus, the development of the intellect and of human misery go hand in hand. Finally, the development of the intellect means a progressive liberation from natural constraints, paving the way for perversion, degradation, cruelty, and murderousness of a scope unparalleled in the order of nature.[10]

Clearly, no simple refutation of these charges would be plausible. But some objections are at least germane. First of these is that the antithesis between intellectual development and necessary belief rests on one of two premises: either reason is incapable of providing justifications for particular courses of action, or rational guidance can be understood and acted on by only a few extraordinary individuals, leaving the majority doubting and bewildered. Neither of these is self-evidently true. If substantive moral theory is possible, then the first is false. And if enlightenment, even though incomplete, inclines us to believe what is in fact true, the latter is false as well. For example—although admittedly this, and indeed any, case is controversial—many historians have seen a connection between the relatively high level of average intellectual development among the American colonists and their willingness to accept as valid the principles of the Declaration of Independence.

The second objection is that the antithesis between intellectual awareness on the one hand and passionate commitment or activity— military, political, artistic—on the other seems overdrawn. Awareness sometimes kills love, sometimes deepens it. Far from destroying courage, knowledge may be the only secure basis of the willingness to die. The commitment to lucidity and to politics have frequently been combined (consider Cicero and Marcus Aurelius). Allegations of tension between the intellect and artistic creation, though not entirely groundless, seem to stem more from a particular theory of art than from inspection of actual artistic activity (consider the fusion achieved by, for example, Plato or Sartre).

Third among the objections is that the claim that "natural," unreflective relations among human beings are characterized by unity and mutual sympathy is at least questionable. One does not need to swallow Hobbes whole to believe that the unreflective pursuit of natural inclinations leads to antagonisms the overcoming of which requires awareness and reflection. As a product of reason, the bond of justice is midway between the uncalculating union of pure friendship and unfettered hostility. To the extent that friendship exists, justice is unnecessary.[11] But it does not seem possible to achieve, or to maintain for any significant period, friendship among members of a group of even moderate size. Sustained peace and cooperation thus cannot exist without reflective regulation.

One might also note the relation between reason and universality. Even Rousseau was compelled to admit that enlightenment can be a source of unity by helping us to overcome unreasoned preferences for ourselves or for what is nearby and familiar—preferences that all too frequently lead to conflict. Finally, if secure bonds among human beings rest on enduring sharing, then what is intrinsically most capable of being shared would seem to provide the securest basis. Activities whose goal is some kind of awareness are of this character; unlike military alliances, business partnerships, and private relationships of pleasure or mutual convenience, whose objects are both transitory and scarce, such activities as aesthetic contemplation and intellectual exploration are enhanced by being shared (or at least do not raise the same kinds of distributional questions) and reflect the human characteristics least subject to variation.

Fourth, the antithesis between reason and sensuality is overdrawn. It is not true that the development of reason leads to, or mandates, asceticism, although reason will almost certainly place some limits on pleasure if only through counsels of prudence. It is the case, however, that reason raises doubts quickly but answers them slowly if at all. If we pause before every potential pleasure to examine its merits and consequences, we are likely to miss most of the experiences that give life its charm and excitement, later to spend time consumed with regret and self-pity. Thus reason itself suggests some limits to reasoning. Similarly, an excess of deliberation can be politically disastrous.

Neither is it the case that reasoning is inherently ascetic or painful. It does have a painful component, to the extent that it is laborious and requires the overcoming of difficult obstacles. But the perception that one is overcoming, or even doing one's best to overcome, can be a source of compensating pleasure. Besides, the occasional periods when reason is functioning smoothly, powerfully, and adequately can produce an unparalleled exaltation. Even Hobbes, whose account of reason as "reckoning" is in no small measure responsible for recent tendencies to view reason ascetically, has this to say about the roots of human reasoning:

> Man is distinguished, not only by his reason but also by this singular passion [curiosity] from other *animals;* in whom the appetite of food, and other pleasures of sense, by predominance, take away the care of knowing causes; which is a lust of the mind, that by a perseverance of delight in the continual and indefatigable generation of knowledge, exceedeth the short vehemence of any carnal pleasure.[12]

Another source of the belief that reasoning is painful is the contention that existence is disordered, brutal, ugly, or contemptible and that these characteristics of what is to be known are necessarily translated into aversion on the part of the knower. Our earlier discussion provides a partial answer. If we value our own existence, it cannot be the case that, on balance, our perception of our activities of perceiving or knowing is a negative experience that we would rather be rid of. Whether this is so because the world is not experienced as negative or because knowing and perceiving are valued, whatever the characteristics of their object, is a fascinating question with which we cannot now deal.

The fifth objection is that, even if there were a serious tension between reason and happiness, this would not be a decisive consideration unless the worth of an activity were simply equated with its happiness producing properties. Although, as we shall see, there are good reasons to give happiness great weight, monistic eudaimonism is probably a mistake. We can admire acts of courage that misfire, benefiting neither the actor nor anyone else. It is not absurd, logically or psychologically, to imagine someone choosing a life of discontented rational awareness over blissful obliviousness. Rousseau recognized—or at least reflected—this. After criticizing the development of rationality in the *Second Discourse,* he praised it in the *Social Contract.*[13] The former rests on the criterion of happiness; the latter, on the "elevation" or intrinsic worth of being fully human.

Sixth, it is true that reason, negating our unself-conscious experience of the world and unreflective sense of what is good and true, fills us with doubt and can thus render us dependent on the opinions of others. In many ways intellectuals are more slavish and more vulnerable to fads than those who are involved in politics or production. But this is only half the story. Reason is the source, not only of dependence, but also of what is probably the only genuine freedom. To achieve it we must extend reason to its limit, rejecting the authority not only of the immediate or conventional but also of the novel and dramatic. We are free only when no premise of our thought or action is hidden and each one that determines our activity has been rationally accepted. And, as Aristotle noted, reason also liberates us from dependence on external goods and chance, to the extent humanly possible.[14]

Seventh: The Greeks had already observed that the liberation from nature reason engenders also makes possible unprecedented degradation and cruelty. But this was not taken to be a compelling argument for the depreciation or abandonment of reason. If the abuse of reason degrades humanity, the perfection exalts it. On balance, the opportunities outweigh the dangers. It should be added that liberation from nature entails neither a negative attitude toward nature nor its conquest, although much modern thought has drawn precisely these inferences. Through reason we can extend or correct nature without contradicting it. Eyeglasses are a contrivance of reason, but they merely supplement the given natural material to achieve a natural norm of activity. This is true for internal nature as well. Some mental illnesses can be ameliorated only through the same pharmacological competence that allows us to distort consciousness.

Let us suppose that the foregoing arguments make plausible the general contention that the development of capacities is an important element of the human good. Even so, these arguments are incomplete in a crucial respect. We cannot be satisfied with a mere enumeration of kinds of capacities. There are enormous differences among them, and much depends on the relative weight given to the development of each. We must, then, try to discover some ordering among them as a basis for choice.

There are, of course, many different kinds of orderings. Let me briefly sketch the possibilities most relevant to the present discussion.

1. *Quantitative orderings.* Goods are ranked according to the extent that they possess some attribute taken as the measure. Pleasure and utility are traditional candidates, but intuited or "nonnatural" attributes are also possible.

2. *Teleological orderings.* Some good serves as the "end," and all others are ranked in accordance with their propensity to further this end. There are two types within this category: *dominant-end orderings,* in which some homogeneous good serves as the end (an example of this is Aristotle's argument at the end of the *Nicomachean Ethics* for the perfection of the theoretical faculty as the highest good); *inclusive-end orderings,* in which some heterogeneous set of goods serves as the end (an example of this occurs in Aristotle's *Eudemian Ethics,* in which moral virtue and intellectual perfection are together said to constitute *eudaimonia,* the goal of human endeavor).[15]

3. *Heterogeneous orderings.* Goods are taken to be qualitatively different and independently defined, ranked on the basis of intuition, consensus, "dialectical argument," etc. Within this kind of ordering there are two variables: *item-orderings* v. *class-orderings* (in item-orderings each good stands in a strong preference relation to every other good— that is, it is either higher or lower than the others; in class-orderings classes of goods stand in preference-relations to one another, but items within classes are unranked); *continuous* v. *lexical orderings* (in continuous orderings each good is linked to every other good by indifference curves, while in lexical orderings lower goods may be added to but cannot be substituted for higher goods, whatever the relative quantities).

The interaction of these variables produces the possibilities shown in Figure 1.

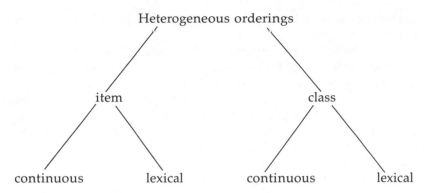

Figure 1. Types of heterogeneous orderings

Capacities are, I would argue, most sensibly ranked in a continuous class heterogeneous ordering, for the following reasons.

1. Quantitative orderings are inappropriate because capacities do not possess a common measure. Each capacity represents a different dimension of human existence. Groups of capacities, for example, the senses, share some common features, but these features do not afford an adequate basis for measurement.

2. Teleological orderings are inappropriate because most capacities cannot be adequately understood as directed toward other goods. In Aristotle's dominant-end argument at the conclusion of the *Nicomachean Ethics*, all practical activities—political and moral—are reinterpreted as means to the end of contemplation, a move that contradicts his compelling earlier description of moral activities as performed for their own sake on account of their intrinsic "nobility."[16] This difficulty is not averted by the inclusive-end strategy. Even if, for example, the contemplative end is broadened by the addition of moral capacities, it remains implausible to say that we value the senses, or productive activities, or the arts, or the life of the family, simply as means. And if the end is so broadened as to include all capacities, it can no longer perform an ordering function.

There are, in addition, substantive arguments against dominant-end positions; there is no a priori reason to believe that the highest good consists in the development of a single capacity, and our experience suggests otherwise. It would be bizarre, except in special circumstances, to embark on a program of exercise that developed one muscle while allowing the others to atrophy. Our souls contain many heterogeneous capacities and, by analogy, our good lies in the systematic exercise of each so as to produce a harmonious, mutually supporting totality. Further, as Aristotle himelf suggested, it is not possible to perform one activity continuously without tiring of it and ceasing to do it well.

3. Thus, both direct arguments and the defects of the other alternatives point toward a heterogeneous ordering as the most plausible possibility. Further:

a. It seems unlikely that we can move much beyond a class ordering. Perhaps, for example, we can agree that there is a group of higher capacities—religious, political, artistic, contemplative. But how can we nonarbitrarily rank within this group without presupposing what is at issue? The Platonic critique of poetry appeals to the criterion of truth; the Aristotelian subordination of statesmanship to contemplation rests on an arguable analysis of leisure. It seems ridiculous to be asked to choose among Jesus, Da Vinci, Caesar, and Socrates; without doing so, we can respect each for having fully developed an important kind of human possibility.

b. It is counterintuitive to contend that capacities are lexically ordered; at some point, the additional increment of time and effort devoted to the higher capacity forces us to forgo too much of the lower.[17] Of course, individuals differ. Some behave for extended periods as though only one capacity matters, practicing an instrument or working in a laboratory every waking hour, indifferent to family and friends, politics, even their own bodies. But in most cases this eventually becomes an insupportable strain as the demands of the repressed aspects of the self escalate in urgency and intensity. And even if the agent is able to persist, outside observers can judge the life that results to be unenviable. To be sure, a lexical ordering forces us to choose only when time and effort are scarce. Some are so gifted that they can develop their highest capacities without being compelled to sacrifice anything else. Others (most of us) must choose between a single excellence and lower but more even development in various spheres. If we were nothing but tools or functions, the path of single excellence might be sensible; an ensemble of specialized, single-function tools may collectively work better than a single large tool the design of which reflects the compromises inherent in multiple functions. But of course we are not simply functions. Our capacities are aspects of our character or self and cannot be accurately weighed in abstraction from this relation. I would suggest, though I cannot prove, that in developing our character there is a substantial convergence between the aesthetic criteria of unity, coherence, and balance and the subjective criterion of long-run satisfaction.

If all this is generally acceptable, I must now try to give some substance to the distinction between higher and lower capacities. A full discussion would require another book. Let me simply list some criteria that appear to capture widely shared intuitions. Higher capacities:

- —are features of our distinctive humanity (for example, morality, complex production, theoretical inquiry) as opposed to "vegetative" functions or the senses
- —are, in their well-developed forms, relatively rare
- —are thought to be difficult or demanding
- —are relatively inclusive—that is, are capable of serving as principles of order around which a life may reasonably be constructed—because they stand in teleological relations to a large number of subordinate goods or activities
- —have, when exercised, a wide range of significant effects on other human beings (effects that need not be intended, or intrinsic to the activities *per se*)
- —have been accorded wide and enduring respect

If, as I believe, the systematic application of these criteria produces a reasonably determinate, continuous class heterogeneous ordering of capacities, we arrive at a principle of choice that is both objective and sensitive to the differing endowments of individuals:

Develop one or more of the highest capacities within your power, subject to the constraints of unity, coherence, and balance between these capacities and those in other classes.

Note one attractive feature of this principle: it enables us to say that it is not rational to pursue the development of a higher capacity with which we are not generously endowed in preference to a lower capacity that we can develop adequately if the effort the former requires will distort our life, considered as a whole.

3.5. The Worth of Happiness

In considering happiness, let us begin with the obvious. Man is a being of desires. Desire implies lack or absence, coupled with the impulse to overcome this lack. Not everything that is lacked is desired, but only that which appears good. If happiness is comprehensive satisfaction, and if satisfaction is the fulfillment of desire, then happiness is the presence of the totality of what appears good. Two conditions must be satisfied. The presence must be secure and enduring; we are not satisfied if what appears good is (or is felt to be) in danger of being removed from us. Second, what appears good when absent must continue to appear good when present.

The worth of happiness follows directly from this analysis. If x appears good, then its presence appears good. But then happiness, the perception of the presence of the totality of apparent good, is felt to be good. Thus, if a person explains personal actions by subsuming them under the pursuit of happiness, questioning comes to an end. The query, "Why do you want to be happy?" is ordinarily thought to be superfluous, since it amounts to asking, "Why do you want what appears good to you?" Of course, various accounts of why particular objects appear good to particular individuals can be advanced, but the general question can be addressed only by pointing once again to the factual connection between desire and the apparent good. And if it is asked why this fact implies the worth of happiness, we can answer only that what we *are* is so intertwined with our desire that we cannot withdraw weight or significance from it.

Thus far, the analysis has been completely formal. Now let us consider a simple example. From a prereflective standpoint, if we are thirsty, we want to quench our thirst, and we accordingly seek any object that will enable us to attain that goal. (If a plurality of such objects is available, other criteria may come into play.) The state of desiring is undesirable; we desire the annihilation of desire, and we prize that which annihilates it. But clearly this view is too simple. We also value the process by which thirst is quenched; indeed, within very broad limits drinking appears good in relation to the extent of our thirst. Thirst cannot be wholly undesirable, for it is the basis of something desirable. Further, it is only on the basis of desiring that we anticipate satisfaction, and the anticipation of the presence of what is desired is itself desirable. These facts are the ground of pervasive modes of behavior. Many people seek to prolong the process of gratification by, for example, eating or drinking very slowly. Others seek to delay satisfaction in order to prolong the delights of anticipation. Many sexual *mœurs*, now unhappily quite rare, had this effect. Current practices reflect an imperfect understanding of what desire is for and thus, in the name of unfettered satisfaction, eliminate one of its primary sources. Finally, desires are deliberately created. Sated Romans made themselves vomit so they could return to the feast with renewed zest. And some people who are unusually impassive sexually seek out situations that will stimulate them. They desire to desire.

These considerations suggest the following conjecture. Sometimes we prize desire without regard to its fulfillment, as when someone, after a long period of indifference to food, realizes that he is hungry. Perhaps the desire is valued as an intensification of life. Sometimes we do want the annihilation of desire through the presence of its object. More frequently, we want neither pure desire nor pure satiation, but rather the simultaneous copresence of desire and its object. This accounts in part for the classical defense of contemplation. Contemplation allows us to possess the object without destroying it. Conversely, this mode of possession seems, to an unusual degree, not to destroy the desire to contemplate.[18] To put the same point another way: we primarily desire a form of activity, coupled with consciousness of that activity. In this respect, at least, Callicles' position is perfectly correct:

SOCRATES.   Then the view that those who have no wants are
            happy is wrong?
CALLICLES. Of course; at that rate stones and corpses would be
            supremely happy.[19]

There are two sets of distinctions that illuminate the heterogeneity of desire. First, one can distinguish between "physical" desires and "psychological" desires. Physical desires are direct expressions of organic requirements or impulses: food, warmth, procreation. It is in this sense that animals can be said to desire. Psychological desires, on the other hand, are mediated by consciousness. Three types are immediately apparent: awareness of physical desire; desires freely chosen or posited through the imagination; and desires inherent in and specific to consciousness itself. Physical desire is the ground of the quest for annihilation of desire; the psychological, of enduring gratification of enduring desire. Second, desire points in two directions. On the one hand it implies lack; the overcoming of lack is fulfillment, the supplying of what is missing. On the other, it implies pain; consciousness of lack is pain, which is not to say that all pain is consciousness of lack. Pain can be negated in two ways: through cessation (the state of not-feeling-pain) or through pleasure. Both the overcoming of lack and the cessation of pain are correlated in different ways with the annihilation of desire. But enduring pleasure must be correlated with some enduring process or activity.

The worth of happiness has been subjected to a number of lines of criticism. For our purposes two are important: the claim that happiness as a goal of striving is inherently unattainable, even illusory; and the claim that happiness cannot be judged good without qualification.

The claim that happiness is unattainable or illusory has a number of variants. First, it may be argued that desires contradict one another, so happiness as total satisfaction of desire makes no sense. To evaluate this thesis we must note that desires contradict one another in different ways. Perhaps the most common is *temporal* contradiction: we want to engage in activities that cannot be performed simultaneously. But this is not in itself an insoluble difficulty. We resolve to perform the activities sequentially—writing an article, then playing the piano, then going to the movies. Temporarily deferring one activity does not impede happiness if we are fairly sure that that activity is available to us whenever we decide to perform it. This can be seen even in very young children. They may scream when prevented from doing something at a particular moment, but once they learn that deferral is not denial (not a simple process, since it implies the development of time-sense) the sting of deferral is greatly reduced. And if Aristotle's contention that no activity can be performed indefinitely without losing its savor is correct, then sequential performance of desired activities is not only necessary but also best from the standpoint of happiness itself.

If conflicting desires cannot be performed sequentially, then *existential* contradiction occurs. A young woman wishes both to be a first-rate ballet dancer and to have a family. Let us suppose that these desires cannot be gratified simultaneously and that deferral means denial. If she pursues ballet to the height of perfection and success, she will be too old to have children. Clearly, she must make an exclusive choice. But to conclude that such a choice necessarily implies unhappiness, we must assume that repressed desire persists undiminished through time, producing longing and regret. This assumption is arbitrary. It rests, first, on the belief that desire is not affected by the reasoned choices we make. But if, in choosing between x and y, we come to realize that x matters to us more than y, this realization has an effect on the way y appears to us and on the force of the claims it makes on us. And second, it assumes that desire is unaffected by the impossibility of its gratification. But if we really come to believe that an object of desire is unattainable, we cease to desire it. (When analyzed closely, the usual counterexamples reveal that the desire for the unattainable is felt to be desirable in itself, hence is a source of gratification. But then the unattainable ceases to be the real object of desire, and the desire ceases to be an impediment to happiness.) That the "impossible" is here defined in part by our own choice makes no difference. *Ex hypothesi,* the need to make an exclusive choice is as unavoidable as laws of physics or requirements of logic.

The foregoing is not intended to show that existential contradiction cannot produce frustration of desire, but only that it need not do so. Two important clarifications of our initial characterization of happiness have come to light. For one, the concept of *totality of desire* is ambiguous. It can refer either to the sum of unexamined particular desires or to the organized whole of desires we can develop through reflection, comparison, rank-ordering, and choice. If happiness is defined relative to the former (merely additive) totality, it is almost certain to be unattainable. But there is no good reason to take prereflective desire as our benchmark. Indeed, most human action presupposes an ordering of desire; far from being imposed on desires, reflection brings out their immanent relations. Nevertheless, reflection on the desires does not leave them unaffected. Contradictions are resolved, priorities and trade-offs established. Happiness is relative to this organized totality.

For the second, it now appears that the lack correlated with desire may be removed in two ways. Either what is lacking may be obtained, or the perception of something as lacking may be altered, so that we no longer desire it. The attainment of happiness requires us to combine these modes. Purged of all lacks, we cannot enjoy anything. But if our unexamined feelings of lack are allowed to determine our behavior, our striving will be frustrated.

To return to the claim that happiness is unattainable or illusory: Hobbes argued against the possibility of happiness as total gratification of desire by placing special emphasis on the consequences of the desire for continuing, enduring gratification. In a famous passage he argued that

> felicity is a continual progress of the desire, from one object to another; the attaining of the former, being still but the way to the latter. The cause whereof is, that the object of man's desire, is not to enjoy once only, and for one instant of time; but to assure for ever, the way of his future desire. And therefore the voluntary actions, and inclinations of all men, tend, not only to the procuring, but also to the assuring of a contented life. . . . So that in the first place, I put for a general inclination of all mankind, a perpetual and restless desire of power after power, that ceaseth only in death. And the cause of this, is not always that a man hopes for a more intensive delight, than he has already attained to; or that he cannot be content with a moderate power: but because he cannot assure the power and means to live well, which he hath present, without the acquisition of more.[20]

Hobbes was right. The desire to assure the possession of what one values leads to endless striving, since perfect assurance is unattainable. A consequence of this, left unstated by Hobbes, is that the desire for secure possession of the good undercuts the gratification of possessing it. Consider some examples. The healthy person who seeks assurance of continued health turns into a fearful hypochondriac. The worried owner of property, investing in ever more complex security systems, at length cannot even bear to leave his property or to fall asleep. The lover seeking assurance of eternal fidelity can destroy love through obsequiousness or jealousy. The scholar who begins to worry about the possibility of a stroke that would deprive him of his mental acuity is deflected from his inquiries.

But Hobbes's description poses the problem without solving it. If the goal of absolute security is unattainable and conflicts with our enjoyment of what we can attain, it would seem to follow that the desire for absolute security is in the strictest sense irrational. If so, one task of reason is to moderate this desire by teaching us to accept the element of contingency and uncertainty in our existence. A delicate balance must be struck. Up to a point, the desire for security is proper and productive. It is as unreasonable never to have a medical examination as to insist on undergoing one every week. Love can be killed by the blithely oblivious confidence that it will endure, come what may.

There is, then, a tension between the present-oriented and future-oriented components of happiness. But it is neither logically nor empirically necessary that this tension become a contradiction. The desire for absolute assurance is neither universal nor unalterable. It reflects a combination of illusion and excessive fear, the former in principle curable through rational instruction, the latter through moral training. But Hobbes was right to point to classes of situations in which real external threats to secure possession are very serious disruptions to the balance between the present and the future, making it impossible to enjoy happiness in the full sense. This is one of the important ways in which the individual's concern for personal happiness leads toward politics—that is, to the cooperative attempt to reduce real external threats to the greatest possible extent.

As to the third variant of the claim that happiness is unattainable or illusory: Sartre has offered the most radical denial of the possibility of happiness or satisfaction. The impossibility has nothing to do with the content or intensity of particular desires; rather, satisfaction is predicated of *consciousness*, but the proper understanding of consciousness reveals that it is in principle incompatible with satisfaction.

We cannot avoid the complex details of Sartre's argument if we wish to evaluate his conclusion. Let us begin with a vivid passage, parallel in many ways to Hobbes's statement:

> Picture an ass drawing behind him a cart. He attempts to get hold of a carrot which has been fastened at the end of a stick which in turn has been tied to the shaft of the cart. Every effort on the part of the ass to seize the carrot results in advancing the whole apparatus and the cart itself, which always remains at the same distance from the ass. Thus we run after a possible which our very running causes to appear, which is nothing but our running itself, and which thereby is by definition out of reach. We run toward ourselves and we are—due to this very fact—the being which can not be reunited with itself.[21]

This passage raises two major questions. In what sense are we pursuing ourselves rather than what we are not (or have not)? And why is the self that we allegedly pursue a moving target in no way distinguishable from the act of pursuit?

All that exists, Sartre asserts, can be divided into beings and consciousness. Beings are self-enclosed, self-subsistent, nonrelational. Consciousness exists only in relation to what it is not. Consciousness is of two types: consciousness of beings and consciousness of consciousness of beings. Acts of consciousness affirm both a connection with and distinction from their objects. Thus, to be conscious of a table is to affirm a distinction between that consciousness and the table; to be conscious of being conscious of the table is to affirm a distinction between being conscious of consciousness and being conscious of the table. Following Sartre, let us call the affirmation of distinction *negation*.

There are two types of negation, external and internal. In external negation, the difference between x and y leaves both unaffected: x is neither defined nor moved by not being y, and vice versa. In internal negation, on the other hand, x is affected in both those ways by not being y. Internal negation can exist only through *refusal*; x rejects being x, refuses not to be y, and wrenches itself away from x toward y.[22] To refuse not to be y is to "lack" y. Since no being is capable of refusal, no being lacks anything else. Only consciousness lacks; and it itself engenders the lack it imputes to beings. Since consciousness is the source of lack, it *is* lack. The "existence of desire as a human fact" is enough to confirm, or prove, the adequacy of this theoretical deduction.[23]

The analysis of lack reveals its triadic structure. The *existing* is the particular concrete consciousness, or desire; the *lacking* is what the existing refuses not to be; and the *lacked* is that by which the existing must be supplemented in order to become the lacking. Satisfaction is the realization of the lacking: the simultaneous copresence of the existing and the lacked. In general, the lacked of consciousness is what consciousness is not: the kind of being that characterizes objects. But since the lacked of consciousness can only be consciousness, it is consciousness-as-object. Thus, the satisfaction of consciousness is the simultaneous copresence of consciousness-as-object and consciousness of consciousness-as-object. The former by itself would not be sufficient, since satisfaction has as a necessary condition awareness of the presence of that which was lacked. No consciousness desires its annihilation.

But, Sartre concludes, the simultaneous copresence (or "totality") that constitutes satisfaction is impossible, for two reasons. First, self-consciousness stands in a destructive relation to the self of which it is conscious. For example, when we are aware that we are suffering, we cannot suffer adequately. Our norm of suffering is to be seized and overwhelmed by it. But to be aware of it is precisely not to be overwhelmed. In fact, our awareness reveals that we are responsible for it, bring it into being. Second, the unity of self-consciousness and self is another consciousness. But this means that it exists only in relation to what it is not, that is, what stands outside the circle of the achieved unity. "Hence the constant disappointment which accompanies reple-tion, the famous 'Is it only this?' which is not directed at the concrete pleasure which satisfaction gives but at the evanescence of the coinci-dence with self."[24]

We are finally in a position to answer the questions raised by the metaphor of the ass. We are pursuing ourselves because the satisfaction we seek is nothing but the unity of the two elements of our own con-sciousness. And, as consciousness, the self we pursue is pursuit, that is, desire. The annihilation of desire requires the annihilation of con-sciousness, but this destroys all possibility of satisfaction.

A number of objections can be raised against this analysis. First, the claim that human consciousness is the sole source of lack makes it impossible to view animal desire as anything but a human interpreta-tion superimposed on a mechanical process. The allegedly exhaustive antithesis of consciousness and being forces Sartre to affirm the Carte-sian view of animal existence. But if we begin, not with theory, but with the phenomena, it is more plausible to say that animals have desires.[25] This has important consequences. For instance, if we assume that animals have consciousness of beings but not consciousness of that consciousness, then the latter cannot be a necessary condition of desire. In addition, at least some animal desire is for specific beings to fill up an organically defined emptiness. Although the emptiness is not identical to the desire, it produces it directly. The absence of food or shelter is translated into a quest which is for those beings, not for the experience of having them. As the emptiness is succeeded by repletion, the desire vanishes. As we saw earlier, some human desire closely resembles this. Sartre focuses on the mediation of the organic by consciousness, the extent to which a physiological state does not become desire until we affirm it as lack. But the fact that some human desires have this origin does not mean that all do. Affirmation frequently mediates, not be-tween physiological state and desire, but between desire and action. Under certain circumstances, for example, nearly everyone will feel thirsty and desire relief; but not everyone will seek relief. This is the basis of the classic distinction between strength and weakness of will.

Second, Sartre fails to prove that human existence is (nothing but) lack. The fact of desire shows only that lack is a feature of human existence, not that it is the totality of that existence. And even if it were granted that man is the source of all lack, it would not follow that man is nothing but lack. Consider Plato's *Symposium:* The poet Agathon asserts that eros (desire) is an overflowing plenitude of good. Against this Socrates makes the point that all desire is directed toward an object from which it is distinguished and which it lacks. Desire for the good cannot be good because it is an active recognition that the desire lacks the good. But, Socrates continues, this simple "negative" thesis is not adequate either, for two reasons. From a logical standpoint, to be distinguished from x is not necessarily to be contrary, or opposed, to x. The not-beautiful is not ipso facto ugly. Further, to say that x stands in some relation to y is to assert that there is something that x and y share, some resemblance between them. If desire is a particular kind of relation between the desiring being and what it desires, then the desiring being somehow resembles what it desires. Thus, desire stands between indifference to x and possession of x. It resembles x in and through that capacity that allows it to care about x. Desire is neither lack nor plenitude, but rather a combination of lack and plentitude. For human beings, desire has an element of plenitude because the desiring being already *has* what it desires in the mode of imagination, opinion, or conception.[26]

Insofar as Sartre equates human existence with lack, he embraces Socrates' superseded "negative" thesis. Preoccupied with the distinction desire reveals, he neglects the relation on which it rests. Curiously, this neglect is contradicted in his own theoretical characterization of the link between consciousness and beings:

> I can not determine myself not to be an object which is originally severed from all connection with me. I can not deny that I am a particular being if I am *at a distance* from that being. If I conceive of a being entirely closed in on itself, this being in itself will be solely that which it is, and due to this fact there will be no room in it for either negation or knowledge. It is in fact in terms of the being which it is not that a being *can make known to itself* what it is not. This means in the case of an internal negation that it is within and upon the being which it is not that the for-itself appears as not being what it is not. In this sense the internal negation is a concrete ontological bond.[27]

Even if, as Sartre contends, consciousness does not add to beings but merely reflects and affirms their existence as they are, it cannot reflect them without resembling them. The capacity of a mirror for reflection rests both on what it has in common with what it reflects and on its own constitution. A mirror does not reveal sound; nor, if melted, would it reveal images. Thus, although consciousness does not have the being of an object, it is not nonbeing but rather something, and that something has some resemblance to objects.[28]

3. Elements of the Human Good

Third, as we have seen, Sartre himself distinguishes between difference and lack: the difference between x and y is transformed into the lack of y for x only if x refuses to accept the difference. Thus, the fact that consciousness is not an object does not by itself imply that consciousness lacks or desires the mode of being of an object. Sartre must somehow show that consciousness refuses not to be an object.

Let us concede for purposes of argument that Sartre establishes that the relation between consciousness and its object is internal negation. The difficulty is that Sartre never proves that all internal negation is or implies the relation of lack. In fact, he suggests the reverse, both by describing lack as *one kind*—albeit the most fundamental—of internal negation and by offering as an example of internal negation "not being handsome." The handsomeness that I do not have is not merely external or privative but affects what I am through its absence. But the absence is in a way accepted. The acceptance may occur through melancholy, but I do not refuse not to be handsome.[29] There are many other examples. What I am now is affected by the fact that I am no longer a child, but I need not refuse not to be a child.[30]

We can say, then, that internal negation is a necessary but not sufficient condition of lack. Lack is internal negation coupled with refusal. The question then arises: Is the occurrence of refusal an unexplainable brute fact, or is it derived from deeper considerations? In Aristotle's analysis, the refusal not to have or to be x is derived from the desire to have or to be x, which in turn rests on two facts: x appears good to the desirer, and the desirer does not believe that x is unobtainable. For Aristotle, refusal is based on desire, while for Sartre desire is based on refusal.

This difference can perhaps be understood in the following way: Sartre claims that desire is not a given, natural fact. We do not desire x unless we choose x. But choice is not determined, conceptually or practically, by any or all facts or beings. Choice goes beyond beings; it is a refusal to be bound by beings, a determinate refusal the content of which is self-determined. The choice occurs, but it is ultimate and unexplainable. For Aristotle, on the other hand, we choose x because we desire it and desire it because it appears good. What appears good to us is given, ultimate, unexplainable. We do not choose the fact that happiness appears good, and we do not ordinarily seek to explain it. We seem to be faced with an unexplained choice on the one hand, an unexplained appearance on the other. From a theoretical standpoint there is some reason to prefer the latter. It is logically coherent—in fact, logically necessary—that some facts are unexplained or "brute," and appearance is a fact. But it is not clear that an unexplainable choice is conceivable or logically coherent.

In the *Symposium* Aristophanes contends that desire is directed toward the reuniting of a sundered totality.[31] Socrates responds that no totality, present, remembered, or imagined, is desired unless it appears good.[32] Even if, as Sartre contends, it makes sense to interpret consciousness and being as a sundered totality, it would not follow that the goal of desire is the complete overcoming of this split. And if we can know, as Sartre claims, that this overcoming is impossible, how can we (continue to) desire it? Can desire and possibility really be disjoint?

Fourth: In describing the self-contradictory goal that consciousness pursues, Sartre insists that this ideal totality necessarily includes self-consciousness as an element: "Consciousness does not surpass itself towards its annihilation."[33] There is nothing logically wrong with this proposition, but experience does not support it. We desire the annihilation of consciousness daily when we seek relief from fatigue in sleep. Suffering from excruciating pain, we sometimes choose to take painkillers that knock us out. For various reasons we may seek to "lose ourselves" (that is, temporarily annihilate self-consciousness) in drink. To be sure, all of these can be reinterpreted as instrumental to self-consciousness within a larger totality, marked by a longer time horizon. But not even this verbal escape route is open in the case of suicide, which can be consciously chosen. Whatever the intratheoretic merits of Sartre's claims that suicide is an absurdity and death is not one of an individual's possibilities,[34] the fact that self-consciousness can choose and effect its own permanent annihilation cannot be sensibly denied, except from a theological standpoint—hardly a Sartrean refuge! Thus, there cannot be a necessary link between self-consciousness and a projected totality in which it is preserved.

Fifth, Sartre's proof that self-consciousness is incapable of satisfaction may be restated as follows: Self-consciousness desires itself as self-sufficient. But self-sufficiency characterizes only the being of objects. Thus, what is self-sufficient is not self-conscious, and what is self-conscious is not self-sufficient. The desire of self-consciousness for itself as self-sufficient is a contradiction in terms, an impossible totality.

Let us grant that, for the most part, self-consciousness does see itself as an element of its satisfaction and that it desires self-sufficiency. Sartre's crucial claim that only objects are self-sufficient in the desired sense is questionable. If by self-sufficient one means that which is complete in itself and does not point beyond itself to its transcendence, then it is at least possible that certain relations between consciousness and objects, that is, certain activities, may be self-sufficient. The Platonic–Aristotelian conception of contemplation meets these requirements. Contemplation is a relation of nonidentity between the self that contemplates and what is contemplated, and between the activity of contemplation and the consciousness of that activity. The three poles of these relations have no desire to seek the unity of identity; the totality of activity defined by these relations is self-enclosed and satisfying. In the most general terms: the Platonic–Aristotelian analysis leads to the conclusion that man desires to know God; the Sartrean, that man desires to be God.

If we ask why Sartre rejects the possibility that contemplation brings satisfaction, we receive the reply that

> knowing has for its ideal being-what-one-knows and for its original structure not-being-what-is-known . . . in order to know being such as it is, it would be necessary to be that being. But there is this "such as it is" only because I am not the being which I know; and if I should become it, then the "such as it is" would vanish and could no longer even be thought.[35]

But this contradiction emerges only because the crucial premise is overstated. In knowing we want neither to distort nor to add to what is to be known. We want to bring nothing to the to-be-known except pure receptivity. But even if we grant that this receptivity implies perfect plasticity, the ability to take on the form, structure, or appearance of the to-be-known, this does not require the identity of knower and known. It may be objected that this analysis leaves knowledge incomplete. Through receptivity we grasp at most what kind of object we are presented with. Its mode of being escapes us; we do not grasp how or in what sense the object exists. This objection can also be formulated as follows: The interpretation of knowledge as receptivity means that knowledge is what appears, but the being of the object is not exhausted in what appears, even in the unrealizable totality of possible appearances. This does not necessarily imply the Kantian phenomenon–noumenon distinction. Rather, we realize that appearance *is* and that the being of appearance cannot be identified with appearance.[36]

This objection, though valid, is not decisive. The way it fails illuminates the fundamental excess or error of Sartre's philosophical stance. Let us suppose, with Sartre, that reflection reveals that knowledge is in principle incomplete. As relational it cannot encompass what is self-enclosed or nonrelational; at most it can disclose *that* the nonrelational is, but never *what* or *how* it is. But if this limitation is inherent in knowledge, and knowable as such, in what sense is the transcendence of this limit the "ideal" of knowledge? Even Kant admitted that if something is known to be impossible it ceases to be an ideal. In both theoretical and practical analyses, Sartre's guiding assumption is that consciousness is stupid. We are free to be everything except rational. Having demonstrated to ourselves that our striving overreaches itself, we cannot act on this knowledge but rather continue to strive precisely as before. This is the *reductio ad absurdum* of Sartre's analysis; Don Quixote without illusions would no longer be Don Quixote.

Sixth, having suggested that Sartre has failed to establish the impossibility of happiness theoretically, let us now consider the evidence he offers.

1. Sartre is right to point out the normative component of experience; we do have a concept of adequate suffering, on the basis of which we indict ourselves and others for selfishness or indifference. But this norm is not unrealizable, as Sartre thinks. The relation between suffering and awareness of suffering need not be destructive of suffering, though it may be. Sartre describes, not suffering in general, but failed suffering, and (if it is permitted to hazard this) from the standpoint of someone who has never experienced genuine suffering or has never recognized it as such. Most of us have on occasion been overwhelmed by grief or despair, experienced as eruptions from within us or as assaults from without. To be sure, these feelings do not endure, but while they persist our awareness of them is neither ironic nor destructive. More generally, there is a wide range of phenomena that might be called "being possessed": religious enthusiasm, certain moments of artistic creation or intellectual discovery, love. These forms of consciousness are not chosen, willed into being, constructed. They occur, they happen to us. While they persist, they are intensely satisfying. We have a heightened sense of being alive; our capacities are exercised fully and harmoniously; and our doubts are suspended. Within limits, then, Sartre is right to suggest that the satisfaction of consciousness rests on its encounter with itself as self-sufficient, objectlike. But his claim that such an encounter can never occur seems unwarranted.

2. Sartre's appeal to the constant disappointment that accompanies repletion captures a real and pervasive aspect of human experience. But he insists, without justification, that we take this part for the whole. The claim that every uniting of consciousness and its object of desire leads to a new range of possibilities for that consciousness is a sheer *petitio principii*. Tacitly conceding the one-sidedness of his thesis, Sartre himself contradicts it. Human reality is, it is alleged, "an unhappy consciousness with no possibility of surpassing its unhappy state."[37] Much later we are told that "whatever may have been its ultimate vanity, the fact remains that Sophocles' life was happy."[38] We are presented, then, with a curious spectacle: an author who furnishes us with both a general impossibility theorem and an empirical instance of what has been demonstrated to be impossible. But since most of us have encountered instances of human satisfaction, fidelity to the phenomena and simple honesty necessitates Sartre's concession, whatever its theoretical consequences.

The foregoing remarks have been very largely critical. But although

Sartre's extreme conclusion must be rejected, his analysis contains many correct and illuminating elements: the description of desire as triadic; the centrality accorded the quest for satisfaction; and the characterization of that quest as the escape from dependence toward self-sufficiency and from negation and flux toward stability and permanence. His description of the self's desire for itself-as-object suggests an important unexplored possibility. Perhaps satisfaction rests, not on becoming an object (an impossibility), but rather on generating and contemplating with approval a product that is separable from oneself yet is in a sense oneself. Would it not be a source of permanent contentment to know that one had produced a book, a work of art, or a system of political institutions that measured up to one's own standards of excellence? Neither time nor the world could take this away from us. As the *Symposium* suggests, it may be sensible to view one's children or the totality of one's past deeds in this manner.[39]

We now turn from the question of the possibility of happiness to that of its worth. Kant's moral theory rests on a complex, perhaps ultimately self-contradictory, critique of happiness. We shall not here deal with that critique as a whole.[40] Rather, we shall focus on one of his important claims: the conjunction of virtue and happiness constitutes a higher or more complete good than virtue alone, but the conjunction of happiness and vice is worse than that of unhappiness and vice.

Two preliminary points. First, for the purposes of this discussion *virtue* will remain formal and undefined. We shall accept as a working hypothesis Kant's claim that virtue exists and is definable and shall explore the relation between the concept of virtue and that of happiness. This procedure will lack cogency for anyone who denies the existence of at least one of the poles of the discussion. Second, we shall accept Kant's view that virtue and happiness are distinct and that each can exist independent of the other. This is distinguished from the Stoic position, which equates virtue and happiness, and from the Aristotelian, which distinguishes them but claims that virtue is a necessary condition for the existence of happiness. We need not linger over Stoicism. As Kant said, if the Stoics had listened to and honestly reported "the voice of their own nature," they could not have maintained their position.[41] Aristotle wavered between defining happiness as requiring virtue and trying to show empirically that vice renders contentment with self impossible. Neither tack is wholly satisfactory. The former merely forces us to reformulate the issue: What are we to make of contentment with self unaccompanied by virtue? The latter rests on highly selective evidence and fails to resolve our doubt. So Kant's "subjective" definition of happiness as contentment with self not empirically linked to any particular acts or moral states seems preferable. It is less moralistic and closer to common opinion (or suspicion), and it forces us to focus on the claims, if any, that virtue can sustain by itself without external adornments.

The Kantian thesis we are examining may be summarized by the following preference ordering:

1. happiness plus virtue
2. unhappiness plus virtue
3. unhappiness plus vice
4. happiness plus vice

where the first is the most preferred, the fourth the least. Let us compare this with the preference ordering of the "benevolent moralist":

1. happiness plus virtue
2. unhappiness plus virtue
3. happiness plus vice
4. unhappiness plus vice

The benevolent moralist's principle is that both virtue and happiness are intrinsically good but that the claims of virtue dominate; that is, any conjunction in which virtue appears is preferable to any conjunction in which it does not. Kant and the benevolent moralist would agree about their first two preferences, disagreeing only about whether it is preferable for the vicious person to be happy or unhappy.

The following difficulty arises. Kant's objection to the happiness of the vicious person is that happiness is a reward, and vice ought not to be rewarded:

> The sight of a being adorned with no feature of a pure and good will, yet enjoying uninterrupted prosperity, can never give pleasure to a rational impartial observer. Thus the good will seems to constitute the indispensable condition even of worthiness to be happy.[42]

But the claim that happiness is a reward implies the premise that happiness is intrinsically good. Indeed, its value must be very great if only the possession of the one thing that Kant was willing to call "good without qualification" can make us worthy of it.[43] If so, how could Kant avoid the benevolent moralist's conclusions?

Consider a related example. A wealthy businessman formally establishes a competition to solve an important, long-standing mathematical problem and promises a large cash prize to the first entrant who can present a valid solution. Now compare three possible outcomes: the businessman gives the winning entrant the prize; after the winner presents the solution, the businessman announces that no one will receive

3. Elements of the Human Good

any money; after the solution is presented, the businessman gives the prize money to another entrant. Clearly, ceteris paribus, the second and third outcomes are wrong and bad. Equally clearly, the third is worse than the second, even though, *ex hypothesi*, the monetary transfer from the businessman to the nonwinner produces a net benefit.

There are, it seems, not two but three "goods" in this situation: mathematical competence, money, and a particular relation between them, the denial or destruction of which is wrong. More generally, certain relations among good things may be bad, but *bad* is predicated of the relation, not the things related.

Thus, Kant's implicit affirmation of the worth of happiness need not have led him either to self-contradiction or to the position of the benevolent moralist, for he asserted the existence of a relational good that the other ignored. Kant was able to distinguish between "Happiness is good" and "It would be good for A to possess happiness" and to deny that the former, by itself, entails the latter.

One might object that this distinction is artificial. Since happiness exists only when predicated of some definite individual, it makes no sense to consider it in abstraction. This raises a host of familiar and knotty questions that we cannot deal with here. The best we can do is to appeal to the plausibility of the Aristotelian distinction between analytic and real existence: Many predicates have no real existence unless predicated of some existing thing but nevertheless have characteristics of their own that can be considered in abstraction. (It is possible that all "appearances" can be treated in this manner.) It does not seem unreasonable to believe that happiness has formal or conceptual features that can be examined without reference to the conditions of its existence.

One might also object that the existence of a relational good is one thing, the dominance Kant ascribed to it quite another. There is no relation of entailment from

(1) If A is virtuous, then it is good for A to possess happiness

to

(2) If and only if A is virtuous, then it is good for A to possess happiness.

It is easy to grant that virtue is a sufficient condition for being entitled to happiness, but much more difficult to agree that it is a necessary condition. In the passage quoted earlier, Kant in effect argued (validly) from (2) to (1), but his language betrays some equivocation about (2). He did not say that the good will constitutes the condition but rather that a being displaying "no feature of" such a will does not satisfy the

84

condition. But, especially in light of the analysis of the good will Kant himself provided, it is doubtful that any human being completely lacks all its characteristics. In addition, much depends on the specific analysis of virtue. If we believe that it is possible for someone to be vicious through no personal fault, then the moral worth of depriving that person of happiness (especially if that deprivation will not effect any change for the better) seems very questionable.

Kant's position suggests the following hierarchical typology of the "human good":

1. The complete good: that which it is right to desire and to possess in all circumstances and which cannot be made better by any addition
2. Intrinsic, nonrelational goods: those which it is right to desire and to possess under all circumstances, for example, virtue
3. Intrinsic, relational goods: those which it is right to desire under all circumstances but to possess only in certain circumstances, for example, happiness
4. Nonintrinsic, relational goods: those which it is right to desire and to possess only in certain circumstances, for example, all "instrumental" goods
5. Complete bad: that which it is never right to desire or to possess

According to Kant, the appropriate circumstance for the possession of happiness is that of worthiness or entitlement, defined in relation to the possession of an intrinsic, nonrelational good (virtue). This raises two points of importance for our inquiry. First, if the problem of distribution is that of determining appropriate bases of possession, then happiness is among other things a distributional problem; second, it follows that not all distributional problems are interpersonal or involve division of goods and bads. It may well be considered unjust that a wicked person enjoys happiness even if the happiness does not come at the expense of anyone else.[44]

3.6. The Worth of Reason

Morality rests on what I shall call the principle of rational action. A preliminary formulation runs: Take or do only what you are entitled to. To be entitled to x is to have a warranted claim on x; to have a warranted claim is to be able to advance a satisfactory reason to have or to do x.

What can count as satisfactory is subject to a number of formal constraints. First, the assertion that x is good (for me) is not sufficient. It must be supplemented by some proposition of the form: I am entitled to

3. Elements of the Human Good

whatever is good for me. Such propositions are commonly thought to be self-defeating because they can generate conflicting entitlements when employed by more than one individual. This objection is not decisive, however, for it rests on the dubious premise that valid entitlements cannot come into conflict. This seems arbitrary. Consider a system in which a fixed number of medical school slots are to be allocated by competitive examination. If two or more individuals competing for the last slot receive the same score, it makes sense to say that each of them is equally entitled to enter medical school even though only one of them can do so.

Second, no tautology can constitute a sufficient reason. If someone asks why you are entitled to what you are requesting and you reply, "Because I am I," or "Money is money," your claim is unwarranted on its face. All reasons are substantive or synthetic. They establish a connection between the particular and the general in two senses: between an individual act and a class of acts; and between an individual agent and a class of agents.

Third, the agent must accept or believe the reason offered in support of a claim. There is a common form of justification that may be called rhetorical: subsuming one's act under premises accepted by the audience but not by the agent. A genuinely rational or moral justification involves an appeal to premises that the agent accepts and believes others ought to accept. This is not to say that public reasons should always be the real ones, but only that there must always be real ones. If an agent cannot, on reflection, articulate internally an acceptable reason for an act, then that act is not rationally grounded. This requirement may seem arbitrary.

Suppose an external observer concludes that the public reasons cynically advanced by the agent are in fact valid, for example, redistributive arguments someone actuated by spite or envy might offer. We must, it seems, recur to the familiar distinctions between act and agent and between morality and legitimacy. A legitimate act externally conforms to the dictates of reason; a moral act not only externally corresponds but also is internally motivated by those dictates. An immoral agent can perform legitimate acts but never moral acts. Thus, it is fair to say that someone who proceeds with or repeats an act while believing that no acceptable reason for it can be found has rejected the principle of rational action, whatever the content of the act may be.

We must reject two other criteria frequently advanced as formal constraints on acceptable reasons.

First, it is not the case that proposed reasons must be able to withstand the effects of publicity. The criterion of publicity is frequently used against "egoistic" principles: Since it is usually contrary to self-interest to announce that self-interest is the basis of one's acts or to urge others to act on that basis as well, egoism is self-defeating, hence not an acceptable reason for acting. The difficulty is that one can easily imagine situations in which highly desirable results can be achieved or disaster averted only if the real reasons for an action are concealed. There does seem to be a close relation between the need for concealment and the lack of justification, but the criterion of publicity is too broadly drawn. Moreover, the requirement of publicity cannot be derived simply from the generality characteristic of reasons; the former is social, the latter logical. The rejection of publicity is consistent with adherence to reasons.[45]

Second, it is not the case that acceptable reasons must be nonegoistic. The case for this claim begins with the true proposition that egoistic premises of action must be generalizable. If I defend my acts by asserting that I am entitled to whatever benefits me, then I cannot resist the extension of this principle to others. But, it is alleged, this leads to a contradiction: We desire both that we achieve our own interests and that others achieve theirs, and we have no way of coping with the common situations in which interests come into conflict. This argument fails because we can consistently grant that self-interest constitutes an acceptable reason for another's acts without wanting that individual to achieve personal objectives. In politics, for example, competitors for influence, office, or spoils accept one another's pursuit of self-interest as legitimate (at least within very broad limits) while trying to thwart one another's plans. The fervent politician may even believe that all others *ought* to put themselves first ("They're suckers if they don't") without diminishing his efforts to thwart them.[46]

Alan Gewirth has argued that universalized egoism is self-contradictory and that it cannot consistently distinguish between what others ought to do and what we want them to do. If the egoist

> maintains his universal egoism with its primary, definitive commitment [to the principle: each and every person ought to act only for his own respective self-interest], then he is not really an egoist in the sense of a person whose primary, definitive commitment is to the pursuit and maximization of his own self-interest, for he would endorse directives that violate his self-interest. If, on the other hand, he maintains this latter, egoistic commitment as his primary and definitive one, then he cannot maintain his universal egoism with its primary, definitive commitment to the universal life of struggle and conflict.[47]

This argument is not decisive. It is of course the case that the commitment to reasons for action in itself implies some constraints; the rational human egoist does not pursue self-interest in precisely the way an animal would. But the commitment to reason does not necessarily contradict egoism. Reason compels the egoist to acknowledge the *legitimacy* of competing interests but *not to give in to them* in any way. The egoist is even permitted to employ dishonest moral arguments against opponents. Gewirth's argument turns on this ambiguity of what it means to endorse the activities of a competing agent.

Gewirth's contention that universal egoism generates incompatible directives (I ought to violate your interests, and you ought to violate mine) fares no better.[48] First, these directives are not *logically* incompatible; they imply a possible, though competitive, state of affairs. Second, universal egoism need not express itself in positive ought statements. It requires only the negative proposition that there is *nothing wrong* with any self-interested action, although agents may behave otherwise. The egoist hopes that the egoism of others will be diluted but need not think that every qualification is a violation of some directive. Thus, egoism is not logically self-defeating, and in some circumstances it does not even lead to competition.

The principle of rational action may appear to be a weak and uninformative truism. In fact, it represents a fundamental choice among possible ways of life. It is a moral rather than a logical truth, since the rejection of the imperative, "Never perform an act for which an acceptable reason cannot be provided," does not lead to a contradiction, pragmatic or otherwise. The *Gorgias* demonstrates this graphically. Callicles cannot formulate an acceptable principle that justifies the course of action on which he is embarked. But rather than reject this course, he rejects the process of justification, retreating into silence in the face of Socrates' argument. There is no evidence that Callicles' commitment to his objectives or his ability to obtain them was damaged by this retreat.

This can be understood in various ways:

1. There is a discontinuity between actions and propositions. Actions are said to be "opposed" to or to counteract one another. Only propositions can be said to contradict one another. Actions can contradict neither other actions nor propositions. Thus, if we have

(P1) It is always wrong to kill

and

(A1) x is a killing,

A1 is logically compatible with P1; their conjunction produces the conclusion that x is wrong. (For the purposes of this analysis we will ignore the fact that A1 is not an act but the description of an act.) The logical contradiction emerges only in the attempt to *justify* A1, for any justification must contain or imply the premise that "it is sometimes right to kill," which directly contradicts P1.

It may be objected that this analysis overstates the gap between actions and propositions. After all, it is possible to utter a contradiction; it is impossible only that it be true. Contradictions are improper only when speech is understood as pointing beyond itself, to truth, that is, as making affirmations. Contradiction makes it impossible for speech to attain this objective, by impeding the process of affirmation. Similarly, actions embody goals or purposes, and they oppose one another when they mutually impede the attainment of goals.

This objection has the merit of pointing out the shared teleological structure of action and speech, but it is not decisive. In the first place, the opposition characteristic of actions can be a question of degree or quantity. In the limit case, we can say that actions x and y are opposed, even if x attains its objective in spite of y. There is no quantitative element of contradiction: propositions x and y either contradict each other or they do not. Second, only propositions can be said to be true or false. An action can aim at revealing the truth, but it cannot itself be called true. This is why actions cannot contradict propositions or vice versa: only truth-claims can be contradictory, and action *simpliciter* does not make truth-claims.

2. As we have seen, to justify x is to give a reason for x. But every reason is general. Reasons define classes of acts of which judgments are predicated, establishing limited spheres of similarity and equality. Thus, justification always points beyond the particularity of the act that gives rise to it, even if only the act in question happens to satisfy the criteria for inclusion in the justified class. Callicles' withdrawal from the process of justification may then be interpreted as asserting that the generality of reasons is arbitrarily superimposed on, and perverts, the particularity of action. It is, for example, quite possible to act on the basis of the maxim that one's own interests are always to be given greater weight than the interests of others. But it is not possible to justify that maxim without legitimating similar behavior by others. If self-preference is defended by ascribing some merit to oneself, then anyone else possessing that merit may make the same claim. Thus, a course of action may be simultaneously coherent and indefensible; the coherence of a course of action consists only in a harmony between actions and their objective.

3. The rejection of justification is a real human possibility. Animals act without justification and without sensing this absence as a lack or defect. We can seek to become animals in this sense, and some of us can succeed. We can close ourselves off from the appeal to reason, allowing

force and fraud to determine our relations with others. Locke perfectly described the consequences of this:

> A criminal, . . . having renounced reason—the common rule and measure God has given to mankind—has . . . declared war against all mankind, and therefore may be destroyed as a lion or a tiger, one of those wild savage beasts with whom men can have no society nor security.[49]

But if we believe that replacing relations of reason with those of force and fraud will be to our advantage, we shall be willing to accept these consequences.[50]

It may be argued that the rejection of justification must itself be rejected because it is irrational: rationality implies rational action, which in turn implies action in accordance with reasons. In support of this claim, one might argue that doing x implies the belief that I am justified in doing x; I cannot reject all possibility of justifying the action without rejecting the action itself. Unfortunately, this assertion is empirically false. The phenomenon of weakness of will testifies against it, unless one adopts a hyper-Socratic interpretation. Further, unless one supposes that all action stems from choice and that all choices are made in light of reasons, it must be conceded that some actions can be undertaken without reference to reasons, that is, without any awareness of the problem of justification. Our experience confirms this. Most of us have met individuals whom we think of as "elemental" or as "forces of nature." They act boldly, spontaneously, and with minimal regard for the opinions of others. Impulses are translated directly into deeds, and every act becomes a form of self-expression. Such individuals, we suspect, never reflect on whether or how they are to express themselves, and they greet criticism with incomprehension or mockery.

There are two senses in which an action may be said to be rational. It is internally (instrumentally) rational if it furthers the attainment of the goal that underlies it. It is externally rational if it can be subsumed under an acceptable reason. An action that is internally irrational is characterized by a kind of self-contradiction, or pragmatic contradiction: it comes into being to do something that it does not do. An externally irrational action does not fail in its own terms, but only in light of an external standard that is superimposed on it. We can, without contradiction, reject this standard.

This can be restated in slightly different terms. The premise of internal rationality is that the goal of an action constitutes a sufficient or acceptable reason for the action and the criterion for judging its adequacy. External rationality denies that goals constitute sufficient reasons. But, while goals are necessary conditions of actions, the kinds of reasons demanded by external rationality are not. We can act, determinedly and coherently, without external rationality. On what basis, then, should we subordinate ourselves to its demands?

We can clarify this problem of "practical rationality" by considering the related problem of theoretical rationality. Let us define theoretical rationality as the outcome of two imperatives: the avoidance of contradiction, and the provision of the most adequate possible basis or warrant for whatever we assert. These demands are nothing but the requirements for the attainment of knowledge. Theoretical rationality, then, is instrumental, and it loses its justification if the goal of striving for knowledge is rejected.

Our question about practical rationality can now be rephrased: to what goals is external rationality necessary? First, as Aristotle pointed out, human speech seems to be unique in its ability to formulate opinions about justice and injustice. But these opinions come into conflict with one another, raising doubt and perplexity. External rationality tries to resolve these difficulties by tracing opinions back to a mutually acceptable ground. Second, the human ability to form moral opinions makes possible a distinctive kind of community based on shared opinions. External rationality contributes to this by helping to secure agreement. As a source of community, it constitutes the most important alternative to force and rhetorical manipulation. Third, it is natural to be perplexed by and curious about behavior that appears unjustifiable and incomprehensible. Even when agreement is not possible, external rationality helps human beings explain their actions to one another. Fourth, external rationality helps us to attain lucidity and insight into ourselves. Its employment implies the rejection of the self as simply given, a fact of nature, a bundle of goals over which we exercise no control and which we are condemned to pursue. If we cannot justify a desire, external rationality obliges us to resist its demands and to attempt to weaken our attachment to it.

We see, then, that external rationality implies the choice of a particular way of life—a life of self-understanding and -control, of mutually giving and receiving explanations, of striving for moral knowledge and for human community based on that knowledge. The rejection of this choice is not incoherent. But it is very difficult and, indeed, rarer than one might think. Most "amoralists" are disguised moralists. This is the underlying strength of the Socratic position: The tendency toward moral justification is deeply embedded in what makes us human, and the general commitment to the process of justification carries with it some implicit substantive limitations on acceptable moral opinions. Still, no argument can prevent someone determined to shed this portion of his humanity from becoming what Aristotle feared, "the worst of all animals." All rationality requires a commitment for which it cannot provide the ground.[51]

3.7. Principles of Worth and the Problem of Justice

I began this chapter by asserting that a set of basic principles could be propounded and defended in such a manner as to provide an adequate foundation for a theory of justice. Having laid out those principles, we must now begin to explore their relation to the question of justice.

Our inquiry assumes that justice is good. If something is determined (on whatever grounds) to be bad, we may conclude ipso facto that it is not just. (Of course we may not go on to conclude that it is unjust, since justice is not the sole good.) It is thought, however, that some acts benefiting neither their agents nor their recipients may be just. This common opinion has its basis in the fact that neither of the propositions, "A would benefit from having (or doing) y," and "A's having (or doing) y would be good," is entailed by the other. In particular, if A is not entitled to y, then A's having or doing y is not good. The goodness of justice is the goodness of having or doing in accordance with one's entitlement. As we have seen, this is simply the principle of practical reason. Justice is a subset of practical rationality. Its goodness is a consequence of the worth we ascribe to rational activity.

A theory of justice has two essential elements: a specification of what is beneficial for individuals; and principles of rational entitlement to govern cases in which (a) individual benefits come into conflict with or exclude one another or (b) there is a conflict between the desired benefit and some characteristic of the individual who desires it. To pose a particular problem of justice precisely, we must resolve three questions:

1. Would A's possessing y exclude any others from possessing y (or something not relevantly dissimilar to y)?
2. Would possessing y be beneficial to A or to anyone else?
3. Does A or anyone else have a rational claim on y?

This formal analysis suggests that there are two cases in which A's having y is unquestionably just: when y is beneficial and possessed nonexclusively, on the basis of a rational claim; and when y is beneficial and possessed exclusively on the basis of a rational claim that only A is able to make. All the other cases present difficulties of various kinds. It might be thought, for example, that nonexclusive possession raises no problems of justice. But there are circumstances in which we may seek to deprive individuals of nonexclusive possession. We may, for example, prevent children from staying up late, eating certain foods, or watching particular television programs. Nor are these circumstances limited to cases in which the possession would not benefit the potential possessor. Someone who wishes but does not deserve to be happy may justly be thwarted (for example, through punishment) even though the punishment is less beneficial than happiness and the deprivation does not remove an impediment to the happiness of anyone else.

The necessary distinction between benefit and entitlement also generates problems. How are we to weigh benefits against rational claims when the class of potential beneficiaries does not coincide with the class of rational claimants? Are rational claims wholly disjoint from considerations of benefit? How are we to decide among conflicting rational claims? Obviously, these and related questions cannot be resolved without specifying more precisely the content and ground of possible rational claims.

As a first approximation, though, we can say that some view of individual good serves as the point of departure for a theory of justice. That y is good for A constitutes a rebuttable presumption that A is entitled to y. It may be challenged from two directions: A may be said not to deserve y, or y may be good for B as well. If justice is in part reward in accordance with merit, however defined, then justice cannot be known or done without understanding what constitutes a reward, that is, what is good for the individuals whom one wishes to benefit. And it is reasonable to suppose that substantive features of what we say to be good will influence although not completely determine the sorts of rational claims we can make. For example, among its important features, life has variable duration and must be engendered through the creation of new living beings. If not all passengers on a sinking ship can be saved, then, ceteris paribus, children ought to have priority. If the ship were filled with terminally ill children and highly trained doctors, our judgment would probably be different. And if limited resources to sustain life remained after a nuclear holocaust, then, within limits, the claims of women would appropriately be accorded priority.

Our argument has advanced life, development, and happiness as the basic principles of the good for individuals. We desire everything, either as integral parts of these basic goods or as means to them. These basic goods are independent of one another. We do not desire one of them simply for the sake of any other; the worth we ascribe to each is intrinsic, not instrumental. If the worth of means is derived from these basic goods, then the human good is not infinite but, rather, circumscribed in various ways. For example, if money is valuable only insofar as it conduces to the attainment of basic goods, then it is not reasonable to suppose that rational beings will always desire more.

Our distinction between benefit and entitlement implies that human beings are not simply entitled to life, development, or happiness. There is, for example, no absolute right to life. Ordinarily, the prima facie claims generated by basic goods are overriding, but in some circumstances they may not be. Hostages in political kidnappings cannot claim as a matter of right that their government ought to comply with the kidnappers' demands, even if it is certain that noncompliance will result in their deaths and less than certain that compliance will lead to other deaths.

None of the basic goods has absolute priority over any of the others. There is no lexical ordering among them. Moreover, their mutual independence, coupled with their heterogeneity, makes it impossible to find any common denominator by which they could be quantified and compared. But this is not to say that relative judgments are either impossible or simply subjective. It is entirely possible to make trade-offs among goods that lack a common measure.

Most of us, for example, would reject the claim that only the developed and happy life has worth. Life retains some worth even if an individual life is stunted and wretched. Still, that individual may sensibly decide at some point that life has lost worth altogether. Development may have been thwarted or reversed through disease, age, or accident. Happiness may have been rendered impossible by extreme physical pain, the deaths of those one cares for, or the irreversible defeat of hopes and purposes.

We also reject the claim that the developed life is good only if it brings happiness. It makes sense to say that one prefers fuller awareness even if it brings permanent dissatisfaction: better to be a human being dissatisfied than a pig satisfied. Nevertheless, at some point the worth of development is called into question. A highly developed insight into the misery of others may make life unbearable. The worth of the senses themselves is dubious in a concentration camp. The cultivation of powers that circumstances prevent one from employing need not be viewed as beneficial if frustration rises too high.

A kind of ordering does seem to exist among basic goods. Consider the following thought experiment: You are a healthy, talented young adult forced into a booth with three buttons on a panel. The first will bring you instant death; the second, lifelong imbecility; the third, wretchedness that increases with the duration of your life and the development of your powers. If you fail to push any button within a specified interval, a computer will select and execute one of the alternatives, at random. It seems clear that most of us would select the third. Each of the others implies the annihilation of our existence and identity, the cessation of our humanity. I suspect that most of us would be nearly indifferent between the first and the second—at least if we believe that death is the final extinction of consciousness.

Now imagine that the second alternative is gradually made less severe by slowly increasing the remaining degree of awareness, intelligence, and development of capacities. At some point most of us would cease to be indifferent between the first and second alternatives; if we were forced to choose between them alone, we would select the second rather than accepting a random outcome. It is possible to imagine exceptions to this generalization: a great musician might choose death rather than risk even a slight stroke that would reduce necessary abilities to the level of mere competence. Such cases, though neither politically nor morally irrelevant, would be quite rare.

Finally, imagine being forced to make a choice among the same three alternatives, but for someone else rather than for oneself. We would continue to prefer the third. If that were excluded, we would not be indifferent between the first two. We would ascribe some value even to the continuation of life wholly deprived of self-consciousness. If this is not the case, we have only the most dubious or pragmatic reasons for institutionalizing rather than killing the severely retarded and for limiting and regulating the killing of animals. The discontinuity between choosing for oneself and for others has two bases. First, we stand in a relation of possession to our own life that we bear to no one else's. Suicide is distinguishable from murder and less blameworthy; we are entitled to make some life-and-death decisions for ourselves that we cannot properly make for others. Second, the worth of existence is not simply a product of the desires of the one whose existence is called into question. It is also influenced by the beliefs of others and by general rational principles. Your existence may have worth *for me* even if it lacks worth for you. In ordinary circumstances it is appropriate to defer to the individual's own desires if they appear to be stable and well grounded. But even if we have no obligation to prevent someone from committing suicide and no right to try, it does not follow that we are obliged to kill that person if the individual wishes to die.

These remarks have dealt mainly with the question of intrapersonal trade-offs among basic goods. Similar considerations are at work in interpersonal trade-offs. No basic good possessed by one individual has absolute priority over different basic goods that others may wish to acquire or defend. It is not the case, for example, that the sacrifice of life may be demanded only to preserve life. If a hostile power threatens to reduce an entire nation to primitivity and wretched servitude, that nation may justly ask some if its citizens to die to forestall this eventuality, even if peaceful submission would not lead to the loss of a single life.

It is clear, however, that in both intra- and inter-personal cases life enjoys a kind of priority over the other basic goods; the quantity of the other goods that can validly be substituted for life must be very considerable. Using fixed resources to take a vacation rather than to save someone from starving is absolutely indefensible, even if giving up the vacation would make us very unhappy. To a certain extent the worth of development enjoys a priority over the worth of happiness as well. If we can stave off malnutrition-induced brain damage to young children by giving up our vacation, we ought to do so. If we could increase the availability of primary education by driving smaller cars, we ought to do so.

I do not want to place too much weight on the details of these thought experiments. In general, though, they point to a distinction that helps put in order many of our intuitions and practices. In choosing among goods, I suggest, we use two independent criteria: *intrinsic worth* and *urgency*. Intrinsic worth is a basis of ordering that reflects our sense of what is truly elevated or important. A good possessing great intrinsic worth is one we would choose to emphasize in ideal, unconstrained circumstances. Urgency, on the other hand, is defined by three considerations. First, urgent goods are those for which there is no ready substitute. Second, urgent goods reflect facts about individuals that could not easily have been otherwise, that is, are not thought to stem from individual preference.[52] Third, urgent goods are necessary conditions for a wide range of other goods. This relation frequently expresses itself as temporal priority: we must do *this* now if we are to have or do *that* later.

From this standpoint, it is easy to see why the various dimensions of simple physical existence—nutrition, health, shelter, security—make such insistent demands. Life is the paradigm of the urgent good; there is no substitute for it, and without it the others cannot be enjoyed. The relation between development and happiness is more ambiguous. It has frequently been claimed that development is an important condition of happiness. On the other hand, a wretchedly unhappy individual will probably not be able to develop adequately. Thus, a teacher must frequently decide whether to attempt to improve a student's disposition to facilitate learning or rather to induce an unhappy student to accomplish something as a basis for the pleasure of self-esteem.

The tension between urgency and intrinsic worth is reflected in a wide variety of moral and political theories. Mill traced the importance of justice to the urgency of the interests—life and security—it defends while at the same time proposing his much-abused distinction between higher and lower pleasures. The "priority of liberty" in Rawls's theory of justice reflects the greater worth we are alleged to ascribe to it in ideal circumstances but, as Rawls concedes, material acquisition may reasonably be given priority on the basis of its urgency in nonideal situations.[53]

As is the case with the other heterogeneous rankings I have discussed, neither urgency nor intrinsic worth enjoys absolute priority; rather, the marginal rate of substitution varies with circumstances. In general, however, the claims of urgency have a prima facie priority that can be overriden only by a combination of quantitative considerations and very substantial differences of intrinsic worth. This priority of urgency is, I shall argue, one of the major theoretical underpinnings for the concept of need.

3.8. Freedom

I have not included freedom among the basic goods. It can be argued that this omission is so crucial as to render moot my entire analysis. At first glance, the grounds for ascribing worth to freedom seem numerous and powerful. One may begin by pointing to the annoyance that attends the will constantly thwarted, self-assertion regularly repressed. More positively, free agency seems essential to achieve satisfaction. The agent knows, better than anyone else, what tends to produce personal satisfaction and surely cares for those satisfactions more deeply than does any outsider, however benevolent. Moreover, the natural telos of human life is mature adulthood; but the transition to adulthood is marked by the substitution of self-direction for tutelage. Freedom is, as well, a major attribute of developed excellence. The well-developed human being judges on the basis of unfettered reason, acts without being enslaved to passions, and is less than ordinarily dependent on the judgments or opinions of others. One might even contend, as Kant may be interpreted to have done, that freedom properly understood is the essence of what it means to be human, so that the worth of freedom is a direct correlate of the worth we ascribe to our distinctively human existence. Finally, freedom may be said to be the rationally required implication of the premise that there are no "natural" constraints on relations among human beings and that we can be required to refrain from only those acts that we have in some public way consented to forgo.

The cases in which certain freedoms are valued as means to the attainment or retention of basic goods present no difficulties for my analysis. The relation between freedom and happiness, or freedom and development, varies with individuals and circumstances. Sometimes constraints are harmful; at others, paternalistic interventions are obviously required.

The contention that freedom is an attribute of development, hence a basic good and not simply a means, raises deeper issues. I suggest that in this context, when we talk of "unfettered reason" we mean reason that is functioning appropriately—that is, in accordance with the internal constraints suited to it rather than with external, alien forces. If this is so, then the concept of freedom adds nothing to the notion of full or proper development, and it remains purely formal until the characteristics of particular faculties are adduced.

In a well-known argument, Gerald MacCallum has proposed that every usage of *freedom* is implicitly or explicitly triadic:

> Whenever the freedom of some agent or agents is in question, it is always freedom *from* some constraint or restriction on, interference with, or barrier *to* doing, not doing, becoming, or not becoming something.[54]

If this plausible suggestion is accepted, then the worth of a specific freedom would appear to be highly dependent on the characteristics of the purposes toward which it is directed. For example, if an act is wrong, then there is at least a prima facie case that removing what constrains an agent from performing it is undesirable. In many apparent counterexamples to this, freedom to do wrong is increased in the hope that an internal (psychological, moral) constraint will come to be substituted for costly and ineffective threats. More generally, the triadic analysis of freedom implies that it is conceptually impossible to view freedom as an end unless it is illicitly identified with the acts or end-states toward which it is directed. But if freedom is not an end, it cannot—at least in my sense—be a basic good.[55]

From a very different point of departure, Frithjof Bergmann arrives at a similar conclusion. He begins by considering a wide variety of views of freedom and argues powerfully that they all presuppose the same underlying deep theory or structure:

> *An act is free if the agent identifies with the elements from which it flows; it is coerced if the agent dissociates himself from the element which generates or prompts the action.* This means that identification is logically prior to freedom, and that freedom is not a primary but a derivative notion. . . . The primary condition of freedom is the possession of an identity, or of a self—freedom is the acting out of that identity.[56]

But, Bergmann continues,

> Parts of my self or of my nature are bound to be unappealing or mean or retrograde or evil. . . . Expressing those would not just be a slight and easily outweighed advantage, but would be a straight detriment. It is the hindrance or the extirpation of these impulses that represents the immediate gain. So freedom needs to be limited not only for the sake of others.

... The evaluation of the identification (or of my nature) by moral, human, or whatever other standards is therefore always primary and dominant. And this means that freedom is anything but a categorical or unquestionable good. How great or small its value is depends decisively on the value of the force that is to be released.[57]

For my purposes I need no more. But it may be useful to consider two further points. First, from a libertarian standpoint it might be argued that the instrumental character of freedom does not lead to any restrictions because no act—considered in itself, anyway—has characteristics that provide a rational warrant for constraints. I disagree, for three reasons. One, it is the burden of this book that there is at least one category—just and unjust—that can be rationally applied to acts, and it is not easy to see on what basis one could demand the freedom to commit injustice. Two, as Ronald Dworkin has forcefully argued, there are many categories of acts in which individual freedom can appropriately be limited by collective considerations, such as the appeal to utility.[58] Three, as I argued at the outset of this book, it is a mistake to view individuals as "originally" unconstrained, taking on constraints only through the voluntary surrender of freedoms. It is absurd to contend that we may behave as we please toward our parents because we did not choose to be their child. Similarly, the social and political dimension of our existence imposes unchosen limits on us, although there is a range within which we are able to shape them in the light of specific collective purposes.

The second point to be considered is that Kant's concept of freedom has two dimensions. Negatively, man is free because he alone is not wholly causally determined by external forces; positively, man is free because he is rational. As Mary Gregor puts it, "Freedom, for Kant, is the power of pure reason to be practical."[59] Thus, Kant's understanding of freedom is wholly compatible with my analysis of rationality; the unusual emphasis Kant gave to it is the outcome of a general theoretical position that compelled him to accord at most hypothetical or contingent value to other aspects of the human good. The Sartrean view, which denudes Kantian freedom of its positive dimension, poses a more radical challenge. But without *some* positive dimension, the idea of freedom becomes incoherent: the alleged absence of causal determination is rendered incomprehensible, and human action is deprived of any source of agency.

4

Justice
Background Considerations

4.1. The Subject Matter of Justice

David Miller's characterization of justice provides a useful point of departure. He writes:

> We talk of just men, just actions, and just states of affairs. But the last of these uses must be regarded as the primary one, for when we describe a man as just we mean that he usually attempts to act in such a way that a just state of affairs results. . . . If we did not have independent criteria for assessing the justice of states of affairs, we could not describe men as just or unjust.[1]

Although Miller does not define *state of affairs*, he seems to view it as a special kind of fact: an ordering or relation that obtains among human beings or between human beings and other kinds of entities. This suggestion seems intuitively plausible. Socrates' attempt in the *Republic* to offer a purely internal definition of justice as a condition of the soul opens a gap between the just individual, so defined, and just acts and arrangements. Even if psychic harmony strikes us as desirable, we want to know how it will lead us to behave toward others and what effect it will have on the assignment of goods, opportunities, and activities to the just individual and others.[2]

Compare this with other cardinal virtues. We would ordinarily speak of a "moderate" man but not of a moderate state of affairs. If we did use the latter phrase, we would almost certainly define it in terms of the former: a moderate state of affairs might be said to prevail when most members of a group behave moderately or as if they were moderate. Yet it will not do to say that moderation, unlike justice, is self-enclosed or nonrelational. Moderation deals with a relation between the individual and the world, appropriately regulating his desire for sources of gratification.

One might try to account for the difference in the following way: Moderation can be defined absolutely, relative to an isolated individual, without regard to the situation of others; justice, on the other hand, is essentially comparative. To define it, one must look, not only at the relation between an individual and an object of desire or aversion, but also at the relation of other relevant individuals to that object or objects of that kind. Justice is the right ordering or relation of relations.[3]

Clearly this is correct to a certain extent. The last man on earth would still be confronted with situations that called for moderation but few if any in which justice would be at issue. But justice is not only comparative. A class of individuals, relevantly similar, may be treated equally without being treated justly. We can meaningfully say that a penalty for a certain kind of crime is unjust even if all who commit that crime receive it and its severity is reasonable relative to the rest of the criminal code. Nor is justice necessarily comparative. There are certain acts or states of character that in themselves seem to call for particular consequences as a matter of justice to the individual, the justice consisting in the appropriateness or good fit between some feature of the individual and his situation. Considerations of this sort led Kant to observe that common opinion was not wrong in viewing the misfortunes of the virtuous as a kind of injustice because it is natural to see virtue as constituting a kind of entitlement.[4]

Another suggestion, that justice is the social virtue, dealing with relations among human beings, fares no better. First, justice is not the only social virtue. Generosity, gentleness, and many others are concerned to an equal degree with relations among human beings. And moderation has an element of this sort, since it deals with sexual desire. Second, justice is not always social; it does not always deal with actions through which human beings affect one another. It is possible to say, without evident absurdity, that it is unjust for a certain individual to have or to enjoy a particular object or opportunity, even if no one else is harmed by this. Still, this suggestion contains an element of plausibility. Even if some relations between human beings and inanimate objects may be considered unjust, one cannot speak of acting unjustly *toward* such objects. If A cannot be harmed, then A cannot be the recipient of injustice. At most, our behavior toward them reflects traits of character more or less likely in other situations to issue in injustice to those entities that can be harmed.

Aristotle suggested that, unlike the other virtues, justice is concerned with the *share* of objects of desire and aversion for which individuals strive. Unlike cowardice or immoderation, injustice derives from the pleasure that comes from excessive profit or gain.[5] At first glance this does not seem satisfactory. The coward seeks real advantage, the preservation of his life; the immoderate man seeks the advantage of forbidden sensual pleasures. More broadly, Aristotle is famous for endorsing the highly plausible view that we perform every act with a view to securing some advantage for ourselves.[6] If so, how can we distinguish the unjust man, the excessive lover of gain, from any other kind of wrongdoer?

The distinction cannot lie simply in the kind of advantage: both the unjust and the immoderate seek excessive pleasure, as Aristotle acknowledged. It is more plausible to look to the *source* of advantage: the pleasures of the unjust are dependent on something external to the actor, while this need not be the case for the pleasures of the immoderate, although it may be. This points us in the right direction, but it does not allow us to distinguish between them in those cases in which immoderation is mediated by something external. We may also seek to take our bearings from the concept of *share*. It implies that the object of desire is in some sense divisible and that any alteration of a given division will affect the benefits enjoyed by different individuals. On this account, injustice involves the wrongful withholding from some individual of an object of desire. An individual's immoderate act, on the other hand, is wrong whether or not anyone else has been excluded from that pleasure. Undoubtedly, many problems of justice are of this character. It might even be viewed as the focal meaning of the subject of justice, especially if, as Aristotle contended, the term *gain* is taken over from the sphere of exchange.[7] But it cannot be the whole story if, as I argued earlier, we are also inclined to judge that some relation between an individual and something external is unjust even though no one else is harmed by it.

We can account for these intuitions by beginning from the fact that justice deals with a particular kind of relation between the individual and objects of desire or aversion—the relation of "having" or "possession." The form of the typical question, "Is it just for A to have (retain, receive) x?" reflects this. It also underlies the classic definitions of justice offered by Aristotle and Ulpian: "Justice is the virtue because of which all have their own"; "Justice is the constant and unremitting will to render to everyone his own right."[8]

Characteristic of this relation is a sharp distinction between the possessor and what is possessed. The relation connects them without identifying or coalescing them. Moderation, on the other hand, is concerned with being or doing in a certain way. Even if a separable object of desire is present, it is not an independent constituent of the definition of moderation. Rather, attention is focused on the state of character revealed by desiring or by gratifying one's desire for the object.

This suggestion is exposed to a number of important objections. First, it seems to presuppose, as Hume and others in fact have done, that justice is concerned exclusively with transferable external objects, existentially separable from human possessors. But if, as I shall myself argue later, justice deals as well with the distribution of human existence and its modes (development, happiness), then the identification of justice and possession breaks down. We do not ordinarily speak of *having* life or happiness, but rather of *being* alive or happy.

To respond to this, we must distinguish between existential separation and analytical separation. Crudely: existential separation obtains between self-subsistent entities, each of which can be the bearer of predicates or qualities; analytical separation obtains among the different elements of a self-subsistent entity. Justice is concerned with relations among things separated in both these ways. When we inquire, "Is it just that *A* be put to death?" we are effecting an analytical separation between *A* and *A*'s life and then attempting to determine the appropriate relation between the two. For these purposes, *A*'s life is considered as something *A* has; the question is whether possession is preferable to nonpossession, or the reverse.[9] Similarly, when we ask the Kantian question, "Is it just that *A*, a wicked man, is happy?" we analytically separate the kind of person *A* is from his happiness and then try to determine whether *A* has a valid claim to happiness.

This analysis leads to a broader concept of the possessive relation with which justice is particularly concerned. *A* is possessively related to *y* if we see *A* as essentially the same whether or not *y* is predicated of *A*. It is difficult to provide precise criteria for this concept, but the underlying intuition seems clear. An individual is possessively related to, for example, an article of clothing because if we imagine him without it, we believe that he is in all important respects the same person. On the other hand, we think of traits of character as aspects of what we are, not as what we have. If after a gap of some years we meet a former acquaintance whom we remember as generous and outgoing, only to find him selfish and withdrawn, we think to ourselves, "He has really changed." Bodily characteristics occupy an intermediate position. I would suggest that we think of them as essential only if they are correlated with alterations of character. Recently, a man wrote of going to visit a college acquaintance, a former track star, and discovering to his horror that the athlete had been rendered a paraplegic in an automobile accident. But horror turned to relief and then admiration as he gradually realized that his acquaintance had not been made bitter, self-pitying, or disconsolate, that is, that he was "really" the same. Similar considerations are at work in our reactions to the physical processes of aging.

But these considerations lead to a deeper objection to this way of thinking about justice. When we inquire into the justice of relations, actual or proposed, we are frequently concerned about the essential changes that we expect someone to undergo through having or being deprived of some object, activity, or opportunity. When we consider the justice of punishment, it is at least relevant to wonder whether a proposed penalty will improve the offender's character or rather transform him into a hopeless criminal. We cease to worry about this only when we are convinced that someone is already "hopeless," unchangeable in fundamental respects. Similarly, in distributing educational resources we may think justice demands giving opportunities to those whose lives will be most changed by them.

To meet this objection, we must spell out some of the implications of our analysis of possession. First, to say that y is not essential to A (that is, that y is not an essential constituent of what A is) is not to say that the presence or absence of y cannot causally transform something that is essential to A. For example, although we would not say that wealth is part of what someone is, its loss or expropriation may lead to drastic changes in the character of that individual. Second, the transformations of A, actual or anticipated, produced by y enter into judgments of justice indirectly by affecting our view of A. Capacities for change are part of what a person is. Thus, if we believe that someone will be radically changed for the better through education, then we wonder whether it is just that this person be deprived of the opportunity to be educated. Justice here consists in the right relation between present capacities and opportunities. For purposes of analysis, the individual is held constant while the opportunity is—imaginatively—allowed to vary across its range of possibilities until the right fit is obtained.

This analysis may be defended from another standpoint. That the possession of y will change A for the better is only one element in determining whether it is just for A to have y, even if A's possession of y harms no one else. Even if we are sure that A, a murderer, will be permanently rehabilitated if he receives a good job rather than a jail sentence, we may still be undecided about how to treat him. Justice involves the right relation between persons and consequences; it cannot be determined by looking at the characteristics of consequences in the abstract. The person is not only a capacity for change but also a moral actuality, revealed by deed and demeanor. Justice considers both and tries to strike a balance when they seem to point in different directions. In any event, the present provides the baseline for reflection. The justice of a proposed future state of a person cannot be determined without regard to his present state.[10]

I began this discussion in an attempt to clarify the suggestion that justice is primarily concerned with states of affairs, and that just acts are those that result in just states of affairs. The argument has in the main supported this suggestion, but in the process our intuitive view of states of affairs has been altered. The relevant state of affairs is the possessive relation that exists between an individual and some object of desire or aversion; the judgment of justice or injustice is applied to this relation. The projected consequence of a given relation is one element—sometimes dominant—we must consider in determining the justice of that relation, but it is not directly the subject of the judgment. Thus, even if we were to posit, with W. D. Ross, the existence of intrinsically—that is, nonrelationally—good objects of desire, it does not follow that their worth is translated directly into the worth of their attainment by every individual. From the standpoint of justice, it may be preferable for someone to be deprived of what is intrinsically good. Justice is good because we view as good or appropriate the relation it dictates between possessor and possession, not because of the worth of either pole of the relation, considered in isolation.[11]

We shall not now attempt to provide a substantive characterization of the "appropriate," but our discussion has an important formal result. If judgments of justice deal with possessive relations, then justice is *rightful possession*. To possess something rightly is to have a valid claim to it. A claim, we may say, is a reason that is relevant to the question of possession, that is, would establish a rational link between possessor and possessed in the absence of conflicting reasons. A valid claim is the reason we judge to prevail after all conflicting reasons have been taken into account. Thus, for example, if A says to B, "It's just for me to earn more than you do because I'm taller," A has offered a reason but not a claim, because the content of the reason is not relevant to the question of possession. If A goes on to explain by saying that taller individuals are forced to spend more for food and clothing, then a claim has been made, since need is at least relevant to possession. If B retorts that he works harder than A, a conflicting claim has been advanced. Neither is valid on its face, since neither takes the other into account.

The substantive problem of justice, then, consists of two questions: What are the facts, deeds, or premises on the basis of which claims may be advanced? and How are conflicting claims to be aggregated or rank-ordered?[12]

Because justice involves the absolute and comparative evaluation of reasons, it is the most theoretical of the virtues and the most controversial. It is relatively easy for different individuals to agree that a particular act is genuinely courageous; indeed, soldiers of opposing armies, engaged in a life-and-death struggle on behalf of antithetical ways of life, regularly recognize and admire the courage of their adversaries. Philosophical treatments of courage seek to provide an account of shared initial judgments through fuller description, more nuanced typologies, and a subtler psychology. The discussion of justice must proceed differently, because the facts of justice are disputed, that is, shared initial judgments usually do not exist. The attempt to resolve these disputes forces us to ascend from the particular to the general. Moreover, the "facts" of justice already contain a general element—reasons that purport to justify practices. Thus, the philosophical treatment of justice necessarily issues in a "theory" of justice: a principle or set of principles to guide our judgment.

4.2. The Individual as Benchmark of Justice

All judgments of justice and injustice are ultimately relative to individuals. First, consider recipients. When we say that a group has been treated unjustly, we mean that the individuals comprising that group have been so treated. It would make no sense to say that every member of a group has been treated justly but that nevertheless the group has been treated unjustly. This has an important consequence. If most members of a group, however defined, have been treated unjustly but one has not, that individual has no valid claim for redress against anyone. Membership in the group does not constitute an additional basis of entitlement. A law may use group membership as the basis of entitlement. This merely reflects the practical judgment that most members of the group have valid claims and that the costs or administrative difficulties of trying to make finer discriminations among individuals outweigh the increment of justice that might be obtained.

We may go further. If A treats B unjustly, C has no claims against A unless the treatment of B has a significant indirect effect on C, depriving C of something to which he has a valid claim. This is not to say that, in the absence of an indirect effect, C may not prevent A from harming B. A fortiori, if A treats B unjustly, producing an indirect effect on C, C has no claims against D unless D significantly participates in A's act. Thus, if my father kills your father, my father indirectly wronged you, but I did not, and you would not be entitled to seek redress, legal or otherwise, against me. But if, in addition, my murderous father takes your father's justly held property, leaving it to me in his will, I significantly participate in the unjust act if I refuse to surrender my inheritance or at least part of it after you bring the facts to my attention.

The law may designate groups or legal entities as recipients of kinds of treatment. But this is always subject to challenge from the standpoint of the individual. For example, it might be decided to give every family a $100 tax rebate. But families vary widely: in number of members, number of wage earners, income per capita, etc. Treating families equally means treating individuals unequally. This is not ipso facto unacceptable. But those who sought to justify the law would have the burden of proving that the unequal treatment was reasonably correlated with some features of the affected individuals. Similarly, the ultimate standard for judging corporate law is the effect that endowing corporations with particular powers and obligations will have on individuals they affect, members and nonmembers.

Now consider agents rather than recipients. There is no collective injustice or guilt apart from the misdeeds of individuals. We are apt to be misled by ignoring the different ways in which an individual can behave unjustly. If C has the power and opportunity to prevent A from treating B unjustly but does not do so, C contributes to the injustice done to B. Similarly, if C knowingly profits from A's misdeed, C contributes to the injustice even if C had previously done his best to prevent A from committing it. Thus, if over my strenuous objection, A unjustly deprives B of property, I cannot justly accept a portion of that property in any form—direct payment, greater leisure, increased standard of living, exemption from onerous activities, etc.

We may apply this to political acts. Suppose that under completely democratic procedures, the majority passes a law that treats some group other than itself unjustly. Suppose further that the minority opposed to the law is composed of two groups—those who are oppressed by it, and those who, although not directly burdened by it, believe it to be wrong. It is clearly absurd to contend that any citizen in either of these groups has behaved unjustly. Only the individuals in the majority have done so. Our judgment would be different if members of the second minority group subsequently allowed themselves to benefit from the misfortunes of the first.

To be sure, we constantly predicate justice and injustice of collective entities. We speak of unjust laws, unjust institutions. But unjust laws are nothing but the combined will of unjust individuals who successfully claim to be able to make decisions and inflict them on other individuals. Institutions are unjust, either because they inherently deny the valid claims of individuals (for example, to participate in certain ways) or because they are conducive to the regular production of unjust laws and practices, as previously defined.

These contentions lend themselves to misinterpretation, however. Justice and injustice are relative to states of affairs; states of affairs are composed of individuals in particular circumstances. It does not follow from this that in states of affairs involving more than one individual, we simply look at the condition of each individual, considered in isolation from the others, and then aggregate the individual results. Rather, relations among individuals within the state of affairs will usually, though not invariably, enter directly into our assessment of the condition of each individual. There are two ways in which this may occur. The extent of the valid claims of an individual may be affected either by what others possess or by the extent to which the totality of claims exceeds the totality of resources available to satisfy these claims. We shall later consider each of these types of relations in some detail.

4.3. Justice as a Prima Facie Requirement

Justice is not the sole criterion for evaluating the desirability of a community. Two communities may be equally just while the way of life enjoyed by the members of one is clearly preferable to that of the other. Justice, we may say, is but one component of the human good for which we strive, albeit a very important one.

It is not part of my task here to enumerate, let alone discuss and defend, the other components. There is, however, no reason, formal or intuitive, to believe that justice enjoys anything like an absolute priority. Even Rawls admits this. He begins by claiming that justice is the first virtue of social life, that it is uncompromising, that it enjoys primacy. But it quickly becomes apparent that other factors must be taken into account. The principles of justice are "but a part, although perhaps the most important part" of what he calls a *social ideal*, which contains an enumeration of all relevant parts, coupled with a specification of "their respective weights when they conflict."[13]

Justice, then, stands in the same relation to the human good as do the various kinds of claims to justice. A claim, we saw, is a reason relevant to the question of possession that would be sufficient to resolve the question in the absence of competing claims or when the competing claims balance one another. Similarly, the demands of justice are relevant to the determination of the overall worth of acts and states of affairs, but its demands are decisive only in special circumstances. Adopting Ross's terminology, we may say that the demands of justice, considered in isolation, are prima facie rather than absolute.[14] This does not commit us to Ross's claim that no general principles exist to guide us in weighing and comparing conflicting demands.

We must distinguish our position from Ross's in another respect as well. Ross appears to argue that when we are faced with conflicts among prima facie demands, we reflect until we determine which, in the particular circumstances, is more incumbent on us than any other and then affirm that demand as absolute.[15] But this is hardly the most plausible account of moral reflection. Consider the example Ross offers: the classic problem of whether or not A should break a promise to B in order to relieve C's distress. In saying that we must choose between prima facie demands, Ross overlooks the ways frequently open to us of honoring both to a certain extent. Suppose that A, having promised $100 to B, gives him only $90 and buys food for starving C with the remaining $10. A has broken his promise, but to a lesser degree than if he had given B nothing at all. It is implausible to contend that the difference between $90 and nothing is morally irrelevant merely because neither corresponds to what was promised.

There are two kinds of moral situation. In one, our alternatives are fixed, discrete, discontinuous, and we are forced to choose among them. In the other, we are free—at least within a certain range—to allow the mix of different variables to vary continuously. We ask, not "Which should we choose?" but rather "What should we do?" [16] Ross's analysis is more closely applicable to the first, in which each of our alternatives may starkly give full weight to one different moral consideration. But the latter is a much better approximation of the moral or political theorist's circumstances of reflection when attempting to determine what is good *simpliciter* rather than relative to severe practical constraints.

4.4. Justice and Distribution

Our preliminary analysis has suggested that justice deals with what we have called *possessive relations*. But what is the connection between this very general conception and the traditional analysis of justice as concerned with two realms—distribution and punishment?

The major focus of this study is the complex of problems customarily considered under the rubric of distributive justice. I shall not deal directly and systematically with the issues peculiar to punishment or criminal justice. But, I shall argue, a close examination of the notion of distribution suggests a partial convergence of the two. A sign of this is the way in which statements like "He got what he deserved" may be appropriate to both. And, broadly speaking, both distribution and punishment can be viewed as types of *assignment*. But let us begin with distribution and follow the argument.

In ordinary usage the concept of distribution is very broad. We may, for example, speak of the distribution of the elements in the universe; here we measure location and mass. Or we speak of the distribution of ages in a given population, meaning the frequency of occurrence of specific age categories. Generally, then, a distribution is a pattern composed of two elements: a specified unit of analysis and a specified dimension or dimensions among which these units vary. Distributions may arise through natural processes or as the consequence of conscious acts. These consequences may be intended, unintended, or a combination.

4. Justice: Background Considerations

Obviously, not every distribution is relevant to the question of justice. First, we do not consider distributions that do not affect human existence or the effects of which cannot be measured, even approximately or qualitatively: for example, distribution of metals in distant galaxies. Second, we do not consider distributions that do affect human existence but cannot be significantly altered through human action. This criterion is in part relative to technological capabilities. For example, at present we cannot significantly alter the distribution of sunlight reaching the earth's surface, but it is possible to imagine immense mirror satellites that could do so in the future.

In addition, the origin of such distributions affects our judgment. If they are seen as natural, they are excluded from the realm of justice. But if we view them as the products of conscious acts, we may include them within that realm. Even those who believe that the ratio of the damned to the saved cannot be changed by man may ask whether the existence of individuals who are damned is compatible with divine justice. Most of the traditional problems of theodicy have a similar status. We may say, however, that a distribution does not raise problems of human justice unless it can somehow be affected by human contrivance.

There is an important ambiguity here, however. Even if we cannot alter a particular distribution, we may be able to respond to it or to its effects in a variety of ways, the choice among which will raise questions of justice. For example, even if we suppose that the distribution of innate intelligence or ability is unalterable, we can seek either to foster or to mute innate differences through differing allocations of educational or training resources, and we can vary the relation between ability and occupation or economic status. Indeed, the proper role of natural facts, of which natural distributions form a subset, is one of the basic questions with which any theory of justice must deal.[17]

Third, some alterable distributions that affect human existence are nevertheless outside the realm of justice. Imagine, for example, a drug that would allow prospective parents to determine their unborn child's hair color without changing the fetus in any other respect. One can specify circumstances (for example, Nazi Germany) in which questions of justice might arise, but for the most part they would not. In general, for questions of justice to emerge, the units of distribution must be—or be bound up with—objects of widespread concern and significance. This criterion is far from absolute. We can, however, intuitively divide units of analysis into three broad categories: those that are very likely to be objects of concern, whatever the character of the individual or group; those whose status will vary greatly with the individual or group; and those that are very unlikely to be objects of concern, whatever the individual or group.

Fourth, some alterable patterns that arouse passionate disagreement do not ipso facto raise questions of justice. Consider, for example, a husband and wife arguing about the arrangement of furniture in a room. A complex of practical, aesthetic, sociological, and even moral issues might arise, but the *justice* of the arrangement is not likely to be among them. But if one party broadens the dispute with statements like: "This is my study and I ought to be able to arrange it the way I want," or "All the other rooms in the house are arranged to suit you, and I'm entitled to one that suits me," or "I've given way to you in every significant dispute lately, and it's about time you gave in to me," then justice or fairness has become an issue. The additional statements invite us to consider the furniture arrangement as, in part, a problem of division among or assignment to competing individuals.

We might be tempted to conclude that the realm of justice is that of disputed divisions. But this must be qualified in several ways. First, a division may be unjust even if none of the affected parties has ever disputed it: Imagine an exploited class that has never received fair treatment and has been taught to regard existing arrangements as facts of nature. Second, questions of justice can arise when division is not the issue. Consider the case of the teacher who has hundreds of students and who grades all of them impartially in accordance with publicly announced standards except for one student who receives a much-higher-than-earned grade. This act does not deprive anyone else of anything (it is not a transfer), yet in the absence of mitigating circumstances it must be considered unjust. This case turns into a problem of division if the teacher through fear or generosity awards unearned grades to a large number of students and this fact becomes generally known, because the value of the grades the deserving students receive is thereby depressed. We may conclude that the realm of justice is the assignment of entities to individuals and that division is a special case of assignment. Third, the notion of division inclines us to distinguish sharply between *what* is to be divided and *how* it is to be divided and to think of the *what* as static or fixed, unaffected by the particular mode of division we select. In some cases this view makes sense, for example, the classic problem of dividing the cake, in others—probably more frequent and significant—it does not. In the economic sphere, for example, the type and quantity of goods available for division is decisively affected by the principles of division a community employs. To ignore this relation is to court disappointment and disaster. In general, one may conjecture that this relation is likely to obtain in some form whenever what is to be divided is substantially the product of human endeavor.

Provisionally and formally, we can say that justice is the appropriate assignment of entities to individuals; *appropriateness* encompasses both the relation between some features of the entities and individuals under consideration and the relation between those entities and possible modes of assignment. The domain of entities may include objects, qualities, positions within a system, or even human beings. We may speak of an unfair division of players among sports teams. The domain of individuals includes all human beings and, for some purposes, animals and superhuman or divine beings but excludes all inanimate objects and qualities: we do not speak of treating rocks or the color "red" unjustly.

To bring out the force of this formal analysis, we may contrast it with that of Hume. Hume began by arguing that the disproportion between human needs and the ability of individuals to satisfy them can be overcome only through society, but that individual selfishness threatens to make society impossible. He then took over an Aristotelian distinction:

> There are three different species of goods, which we are possess'd of; the internal satisfaction of our minds, the external advantages of our body, and the enjoyment of such possessions as we have acquir'd by our industry and good fortune. We are perfectly secure in the enjoyment of the first. The second may be ravish'd from us, but can be of no advantage to him who deprives us of them. The last only are both expos'd to the violence of others, and may be transferr'd without suffering any loss or alteration; while at the same time, there is not a sufficient quantity of them to supply every one's desires and necessities. As the improvement, therefore, of these goods is the chief advantage of society, so the *instability* of their possession, along with their *scarcity*, is the chief impediment.[18]

On this basis Hume argued toward a general conception of justice:

> Justice takes its rise from human conventions; . . . these are intended as a remedy to some inconveniences, which proceed from the concurrence of certain *qualities* of the human mind with the *situation* of external objects. The qualities of the mind are *selfishness* and *limited generosity:* And the situation of external objects is their *easy change*, join'd to their *scarcity* in comparison of the wants and desires of men.[19]

We shall return to the question of scarcity. The prior question is whether Hume was justified in restricting the scope of justice to the distribution of external goods. The differences he noted among the types of goods are decisive only if we assume as a point of departure human beings in possession of these goods, preoccupied with preserving or safeguarding them. But this assumption leads us to overlook some important considerations. Society plays an essential role in the development of bodily and internal goods as well as of property. To be sure, once developed, they are less transferable and, in the case of internal goods, less vulnerable to outside intervention. But unfavorable social circumstances can stunt their development. To the extent, then, that they are objects of human concern and striving, it is not necessarily the case that the increase and stabilization of property is the "chief advantage of society." Further, goods other than property are subject to direct distribution through social mechanisms: for example, the allocation of health services, of education, of freedom from distraction, and leisure for contemplation. Nor did Hume note that access to goods other than property is to a large extent indirectly regulated through the distribution of property and that the importance so widely attached to property is mainly a reflection of the opportunity it provides to enjoy and secure other kinds of goods. His relative deemphasis of the Hobbesian concern with physical security seems to rest on the dubious premise that bodily violence is occasioned only by conflicts over property.

But even if we were to set aside all these difficulties, Hume's claim is exposed to a decisive objection: property is not the only kind of transferable possession subject to violent alteration. In some circumstances, for example, political power or position satisfies Hume's criteria: B may deprive A of power through violence, and B may appropriate it from A, gaining the same advantages that A enjoyed. For this reason, it is completely intelligible to characterize the distribution of power or positions within a community as just or unjust. Indeed, the structure of our judgments in this area is virtually identical to that of judgments about distribution of property, although the content of our substantive principles may be quite different in these two cases.

Rawls's view of the scope of justice is in some respects more satisfactory. Distributive justice regulates the allocation of *primary goods:* rights and liberties, powers and opportunities, income and wealth, and self-respect. These goods are not ends but rather means: whatever our purposes may be, it is instrumentally rational to prefer more rather than less of them. From the standpoint of justice, one's relative position is determined by the intersubjectively measurable quantity of primary goods one possesses or controls.

Although Rawls admits political and social goods into the realm of justice, his proposal is still open to a number of objections. First, with the exception of self-respect, all of Rawls's primary goods fall into Hume's third category. We may then inquire of Rawls, as we did of Hume, why the other kinds of goods are excluded. This query is particularly unavoidable because Rawls himself distinguishes between primary social goods and primary natural goods, such as health and intelligence, admitting that the latter are influenced by collective determinations.[20] The claim that only social goods are completely controlled by society is neither persuasive nor decisive. As Hume pointed out, society's efforts to distribute income and wealth in accordance with abstract patterns will always be partly frustrated by factors over which society has no control.[21] It is not the case that, as Rawls seems to believe, self-respect is purely a social product or fully manipulable. But even if we set aside these objections, Rawls's unstated premise that justice deals only with goods that are fully socially determined is neither defended nor defensible.

Second, Rawls offers only the most casual support for the contention that his primary social goods are *universal* means,[22] and it is easy to discover counterexamples. If it is rational to want to go to heaven, and if Jesus' claim about the relation between wealth and the attainment of heaven is true, then there is at least one important plan of life that wealth impedes rather than furthers. And if it is rational to want to be good, as Rawls supposes, then self-respect is instrumentally good only when goodness has for all practical purposes been achieved. This is especially true because Rawls associates self-respect with contentment or self-satisfaction.[23] If one is not yet good, then unalloyed self-respect can be an impediment to self-improvement, and the ability to feel and respond to shame must be considered beneficial.

Third, Rawls's decision to view justice as the allocation of means rather than ends is unfortunate. He does not ground this decision on the standard relativist position that rational discrimination among ends is impossible; indeed, he explicitly affirms the possibility of such judgments. Rather, he argues that those who disagree about ends would not agree to a general principle that forces them to "risk their freedom" to pursue their disparate objectives.[24] This argument transforms freedom from a primary good into an end in itself, indeed the highest end, constituting a restriction on the pursuit of all others and restrictable only through its own internal demands. Rawls never adequately defends this claim, and it probably cannot be defended.[25] In addition, Rawls's focus on the distribution of means prevents us from taking into account the use individuals make of these means or the variations of worth that the same means can have for different individuals, differently situated. Brian Barry offers a decisive objection to this approach: "It rules out any extra provision for those with special needs.... The result of this dogma is to prevent anyone from being able to claim that because of special handicaps or disadvantages he needs more income than other people to achieve the same (or less) satisfaction."[26] To be sure, questions of need raise notoriously thorny theoretical problems and engender practical disputes. But the fact—if it is a fact—that greater quantitative precision and agreement can be achieved if we restrict our attention to Rawlsian means is not an adequate reason to define important human and moral considerations out of existence.

Fourth, Rawls derives primary goods from *individual* rationality but uses them as the basis of *collective* principles and determinations. Barry acutely identifies the dubiousness of this strategy:

> Even if it is accepted that primary goods are things each person would (other things being equal) sooner have more of than less of, it does not follow that it is rational to choose . . . principles of general application for the distribution of as much as possible of these primary goods. . . . All else remaining equal, a motor car is something that it would be rational for almost everyone to want rather than not to want. . . . Does it follow from this that it would be rational to wish that everyone had a car? From a self-interested angle the answer is clearly no. The ideal arrangement for each person individually would be that there should be enough cars to warrant tarred surfaces and a reasonable network of garages but no more, and that he should be one of the minority of car-owners . . . it might be rational to say that, if one cannot specify that one will belong to a privileged minority of car-owners one would sooner have the private ownership of cars prohibited.[27]

Thus, the choice among allocative principles necessarily involves some consideration of the overall way of life for the community that each implies. In so doing, variables such as the kinds of goods a society encourages, the quantity of these goods, and the character of the interaction among individuals possessing them must be taken into account.

Fifth, Rawls deals with the problem of distribution of political goods incompletely. Citizenship—full membership in the political community—is accorded every adult in the society and implies the same substantive rights and powers for each individual. But access to public office is equal only in the "formal sense," and may be regulated by restrictions that are "reasonably related to the tasks of the office," since these restrictions are in the "common interest."[28] But then, a full theory of distributive justice must investigate the nature of political tasks and seek to determine, at least in general terms, how various features of human beings are related to these tasks. Aristotle's distinction between making policy decisions and evaluating the outcomes of these decisions constitutes the point of departure for our reflections.[29]

To sum up: Distributive justice is not restricted to external goods but deals as well with bodily and internal goods. External goods include, not only economic goods, but also opportunities, activities (for example, military service), and political goods. Political goods include both citizenship and leadership or authority. This is not to say that every community will collectively determine all allocations in these sectors. It is, for example, entirely possible to allow certain allocations to be arrived at through private exchanges among individuals. Nor is it to say that moral or practical restrictions on the appropriate sphere of collectively determined allocations do not exist. It is only to say that our definition of the problem of justice must take into account all of the areas in which judgments of justice and injustice are customarily made.

4.5. Scarcity

In considering the relation between justice and the quantity of goods available for distribution, Hume invited us to compare three different cases. If goods were so abundant that everyone could satisfy all claims and desires without exhausting the available supply, no questions of justice would arise, and no rules would be necessary. If goods were so scarce that some must perish and all be wretched, then the "strict laws of justice are suspended." Thus, justice corresponds to the situation of moderate scarcity, in which claims and desires exceed available resources but no individual need be deprived of existence or of the bare necessities of life.[30]

Hume's analysis is intuitively plausible. In periods of economic expansion, distributive questions are frequently muted. And the suspension of normal laws of property during emergencies frequently occurs and is usually approved. Nevertheless, I would suggest that this view is so incomplete as to be seriously misleading.

In the first place, Hume assumed that all distributional questions involve divisions of potentially transferable goods. But as we have already seen, this is not the case: some allocations may be considered unjust even if no individual is deprived of the goods in question and if the goods could not be transferred to anyone else. In this respect, justice is not completely interpersonal or comparative. Problems of justice can therefore arise in circumstances of abundance, although the more common disputes will not.

Second, Hume's tendency, considered above, to restrict the scope of justice to material goods permitted him to imagine that abundance is at least a logical possibility and thus that the bounty of nature could make the problem of justice disappear. But this overlooks the existence of goods not subject to natural increase, competition for which *in principle* produces a shortage: political power, positions of authority, and in general all relative or "positional" goods. One reading of Hume would make him reply that, in the absence of disputes over material goods, the need for coercive collective organization (politics as we know it) disappears. (Rawls explicitly adopts this position.) But this is very questionable. Politics is concerned not only with securing means but also with determining the ends for which they are to be used, at least in some cases. And many political disputes center, not on the allocation of scarce resources among competing alternatives, but rather on whether we *ought* to do something that we have the power to do.

Finally, in situations of extreme necessity we may wonder whether justice as a whole is suspended, or only the rules that usually obtain. This is not merely a terminological issue. The question is whether any moral limits on means for self-preservation exist in extreme situations. We should first note that there is nothing peculiar or contradictory about the proposal that principles of right conduct may vary with changing circumstances without ceasing to be linked to and to resemble one another through their "rightness." It is only because Hume linked justice and property so closely that the emergency use or expropriation of property seemed to him not-just. But if it is sensible to regard need as a principle of entitlement, then it is reasonable to suppose that in some situations it might come to dominate conflicting principles and emergency use be defended as just in its light. In addition, we can meaningfully distinguish between just and unjust conduct even in the most extreme situations. Consider the famous case of the two men on the raft that can support only one. If one has a terminal illness while the other is healthy, or if one is eighty and the other twenty, or if one is a doctor who has just discovered a cure for some serious and widespread disease, then the appropriate outcome is at least inclined in a particular direction. If no relevant difference exists, then the outcome can be fairly arrived at only by lot or chance. It would be right to use force only to enforce the correct outcome if the other party resists.

It is certainly true that in extreme situations the participants are less likely to be able to govern their acts by reason, even if they try hard. But a rational principle does not cease to be just, or applicable, when it ceases to be easy. Hume assumed, with Hobbes, that reason and self-preservation cannot come into conflict and that if a principle of justice instructs us to sacrifice ourselves it ceases ipso facto to be rational or binding. At the same time he betrayed some uneasiness, mentioning in passing that the means we use to preserve ourselves are limited by "humanity."[31] If Hume was not willing to endorse Hobbes's conclusion that all means are permitted in extreme situations, then it is difficult to see how he could deny that we must take reason as well as sentiment into account in determining what we ought, and are allowed, to do.[32]

4. Justice: Background Considerations

Recently, two modifications of Hume's analysis have been proposed. Rawls accepts the threefold schema but divides the goods with which justice is concerned into two broad categories: economic and political. He is thus able to distinguish two conditions within the situation of moderate scarcity. In the first, economic goods are available in quantities sufficient to provide basic necessities and at least a modicum of comfort to the entire population of a community. Under these circumstances, no sacrifice of political goods is warranted to raise the level of economic well-being still higher. In the second, economic goods are not present in sufficient quantities, and various deviations from the distribution of political goods required by justice in more favorable economic circumstances are permitted. Hierarchy, coercion, unequal rights, even denial of citizenship can be defended as just if they are necessary to raise the level of economic well-being to the point that political goods can be effectively used by all.[33]

For the moment let us set aside the various complications lurking in this suggestion.[34] Its basis is intuitively plausible and can be traced back to the Aristotelian distinction between the two great purposes of collective existence, preservation and the good life. The exercise of citizenship and leadership requires considerable leisure and at least partial exemption from the process of production. If political activity is a good to which nearly all are entitled, then full justice requires a system of production and a general level of well-being that affords everyone a surplus—that is, the ability to purchase leisure without surrendering the necessities of life. The alternative is the permanent division of the community into a leisure class that rules and a productive class that labors more or less full time to provide necessities for all.

The theoretical basis of Rawls's position is the classic distinction among scarcity, sufficiency, and luxury.[35] It is sometimes argued that these categories are arbitrary or relative to particular historical circumstances. But, at least within broad limits, it does seem possible to identify that sufficiency on the basis of which the other alternatives may be defined. Surely sufficiency of food, clothing, and shelter can be specified in general functional terms; transportation, communication, and education introduce greater complexity of judgment but no real difference of principle. It is, however, necessary to distinguish between absolute and relative (that is, psychological) sufficiency. A felt sense of insufficiency derived from a comparison of one's own position with that of others may exist even when all the conditions of absolute sufficiency have been satisfied. Although this constitutes a serious moral and political problem, it does not warrant the conclusion that the theoretical concept of absolute sufficiency is meaningless. Indeed, the immoderation or loss of the sense of appropriate limits characteristic of modern societies is coming to appear not only morally questionable but also practically dangerous.

The real difficulties lie elsewhere. Since raising the average level of economic well-being to sufficiency usually requires a high rate of capital investment and the repression of present consumption, intractable intergenerational issues arise. This repression requires a coercive ruling class that neither views itself in Rawlsian terms nor is willing to relinquish control, once its historic mission has been fulfilled. Moreover, new problems emerge with the achievement of sufficiency. Systems of production capable of abolishing scarcity appear to have internal requirements of coordination and direction that stand in tension with the moral requirements of Rawlsian political justice.[36] Finally, sustaining a relatively noncoercive sufficiency-engendering system of production seems to require the liberation and moral legitimation of immoderate acquisitiveness, risking (as Rousseau foresaw) a dangerous devaluation of political goods.[37] These difficulties suggest, not that Rawls's underlying conception is wholly wrong, but that the subordination of production to politics cannot be achieved as simply and directly as he wants. The appropriate "instrumentality" of the economic sphere is always breached to a certain extent by unanticipated internal requirements and unintended external consequences.

Nicholas Rescher offers a suggestive typology of the broad types of supply conditions that influence principles of justice. There are, he argues, four levels: *superabundance*, in which the problem of justice disappears; *abundance*, in which the total available for distribution exceeds the totality of valid claims and inequities are justified if they are to everyone's advantage, *sufficiency*, in which the available total roughly equals valid claims and distribution must be determined by them alone; and *scarcity*, in which the available total falls short of valid claims and highly disproportionate distributions may be judged optimal.[38]

Rescher's account is superior to Rawls's in two ways. First, he reintegrates the situation of extreme shortage into the theory of justice. If there are three persons alone on a desert island with food enough for two, reason tells us that an equal distribution leading to the slow starvation of everyone cannot be morally required but that an alternative other than Hobbesian conflict exists: ceteris paribus, the food should be divided in two and some agreed-on operation of chance determine who is to go without. Second, he recognizes that the accurate description of supply conditions rests not only on the absolute quantity of available goods but also on the kinds and quantities of valid *claims* that individuals have to them. Valid claims are based on principles of entitlement whose moral force derives from reason rather than agreement: human beings ought to agree to them, whether or not they are so constituted as to do so in most (or any) choice situations.

We may summarize the results of this discussion of scarcity in the following propositions: (1) It is theoretically sensible to distinguish among scarcity, sufficiency, and abundance in relation to particular goods, even if quantitative precision is not possible. (2) The content of principles of justice must to a certain extent be responsive to differences in supply levels of particular goods. (3) Justice is altered but not suspended in circumstances of scarcity. (4) To the extent that justice embodies rational claims or is concerned with desert, problems of justice do not wholly disappear in circumstances of abundance. (5) Any discussion of scarcity must take into account the distinction among types of goods. Some political and positional goods are intrinsically scarce. Thus, even if we were to accept the contention that the problem of justice disappears in circumstances of abundance, since such circumstances can never be fully realized, issues of justice are coextensive with the existence of coordinated communities. (6) The most important distinction seems to be between political and economic goods. A theory of justice requires theoretical and empirical clarity about the relations between systems of production of economic goods and forms of political organization, in particular, the implication of the commitment to overcome rather than redistribute economic scarcity for structures of authority.[39]

4.6. Justice and Reference Groups
4.6.a. Political communities and individuals

Barry criticizes Rawls for assuming without argument that existing states are the units within which principles of justice operate: Whatever standards of justice we employ, "the question of distribution between societies dwarfs into relative insignificance any question of distribution within societies."[40] The most appropriate response to this fact is, however, far from clear. We may begin by considering two extreme suggestions. One, the Hobbesian, is that principles of justice are binding only within communities; relations between nations or between citizens of different nations are ultimately guided only by prudence. The other is that at least some principles of justice are properly defined relative to individuals without regard to the existence of separate communities or the different affiliations of individuals. For example, Barry suggests that most of us subscribe in theory to the proposition that the evaluation of acts must take into account all those who are affected by them. But when we consider, for example, charitable contribution to refugees, it is difficult to see why we do not ask at what point the potential recipients will cease to benefit more from receiving the next dollar than we shall from retaining it and, accordingly, regulate our contributions. The strict application of this principle would, Barry observes, increase charitable transfers at least tenfold, perhaps as much as one hundredfold.[41]

Neither of these extremes is wholly tenable. Consider, for example, two individuals, A and B, citizens of different countries, who enter into an agreement thought to be fair by each and by outside observers. Subsequently, A performs his part of the bargain, but B reneges and flees to his own country, where the laws of A's country are without force. We must, I think, conclude both that B has behaved unjustly and that B's country would behave unjustly were it not to facilitate B's return to A's country to undergo a judicial determination of his obligations. More generally, the existence of legal relations is neither a necessary nor sufficient condition for a principle of justice to be binding, although obviously enforcement will be difficult in the absence of formal, settled arrangements.[42] In addition, the Hobbesian position rules out principles of just war or justice in war, a counterintuitive result.

On the other hand, it may be argued that giving greater weight to the claims of members of one's own community is not ipso facto unreasonable or unjust. In the first place, experience suggests that communities cannot be held together or function effectively without shared loyalties among their members and that these loyalties are necessarily exclusive to a certain extent. Further, to the extent that a community is a shared venture based on a kind of agreement, special responsibilities arise among the parties to the agreement. Finally, we have already observed that, from the standpoint of just claims, distribution and production are not wholly disjoint. To the extent that we view members of a particular community as jointly engaged in the production of economic goods and an overall way of life, we must grant that these individuals have special though not exclusive claims on their product.

But, one might object, these arguments assume the validity of the division of the human species into separate and partly closed communities. Can it not be argued that this division is itself unjust or a source of injustice? We no longer believe that race constitutes a morally relevant difference that can justify preferential or discriminatory treatment. Citizenship is for the most part, like race, an accident of birth about which, given exclusionary policies, the individual can do very little. Like race, it is not correlated with substantive differences among individuals that would warrant systematically different treatment. To the extent that the division of the species requires and legitimates differences of treatment, it is unjust. Further, this division forces individuals to inflict unnecessary harm on one another through war. The conflict situation is unjust, even if we concede that individuals who must act violently within it are not behaving unjustly. Consider the following analogy: Someone contrives to place two men on a deserted island and to convince each that the other is trying to kill him. The island denizens do not act wrongly in trying to strike preemptively against each other, but the contriver is guilty of wrongdoing—specifically, dividing human beings artificially and unnecessarily in a manner that provokes senseless violence. Of course it would be difficult to claim that most political divisions are intentionally contrived by third parties. The analogy still works, however, for a situation can be judged unjust even if it is the unintended consequence of blameless acts.

There are, I fear, no conclusive replies to these charges. Some possible defenses of political divisions do however suggest themselves. First, given existing racial, cultural, and linguistic differences, political divisions may be more conducive to morally appropriate behavior than unification would be. At present, at least, the most violent, destructive, and intractable political conflicts seem to occur not across but within political boundaries—Northern Ireland and Lebanon, for example. Moreover, existing political divisions appear for the most part to be solidly based on popular consent, with some sentiment in favor of further divisions but very little in favor of greater unity. It is not clear that the coercion required by unpopular unification would be preferable to the violence that occurs from time to time across political boundaries. Second, if, as many have argued, every political community embodies a choice among possible ways of life or at least a restriction on the full range of possibilities, then the existence of a multiplicity of communities tends to promote variety and—assuming some freedom of movement across boundaries—to allow a greater degree of individual choice. Moreover, multiplicity guards against the worst possibility: the worldwide dominion of a tyrannical regime. Third, even if we were to assume a world of perfectly just and impartial individuals, there may be a correlation between the size of political associations and the existence of certain social and political goods. It is clear that the relation between population and coordination is not just linear. At some point, the fraction of total resources that must be devoted to coordination begins to rise rapidly, new forms of communication replete with unintended consequences must be employed, and certain kinds of political organization become easier to institute and maintain, others much more difficult.

The foregoing discussion has not proved but has made intuitively plausible a set of principles that can serve as the basis for the analysis of particular problems. To summarize: the division of the human species into various communities is not ipso facto unjust or a source of injustice, although it may be in particular cases; the requirements and consequences of division provide rational bases for giving greater weight to the interests of the members of one's own community than to others; but the preference for one's own is limited by the claims that others can make as fellow human beings, not only by considerations of long-run prudence. Without here trying to be precise, we may link this limitation to the question of scarcity. Addressed to nations awash in goods and services, the claims of those in dire need have great force, even if the prosperous nations are thought to have earned rather than extorted what they possess. Something similar is true for political goods as well. If a reasonably just nation can preserve other communities from tyranny or grave injustice only at the cost of a limited deterioration of its own political institutions and practices, a strong case can be made that it ought to do so.[43]

In considering the problem of justice among political communities, Rawls employs an expanded version of the original position that posits communities rather than individuals as choosing principles to regulate conflicting claims. But, setting aside our skepticism about the original position, the principles of external justice deal exclusively with political questions rather than with the combination of political and economic issues characteristic of internal justice. Since conflicting economic claims among nations constantly arise, it is very difficult to see how this omission can be justified. In addition, the content of the political principles Rawls proposes—equality, nonintervention—is most dubious.[44] Sovereign communities may be said to be qualitatively equal in that they have similar sets of fundamental needs and concerns. But they are quantitatively unequal in population, military strength, per capita income, etc., and these differences are hardly irrelevant from the standpoint of international justice. Whatever its original intentions, the charter of the United Nations in effect strikes a reasonable balance between equality and inequality by basing one voting body on equality of sovereignty, the other on inequality of strength and contribution.[45] Nonintervention can hardly be considered an absolute principle. If a civil war breaks out, or if a regime tortures, starves, and murders large numbers of its innocent citizens, outside intervention may be both necessary and proper. In considering internal justice, Rawls insists that unjust claims and desires of individuals must be resisted by law and, if necessary, by force. But a regime or nation cannot be said to be just unless it is internally as well as externally just. Thus, a regime could well adhere to Rawlsian principles of external justice while practicing the extreme of Rawlsian injustice internally. If individual injustice can be forcibly resisted by others, on what basis can collective injustice be cordoned off and protected? The content of external justice cannot be defined without some regard to substantive moral differences among regimes, although prudential considerations will dictate a significant degree of tolerance and restraint in acting on these judgments. To the extent that the original position forces us to ignore these differences, it distorts the issue.[46]

This conclusion is only strengthened by the proposition, central to Rawls's own approach, that the political community is a collective venture whose basic purpose is to further the well-being of all its participants. Principles of external justice must be determined in light of this. Thus, the analogy between internal rights of citizens and external rights of states is imperfect. Individuals are ends, states means. When political arrangements within a community grossly contradict the end in light of which they must be justified, they lose legitimacy and all claim to noninterference. Of course, conceptions of individual well-being can vary widely from community to community, but unless the human good cannot be delimited in any way, some practices may be presumed to contradict it on their face.

4.6.b. Justice toward animals

Recent years have witnessed a resurgence of interest in the question of moral relations between human beings and animals.[47] Various sources have contributed to this renewed interest: the ecology movement; increased theoretical and moral skepticism about the drive toward the domination of nature characteristic of modern societies; scientific evidence pointing to greater continuity between human and nonhuman animals than hitherto suspected; habits of mind carried over from the contemporary delegitimation of unequal treatment among different human groups; and the extension of the humanitarian tradition that has roots in both Rousseau and classical utilitarianism.

The contention that we are not free to treat animals in any way we choose has great intuitive force. But we must inquire into the principles of right conduct toward animals to determine whether animals stand within the sphere of justice, for not all moral restraints are founded on justice.

We note, first, the existence of a class of objects to which we stand in a purely instrumental relation. Pure instruments have no characteristics that provide bases for claims against potential users. Considered in isolation, for example, we may do anything we like with rocks or rivers without violating any of their entitlements, because (intuitively) they cannot in principle be entitled to anything.[48] This is not to say that our use of the instrumental is wholly exempt from moral restriction. It would be wrong to hit an innocent person with a rock. It would be wrong to beat a river angrily in the belief that it was responsible for its motion.[49] In some circumstances it would be wrong to destroy the beauty of an instrument for other purposes. In addition, it is meaningful to speak of "abusing" a tool—that is, damaging it by using it for a purpose it was not intended to serve. But in none of these cases does the moral prohibition stem from a "wrong" or "harm" inflicted on the instrumental object. Rather, we may not use them to harm others or degrade ourselves.

It is clear that animals cannot be viewed as pure instruments. We may harm them directly. The reason is that animals have *interests*—things that they seek to attain and preserve, the totality of which constitutes their good. This good is independent of human purposes and interests; an animal has a good even if it is not a good for *us*. Broadly speaking, these interests may be divided into three categories: life, a genetically preformed way of life, and exemption from pain. Thus, we may harm animals in three ways: by killing them; by forcing them into circumstances that impede their natural mode of existence; and by inflicting pain on them.

To say that animals may be harmed in these ways is not to say that we should never do so but rather that we should be prepared in each case to offer an adequate justification. We may, for example, kill an animal that is killing others wantonly, beyond the requirements of its own survival; we may kill an animal racked by pain from an incurable disease; we may also kill for food if our own survival is at stake. Note that we might well offer these as valid reasons to kill human beings in certain circumstances. It is, however, difficult to justify most of our existing practices. There is no evidence that either human survival or human well-being requires the widespread use of animals for food, and the claim that eating animals benefits them by allowing more of them to exist leads to unacceptable consequences.[50] If the normal circumstances of existence cannot be adequately replicated, animals should not be forced into zoos merely to satisfy the passing curiosity of human beings. Our experimental practices are far from being limited by even long-run considerations of the greater good.

If we grant that animals have interests the moral weight of which is considerably greater than zero, then they must for some purposes be included within the sphere of justice when distributional problems arise. Suppose, for example, that a fixed flow of food is divided among four human beings and a dog. Under alternative x, the humans would have more than they needed for an active life, gradually gaining weight, while the dog gradually starved to death. Under y, all could be sustained at a level of reasonable activity; x is, I submit, literally and not merely analogically unjust. The dog is *entitled* to sustenance, not on the grounds of generosity or sympathy, but for the same reasons as the humans. The added pleasure humans receive under x falls far short of outweighing the harm done to the dog.

The question becomes more complex when human beings stand to gain significantly. Consider a poor country with only one valuable resource—a species of animal much prized by foreigners for decorative purposes and fur clothing. The government wishes to build roads and schools but lacks foreign exchange and can neither attract investors nor qualify for loans. The government's decision to allow the slaughter and export of the species can be defended by claiming that the increase in the quality of human life, particularly for children, is of greater weight than the animals' loss of life. This claim may be disputed, but the underlying intuitive point seems clear. Animals and human beings both have interests, but human beings have some interests that animals lack. These distinctively human interests impart a greater weight to human existence, but not an infinitely greater weight. Although these different kinds of interests cannot easily be made commensurable, we are willing to make trade-offs among them. As we imaginatively vary the balance, at some point the human good derived from a proposed course of action will come to seem either frivolous or insignificant in comparison with the harm done to animals. Thus, as even Nozick eventually concedes, it is not defensible to claim there is an absolute prohibition against harming human beings in order to benefit animals.

It may be objected that the entire basis of this discussion is mistaken. Something is not "good" merely because it is prized and sought after, let alone because there is a natural instinct to attain and preserve it. Thus the fact, if true, that animals very generally seek certain things is not sufficient to prove that these things or their possession are good. We therefore have no compelling reason to conclude that we are decreasing the amount of good in the world by depriving animals of what they pursue or possess.

The previous chapter contains the fullest response I can make to this objection. Let me briefly recapitulate the basic point: The concept of justice we ordinarily employ implies a view of the human good and is vacuous without that view. When we make the elements of that view explicit and ask how they can be defended, the answer can only be framed on the basis of widely shared human desires, impulses, and beliefs. To deny the significance of these is to undercut the only basis for substantive moral thought. But if we grant their human significance, then we cannot rationally refuse to extend this strategy of argument to animals.

4.7. Justice and Rights

In the past ten years a major debate has occurred between utilitarians and proponents of rights-based political theories. The real and imagined defects of utilitarianism have been much discussed and need not be rehashed here. But the proponents of rights have taken the offensive so vigorously that the underpinnings of their position have not been scrutinized with equal rigor. In the following remarks I shall investigate the concept of rights and some of its characteristic applications. I arrive at two broad conclusions. First, rights as ordinarily understood cannot be central to political philosophy because they do not constitute an independent moral claim. The language of rights is at most a convenient proxy for a heterogeneous collection of familiar moral reasons. Second, rights to particular objects, deeds, or forms of treatment cannot be absolute or inviolable.

I shall spare the reader the now-ritual recitation of the Hohfeldian quadrichotomy and proceed directly to rights "in the strict sense." It is generally agreed that the following are necessary conditions for the possession of such rights: (1) If A has a right to do, have, or be treated as x, then A does not have a duty not to do, have, or be treated as x.[51] (2) If A has a right to do, have, or be treated as x, then all individuals other than A have a duty not to interfere with A's doing, having, or being treated as x.

We may now ask: under what circumstances may we affirm that these conditions are satisfied? One element of the answer is clear: only when x is not morally wrong. First, if x is morally wrong, to affirm x as a right is to say that A does not have a duty not to do what is morally wrong. But clearly A does have a duty not to perform such acts. This is indeed the clearest, least controversial employment of the concept of duty. To deny duty in this case would be to imply that we never have duties.

Second, if x is morally wrong, then to affirm x as A's right is to say that all other individuals have a duty not to interfere, that is, that it is morally wrong for them to seek to prevent a wrong. I can imagine only one basis for this assertion: the belief that the preservation of A's freedom to act wrongly is morally weightier than the good achieved through the prevention of the wrong. But why should this be so? As I argued earlier, the worth of freedom cannot be ascertained without regard to the character of the acts in which it issues. Moreover, from the standpoint of ordinary moral judgment, the immoral act freely committed is the worst possible kind of act. It is in this sense that Kant spoke of "radical evil" and Aristotle described human beings without moral restraint as the worst of all animals.

If we refrain from preventing the commission of a wrong act, our restraint is merely prudential, not something that the actor can demand of us on moral grounds. We may believe that the actor will be less likely to repeat the action in the future if allowed to confront its consequences. Or we may judge that the side effects of the means needed to prevent the wrong are, on balance, worse than the consequences of the act itself. Thus, we may deplore looting without being willing to sanction shoot-to-kill orders, or child- and spouse-abuse without expanding legal mechanisms for intervention into family life. Politically, many rights arise through the collective decision to treat certain categories of acts, for example, choice and exercise of religion, as morally neutral for prudential reasons. Underlying such decisions is usually some form of maximin calculation: each individual or group declares its willingness to forgo whatever advantages may accrue from imposing its moral beliefs on others in order to ward off the worst possible outcome, having others' beliefs imposed on them.

The consequence of this line of argument is to demote rights from moral or conceptual centrality by making them contingent on an antecedently defined "right" and "wrong."

At this point there are several moves open to the rights theorist, all unsuccessful.

First, the defender of rights may simply deny the existence of any substantive notion of right and wrong. Ronald Dworkin comes close to this when he insists that genuine liberalism, which rests on the concept of rights he endorses, must be "neutral on what might be called the question of the good life."[52] Of course, this is perfectly compatible with what might be termed the "subsequent" theory of right and wrong. As we have seen, the possession of a right entails a concept of right and wrong acts relative to it. Moreover, the sincere (rationally consistent) affirmer of rights must grant that the range of claimable rights is limited by the rights of others. If you have a duty not to interfere with someone else's enjoyment of x, then a fortiori you cannot have a right to x, and it is wrong to advance or pursue it.

The difficulty with this thesis, at least in its strong form, is that it arbitrarily dismisses the virtues. The acts stemming from the absence of charity, generosity, moderation, or courage may reasonably be said to be wrong even though quite possibly it would not make sense to say that such acts violate anyone's right.

A weaker version, advanced by Rawls, is that antecedent notions of virtue and excellence do exist but are irrelevant to the determination of what we have a right to do or be.[53] This thesis rests on the ascription of worth to individual freedom without regard to the uses of freedom and is accordingly rebutted by the considerations we earlier adduced against freedom, so conceived.

Second, A. I. Melden concedes that any alleged "right to do the immoral" would be "morally absurd."[54] He seeks to defend the primacy of rights, defined without reference to antecedent moral standards, by distinguishing between having a right to do x and exercising that right: "There is no contradiction involved in saying that it would be wrong for someone to . . . exercise his right."[55] Antecedent moral considerations have a direct bearing on the propriety of exercising a right but do not determine what rights we have.

The difficulty with this suggestion may be simply stated. To exercise one's right to do x is to do x. If, *ex hypothesi*, exercising one's right is wrong, then doing x is wrong. But if doing x is wrong, then one has an obligation not to do x. If one has an obligation not to do x, then one cannot have a right to do x.

Third, the rights theorist may point to the ambiguity of the "morally wrong." There are, it may be said, two kinds of wrongs—public and private. Public wrongs damage some individual other than the agent, while private wrongs damage only the agent. Public wrongs may be prohibited and, when committed, forcibly redressed or punished. Private wrongs, on the other hand, concern only the agent, who has the right to harm himself in any manner whatever. The affirmation of rights, then, is coextensive with the rejection of "paternalism."

The inadmissibility of paternalism is hardly a moral first principle, however. Paternalism (more properly, parentalism) is the essence of the family, but there is no hard-and-fast line between the functions of the family and those of the public authority. There are, moreover, many paternalistic practices directed toward chronological adults who are presumed not to be able to care for themselves, temporarily or permanently. The most cogent arguments against paternalism are, I suggest, empirical. Constant intervention may diminish the individual's chances of developing fully, and it may be reasonable to restrict such intervention *in toto* rather than legitimating it, only to see the power of interpretation and enforcement fall into the hands of the incompetent or malevolent. But the force of these considerations varies with circumstances, and they hardly provide warrant for asserting the existence of an inviolable private sphere.

Robert Nozick bases an argument against paternalism on the

> Kantian principle that individuals are ends and not merely means; they may not be sacrificed or used for the achieving of other ends without their consent.[56]

The obvious difficulty with this argument is that paternalism does indeed treat the individual as an end, merely refusing to identify the individual with a specific choice made at a particular time. I prevent my tipsy friend from driving home at the end of the party and say, "You'll thank me in the morning." I am not substituting my interests or my conception of his interests for his. Rather, I am responding to a discontinuity between his interests and his acts. Obviously, this claim can be abused, advanced in bad faith, in both public and private life, but it is not for that reason always invalid.

Fourth, the rights theorist may deny that the existence of a demonstrable "public wrong" constitutes an adequate basis for interfering with individuals. Nozick, for example, argues that rights (in his terminology, side constraints)

> express the inviolability of other persons. But why may not one violate persons for the greater social good? Individually, we each sometimes choose to undergo some pain or sacrifice for a greater benefit or to avoid a greater harm: we go to the dentist to avoid worse suffering later; we do some unpleasant work for its results; some persons diet to improve their health or looks; some save money to support themselves when they are older. In each case, some cost is borne for the sake of the greater overall good. Why not, *similarly*, hold that some persons have to bear some costs that benefit other persons more, for the sake of the overall social good. But there is no *social entity* with a good that undergoes some sacrifice for its own good. There are only individual people, different individual people, with their own individual lives. Using one of these people for the benefit of others, uses him and benefits the others. Nothing more.

> . . . The moral side constraints upon what we may do, I claim, reflect the fact of our separate existences. They reflect the fact that no moral balancing act can take place among us; there is no moral outweighing of one of our lives by others so as to lead to a great overall *social* good. There is no justified sacrifice of some of us for others.[57]

Put formally, Nozick's argument seems to be the following:

(P1) Every justification for penalizing some individuals to benefit others rests on the existence of some "social entity" of which benefit and harm can be predicated.

(P2) No such social entity exists.

∴   There is no valid justification for penalizing some individuals to benefit others.

Nozick is justified in asserting P2. On the lowest level (pleasure, pain, happiness), he is obviously correct. Aristotle made this point in his critique of the *Republic:* if you understand what "happiness" is, you see immediately that it makes no sense to predicate it of a community unless all or most of the individuals that constitute it are happy. The case of collective endeavor is more complex. In sports, for example, the good sought by individuals (victory) can be predicated only of the team: *not* "Wilt Chamberlain won the championship," but rather, "The Lakers won the championship." But the victory is good only insofar as it is prized and sought by the individual players. In this situation, conflict is endemic: If the player prizes other goods above victory, he may, for example, pick unnecessary fights with other players, hog the ball, or resist being benched. In short: the collectivity can function successfully only if the demands of the collective good are highly congruent with the good of individuals, *as they perceive and define it.*[58] Of course, these perceptions can be affected by certain kinds of collective—educational, social, cultural, political—influences.

But P1 seems arbitrary and implausible. Consider the oft-discussed case of the innocent individual whose life is deliberately sacrificed to save ninety-nine other innocents. Those who are willing to justify this act, in spite of its manifest unfairness, do not need to claim that the one hundred individuals form a social entity that feels pleasure and pain; rather, the decision is between two *states of affairs,* each involving the same disjoint individuals. To conclude that "it is better that" the ninety-nine live is not necessarily to engage in illusory reification. Nozick's claim that the dead man "does not get some overbalancing good from his sacrifice" may well be correct in many cases; but how does it follow from this that "no one is entitled to force this [sacrifice] upon him"? To say that this treatment of an individual does not sufficiently respect the fact of a separate existence begs the question, because the issue is precisely to determine what claims or entitlements separate existence generates. Thus, when Nozick says that side constraints reflect our separate existences, the vague connection between conclusion and premise obscures the wide range of possible relations. We may grant that side constraints are consistent with separate existence, but it is difficult to see how they are entailed by this fact.

Dworkin advances a more temperate version of Nozick's argument. The idea of individual rights is, he says,

> parasitic on the dominant idea of utilitarianism, which is the idea of a collective goal of the community as a whole. Individual rights are political trumps held by individuals. Individuals have rights when, for some reason, a collective good is not a sufficient justification for denying them what they wish, as individuals, to have or to do, or not a sufficient justification for imposing some loss or injury upon them.[59]

4. Justice: Background Considerations

This formulation of the problem has several noteworthy features. First, it presupposes that if collective goals do not provide a justification for interfering with individuals, then nothing does; that is, it assumes the invalidity of paternalistic considerations and of arguments based on desert or appropriateness. Second, it concedes that rights are not really morally "primitive" reasons; rather, rights claims are validated by some reason that antecedently blocks the force of collective considerations. Third, it implicitly adds a new formal condition for rights to the two already noted. As Dworkin himself suggests, it would be logically possible to define the content of individual rights in relation to specific collective goals.[60] So related, rights and goals could never come into conflict. But for Dworkin, such rights are not rights *simpliciter*, even though they satisfy the conditions of being nonobligatory for the agent and entailing obligations for others. In addition to being necessary if rights-based theories are to provide a basis for opposing utilitarianism, Dworkin's reservation is intuitively plausible, for two reasons. First, in ordinary political argument, rights are very frequently invoked to blunt the force of collective considerations. Second, we think of rights as relatively insensitive to changes of circumstances. This is obviously the case for "universal human" rights. But teleologically defined rights necessarily vary with such changes, because the best means to a fixed end are variable. In classical utilitarianism, for example, rights and obligations would shift with every change of policy.

Let us agree on Dworkin's description of the philosophical task rights must perform. But are there any such rights? Before examining the details of Dworkin's affirmative answer, we must note that the content and, perhaps, the structure of any affirmative claim will be highly dependent on the specific collective goals that rights are said to block. A nation that devoted all its efforts to plundering and subjugating its neighbors would give its citizens orders that they could resist on all sorts of appealing grounds. In the case of a more defensible collective goal, the range of legitimate objections would probably contract. If so, it follows that to show that certain objections advanced by individuals prevail against classical utilitarianism is not necessarily to say that they would dominate other specifications of collective goals. I shall return to this point.

Dworkin summarizes his argument as follows:

> I presume that we all accept the following postulates of political morality. Government must treat those whom it governs with concern, that is, as human beings who are capable of suffering and frustration, and with respect, that is, as human beings who are capable of forming and acting on intelligent conceptions of how their lives should be lived. Government must not only treat

people with concern and respect, but with equal concern and respect. It must not distribute goods or opportunities unequally on
the ground that some citizens are entitled to more because they
are worthy of more concern. It must not constrain liberty on the
ground that one citizen's conception of the good life . . . is nobler
or superior to another's.

This government obligation reflects the underlying fundamental *right* of
every citizen to equality of concern and respect. But, Dworkin continues,

there are two different rights that might be comprehended by that
abstract right. The first is the right to equal treatment, that is, to
the same distribution of goods or opportunities as anyone else has
or is given. . . . The second is the right to treatment as an equal.
This is the right, not to an equal distribution of some good or
opportunity, but the right to equal concern and respect in the
political decision about how these goods and opportunities are to
be distributed. . . . I propose that the right to treatment as an
equal must be taken to be fundamental . . . and that the more restrictive right to equal treatment holds only in those special circumstances in which, for some special reason, it follows from the
more fundamental right.[61]

Let me begin my analysis of this argument by sketching a distinction
that I shall develop more fully in the next chapter. All rational moral
theories have an element of formal equality because formal equality is
inherent in the notion of rationality. If characteristic x is a sufficient
reason to treat individual A in a particular manner, then it is a sufficient
reason to treat B in the same manner unless some relevant distinction
between A and B can be adduced to block this inference. In one sense,
then, a formal right to treatment as an equal is a part of all moral
theories. But this right adds nothing to the concept of moral rationality
and is perfectly compatible with goal-based theories—for example,
classical utilitarianism—that deny the existence of rights in the strict
sense. Moral theories differ in the *kinds* of characteristics thought to
bear on the treatment of individuals and the *ways* in which these
characteristics are taken into account.

Dworkin's theory begins by specifying two types of relevant
characteristics—capacity for suffering and frustration, which I shall call
sensitivity, and capacity for forming and executing life plans, which I
shall call *purposiveness*. He does not justify these choices, but the missing premise must go something like this: There are certain kinds of
basic goods—avoidance of pain and attainment of objectives—that all
human beings deeply prize and that social policy necessarily adopts as
benchmarks. Dworkin's point of departure, then, gains its plausibility

133

from an implicit appeal to an underlying theory of the good. If pleasure and the attainment of what we desire were not independently and antecedently valued, being deprived of them—by either the government or by private individuals—would not matter.[62]

So far so good. But the transition from kinds of relevant characteristics to the way in which they are taken into account—that is, from concern and respect to *equal* concern and respect—is highly questionable. If, as Dworkin states, respect is based on the capacity to form intelligent life plans, then the extent of respect owed would appear to be subject to variation, because intelligence varies quantitatively and qualitatively. Even if intelligence is intended only to establish a bimodal index or threshold (a life plan is either intelligent or it is not), then unless *all* life plans are intelligent—a contention that would have to be grounded in definitional fiat rather than in experience—respect is unequally owed. Concern is also subject to variation. For most practical purposes, perhaps, it makes sense to assume that human beings suffer equally. But consider the example of a medic, short of morphine, who encounters two soldiers lying wounded on the battlefield. If he happens to know that one of them has an unusually high pain threshold, he may rightly be more concerned about the other, and this may lead him to give the other the bulk of the morphine.

The ambiguity of equal concern and respect may become clearer if we distinguish three different levels of analysis. The most general—formal equality—is uncontroversial, as we have seen. The most specific—actual allocative policy—presents no difficulties here; Dworkin specifies that equal rights need not lead to equal allocations of benefits and burdens. The difficulty is located at the intermediate level, which specifies the weight each individual is to be given in the evaluative process that produces morally acceptable social policy. Dworkin interprets "equal concern and respect" as a principle of substantive equality: each individual is to be given the same weight in determining the social outcome. But this is incompatible with his account of why, or in what respects, individuals are to be accorded moral weight. If human beings are unequally characterized by the alleged bases of concern and respect, then it is not possible to conclude that they should be given the same weight. A more consistent interpretation of equal concern and respect would be: equally acute cases of suffering, or equally intelligent life plans, are to be given equal weight in determining social outcomes. The locus of equality is *claims,* not individuals considered without regard to the features that allow them to be claimants. So interpreted, equality of concern and respect is nothing more than the principle of formal equality, supplemented by a partial theory of the human good.

This outcome points toward a deeper result. There are two ways of arguing that human beings have rights. The first is simply to assert it, as a moral first principle: "We hold these truths to be self-evident. . . . " The defect of this strategy is that it cannot convince skeptics that rights exist or that there is any reason to take them seriously. The second is to anchor rights in certain fundamental facts. This strategy implies that the content of rights cannot be cordoned off from the characteristics of the facts that are said to underlie them. Dworkin tries to avail himself of the philosophical advantages of the second strategy without fully observing its inherent limits.

The appeal to the facts of sensitivity and purposiveness is problematic from another standpoint as well. As we have seen in considering Gewirth's argument, there is no smooth inference from "x is an element of my good" to "I have a right to x." It would be logically possible for a government or another individual to acknowledge that x is a part of my good while depriving me of it. In practice, this disregard for individual interests is blocked by three different considerations: by the intuition that a reduction in aggregate good is at least prima facie wrong; by the belief that individuals are prima facie entitled to, or deserving of, what benefits them; and by the requirement of moral consistency. I have a right to some good because it is wrong to reduce aggregate good, or to ignore what I need or deserve, or to treat me differently from individuals whose cases do not differ relevantly from mine. If this analysis is correct, then rights are not independent moral reasons at all, but rather an elliptical way of talking about claims based on utility, need, desert, or rationality.

As Jules Coleman demonstrates, Dworkin's argument has a most ironic outcome. "Equality of concern and respect" is indistinguishable from the utilitarian principle that everyone is to count for one, no one for less than one. Indeed, Dworkin's principle is in one sense pure Benthamism, for it dismisses Mill's distinction between higher and lower pleasures and reinstates the equivalence of pushpin and poetry. Dworkin rejoins Mill—as he interprets him, anyway by distinguishing between personal and external preferences. An individual's personal preferences "state a preference for the assignment of one set of goods or opportunities to him[self]," while his external preferences "state a preference for one assignment of goods and opportunities to others."[63] According to Dworkin, an aggregative procedure that counts personal, while disregarding external, preferences is the "only defensible form of utilitarianism."[64] Let us ignore the difficulties inherent in the personal/external distinction and simply ask how individual or particular rights can emerge from utilitarianism, so restricted. Dworkin's answer:

> The concept of an individual political right . . . is a response to the philosophical defects of a utilitarianism that counts external pref-

erences and the practical impossibility of a utilitarianism that does not. It allows us to enjoy the institutions of political democracy, which enforce overall or unrefined utilitarianism, and yet protect the fundamental right of citizens to equal concern and respect by prohibiting decisions that seem, antecedently, likely to have been reached by virtue of the external components of the preferences democracy reveals.[65]

Coleman's commentary on this move is exactly to the point: Dworkin's defense of particular rights

> hangs on a mere contingency. There would be no need for political rights were we capable of sorting personal from external preferences. Because Dworkin believes that the impossibility of distinguishing external from personal preferences is a practical problem rather than a conceptual or logical one, a political sovereign with Herculean powers would be able to sort through individual preferences and reach political decisions solely on the basis of personal preferences. Such a political arrangement would treat as basic only two dimensions of morality: utilitarianism and the right to treatment as an equal. The result would be a restricted utilitarianism with no additional political rights.[66]

Thus, the most systematic recent effort to take rights seriously sets out to combat utilitarianism and concludes by endorsing it. Particular rights are not inviolable; they are derived through an aggregative, maximizing evaluative process and express the requirements of social organization that generally and usually prevail, just as Mill had contended. The general right to equal concern and respect can, as we have seen, be no more than the principle of formal equality supplemented by an account of the human good, which is precisely what all utilitarians have always contended.

I do not believe that this outcome is either accidental or avoidable. Nozick's argument from separateness fails, as do all varieties of the argument from freedom. As Richard Flathman has argued, and as Dworkin implicitly concedes, to take rights seriously is to show how they are linked to fundamental human interests. But once the problem is posed in this manner, it is inevitable that some form of aggregative, teleological theory will emerge in which rights will at best enjoy a derivative theoretical status.

I now turn to the question of whether any particular rights may properly be said to be fixed or inviolable. In light of the foregoing analysis, this discussion may well be considered theoretically superfluous. But even though the answer is in general terms predetermined, there is much to be learned from working systematically through some specific issues. I shall consider two kinds of particular rights: negative rights—the right not to be the recipient of certain kinds of acts; and claim-rights—rights to specific kinds of goods, services, or opportunities.

For an individual to have an absolute negative right, it must be the case that everyone else has a duty in all circumstances not to make that individual the recipient of the act in question. If an absolute negative right is to be universal, everyone must have the duty to refrain from that act in all circumstances. Joel Feinberg argues that such rights are at least logically possible, offering the example of torture. He considers the standard objection, a situation in which our failure to torture A will lead to the torture of B and C by someone else, and concludes that our refusal to torture A does not mean that we have violated the rights of B and C. Only their torturer has done so.[67]

There are a number of difficulties with this conclusion. In the first place, it rests on an unacceptably narrow account of responsibility or agency. It is reasonable to distinguish between situations in which only our own decisions and actions are required to bring about a given effect and those in which the decisions and actions of others are necessarily involved as well. In some—though surely not all—circumstances, the fact of multiple agency may be said to reduce the responsibility of one or more agents. But it is never the case that an agent is entirely without responsibility for an outcome that he has consciously decided to prefer to another and has made more probable, however reluctantly, through his act. Thus, typically, one is confronted with a choice between a lesser evil for which one will be wholly responsible and a greater evil for which one will be partly responsible. There is no abstract rule that will resolve this dilemma, independent of circumstances. It is, to say the least, highly implausible that the latter should always be preferred.

Second, even if we were to grant that we have not participated in torturing B and C, it is not clear why Feinberg believes that the question of agency is crucial. From the standpoint of B and C, what matters is what happens to them. They will neither gain from, nor be particularly interested in, the fact that we have preserved our moral purity. In fact, B and C may well feel entitled to complain that we have selfishly preferred our own interest to theirs.

This leads to a broader consideration. In evaluating every action, two major features must be considered: its consequences, and what may be called its "intrinsic" characteristics. The former will vary widely with circumstances, the latter remains relatively invariant. Thus, it makes perfect sense to say that some kinds of action, like torture, are intrinsically highly repugnant. But to conclude from this that it is our duty never to torture anyone, we must contend either that the consequences of refraining from highly repugnant acts are wholly irrelevant or that the intrinsic evil of the act more than counterbalances the net worth of any conceivable consequences of its commission. The first contention is simply arbitrary, the second always vulnerable to counterexamples whose consequences include the prevention of more or equally repugnant acts.[68]

But even if we were to devise adequate responses to these objections, there is a logically independent difficulty that is, I believe, decisive. As Feinberg makes clear, it does not make much sense to speak of an "absolute" negative right unless that right is unalterable or inalienable. But it seems that in certain circumstances any right, no matter how fundamental or well entrenched, may be forfeited or vanish. To return to our example: suppose that a police chief, a faithful servant of a cruel tyrant and a well-known torturer in his own right, seizes a number of innocent citizens, chosen at random, transports them to a secret hiding-place, and then announces over the national radio station his intention of torturing them as a reminder of the omnipotence of his master. Friends of the hostages search frantically but fail to turn up any trace of them. In desperation, they seize the police chief, but he refuses to divulge the hostages' location and dares his captors to kill him. Correctly believing that all other alternatives have been exhausted, they decide to torture him to obtain the information. I begin with the premise that they are morally justified in doing so. The most plausible analysis is that the police chief has forfeited his right not to be tortured. The right presupposes background conditions of normality and reciprocal restraint; the police chief is directly responsible for the destruction of these conditions. More broadly: unless rights are supported by unchallengeable theological claims, they are at most part of the fabric of human existence, existing in a complex relation to both circumstances and individual merit or desert, broadly interpreted. It would be misleading to say that the right not to be tortured must be earned, but it is reasonable to say that under certain circumstances an individual ceases to deserve it. Similarly, a mass murderer forfeits his right to live. Permitting him to continue living may be an act of mercy or prudence, but it is not a moral obligation.

Negative rights are a compressed approximation of our belief that certain objects or states are good for and important to most individuals in a very fundamental way and that to impede individuals in their enjoyment of them is on its face a significant evil. (Consider how the right not to be tortured would be viewed in a world populated largely by masochists.) But to recognize that negative rights are embedded in a teleological context is to concede in principle that considerations of the "greater good" may warrant their abrogation and that the assignment of goods to individuals they effect may be altered by considerations of distribution and desert.

Let us now consider what some have called *claim-rights*—rights to specific kinds of goods, services, or opportunities. David Miller seeks to defend the autonomy and distinctiveness of claim-rights by refuting attempts to reduce them to other considerations. First, he asserts, it is not the case that "*A* has a moral right to *x*" is merely another way of saying, "It is morally right that *A* be given *x*."

> Consider a typical situation in which moral rights are created: the making of a promise. *A* promises *B* that he will give *B* a certain object; this creates in *B* a moral right to be given the object, and the right persists until *B* receives it *unless* he voluntarily releases *A* from his obligation. But suppose it turns out that the object concerned will be extremely harmful to *B*, or that *B* will use the object to harm others. It is then no longer right to give *B* the object—but his moral right to it persists (the moral right is overridden by the requirement that we avoid causing serious harm whenever we can).[69]

It seems much more direct and less artificial to say that the act of promising occurs in an assumed background and that the right it creates is merely provisional and relative to that background. If it is wrong for *B* to do *x*, then *B* can have no right to the means that make it possible for him to do *x*. If *B* threatens *A*'s life with a gun when *A* has done nothing wrong, then *A* or anyone else may properly confiscate the gun. The fact that *B* owns the gun creates, not a moral right, but only a rebuttable prima facie claim. Social practices such as promising and property relations are normally a basis for claims because they are very generally useful in promoting coordination, harmony, and security. But if in specific instances they cease to promote these goals, they can validly be overridden, since their worth is simply instrumental. In practice, of course, we tend to minimize overriding, both because we do not trust the collective mechanism to be impartial and because we fear the long-run effects of even valid overridings on generally useful institutions. These considerations complicate, without qualitatively transforming, their utilitarian basis.

Miller reformulates his argument in an interesting manner.

> If we say "*A* ought to be given *x*, because he has a moral right to it," the second claim does not simply reiterate the first. There are other types of reasons which might be advanced instead—for instance, that giving *x* to *A* will maximize the general welfare. If there are six men in a boat at sea, and only one of them can row, it may be right to give the whole of the last loaf of bread to that one,

in the hope that he can row them ashore. But has he a right to it? Could he complain if a general decision was taken to divide the bread equally and to forgo the added chance of reaching land? I think not.[70]

We may observe, first, that in some circumstances Miller's denial would not be plausible. Let us suppose that the sole rower is also a skilled navigator and is certain about the location of the nearest land and further, that he knows that if he gets all the bread, he can row the boat there before the others die, but if it is split evenly, all will die. A democratic procedure may well lead to an equal division, both because the others may mistrust his claims as a ploy to get all the bread and because short-range considerations, such as acute hunger, may blind the majority to its long-run interest. Given these assumptions, he is indeed entitled to complain about an equal division, since it is very likely to have the effect of depriving him of his life without significantly benefiting anyone else. The rower, I submit, then has a "right," in that he would be justified in using force to make his claim prevail.

But let us concede that, intuitively, rights-claims cannot always be converted into utilitarian propositions. It does not follow that rights constitute an independent sort of moral claim, since it could be argued that "to have a right to x" is nothing but "to deserve x." Miller rejects this possibility. A devoted nurse who cares for a sick person for many years but gets no part of the inheritance deserves the inheritance but has no right to it. A right would exist if the invalid had at some point promised or indicated that the nurse would receive a share.[71] More generally, desert is a "matter of fitting forms of treatment to the specific qualities and actions of individuals," while rights "make no reference to the particular qualities of the individuals concerned." If I acquire a right through a promise, this happens "irrespective of what I am or do."[72]

Our response to this has already been indicated. From a moral standpoint, there are no claims whose validity is independent of what I am or do. It may be convenient to set up procedures and practices that abstract to a certain extent from differences among individuals, but, as our experience of both law and social policy reveals, it is always necessary to find some way to take individual differences into account when the consequence of ignoring them is gross stupidity or blatant injustice. More generally: A right is never an ultimate appeal.

Systems of rights are a kind of imperfect procedural justice, subject to modification in light of underlying principles. To have a right is to have a valid claim; a valid claim is based solely on reasons that prevail over all competing reasons. Feinberg puts this well: A man has a moral right "when he has a claim, the recognition of which is called for . . . by moral principles, or the principles of an enlightened conscience."[73] Thus, a right is not a moral reason, but rather the outcome or result of moral reasons. The language of rights is at most a convenient abbreviation. Habit and social stability may incline us to ascribe logical independence to this language, but change and extreme situations force us to deal explicitly with its underlying premises.

4.8. Rights, Goals, and Moral Structures

It may appear that the argument has led us to an impasse. Theories based on rights were advanced in response to the defects of utilitarianism, but they are exposed to equally powerful objections. Indeed, from the standpoint of justice they are exposed to the *same* objection—unresponsiveness to distributional considerations. Whatever its errors of detail, Nozick's attack on "end-state" and "patterned" theories clearly demonstrates what the rigid separation of rights and goals would entail.

This apparent impasse stems, I believe, from an excessively narrow construe of philosophical alternatives. Utilitarianism is but one kind of goal-based theory, and its defects are not necessarily shared by all others. For example, many objections to utilitarianism can be traced back to the character of its maximand, subjective preferences. These difficulties can be overcome by replacing preferences with an objective theory of the human good. Another characteristic objection is that in utilitarianism numbers count in the wrong way, legitimizing grave deprivations for a minority in the name of trivial advantages for a majority. As we have seen, the force of this objection is blunted when we note the heterogeneity of the human good. Some aspects of the good are more urgent than others; depriving a few of an urgent good will frequently reduce total good by more than the sum of the trivial advantages for the many. But not always. At the outset of this book I argued that human beings necessarily share their fates with one another, by nature and not by choice. One consequence of this is that what legitimately befalls us is not independent of collective considerations. Once appropriate weights have been attached to the different aspects of our individual good, we must be prepared to accept whatever consequences are dictated by according the good of others its appropriate weight. To demand inviolable protection against the worst outcome is to claim an unjustified priority for our own interests.

Finally, utilitarianism has been faulted for its untrammeled pursuit of a nonmoral good, on the grounds that this leads to a kind of moral obtuseness. This objection most frequently surfaces in discussions of punishment; the retributivist view draws its strength from the intuition that what rightly befalls offenders is not simply a function of collective, maximizing considerations. As T. M. Scanlon has recently suggested, the best way to cope with this is to introduce suitably defined moral goods into the maximand of a consequentialist theory. Such goods

> often figure in moral argument as independently valuable states of affairs. So considered, they differ from the ends promoted in standard utilitarian theories in that their value does not rest on their being good things *for* particular individuals ... [they] do not represent ways in which individuals may be *better off*. They are, rather, special morally desirable features of states of affairs.[74]

As I have already suggested, the moral goods required for an adequate view of justice are *relational goods:* the fitness or appropriateness of a possessive relation between a particular individual and a specific non-moral good. In moral arguments, relational goods are expressed as claims—that is, reasons purporting to establish the appropriateness of specific possessive relations. Genuine relational goods are valid claims, claims based on adequate reasons. In Chapter 5 I shall argue that *need* and *desert,* suitably interpreted, constitute such reasons. Because such claims, though moral goods, include nonmoral goods as a basic element, the view of justice based on them can hope to harmonize some of the strengths of traditional nonmoral consequentialist theories with some of the deontological intuitions such consequentialism usually violates. A just state of affairs prevails, I shall say, when the satisfaction of valid claims is maximized.

The theory of justice I present in the next two chapters is goal-based and maximizing. Its basic elements are:

1. An objective theory of the human good, a heterogeneous set of valued ends that differ in both nobility and urgency (Chapter 3)
2. A theory of reasons that constitute valid claims to that good (Chapter 5, sections 3–6)
3. A theory of how valid claims are to be aggregated into a distributional result—the Aristotelian principle of proportionality (Chapter 5, sections 1–2)
4. A concrete application of the concept of proportional claims to different categories of distributional questions (Chapter 6)

For the most part, I shall argue, the nonmoral goods for which we strive are governed by relational considerations. In circumstances in which no such considerations exist—that is, when there is no rational basis for assigning a specific good to a particular kind of individual—all dispositions of the unassigned good are equally just, although some may be deemed preferable for other reasons.

5
Justice
Formal and Material Principles

5.1. Justice and Rationality

Principles of justice are *reasons* or *criteria* for assigning particular things to particular individuals. As a species of universal propositions, they have the following property: Judgments concerning individuals falling within their domain are determined entirely by the extent to which they conform to the designated criteria. R. M. Hare puts this clearly:

> If a person says that a thing is red, he is committed to the view that anything which was like it in the relevant respects would likewise be red. The relevant respects are those which, he thought, entitled him to call the first thing red. . . . To say that something is red is to say that it is of a certain kind, and so to imply that anything which is of that same kind is red.[1]

This is equally true of moral propositions:

> If I call a thing a good *x*, I am committed to calling any *x* like it good. . . . When we make a moral judgment about something, we make it *because* of the possession by it of certain . . . properties.[2]

From this, the formal principle of justice follows directly: Like cases are to be treated alike and different cases to be treated differently.[3] This is the commonsense core of Hare's universalizability criterion: If I grant that a moral principle specifies appropriate criteria for judging or treating individuals in a certain way *and* that a particular individual satisfies those criteria, I cannot without self-contradiction fail to accord that individual the judgment or treatment in question. In the absence of other considerations, I am equally debarred from arbitrary *discrimination* against others and from unwarranted *exceptions* in my own favor.

Taken by itself, the formal principle of justice cannot lead to substantive principles.[4] Recently, two different—but equally mistaken—attempts have been made to move directly from form to substance. Let us briefly consider each.

In one, S. I. Benn and R. S. Peters claim that the formal principle is logically equivalent to the principle of *equality of consideration*, which is "a presumption against treating [human beings] differently, in any respect, until grounds for distinction have been shown. . . . The onus of justification rests on whoever would make distinctions."[5] Feinberg skewers this neatly. First, there are some situations in which a presumption in favor of different or unequal treatment exists. For example, a testator must offer a special justification for treating nonfamily members as well as family members. Second, while the formal principle gives us no guidance when we are ignorant of the (relevant) characteristics of individuals, Benn and Peters's formula would have us presume that equality of treatment is just in these circumstances. This is both substantive and arbitrary.[6]

In the other attempt, Hare has claimed that the formal principle leads to a position that has important affinities with traditional utilitarianism. The formal principle has as a direct corollary the utilitarian principle: Everybody to count for one, nobody for more than one.

> For what this principle means is that everyone is entitled to equal
> consideration, and that if it is said that two people ought to be
> treated differently, some difference must be cited as the ground.[7]

Now, first, we have already indicated why the formal principle cannot imply, as Hare appears to argue, a presumption in favor of equal treatment. Hare's formulation is incomplete; the formal principle also means that whenever it is said that two people ought to be treated similarly, some similarity must be given as the ground. Second, Hare achieves convergence between the formal and utilitarian principles only by misinterpreting the latter. Bentham and Mill were attempting to provide a basis for moral calculation, summing across individuals. To make this possible, that is, not to preclude from the outset the possibility of a determinate outcome, they were compelled to postulate that the complete satisfaction or dissatisfaction of each individual was to be given a weight or numerical value equal to that of every other. If, in one situation, A is wholly satisfied while B is completely dissatisfied, and in another the reverse is the case, the two situations are of equal moral value, equally choiceworthy. (For simplicity, I set to one side the vexed question of "higher" versus "lower" desires.) Clearly, this postulate is not equivalent to or derivable from the formal principle, since the formal principle leaves open the possibility that differences along relevant criteria could provide a basis for attaching unequal moral weight to the satisfaction of various individuals.

This leads us to the second part of Hare's argument—the introduction of preferences, desires, or interests. He invites us to consider the division of a chocolate bar among three individuals who have an equal liking for chocolate in a situation in which no other considerations are thought to be relevant.

It seems to us obvious that the just way to divide the chocolate is equally. And the principle of universalizability gives us the logic of this conclusion.[8]

But Hare's argument presupposes a crucial premise that he does not bother to state explicitly. It is not sufficient to say that no *other* considerations are relevant; it must also be the case that we have decided that intensity of desire is a relevant distributional criterion. The arguments in favor of this criterion, however powerful, are surely not contained within the formal principle!

But even this invalid argument is not enough to establish the convergence between the formal principle and utilitarianism. Hare must go on to claim that the satisfaction of desire is not only *a* criterion but *the* criterion. His argument in support of this claim is little more than an arbitrary assertion:

It is in the endeavor to find lines of conduct which we can prescribe universally in a given situation that we find ourselves
bound to give equal weight to the desires of all parties (the foundation of distributive justice) . . . the considerations that weigh
with me in this inquiry can *only* be, How much (as I imagine
myself in the place of each man in turn) do I want to have this, or
to avoid that?[9]

I do not mean to suggest that the ideal observer thesis, of which this is a version, is necessarily mistaken, although by now its philosophical defects are well established. The point is, rather, that the centrality Hare accords to satisfaction of desires is the consequence of a substantive view, not of the formal principle. In effect, Hare later concedes this. It is logically possible to act consistently, within the bounds of universalizability, in accordance with ideals that, in cases of conflict, give little or no weight to the desires of others.[10] Moreover, such behavior is not always, even from Hare's standpoint, reprehensible, illiberal, "fanatical." When we restrain drug addicts, we think this to be legitimate *"in the interests of the addict."* [11] But this is to introduce a distinction between *desires* and *interests* and to concede that the latter may in certain circumstances constitute a relevant criterion not wholly congruent with the requirements of desire.[12]

5.2. Substantive Justice: General Formulae

We have argued previously that a just situation exists when what individuals come to have or to undergo corresponds to their *valid claims*. We must now undertake to lend some precision to this very general assertion.

5. Justice: Formal and Material Principles

Claims may be divided into two categories, absolute and relative. Absolute claims do not contain, as essential elements, references to treatment that those other than the claimant may receive. For example, an individual may assert that he needs 2,200 calories per day to remain healthy and productive and on that basis may claim that amount of nourishment. Relative claims do contain references to the treatment of others. Such references may be explicit, as when a police union fights for a contract giving its members wages equal to 110 percent of those paid to firemen and garbage collectors, or implicit, as when shareholders expect dividends in proportion to the number of shares each owns. Whether absolute or relative, claims are based on specific criteria alleged to be relevant to the specific situation in which the claims are advanced.

The broad outlines of substantive justice may be expressed in three principles:

1. *The Ordinal Principle*. Individual *A* has a larger valid claim than *B* if and only if *A* satisfies the relevant criteria to a greater extent than *B* does.

2. *The Supply Principle*. Valid absolute claims must be modified if and only if in a specific situation the total of such claims exceeds what is available for distribution.

3. *The Nonviolation Principle*. A just situation exists when no individual possesses or enjoys less than his (modified) valid claims.

The Ordinal Principle merely makes clear the logical implications of linking claims to criteria: nothing except variations along the continua picked out by the criteria is relevant to determining the extent of rationally grounded (valid) claims.

The Supply Principle points out that the force of all claims depends in part on the possibility of satisfying them. Thus, absolute claims implicitly contain presumptions and can be expressed as hypothetical propositions: If the means exist, I am entitled to the full satisfaction of this claim. For example, the laws of bankruptcy contain rules for modifying the claims of creditors in response to the realizable assets of the debtor.

For this reason, we must reject N. M. L. Nathan's attractive suggestion that for a state of affairs to be just, it is necessary and sufficient that the treatment individuals receive be equal in value to the attributes, that is, fulfilled criteria, serving as the basis of claims.[13] Nathan is concerned about, for example, cases in which punishments are thought to be unjust—disproportionate to offenses—even though they are applied fairly to classes of individuals committing similar crimes. But the Supply Principle can handle this case: Since (except in rare or contrived circumstances), the fair punishments to which individuals have absolute claims cannot be said to be in short supply (there is not a fixed store of fair punishments), the presumption in favor of the absolute claim is not rebutted. Nathan also considers the case of two individuals, equally hard-working and highly qualified, who are paid "exactly the same but not enough to keep body and soul together," that is, less than they need.[14] This is more complex, but equally amenable to the Supply Principle. If more money is available for wages, for example, the owner is reaping huge profits and living luxuriously, then they are being treated unjustly. If, on the other hand, the owner is not living much better than his employees and accurately contends that even a small wage increase will force his business into bankruptcy, then the two individuals are indeed unfortunate, but not victims of injustice. Nathan makes the mistake of supposing that because justice is preferable to injustice, just situations must always be good or desirable. But unfortunately, although justice is a necessary condition of fully choiceworthy human situations, it is hardly sufficient.

The Nonviolation Principle reminds us that in some respects justice is a negative principle. Individuals are not necessarily treated unjustly if some, but not all, receive more than their valid claims. For example, consider a group of individuals, each of whom is working for the same company at a wage which he thinks is fair and adequate and to which he has personally consented. The requirements of justice are in no way violated if the employer, having fully paid all the wage claims, privately gives an employee with whom he is friendly an additional amount of money out of his own pocket.

Let us now explore the implications of these principles by considering specific cases.

Case 1. Let A and B be the only individuals with valid claims to a particular good. Assume that f is the relevant criterion and that f_1 and f_2 represent the extent to which A and B, respectively, satisfy f. Assume further that in view of f_1 and f_2, A and B have valid absolute claims to amounts x and y of the good they seek and, finally, that the supply of that good (s) is precisely equal to the sum of x and y. It follows from the Supply Principle that x and y cannot be modified and from the Nonviolation Principle that only one just distribution exists, when A receives x and B receives y.

Case 2. Retain all the assumptions from Case 1, except that now s is less than the sum of x and y, forcing some modification of absolute claims in accordance with the Supply Principle. There are two variants.

a) Assume $x = y$. From the Ordinal Principle, we know that this can be true only when $f_1 = f_2$. Then justice requires that A and B each receive $s/2$. *Ex hypothesi,* no relevant difference exists between A and B. To treat them differently would therefore violate the Formal Principle.

5. Justice: Formal and Material Principles

b) Assume $x > y$. Our task is to find just shares u, v such that $u + v = s$. From the Ordinal Principle we know that $x > y \Rightarrow f_1 > f_2$ and that therefore $u > v$. This outcome, though valid, is less than satisfactory in two respects. First, it is far from determinate or specific: There is an infinite number of pairs (u,v) that satisfy the condition, and they vary across a very wide range. Second, we may well feel that ordinal justice is not fully just, that the extent to which f_1 and f_2 differ ought to be reflected in the difference between valid claims.

We may lend some precision to these intuitions by introducing two further principles. Let f_i represent the extent of an individual's criterion satisfaction and c_i his corresponding claims.

1. *The Principle of Linearity*. Equal increments of criterion satisfaction give rise to equal increments of claims. Formally, $f_1 - f_2 = f_3 - f_4 \Leftrightarrow c_1 - c_2 = c_3 - c_4$.

2. *The Principle of Determination*. If an individual completely fails to satisfy the relevant criterion, then he has no valid claim to any of the good. Formally, $f_1 = 0 \Leftrightarrow c_1 = 0$.

Consider a simple case. An employer and a group of employees agree that overtime work will be compensated through a profit-sharing scheme in which all profits above a certain level will be divided among the employees who have put in overtime. The employees agree among themselves that, as workers, they are approximately equal and that the only relevant difference is length of time spent working. The Principle of Linearity suggests that every hour be compensated at the same rate, and the Principle of Determination, that an individual who has worked no overtime has no claim on the pool of shared profits.

The Principle of Determination is one very plausible interpretation of the meaning or function of criteria in distribution. To say that f is a criterion is to imply that criterion satisfaction is the necessary and sufficient condition of valid claims. Thus, at least in circumstances in which it is sensible to say that an individual registers zero on the continuum picked out by the relevant criterion, the assertion that nevertheless an individual has a positive claim is either groundless or based on other features of the situation that, he argues, have been improperly neglected. Thus, to take our previous example, a worker who has put in no overtime may assert that the foreman discriminated against him, preventing him from doing so. This amounts to the sensible claim that the hours-of-work criterion implicitly presupposed another condition or criterion that was not satisfied.

The Principle of Linearity may appear more arbitrary. I do not mean to suggest that every deviation from it is unjust, but rather that it constitutes an intuitively appealing benchmark or presumption. There is, moreover, an important empirical argument in its favor. Consider a variant of the previous example in which the wage for all overtime hours above the first ten is set at 150 percent of the rate for the first ten. Such arrangements, empirically very frequent, are usually justified through the claim that the additional hours are not simply equal to those in the first group: they require more *effort*, because of increasing fatigue, or more *sacrifice*, of leisure or family. Thus, apparently non-linear claims may represent the sum of claims derived from two or more criteria, each generating claims in a linear fashion. This analysis may also be seen as an answer to objections from the standpoint of the Formal Principle: What is the relevant difference between the individual who works the first hour and the one who works the eleventh, such that the difference of treatment is justified? There is of course the factual difference that one has actually worked the eleventh hour, but this, intuitively, does not seem to be an adequate response. Nor would it be enough to appeal to the fact that, after all, the eleventh hour is not the same as the first, for we want to know what features of the eleventh hour underlie its greater claim-generating powers.

Taken together, the Principles of Linearity and Determination lead directly to what we may call the Aristotelian Principle of distributive justice: A just situation requires that treatment be directly proportional to criteria satisfaction. Formally, justice requires that for all f and c, $f_1 / c_1 = f_2 / c_2$. When the Aristotelian Principle is supplemented by the Supply and Nonviolation principles, a general determinate outcome to distributional problems emerges.

Let us now briefly consider some possible objections to this analysis.

First objection: if f_1 is positive while $f_0 = 0$, $f_1 / c_1 \neq f_0 / c_0$. Response: this is theoretically and practically trivial, since the Aristotelian Principle covers all cases except this one, and the Principle of Determination specifies an outcome for the one excluded case.

Second objection: the Aristotelian Principle is incomplete, since it was developed in the context of absolute claims only and does not deal with relative claims. Response: relative claims *already* embody the principle $f_1 / c_1 = f_2 / c_2$. They differ from absolute claims whenever $s \leq x + y$; the only practical difference is that absolute claims allow for $s > x_a + y_a$, while in the case of relative claims $s = x_r + y_r$ by definition.

Third objection: the Aristotelian Principle is incomplete, since it cannot deal with situations in which $s > x_a + y_a$. Response: it is not clear that such situations exist, since there may be general relative claims that always come into play to soak up the "surplus." But if surpluses do exist, we can say that the Aristotelian Principle, when combined with the Nonviolation Principle, has identified a family of equally just distributions, the choice among which depends on criteria, if any, that lie outside the theory of justice. Such criteria are likely to be derived from a theory of the human good or of the good community, and we may conjecture that utilitarian considerations are likely to be important, if not dominant.[15]

Fourth objection: the Aristotelian Principle is incomplete, since it does not accurately model distributive situations in which criteria satisfactions, or valid claims, or both, vary irregularly or step-functionally, though ordinally. Such situations would include elections and various nonpolitical competitions. Response: an election (at least of the two-person or -issue, majority-rule type) may be viewed as a distributive system in which f_i can assume only two values, one of which is zero. If an n–person competition offers only one prize, we may say that f_i equals zero for $n-1$ participants. If an n–person competition offers more than one prize, then *each* prize can be considered as a separate distribution with a different claim criterion, satisfied completely by one individual and not at all by any of the others.

Of course, this response assumes the relative fairness of the relations between positions and prizes. Even in the case of purely conventional competitions, we may wish to challenge this assumption. It may, for example, seem unreasonable that the first-place finisher in a foot race receive ten times as much money as the second-placer, no matter how small the margin of victory. This intuition rests on the belief that the race comes into being, in large measure, anyway, to manifest and reward *speed*, a quality that varies continuously in a way that relative position does not. A similar, though less tractable, discomfort arises when the major component of the prize varies step-functionally. When a hard-fought World Series between two equally talented and determined teams is decided by a narrow victory in the seventh game, it may strike us as unfortunate or unfair that one team should obtain all the glory and memory of victory.

Thus, the Aristotelian Principle can accommodate step-functional variations, and it can also provide us with a theoretical basis for the intuitive discomfort we frequently feel in such cases.

Fifth objection: either there is some logical error in our derivation of the Aristotelian Principle or some hidden bias in one or more of the postulates, since we have been led, in advance of concrete moral argument, to an antiegalitarian position. Response: the Aristotelian Principle leaves open the possibility of nonegalitarian outcomes, but it does not mandate them. Rather, it enables us to identify the task of an egalitarian theory: the specification of some relevant criterion f such that for all individuals, $f_1 = f_2 \ldots = f_n$. Let us briefly consider some recent attempts to accomplish this task.

5.3. The Grounds of Equality

In this section I want to examine critically two of the most influential recent arguments in support of the claim that there is some relevant criterion that all human beings fulfill to the same extent. Having rejected these as untenable, I shall propose a weaker claim.[16]

5.3.a. Vlastos: Equality of individual worth

Gregory Vlastos begins by distinguishing between merit and worth. Merit refers to "all the kinds of valuable qualities or performances in respect of which persons may be graded." Worth, on the other hand, is relative to the person as an "integral and unique individual."[17]

> If there is a value attaching to the person himself as an integral and unique individual, *this* value will not fall under merit or be reducible to it. For it is of the essence of merit . . . to be a grading concept; and there is no way of grading individuals as such. We can only grade them with respect to their qualities, hence only by abstracting from their individuality. If A is valued for some meritorious quality, *m*, his individuality does not enter into the valuation. As an individual he is then dispensable; his place could be taken without loss of value by any other individual with as good an *m*-rating. Nor would matters change by multiplying and diversifying the meritorious qualities with which A is endowed.[18]

Note that the argument has already taken a very curious turn. *Individuality* has been detached from all differentiating qualities; it is now nothing but sheer metaphysical *otherness*. But everything stands in the relation of otherness to everything else. How, then, can otherness be the ground of a distinctive value attaching to *persons?* We can say this only by picking out some qualities or distinguishing characteristics that *all* persons and *only* persons share; but precisely this move seems to be ruled out by Vlastos's argument.

But, one may feel, this objection is too abstract. Thus far, Vlastos has intended to provide only a formal description of what would have to be the case *if* persons are to be of equal worth; the facts of human experience will tell us whether anything actually satisfies these conditions. Vlastos offers the example of love; the parent's (*P*'s) love for his child (*A*)

> need not fluctuate with the ups and downs in *A*'s achievements. Perhaps *A* had some bad years after graduating from college, and it looked then as though his brilliant gifts would be wasted. It does not follow that *P*'s love for *A* then lapsed or even ebbed. Constancy of affection in the face of variations of merit is one of

the surest tests of whether or not a parent does love a child. . . . There are many relations in which one's liking or esteem for a person are strictly conditional on his measuring up to certain standards. But convincing evidence that the relation is of this type is no evidence that the relation is one of parental love or any other kind of love. It does nothing to show that one has this feeling, or any feeling, for an *individual*, rather than for a place-holder of qualities one likes to see instantiated by somebody or other close about one.[19]

This description of love is profoundly mistaken. In the case of the parent–child relation, the child in fact has an enduring *quality* that provides a basis for love: the child is the parent's own, and to love him is to love one's own. This "ownness," moreover, is of a special type that Aristotle described perfectly: the parent loves the child in the same manner that the poet loves his poem, as a created being the activity of creating which affirms and amplifies one's own being.[20]

As everyone knows, the parent–child relation rests on more than this relational quality. It always reflects, to a certain extent, considerations of merit or achievement. The most unconditional love can be weakened or eroded by acts that outrage the parent's most deeply felt moral principles. Although counteracting ownness, such negative judgments are exacerbated by ownness itself: precisely because the child is in a sense an extension of oneself, its shortcomings are experienced with a special keenness and poignancy.

Vlastos's account works no better for nonfamily love. Who has not been confronted with the most natural and inevitable of all lover's questions: *Why* do you love me? The poet's shrug, "Because I am I, because you are you," is never taken as satisfying, and rightly so. The mere fact of one's existence is never taken as a sufficient ground of love; one wants to be loved for what one is, some prized qualities that distinguish us from others. A love no grounds of which can be described or identified is almost certainly some other sentiment masquerading as love. At the very least, this love will be a source of such lacerating insecurity that it cannot long survive.

There is a further point that appears to undercut Vlastos's approach completely. We do not love everybody, at least not equally. If love is, as he claims, properly directed to a person's individual worth, it follows that we attach different values to the worth of different individuals. But the philosophical motive for distinguishing worth from merit was to find some basis for equality. On the other hand, if it were the case that love were directed to that which all individuals are or have equally, it would be impossible to imagine, let alone provide, an account of the fact that we love some but not others. Love would become an effect without a cause.

Vlastos's attempt to extend the concept of individual worth to the public realm is even less persuasive. He contends that without this concept there is no way of understanding or justifying many of our current practices, such as the commitment to equal citizenship. Even if he were right about this, this relation cuts in two directions; the meritarian might well contend that this merely reveals the error of nonmerit based political participation.[21] But in fact he is wrong. A theoretical meritarian might well believe that, in practice, equal citizenship is the best possible arrangement, since the institutions required to distribute participation in accordance with merit are all too likely to be perverted for class or factional ends, bringing about a result less just than simple equality. A meritarian, that is, might well view equal citizenship as a maximin solution to the problem of distributing political power.

The attempt to find the concept of worth at work in the moral community fares no better. Vlastos contends that

> if I see someone in danger of drowning I will not need to satisfy myself about his moral character before going to his aid. I owe assistance to any man in such circumstances, not merely to good men.[22]

Ordinarily, of course, we presume that we ought to save the drowning person. But this presumption is eminently rebuttable. Suppose you are walking along and hear shouts from the river. Running up to the bank, you recognize the slowly sinking swimmer as the bloodthirsty tyrannical ruler of your country, a man universally condemned by domestic and world opinion but rendered invulnerable to violent overthrow by his secure control of the army. It would, I believe, be morally right as well as practically beneficial to let him drown.

In this as in the other cases of moral behavior Vlastos cites, the presumption in favor of equal treatment may be understood as reflecting the existence of a very low merit threshold. This would then be another instance of the type of distributive situation discussed in the previous section in which both criteria satisfactions and appropriate treatments vary step-functionally.

In spite of all these difficulties, we may still be impressed and disturbed by one part of Vlastos's argument. If, as he claims, regulating our attitudes toward and treatment of others according to their qualities means both that we cannot care for them as individuals, that is, must regard them as replaceable, and that we cannot really care for people at all but only the abstract qualities they happen to instantiate, the premise that leads us to this impasse must be rejected.

But neither of these dire consequences follows necessarily from the premise. We view human beings as unique and irreplaceable for two reasons. First, even though every quality an individual has is possessed by others to some extent, the manner in which qualities are combined and emphasized in each individual is distinctive. (Mathematically, imagine a many-dimensional space, each dimension of which can take on a very large number of discrete values. The number of combinations specifying distinguishable single points will be very large.) Second, a large part of what an individual means to us derives from the history of our relation. In the abstract, I suppose, an old friend could be replaced by someone else with equal sympathy, shared experiences, and knowledge of us; but what difference does this theoretical possibility make, since no one else can *now* possess these qualities in the same way and to the same extent? On the other hand, if we had happened to meet different people twenty years ago, someone else might now be playing the role of the old friend; but this consequence is morally and humanly acceptable. In fact, underlying any sane and balanced view of human existence is the recognition of the large element of contingency in our lives as well as the fact that no one is entirely unique, irreplaceable, or necessary for our own existence.

Nor is it the case that the quality orientation compels us to care for the abstract qualities rather than concrete individuals. For the most part, the qualities we value are *human,* having no real existence or even meaning apart from their instantiation in individuals. Thus, the distinction between valuing qualities and valuing the individuals possessing them is entirely artificial. Of course, if what we really care for is radically separate from human beings, then there is some merit to Vlastos's claim. Some religious and metaphysical accounts of human desire have this consequence. To accept them as true, however, is to reject the very basis of the claim that not caring for others is a moral defect or spiritual impoverishment.[23]

5.3.b. Equality of qualities

If a case is to be made for equality, then, it must be based on some quality or qualities that human beings possess equally. Broadly speaking, there are two possible strategies. First, we may appeal to some nonnatural property. If we are all the "children of God," for example, we are surely equal. We all stand in the same relation to the same creative power, a relation that is not merely a peripheral fact but rather the core of our existence; in light of the infinite gulf between God and man, qualitative differences among human beings shrink into insignificance. Or we may, with Kant, appeal to the transcendental moral personality. Whatever the character of our individual moral lives, whatever the external forces impinging on us, we are all free and possessors of reason that is capable of being *practical*. Transcendental freedom manifests itself as a "fact of reason," a conscience, from which not even the most unregenerate sinner can escape. Existing beyond the bounds of the senses, it is not subject to the quantitative variations that form part of the categorical framework of sense experience; we are not only free, but equally free.

Neither of these claims can simply be dismissed, but each is problematic. The theological argument, of course, cannot persuade those who reject its major premise. To the extent that the transcendental argument arises and gains its plausibility through a regress from ordinary moral experience, it is vulnerable to empirical objections. Some individuals do not feel the pangs of conscience; some are hopelessly determined by heteronomous forces; some have rational faculties so impaired or undeveloped that they cannot be effectively practical. To the extent that the transcendental argument is not empirically grounded or delimited, it tends to become a restatement of the egalitarian intuition rather than a basis for it. Each human being has a dignity based on autonomy, regardless of observable characteristics. But we are asked to accept on faith the contention that every individual participates in autonomy, that is, in practical reason. The way Kant posed the issue makes it impossible to refute his contention, but it is equally the case that without some appeal to experience, only our initial moral intuition can induce us to affirm it.

However this may be, it would be most satisfactory to be able to point to some natural quality—some important, verifiable characteristic that all human beings have in common, to the same degree. It is not clear that any such quality exists. The difficulty goes beyond the often-cited "exceptional" cases of mental illness or retardation; human beings seem to vary quantitatively along every dimension that has ever been specified. These facts have led theorists who wish to preserve an empirical basis for equality to posit thresholds or entitlement points. Below a certain limit, the individual is not equal to "normal" human beings. All who are above the limit, no matter how far, are equally normal and equally the bearers of claims against one another. Rawls, for example, decides to

> select a range property . . . and to give equal justice to those meeting its conditions. For example, the property of being in the interior of the unit circle is a range property of the points in the plane. All points inside this circle have this property although their

coordinates vary within a certain range. And they equally have
this property, since no point interior to a circle is more or less
interior to it than any other interior point.[24]

Similarly, Gewirth concedes the intuitive force of the Aristotelian principle of proportionality but goes on to observe that some dis-
tributionally relevant qualities vary continuously while others do not.
For example, all citizens at least eighteen years of age have the right to
vote; you do not acquire more of the right as you get older. The property
of being "at least eighteen" is distinguished from properties such as
tallness that vary internally. Wilt Chamberlain and Bill Russell are both
tall, but Chamberlain is taller.[25]

This approach is exposed to several difficulties. First, although the
threshold is based on a natural quality, it is not itself a natural quality
but rather a decision. Everything depends on where the line is drawn; a
nonegalitarian might divide the human species into a small number of
natural aristocrats and a large number of slaves. A low threshold,
though intended to provide a foundation for egalitarianism, is more
plausibly interpreted as a reflection of that prior commitment.

Second, there is room for a complex empirical debate about the actual
percentages of human beings who fall above and below a threshold
defined in general terms. Rawls, for example, specifies as a threshold
quality the capacity for "a sense of justice, a normally effective desire to
apply and to act upon the principles of justice, at least to a certain
minimum degree."[26] "I assume," he continues, "that the capacity for a
sense of justice is possessed by the overwhelming majority of mankind."[27] Reflecting on this question, Aristotle came to the opposite
conclusion:

> The natural tendency of most people is to be swayed not by a
> sense of shame but by fear, and to refrain from acting basely not
> because it is disgraceful, but because of the punishment it
> brings. . . . But they do not even have a notion of what is
> noble. . . . Most people are swayed rather by compulsion than ar-
> gument, and by punishments rather than by what is noble.[28]

It is no easy matter to resolve this disagreement, especially as Rawls
hedges by speaking of a capacity that may not be developed or observable rather than actual behavior or psychological characteristics.

The third difficulty is the most serious. It is of course possible to
define range properties that are not subject to quantitative variation,
but this procedure seems question-begging when it conceals variations
that may be relevant. In Gewirth's voting example, chronological age is
obviously a proxy for a set of qualities that every voter is supposed to
possess. As everyone knows, some individuals have these at fourteen;

others do not achieve them until twenty-one; still others will never have them. The legally defined threshold reflects the practical judgment that the costs of making individual determinations of fitness far outweigh the benefits. Further, once we recognize that age is a proxy for other qualities that are variably distributed, we can ask: Why shouldn't greater breadth of vision, or ability to foresee consequences, or benevolence, or civic concern, entitle their possessors to a greater voice in public affairs? Mill's proposal for plural voting is not absurd on its face,[29] even though it may be impractical.

Gewirth's proposed egalitarian threshold is subtle. As we have already seen, his moral analysis focuses on human agency, which has two components: "the ability to control one's behavior by one's unforced choice, to have knowledge of relevant circumstances, and to reflect on one's purposes;"[30] and "the desire to fulfill one's purposes among persons who have these abilities."[31] He assumes that all human beings—indeed, all living beings—are characterized by the second component; the first component functions as a threshold: below a certain level of ability, mentally deficient individuals and, naturally, all animals cannot lay claim to the full range of egalitarian entitlements. The reason for this "proportionality" lies in

the relation between the generic abilities of action and the having
of purposes one wants to fulfill. For the lesser the abilities, the
less one is able to fulfill one's purposes without endangering oneself and other persons.[32]

But why doesn't proportionality hold across the full range of the first component's variation? The answer is that the agent's own standpoint is crucial, and within that standpoint it is not abilities as a whole but rather "that aspect...of abilities whereby he pursues purposes he regards as good" that constitutes the basis of claims:

Wanting to fulfill one's own purposes through action is not the
same as having the ability to fulfill one's own purposes through
action. While it is true that to act requires certain abilities, what is
crucial in any agent's reason for acting is not his abilities but his
purposes.[33]

There is an obvious difficulty with this argument. If purposiveness is crucial, then with what justification can abilities be employed against animals and the retarded as exclusionary criteria? If, on the other hand, the use of the ability criterion is justified on the basis of paternalistic and social considerations—danger to self and to others—then presumably it affects entitlements whenever and to the extent that these considerations come into play. It is no simple matter to determine the practical effect of this criterion; the outcome will depend both on a philosophical definition of "harm" and on complex empirical considerations.

There is another important difficulty with Gewirth's argument. The ability criterion is intended to discriminate between normal agents—the overwhelming majority—and the few exceptional subnormal human beings. Otherwise, it could not serve as the basis for a substantively egalitarian position. But one could well imagine an elitist accepting Gewirth's criterion while arguing that unforced choices made with knowledge of relevant circumstances after due reflection on one's purposes are very rare. This is not an accidental difficulty. Gewirth wants a definition of human agency that will distinguish sharply between animal behavior and human action. If not, animals would have rights, a conclusion he is anxious to avoid. But any definition that emphasizes qualitative differences rather than a quantitative continuum is likely to be rigorous and accordingly runs the risk of leaving large numbers of human beings on the wrong side of the divide.

I do not mean to suggest that the concept of a threshold is entirely without value. It makes sense to establish certain qualifications, for example, for becoming a doctor and to declare that everyone who meets them is equally a doctor. But—and this is the crucial point—our willingness to specify minimum levels of competence does not imply that qualitative differences above the threshold become irrelevant. Faced with a serious medical problem, many people demand "the best." Indeed, similar principles come into play when physicians of ordinary competence encounter rare and complex cases.

5.3.c. Equality of consideration

Are we driven, then, to conclude that equality has no coherent and defensible meaning apart from its purely formal sense? I do not think so.

Let us say that a being has *interests* if it satisfies two conditions: it is capable of being benefited and harmed by actions; it has a conative life, is capable of sensing and responding to benefits and harms. (Conation need not be at the level of developed consciousness.)[34] Beings with interests are equal in one fundamental respect: for every such being, if an action affects it significantly, it is wrong not to consider its interests when one seeks to determine the appropriateness of the action. This does not mean that the interests are equal in content or moral weight. They differ, quantitatively and qualitatively, in ways that properly lead us to attach different moral value or significance to them. Nevertheless, whatever the interests, it is always and equally wrong to say, "I am affecting the interests of this being, but they are irrelevant, and I do not have to take them into account."

It may be objected that in some types of moral evaluation all interests are irrelevant, so that one would not consider the interests of any affected being. First, I doubt whether there is any instance of moral reflection in which interests are wholly irrelevant, although there are some in which other types of considerations may predominate. Second, it would be wholly satisfactory to formulate the principle of equality of consideration as follows: If and when interests ought to be taken into account in moral reflection, all interests must be considered. This may be interpreted as following analytically from the concept of moral reflection: to say that interests are morally relevant is to say that the good or evil consequences of one's act are morally relevant, but these consequences cannot be accurately evaluated unless in reflecting one considers all the evidence. Of course, as in all inquiries, moral and empirical, one is frequently forced to make simplifying assumptions rather than considering every bit of evidence individually, but this does not affect the main point. To make an assumption about evidence is very far from ignoring it.

This kind of equality does not well serve traditional political or moral egalitarianism, for two reasons. First, it is not restricted to human beings; second, it entails no substantive distributive conclusions, since it is silent about the relation between specific interests and their corresponding moral weight. At most, it gives us a way of understanding the traditional claim that moral reflection must be impartial.

5.3.d. Equality of development

I should now like to propose, as a working hypothesis, a limited principle of substantive equality: Considered in itself, the full development of each individual is equal in moral weight to that of every other. Each individual begins with a unique set of natural abilities, the development of which is regulated by fortune, private nurture, and social policy. For any individuals A and B, a policy (p_1) that leads to the full development of A and partial development of B is, ceteris paribus, equal in value to a policy (p_2) that fully develops B while restricting A's development to the same degree as B's was under p_1. This equivalence obtains regardless of the ways in which A's ability set differs from B's. Thus, for example, a policy that neglects the slightly retarded to the extent that they do not learn how to care for themselves and must be institutionalized is, considered in itself, as bad as one that reduces extraordinary gifts to mere normality.

It may be suggested that this principle is incompatible with my own hierarchical account of development. It seems hard to deny that the full realization of high capacities is preferable to the full development of lower, more limited capacities. This is in one sense correct. But we must distinguish between the intrinsic worth of a human characteristic and what we may call its claim-generating properties. All other things being equal, I should prefer greater to lesser innate capacities for myself and should consider a world in which everyone's capacities were higher a distinct improvement over the present situation. But, as we have noted in another connection, capacities are characteristics of individuals and have no existence apart from the individuals in whom they inhere. Thus, even assuming that intrinsic worth of human characteristics could somehow be quantified, it does not follow that the best policy is one that simply maximizes the sum of intrinsic worth, because this is to treat the characteristics of separate individuals as a disembodied unity. Consider a situation in which we must decide who shall die: A, a talented individual, or B and C, much more limited in every respect. Assume that all three are innocent of any wrongdoing and that the sum of the intrinsic worth of B's and C's characteristics is smaller than that of A's. Intuitively, it is not obvious that B and C ought to die rather than A: the simple fact of plurality or individuality makes a difference. It is for this among other reasons that Aristotle introduced a "rectificatory" component of justice in which specific characteristics of individuals are irrelevant to the calculation of benefits, damages, and entitlements.

This may be linked to our discussion of moral structures at the end of Chapter 4. The direct inference from the rank-order of an ability to the rank-order of the policy that promotes it presupposes a form of ideal utilitarianism in which the maximand consists only in nonrelational goods. As we have already argued, this conception is theoretically defective. In the present context, it distorts the analysis by tempting us to think of abilities in isolation from the individuals of whom they are predicated.

We may support this conjecture also by making use of a distinction Kant drew in the *Critique of Judgment* between intrinsic and extrinsic teleology. Intrinsic teleology is the principle of ordering within each living being that permits us to regard that being as an organized whole. Extrinsic teleology is the principle of ordering among beings, or among characteristics within beings, that permits us to form hierarchical judgments: x is for the sake of y. It is intrinsic teleology that allows us to see how equality is compatible with hierarchy. Each living being is equally an organized whole, capable of both healthy functioning or flourishing and sickness or disruption.

Thus, the claim-generating force of every characteristic must be evaluated from two standpoints: the moral weight that it has for its possessor, and its effects on others. Even assuming the equal value of the fully realized good of every individual, in practice the preservation and well-being of some individuals must be preferred to that of others because their existence and activity is more conducive to the good of others. During an epidemic, for example, we would probably seek to keep doctors alive in preference to others by allocating them unequal shares of scarce food reserves. I suggest that this combination of the equality of private good with the distinction between self- and other-directed components of characteristics will enable us to make sensible and consistent judgments across a wide range of cases.

Two serious objections can be urged against this line of argument. First, it may be said, too little weight is given to extraordinary and admirable private characteristics that do not seem to promote the good of others significantly. Do we really want to say that we are not permitted to favor the gifted in the distribution of, for example, educational resources? In fact, I suggest, an inspection of policies favoring the gifted usually reveals the assumption that a significant social dividend will accrue. When the link between individual development and public good is perceived as tenuous, support for investment in the gifted declines. Plato, perhaps the staunchest defender of the intrinsic worth of the contemplative life in the history of philosophy, considered it important to argue against the popular belief that philosophy is useless. On the contrary, philosophers are of all human beings the most able to benefit others. They are prevented from doing so only by conditions over which they have no control.[35] In addition, recall the distinction between intrinsic worth and claim generation. A collectivity may advance an ideal of human excellence and exhort its members to strive toward it insofar as it lies within their power, and it need not gloss over the difference between ordinary and extraordinary individual gifts. It is debarred only from giving preferential treatment to individuals with great natural advantages unless such treatment promotes the public good.

The second objection is in a way the mirror image of the first. It may be argued that my principle of equality is so broad as to blur the differences between human beings and other animals. By giving such weight to intrinsic teleology, a principle of development shared by all living beings, I drastically diminish the legitimacy of using animals for human purposes or of preferring the good of our species to that of all others. I must grant this, but I do not believe that it is a reductio ad absurdum of the principle. As Rousseau noted, testing moral principles by measuring them against existing practices is hardly an unobjectionable procedure.[36] It is not difficult to imagine situations in which the good of certain animals, for example, Seeing Eye dogs or oxen used in agriculture, might reasonably be preferred to that of particular human beings. The preference we give to our own good, when legitimate, is rooted in the benefits it confers. Even Aristotle, who gave such great weight to extrinsic, hierarchical teleology, found it necessary to argue that other animals are improved by human governance: "Tame animals have a better nature than wild, and it is better for all such animals that they should be ruled by man because they then get the benefit of preservation."[37] In circumstances in which Aristotle's worst fears about man are realized, when human beings without restraint become "worse than all other beings,"[38] we cannot rationally prefer our good to theirs.

Let us now turn our attention to the two most important features of individuals on the basis of which distributive claims are advanced: need[39] and desert.

5.4. Need

5.4.a. The concept of need

Brian Barry offers a strong argument against the use of need as an independent principle of justice. All statements of the form "x is needed" or "A needs x" are elliptical, since it always makes sense to inquire what x is needed *for*. Further, no claim that x is necessary to produce y is in itself a reason for doing x. "Before it can provide such a reason y must be shown to be (or taken to be) a desirable end to pursue...the only interesting questions arise in connection with the ends."[40]

David Miller objects to the analysis, arguing that Barry has overlooked the different senses in which *need* can be used. There are, he claims, three different types of need statements: *instrumental* needs, for example, "He needs a key"; *functional* needs, "Surgeons need manual dexterity"; and *intrinsic* needs, "Men need food". Barry's analysis applies perfectly to instrumental needs. In the case of functional needs, the need statement is complete as it stands, and additions are tautological or vacuous. In the case of intrinsic needs, the triadic form of Barry's analysis is appropriate, but it tends to distort the force of the original claim. The means is not a separable, dispensable path to the end but rather an integral part of the end.[41]

Miller's critique must be rejected. The discussion of functional needs rests on a purely verbal point. The concept "surgeon" contains a range of activities that constitute ends. Obviously, need statements in which ends are already implicitly present do not require a supplement. Such statements can always be rewritten in canonical form without change or loss of meaning, as, "Anyone who wishes to perform operations competently needs manual dexterity."

As for intrinsic needs, Miller's claim is not supported even by the examples he provides. The relation between dexterity and surgery is no less integral than the relation between food and life; one cannot become a surgeon and then dispose of dexterity. Indeed, the separation between food and life seems wider, since it would at least be plausible to define life in terms of a complex of states and activities and to view food as instrumental for maintaining them. Miller is right to suggest that the concept of a means–end relation is somewhat ambiguous, but he does not succeed in linking this to the problem of need or in displacing our attention from the character of the ends we seek.

Barry's formal analysis, however, does not provide an adequate account of why we employ *need* to designate a limited sector of the totality of means–ends relations. But only one answer is possible. There are differences among the ends we seek—differences of urgency, importance, objectivity, moral worth. Needs are the means required for the attainment of urgent ends that are widely if not universally desired.

We may link this with our discussion of the good. We may call x a need if it is required either for the maintenance of life or for the development of existence. The concept of need, then, has two components: an invariant end, and a means–end relation that may vary with circumstances. But the variability of needs does not imply, as some have supposed, that need cannot constitute an objective measure or criterion. Consider a society in which employment is the only source of income, in which life-sustaining goods and services can be obtained only through monetary exchange, and in which places of work are far away from family dwellings. In these circumstances, transportation—perhaps even of a certain kind—is a need. Natural differences are also relevant. Ceteris paribus, larger individuals, or those with higher metabolic rates, will need more food to sustain life. In colder climates, more resources may have to be devoted to housing and clothing.

The objectivity of need is grounded in regular features of human existence. For example, one can specify, within broad but definable limits, the kinds and amount of food required for full organic development, maintenance of health, and performance of a normal range of activities. Beneath the lower limit, emaciation, damage to vital organs, and starvation occur; above the upper limit are obesity, impairment of mobility, and a variety of organic disorders. The demand for food can exceed the bounds of need in two ways, quantitatively and qualitatively. A quantity of food that makes us overweight cannot be said to be needed, although some of us may desire that quantity. Similarly, there is no need for a wide variety of foods prepared in complex ways, although we may approve of and seek to justify this variety on other grounds. Since the need for food is not grounded in subjective desire, an alleged "psychological need" for it is an abuse of speech and a misleading causal analysis. Rigorous military training frequently transforms eating habits by requiring the performance of tasks that obesity impedes and by punishing or precluding gluttony. Thus, the Platonic distinction between necessity and luxury in the consumption of food rests on a sound theoretical basis.[42]

Similar considerations apply to clothing. The quantity and variety of clothing we need is determined by climatic conditions and the requirements of the activities we perform. We must distinguish, however, between natural and social requirements. It may be that without expensive clothing an individual may fail to make a good impression and lose his job, becoming unable to support himself or his family. If every job for which that individual could qualify has a comparable requirement, then it makes sense to speak of a need for expensive clothing within that social context. But need *simpliciter* is defined relative to the intrinsic characteristics of activities. Thus, we tend to expect our elected national officials to be well dressed and even criticize them for demeaning the dignity of their offices if they appear in public dressed too casually. But, as countless examples prove, there is no natural connection between style of dress and the respect a public leader must command in order to perform effectively.

We arrive, then, at a threefold classification: natural need, social need, and luxury. From the standpoint of the individual, social needs are as urgent as the natural; if the latter constitute a strong basis for claims, so do the former. But from a collective standpoint, social needs are much weaker. Not only are they mutable; in many circumstances they are wasteful, increasing the resources that must be expended to perform a given activity without yielding a commensurate return. For example, the enforcement of strict business dress codes during the summer either reduces efficiency or increases energy consumption (for air conditioning). Social needs must give way to natural needs whenever the supply of goods and services available to satisfy natural needs is inadequate. In circumstances of shortage, it is wrong to divert energy away from food production to maintain arbitrary dress codes.

Some natural needs are absolute, others comparative. Personal security is a natural need, but the level of security-producing means one needs is in part relative to the threats posed by others. The natural needs for shelter or medical care, on the other hand, are absolute. The fact that the man up the street owns a castle does not mean that you need one; the hypochondriac's daily visits to the doctor do not increase your need for medical services.

Natural needs are the means required to secure, not only existence, but also the development of existence. Developmental needs include at least the following: adequate nurturance (it is an empirical question whether institutions can be devised to provide the same services as a properly functioning family), adequate education; activities that allow for the exercise of a wide range of capacities; and a variety of friendships and social relations.

Needs are proximate means for obtaining certain kinds of human goods. As such, they are links in causal chains and may under certain circumstances transmit their necessitarian character to more remote links. For example, if a community must produce its own food and if the quality of its soil makes agriculture impossible without fertilizer, then fertilizer is as much a need as the food itself. The case is more complex if the remoter link is a product of social organization rather than of nature. If a nation's system of food production is energy-intensive, then cutting off sources of energy will hinder the satisfaction of need. But presumably, given levels of energy consumption are not absolutely required but are, rather, responsive to the relative cost of energy and human labor. In the short run, a given level of fuel must be considered a need; in the long run, probably not. Thus, to cut off or drastically reduce the supply of fuel suddenly is to incur the onus of impeding the satisfaction of needs; to announce a reduction in supply long enough in advance to permit adjustments in the system of production is probably acceptable.

The foregoing analysis allows us to rebut the standard objections to the use of need as a basis of claims. First, it is true that individuals vary. But needs are defined relative to goals or states of affairs that do not so vary. A large individual may need to eat twice as many calories daily as a smaller one to remain adequately nourished. But adequate nourishment can be defined independently and objectively and can be applied to both individuals equally.

Second, it may be argued that "natural" needs cannot be independently defined because the effects of social training are decisive. For example, young Spartan men were systematically trained to withstand the rigors of cold weather, and they came to need less protective clothing than those not trained in this manner. But, first to be considered, are limits to the efficacy of training. No one could be conditioned to endure an Arctic winter without appropriate protective clothing; Eskimos adapt socially to their environment, but they also wear fur suits from head to toe. Further, the effects of training can largely be counteracted by changes of circumstance. In wartime, entire populations discover that they can live without goods they previously considered essential and that there is even a kind of gratification associated with reducing one's dependence on the external. It is rarely the case that man's "second nature" is as powerful or immutable as his first.

Third among the points of rebuttal is that it may be argued that needs vary in accordance with different ways of life. The members of a nomadic tribe that survives by hunting and foraging have requirements for shelter and education very different from citizens of industrialized societies. This objection may be met in two ways: As we have already argued, the variability of required means does not necessarily imply that the ends are different. Presumably, the tribal shelters must provide the same protection against external conditions as do dwellings in industrialized countries. Of course, they must do so within the constraint of mobility, which means either that they must be movable or that they can be built relatively cheaply and easily, making possible a pattern of abandonment and replacement. But this does not undermine the essential similarity. Also, human need is not identical with what is required to maintain, or to act successfully within, a particular way of life. For example, the fact that certain types of education would serve no social purpose within a given society does not mean that they are not needed. Need is defined in relation to a norm of individual human existence. The extent to which a society allows for the fulfillment of this norm is one important criterion of its worth. Need, then, rather than being immanent and relative, is an external, critical concept.

Fourth, it is frequently argued that needs expand or contract in response to changes in material conditions or the availability of opportunities. But, as Miller and others have pointed out, this is a misleading way of expressing an undeniably valid sociological fact. "Wants" do tend to vary in this manner. But wants are neither necessary nor sufficient conditions of needs. We may want what we do not need and need what we do not want. This simple truth is evident to every parent; indeed, much early childhood training is devoted to communicating the existence of the distinction and then helping the child to understand and to apply for itself, the principles that constitute its substantive content. This is not to say that we can have no valid claim to satisfy unneeded wants, but only that we must provide other bases for our claim. But by itself, the statement, "I want x," cannot constitute a conclusive reason for me to have x. One may well doubt that it is a reason in even the prima facie sense.

The implications of our analysis emerge more clearly when we compare it to that offered by Miller. He begins by rejecting any attempt to derive needs from wants. Rather, he suggests, it is most plausible to interpret "A needs x" as "A will suffer harm if he lacks x." To provide more precision to the concept of harm, he introduces the notion of a *plan of life:* a person's central aims and activities. To harm A is to interfere, directly or indirectly, with the fulfillment of A's plan of life. The concept of harm does not rest on a substantive normative theory of human endeavor. There is, however, one proviso: to count as a plan of life, a complex of aims and activities must be intelligible. Intelligibility requires, not that we find the plan valuable, but that we can understand how someone else may value it. Thus, "If confronted with a pyromaniac we are likely to say, not that he needs a plentiful supply of matches, access to barns, etc., but that he needs psychiatric help."[43]

To begin with, this account has the disadvantage of broadening the concept of need far beyond normal usage, at least as a term of distinction. Miller's view amounts to the contention that we need everything the possession of which is essential for the achievement of what we consider good and important. If our plan of life is to conquer Mount Everest, we need Sherpa guides, tents, oxygen tanks, etc. It is difficult to see how such needs could serve as the basis of claims or entitlements; the expansion of need undercuts its moral function. There are two kinds of goods the possession of which is morally appropriate: those to which we are specifically entitled, and those for which we are entitled to strive. Miller's concept of harm encompasses deprivation of both kinds, but the sphere of need, as ordinarily understood, is restricted to the former.

Miller's expanded need also leaves open the possibility of a *need-monster:* an individual whose plan of life is defined in such grandiose terms as to require resources that others need for the satisfaction of simply physical necessities. It seems clear, for example, that it would be wrong to set out to conquer Everest if the extra food you consumed led to someone else's starving. At the very least, this intuition implies a hierarchy of needs along the axis of urgency. It is difficult to see how such a hierarchy can be accommodated within the simple essential/nonessential dichotomy to which the plan of life gives rise.

Miller's criterion of intelligibility is either vacuous or substantively arbitrary. It is quite possible to arrive at an understanding of why a pyromaniac values his activity—a craving for excitement, expression of anger, displacement of sexual desires, etc. We understand without approving or sanctioning. Intelligibility provides a cloak for moral judgments the principled basis of which Miller either cannot provide or does not wish to embrace. This becomes clear when he questions the intelligibility of the desire for status superiority, suggesting that the *real* desire is for the material advantages usually associated with it. His admission that his inability to understand aristocratic values may stem from democratic sympathies gives the game away.[44]

Once allowed as real, Miller contends, the need for status superiority has an awkward consequence: it is logically, not merely contingently, impossible that each individual's need could be satisfied, or even gratified to the same degree. Since justice is commonly thought to require the equal satisfaction of needs, he proposes that all comparative or positional needs be considered irrelevant to questions of justice. This move is almost completely ad hoc. Given Miller's account of need, it is not intuitively obvious that all needs should be accorded the same weight or gratified to the same degree, nor does he offer an independent argument in support of this position. Further, Miller's suggestion rests on the premise, again unsupported, that justice must be possible and hence that no demands incompatible with that possibility can be recognized as legitimate. Finally, the desire for status superiority produces a logical impossibility only if one supposes that it is universally, or at least widely, shared. Miller gives us no evidence that this is so.

All these difficulties may be traced back to the gap between the ordinary intuitive meaning of need and Miller's overly expansive definition. From a commonsense standpoint it is easy to say that while one may want, profit from, and even deserve status superiority, it ought not to be considered a need. The moral force of need-claims is compatible only with a limited range of claimed things, and status superiority lies outside that range. Miller's decision to derive needs from life plans makes this distinction impossible. To render his definition even roughly congruent with normal usage, he is forced to employ a series of arbitrary restrictive devices and judgments.

5.4.b. The force of need-claims

When "I need x" is employed to express a moral claim, it implies that x is a means essential for the attainment of either existence or developed existence. We *desire* these goods as ends; we *need* the means of attaining them. On this basis we can understand the major characteristics of need-claims.

Needs are thought to be widely shared, common to most human beings. This is the case because existence and developed existence are very generally held to be good and because fundamental features of the human condition render certain categories of means generally necessary for their attainment.

Claims based on need are thought to have priority over most others. This is so because the goods in term of which need is defined are among the most important and urgent. Physical existence is the precondition for every other human good; the development of capacities is both an end in itself and the basis of our various activities and projects.

It follows from this that priorities exist among needs as well. Existence-claims are more urgent than development-claims. Thus, if we may use fixed resources either to feed A or B or to feed and educate A, allowing B to starve, we choose the former alternative. The real and important benefit A receives from education is insufficient to outweigh the catastrophic harm inflicted on B. On the political level, defense expenditures are given priority when the lives of citizens are thought to be in jeopardy; it is not accidental that Israel's defense budget consumes such a high fraction of the nation's GNP. Questions of defense are complicated by two considerations. First, one is purchasing, not absolute immunity against violent death, but rather, increments of security. At some point, the increment procured by the next unit of expenditure is likely to seem less significant than the other goods one would have to forgo to obtain it. This is consistent with the priority accorded to life if, as seems sensible, we judge that life is more valuable than other goods but not *infinitely* more valuable.[45] Second, defense expenditures usually safeguard, not only life, but also a way of life. At some point, additional defense appropriations are likely to appear destructive of that way of life, either directly or indirectly.

It is customary to contrast need-claims with desert-claims. The difference becomes clearer when we examine the form of appropriate answers to the questions "Does A need x?" and "Does A deserve x?" In the former case, we want to know whether, given A's specific situation, x is essential for the achievement of certain purposes. In the latter, we want to know whether A satisfies what Feinberg calls "conditions of worthiness"; we are interested in the "fit" between some fact about A and some feature, natural or conventional, of x. We need not be concerned with the use to which x will be put, although we may be. Need always looks to the future; desert is particularly concerned with the past and present.[46]

It is not the case, however, that need and desert are completely independent of each other. A may need x to survive, but it is at least intelligible to inquire whether A deserves to go on living. We may not be swayed by the plea of a mass murderer who begs us for a gun to protect him from the vengeful relatives of his victims. The force of need-claims rests on the assumption that we deserve the ends in terms of which needs are defined.

But we deserve these ends in a special way. In dealing with questions of desert, we normally use as our point of departure a gap between individual and object; we ask whether the relevant facts about the individual justify the elimination of this gap. The burden of proof, so to speak, is on the individual. In the domain of need, we begin by assuming that the individual deserves the basic human goods that constitute the ends of need. The individual does not have to earn them but may, under rare and special conditions, cease to deserve them. It is the presumption of desert that links need so tightly with the principle of equality: the moral force of need-claims is highly insensitive to differences among individuals, although the content of justified need-claims will of course reflect these differences.

5.5. Desert

Recent scholarship has considerably clarified the concept of desert.[47] We may summarize the major findings as follows.

1. Desert does not arise out of existing public institutions and rules. It is prior to and independent of them and may in certain circumstances be used as a criterion for judging them.[48]

2. Desert requires a basis, which must be some fact about the individual alleged to be deserving.[49]

3. Not all facts about individuals are relevant to the question of desert. Every desert-claim is of the form: A deserves x in virtue of f. In general, then, there must be some relation between x and f, and the range of relevant f's will vary in accordance with the characteristics of the x under consideration.[50]

4. Desert-related facts need not be moral characteristics. If one claims, for instance, that A deserves to be the contractor for a particular building because he has the most experience with construction of that type, one is basing the judgment, not on virtue, but rather on instrumental ability. Thus, even if Rawls's claim that virtue or moral worth cannot logically serve as a basis for distributive shares were valid, this would not prove, as Rawls seems to believe, that desert *simpliciter* is an inappropriate basis.[51]

Further, Rawls's argument against the use of moral worth as a distributive criterion fails completely. a) The claim that this criterion could not be chosen in the original position is probably true but wholly without force. Rawls himself declares that the original position is what we arrive at, "once we decide to look for a conception of justice that nullifies the accidents of natural endowment and the contingencies of social circumstances."[52] As Nozick shows decisively, Rawls interprets this nullification so as to include all actual or conceivable moral differences.[53] Thus, it is hardly surprising that moral worth does not emerge as a criterion from the original position; it has been excluded in advance. But why should we "decide" to do so?

b) Rawls quite properly distinguishes between moral desert and "legitimate expectations ... founded upon social institutions."[54] But his argument requires an additional premise, that only institutionally derived expectations can constitute valid claims, at least within the sphere of justice. He merely supposes this to be true, without providing any supporting argument. This procedure begs the entire question.

c) Rawls argues that, within a competitive economy, one's contribution varies with supply and demand, while no one believes that moral worth so varies.[55] This is true; but it implies, not that moral worth cannot be a distributive criterion, but rather that in most circumstances its employment would not be fully congruent with the requirements of a competitive economy. Unless one accepts the distributional consequences of competition as morally canonical—and Rawls does not—this unsurprising conflict hardly constitutes an argument against the criterion of moral worth. Similarly, it is true, as Rawls claims, that considerations of efficiency and need will usually contradict those based on moral worth. But this does not imply that moral worth cannot be *a* distributive criterion but only, if one takes efficiency and need as serious claims, that it cannot be the sole criterion.

d) Rawls argues that moral worth cannot be an independent criterion of justice because it can only be defined relative to a previously determined concept of justice. Moral worth means, is defined as "having a sense of justice."[56] If this were true, it would be decisive, but there are good reasons to question it. As Rawls repeatedly concedes and even emphasizes, justice is not the whole of virtue, or the only virtue. It thus seems arbitrary and strange to define moral worth in terms of justice alone. On this basis, we can construct an alternative to Rawls's approach. Let us begin with the notion of *moral excellence*, defined as the possession of all the virtues. Now let us, with Ross, define the just situation as the due proportion between the extent of moral excellence achieved and happiness enjoyed. The just person, then, is one who recognizes and strives to bring about the just situation.

It may be argued that this argument is circular, in precisely the sense Rawls criticizes: the just situation is defined relative to moral excellence, of which personal justice forms a part, but personal justice is defined relative to the just situation. This appearance of circularity is deceptive. We begin with a formal intuition, that the just situation consists in a certain relation between character and circumstance. On this basis, we can add some substantive precision to the relation with which we began. Our inquiry proceeds, not in a circle, but in stages.

I do not wish to suggest that this "Rossian" schema is correct, but only that Rawls's effort to demonstrate its incoherence does not succeed.

e) Finally, Rawls suggests that those who advocate moral worth as a distributive criterion believe that distributive justice is the opposite of retributive: quite as the criminal law punishes certain offenses, the socioeconomic system rewards certain excellences. But, Rawls continues, this is a fundamental mistake. The function of unequal shares is to cover the costs of training and to ensure that socially useful functions are carried out.[57]

We may note, first, that Rawls again begs the question. If the dispute concerns the function or purpose of distributive shares, it can hardly be resolved by *ex cathedra* pronouncements about the nature of this function. Further, as Feinberg remarks, it is sensible to view rewards as expressing "recognition of . . . excellence."[58] Intuitively, the recognition of excellence is in itself morally satisfying, and it may well promote striving for excellence. Why shouldn't a distributive system be allowed to take this point into account? This is in no way to deny that a system of distribution must try to achieve the purposes Rawls specifies, but only that his purposes are not exhaustive.

Perhaps the difficulty lies elsewhere. Throughout the entire discussion of moral desert, Rawls seems to be concerned primarily with *economic* shares. One may well agree that money, goods, or services do not constitute an appropriate means of recognizing moral excellence; not only is there no internal relation between the desert-basis and what is claimed, but also this form of recognition may cheapen or even pervert what it is intended to reward.[59] But, as we have repeatedly emphasized, the distributive system is concerned with more than economic matters—praise, honor, offices of trust and responsibility, social position. There is a real and plausible internal relation between these goods and moral excellence. In a well-known letter to Adams, Jefferson argued in favor of a political system that would reliably promote the natural *aristoi* to high office; he rightly saw no contradiction between this principle and his belief in the equality of citizens.

5. Desert-related facts need not themselves be deserved—earned, merited, achieved through effort. They may, to use Rawls's phrase, be "arbitrary from a moral point of view," in that there is no moral reason why individual *A* rather than *B* should be characterized by a desert-related fact. But this does not mean that these amoral facts cannot be the basis of moral claims.[60]

This characteristic of desert-related facts has two important consequences. First, as Miller shows, the question of desert is thereby detached from the problem of determinism. Determinism would undermine the concept of desert only if an individual must be morally responsible for the facts forming the basis of his desert-claims. But there is no compelling logical or conceptual reason to impose this requirement, and our ordinary understanding of desert implies its rejection.[61] Second, a desert-related fact need not, as Barry mistakenly claims, be an action or effort of an individual.[62] It may be a quality, such as beauty, the presence of which owes little or nothing to effort. Similarly, there is no compelling reason to accept Barry's suggestion that it is a necessary condition of desert-generating actions that the agent have been "able to have done otherwise."[63] The musical or mathematical prodigy deserves to win the appropriate competition, even if the performance involves no will or choice. In this respect, there may well be an asymmetry between "positive desert" and punishment.

On this basis, Miller is both inconsistent and wrong in excluding beliefs, preferences, and interests as possible desert-bases. We cannot, he argues,

claim that people deserve benefits because of what they believe.... The reason is that there is nothing in the actual holding of a belief (as opposed to the process of arriving at it) which we can appropriately admire.[64]

This is, first, inconsistent with Miller's well-argued claim that the things about people we admire need not be voluntarily acquired; admiration is directed toward "the quality as it now exists."[65] Along this continuum, at least, there is no distinction between beliefs and qualities. Second, his contention is open to counterexample. Consider the following dialogue:

A: John deserves to be the leader of our spiritual community.
B: Why?
A: Because of the unusual purity and sincerity of his Christian belief.

Of course, B is free to argue that leadership requires other characteristics that John lacks. But he cannot reasonably deny that in this context, belief constitutes one appropriate desert-basis.

6. The concept of desert presupposes a general concept of the *good*, and the application of desert in specific cases presupposes a substantive view of the good. As Miller puts it,

Desert is a matter of fitting forms of treatment to the specific qualities and actions of individuals, and in particular good desert (i.e., deserving benefit as opposed to punishment) is a matter of fitting desired forms of treatment to qualities and actions which are generally held in high regard.[66]

Similarly, Feinberg observes that

the deserved object must be something generally regarded with favor or disfavor even if, in some particular case, it is regarded with indifference by a person said to deserve it. If we were all perfect stoics, if no event were ever more or less pleasing to us than any other, then there would be no use for the concept of desert.[67]

We must, however, qualify this in two ways. First, the desert-basis need be generally held in high regard only within a specific allocative context, not universally. Thus, Christian belief may be ignored or even scorned in business and military activities, but, as we saw, within a spiritual community it may be the most relevant criterion. Second, the high regard or admiration we feel for a particular desert-basis need not be either a universal or a moral judgment. We may admire a skill or ability without imputing moral worth to its possessor and while conceding that it can constitute a desert-basis only within specific contexts. It is consistent, moreover, to recognize f as a desert-basis while morally disapproving of both it and the context in which it constitutes a claim. One could, for example, say that the most accurate marksman deserves to win the shooting competition while disapproving of both competitive sports and guns.

Both Feinberg and Miller deny that need can be a desert-basis. Miller offers two reasons: in the case of most needs, everyone has them until they are satisfied; and no one wishes to have them or admires others for having them.[68] These reasons are, I believe, mistaken. First, there is no necessary contradiction between the ubiquity of a quality and holding it in high regard. Consider the Kantian thesis that all human beings are worthy of respect because all are morally free, capable of being determined by practical reason. Second, not all desert is good desert; an individual may be thought to deserve ill treatment on account of qualities that no one admires or wishes to have. The correct reason is implicit in the nature of the relation between deserved treatment and desert-basis. If f is to serve as a desert-basis, it is a necessary condition that x, the treatment appropriate to it, be accorded the same normative or moral evaluation as f. If f is regarded as good or desirable, so is x, and similarly if f is regarded as bad. Clearly, need does not satisfy this criterion; it is regarded as undesirable, but the treatment to which it gives rise is considered desirable. Thus, we cannot say that an individual who performs a wrong or harmful act deserves to be well treated, at least not in virtue of *that* act. If we decide nevertheless to treat that individual well, we may argue that he "needs" good treatment—to become better, more law-abiding, more virtuous—and that considerations of need override those of desert in this case.

There is a further consideration. As Miller points out, "desert judgments are justified on the basis of *past* and *present* facts about individuals, never on the basis of states of affairs to be created in the future."[69] But as we have argued, needs are always defined relative to states of affairs to be created (or warded off) in the future; need-claims are based on a restricted class of *instrumental* relations. Need is, broadly speaking, a utilitarian criterion; desert is not.

7. Feinberg argues persuasively that deserved treatment may be divided into a number of distinct classes. His findings may be summarized in the following list.

Class of treatment	Purpose or distinguishing features
Awards of prizes	Single victor Expression of admiration, recognition, honor
Assignment of grades	Within the context, applies to all Does not express attitude Appraisal of extent to which individuals possess given skills or qualities
Rewarding and punishing	Expresses approval or disapproval, frequently based on generalized gratitude or resentment Intention to confer benefit or harm (suffering)
Praising and blaming	Expresses approval or disapproval, not always or usually linked to (social) consequences of acts or qualities Not regulated by formal or institutional rules
Reparation	Redresses loss or injury wrongly inflicted on some individuals by others
Compensation	Counteracts loss or harm not stemming from wrongful human acts

Feinberg notices, but does not sufficiently emphasize, the extent to which these categories are distributed along the same continua and thus tend to overlap one another. For example, it is a mistake to contend that all prize competitions are directed toward recognizing the single victor. It is possible to imagine, for example, a footrace in which the first across the finish line receives a predetermined sum while the others receive that sum minus an amount proportional to the difference between their elapsed time and that of the fastest. Given a suitable selection of the constant, the resulting distribution of money might be indistinguishable from that of academic grades, but one would hardly want to deny that the payments represent prizes in the full sense. Again, to the extent that participants in a grading situation care about the qualities being measured, the formal process of measurement tends to acquire both prizelike and punitive characteristics, as every teacher knows.

Feinberg's analysis has two important consequences. First, it reveals that the contexts within which desert-claims are made differ from one another in two sorts of ways: the contexts may be different in kind, or contexts of the same kind may differ in the content of the human characteristics or activities with which they are particularly concerned.

Second, our consideration of particular situations in which desert seems to be a relevant allocative criterion will be made more precise by asking, under what kind or kinds of desert contexts should this situation be subsumed? For example, we may ask, as Feinberg does, whether income is best regarded as prize, reward, or compensation, and our decision is likely to have a substantive effect on our theory of distribution.[70] Again, as Feinberg points out, similar difficulties arise in determining the distribution of positions of leadership and responsibility.[71]

8. Desert provides a valid basis for claims, but these claims are not necessarily or even usually against or binding on particular individuals. Nor do they always entail an obligation to act so as to produce situations that conform as closely as possible to desert-claims. As Barry puts it, "To say that a venture deserves success does not necessarily commit one to saying that steps ought to be taken to see that it gets it."[72] Elaborating on this suggestion, Miller traces a continuum of desert-claims. At one extreme is "cosmic" desert that "carries no implications for human actions." At the other is the situation that arises when A freely confers on B a benefit that B desires to receive (B's life is saved or stolen property returned). Here A's desert-claim to a reward does have implications for human action. Indeed, a particular individual (B) is morally bound to perform a particular act. Intermediate are situations in which the translation of desert-claims into reciprocal obligations depends on the relation between the claim and prevailing practices. A government may choose not to establish a system of public honors, as exists, for example, in Great Britain, but if it does, expectations are created that must be dealt with fairly and consistently.[73]

5.6. Desert and Equality of Opportunity

Let me now consider in some detail one of the historically and conceptually most important desert-claims: the notion of merit based on ability. The meritocratic principle may be traced back at least as far as Plato's *Republic*. Over the past two centuries it has been espoused by liberals as the key principle of distributive justice and has been deployed to great effect against claims resting on custom and heredity. Its advocates have argued for institutions that allow individuals to develop their abilities and that distribute certain goods—education, specialized jobs, even high income—in a manner congruent with the patterns of revealed ability. Because talents are distributed unequally, and because standards are established relative to ranges of observed competence rather than a priori, the operation of meritocratic institutions is necessarily both inegalitarian and competitive.

The meritocratic principle entered American political thought under the rubric of "equality of opportunity." A considerable portion of American social history can be interpreted as a struggle between those who wished to widen and those who sought to restrict the scope of its application. Its proponents have worked to eliminate racial, sexual, and religious barriers and to offer universal access to sources of training and development. The former initiative moved toward "formal," the latter toward "fair" or "substantive" equality of opportunity.

For more than a century, open competition was virtually undisputed as the legitimating principle of American socioeconomic development, however it may have been violated in practice. In recent decades, however, equality of opportunity as a principle of distributive justice has come under increasingly sharp attack. Conservatives have denounced it as fostering excessive public intervention in essentially private or voluntary relations; radicals have pointed with scorn to its insensitivity to substantively egalitarian outcomes and its close connection with individualistic competition. Liberals, though clinging to their position, seem bewildered and defensive.

In the following remarks I examine some of the most representative and best-known assaults on equality of opportunity. I shall argue that most of this criticism is unjustified and that much of its plausibility stems from considering equality of opportunity as the sole and universal principle of distribution rather than as what it actually is—one among several principles, the use of which is restricted to the limited range of desert-contexts in which abilities constitute appropriate desert-bases.[74]

5.6.a. Michael Young and the horrors of "meritocracy"

Recent arguments against the principle of equality of opportunity were initiated by Michael Young in his influential book, *The Rise of the Meritocracy*.[75] Young constructs an imaginary account of a society governed by that principle, in the belief that our revulsion against its consequences will constitute a reductio ad absurdum. All opposing principles—heredity, age, equality of result—are swept away. Jobs and material rewards are distributed solely on the basis of ability: the sons and daughters of professionals have no special claim to retain their membership in the professional class, and aging workers who have climbed far up the ladder must compete on an equal basis with those just entering the work force. To ensure that talent does not go to waste, a multitrack school system is established, and children are distributed among the tracks in accordance with a progressively more accurate program of intelligence testing. For the first time in history, ability is concentrated in the elite class; the lower class, deprived of the able leadership formerly provided (unintentionally) by an unjust organization of classes, is increasingly dominated by the elite. Relatedly, the political center of gravity shifts from the representatives of the people toward the natural aristocracy and the administrators. Although all benefit from rapid increases in productivity, class divisions widen. Those with greater ability develop an ill-concealed contempt for those with lesser, and social contacts among classes are reduced. The increasing complexity of the technoeconomic system displaces many unskilled workers, whose only alternative to wretched unemployment is a return to personal service as maids, chauffeurs, and butlers. At length a revolutionary opposition movement arises, preaching equal human dignity and equality of result.

It is certainly true that the society Young describes is distasteful. But it is questionable whether it stems from the principle of equality of opportunity (hereafter, "EO"), correctly understood and applied, or rather from overextending it and combining it with other principles. Let me suggest some points in support of the latter view.

First, few advocates of EO would advance it monistically, as the *sole* principle that ought to govern all aspects of social organization. Young notes, for example, that the family is allowed to persist, in spite of the fact that it works against EO, because without it everyone would be "equally unhappy."[76] But, once considerations based on features of human nature are permitted, many other countervailing practices, for example, some deference to age or some attempt to reduce envy, can be justified as well.

Second, in Young's presentation, EO comes to be justified primarily on the grounds of economic efficiency—the demands of international economic competition in a world dominated by technological change. This has some unfortunate consequences: some significant moral arguments in favor of EO are overlooked, arguments at once more general and more moderate than the one Young emphasizes. Also, many of the features of the world Young asks us to imagine result from technological change and organizational complexity, not EO taken by itself. Not only is it very difficult to disentangle these two vectors, but also we are led to forget that opportunity is purely formal, that the kind of world in which we choose and are chosen determines the character of the outcome just as much as does the principle of selection.

Third, largely as a consequence of the second point, the society Young describes does not cultivate merit or talent in general, but only the narrow segment of it that contributes to scientific–technological progress and the administration of a bureaucratic state. Nonscientific intelligence, or intelligence that cannot be quantified for purposes of testing, is disregarded, as are contributions made by character and experience. The society comes to seem sterile, unimaginative, and inhumane—indeed, for all its worship of intelligence, downright stupid—but this is not the result of EO but rather of forgetting what real human excellence looks like.

Fourth, Young presupposes that inequality of ability to perform functions requiring specialized intelligence implies unequal entitlement to material rewards. There is of course no logical connection, and probably very little psychological connection either. Intuitively, it seems reasonable to believe that many of those who perform such functions derive pleasure and satisfaction from the activities themselves and would continue to perform them even under relatively austere circumstances. Of course, as has been recognized since antiquity, the successful performance of complex intellectual tasks requires a high degree of liberation from day-to-day hindrances and distractions. But Young's tongue-in-cheek extension of this argument to cover wintering in Montego Bay reveals the gap between the requirements of efficiency and the customary life-style expectations of the elite.[77]

Fifth, there is no logical relation between inequality of ability to perform "higher" tasks and an alleged inequality of human worth or dignity that would justify an attitude of amiable condescension on the part of the elite. There is undoubtedly a psychological relation. In order to move from inequality of ability to inequality of worth, an additional argument is required, one that plausibly defines or interprets worth as the vector sum of abilities. As we have already seen, no such argument exists; human worth has at least one component that is wholly unrelated to abilities.

Sixth, most questionable of all is the assumption that technical ability is equivalent to, or leads to, political ability, so that EO leads to political domination by the technical elite. It seems much more plausible to distinguish, with Aristotle, between technical and practical activities and between their corresponding excellences. Moreover, there is a sense in which political competence is widely shared. Finally, as the conclusion of Young's book makes ironically clear, one of the uneliminable practical requirements of politics is consent—of all or most of the population, regardless of differences of technical or even political ability. Hobbes was right to distinguish between the truth of propositions concerning "natural" equality and the content and distribution of *belief* about it and to insist that stable, peaceful consent is impossible without some recognition of demands for equal consideration of interests.[78]

5.6.b. John Schaar: Equality of opportunity as the principle of
competitive oligarchy

The portion of Schaar's attack on EO relevant for our purposes can be
summarized in the following contentions.[79]

1. EO is uncritically conservative, since it operates within and does
not challenge the range of talents and virtues that happens to be valued
by a given society. Every society excludes significant human possibilities through chance, custom, ideology, and force. This is true even
of professedly pluralistic societies, whose tacit discouragement of certain ways of life and rank-ordering of those permitted may be more
dangerous in some ways than obvious, overt restrictions.

2. EO promotes both cruelty and competitiveness. It is cruel because
it stimulates vain hopes and removes all external justifications for failure. It is competitive because it sets human beings apart from each
other, pits them against one another, and produces in them a sense of
self-worth that is at best externally grounded, derived from overcoming
others.

3. EO rests on a false view of morality and politics. It leads us to
return the question of how human beings are to be treated to "nature"
and to forget both that we are responsible for one another and that
social policy can counteract as well as conform to the natural order.

4. EO is frequently defended as a peculiarly democratic principle, but
in fact it is not connected with and even contradicts democracy. It has
been defended by many antidemocratic thinkers; it is compatible with
the maintenance of vast inequalities; and from a democratic point of
view, the hierarchy or oligarchy of merit it authorizes is as bad as any
other. "Realists" claim that there must be specialization of function in
modern political economies. Even if this is true, specialization and
hierarchy cannot be equated, and the former does not justify the latter.

In considering these claims, let us begin by conceding that every
community does tend to promote some activities and discourage others
and that EO alone will not enable us to evaluate these collective preferences. *Which* activities are to be allocated is one question; *how* these
activities, once specified, are to be allocated is quite another. In the
Republic, for example, the range of activities is established through a
combination of moral and "functionalist" arguments, distinct from the
claims about natural inequality that underlie the allocation of these
activities. EO is a hypothetical imperative based upon a principle of
efficiency: *If* a certain activity is deemed necessary and desirable, then
it is reasonable to say that the ability to perform it is an important basis
of the entitlement to perform it. When judged by its consequences, the
instrumental character of EO emerges even more clearly. EO makes a

good community better but a bad one worse. A regime devoted to odious purposes is worse if the jobs furthering these purposes are open to all; efficient evil is worse than inefficient. These considerations do not, however, fully support Schaar's objections. EO is not bad in itself, but only when it is mistakenly viewed as a comprehensive principle for the organization of a community, thereby obscuring fundamental questions about the character of the community.[80] And if, as Schaar contends, every community has a characteristic orientation, EO can hardly be made responsible for this. If EO supports or reinforces these orientations, this is bad only if we already know that every orientation is a humanly harmful restriction and that the correct stance in every case is antinomian opposition.

Schaar's charge of cruelty is perplexing. In a system that really worked in accordance with EO, there would indeed be no external causes of failure. An individual who did not achieve an ambition would have only two choices: to accept the truth of personal deficiencies or to lapse into self-justifying illusions. Being forced to face the truth about oneself is not what we ordinarily mean by "cruelty"; indeed, this is the act of supererogatory benevolence usually associated with genuine friendship. Schaar's case seems to rest on the claim that any system that does not make most of those it affects feel good is ipso facto bad. Taken to its limits, this claim would justify, indeed mandate, a kind of noble lie in reverse—the demeaning popular myth, "I'm all right, you're all right."

No doubt an EO system does stimulate many to strive for what they cannot attain. But this is not necessarily bad. First, such a system induces many who can excel to develop themselves fully. It is not clear that, on balance, a system that increases both achievement and frustration is inferior to one that increases the subjective satisfaction of the less talented only by decreasing the likelihood that the more talented will be able to realize their abilities. Second, many of those not capable of the highest accomplishments will nevertheless develop and achieve more under a system that infuses them with a desire to excel. A permanent gap between what we are and what we want to be need not be debilitating; it can be a barrier to complacency, a source of modesty and self-discipline, an incentive for lifelong effort, and a basis for genuine respect for excellence.

Certainly EO does stimulate competition. But as Schaar admits,[81] competitive impulses are ineradicable, and not all forms of competition are bad. Even if we accept Schaar's dubious premise that antagonism and isolation are ipso facto bad, some competition brings human beings closer together, into communities of shared endeavor and mutual respect. Consider the embrace of two exhausted boxers at the end of a match, or even the spontaneous bond between Sadat and Golda Meir at their first face-to-face encounter. Further, we must distinguish between situations in which what is sought is intrinsically scarce and those in which it is not. Scientific competition may produce simultaneous discoveries; gymnastic competition may inspire two perfect performances. The success of one competitor does not always imply that the other has failed. Indeed, both may do better than either would have, working alone. In addition, the antithesis between competition and cooperation is too simple. Cooperation is made possible by some agreement on goals or principles. Thus, a competitive system can be a form of cooperation if most participants are, on balance, willing to accept the principle and consequences of competition.

Neither is it the case that competition always leads to defining oneself externally, through overcoming others. To be sure, the competitor wants to win and to be recognized as having won. But the competitor wants to come to self-knowledge through the activity as well as to become known by others and to manifest those qualities that entitle that self to victory. Very few believe that victory is worth much unless one deserves to win; hence, the frequent tension between the acclaim of the world and internal self-doubt. It might be added that Schaar's antithesis between external and internal self-worth is overdrawn. We cannot form a coherent theory of how we ought to live without going beyond our own subjectivity and examining the various dimensions along which members of our species have been able to excel. Any meaningful standard will be to a certain extent comparative, relative to the *kind* of being we are. To extend Wittgenstein's point: Our inner sense of worth is in need of outward criteria.

Schaar is right to claim that EO allows natural differences to determine a range of social outcomes. The question is why, or to what extent, is this objectionable? Let us suppose that everyone has the same opportunity to develop skills as a sprinter. All other things being equal, the naturally gifted sprinter will develop furthest and win most races. The sprinter does not "deserve" his speed, but he certainly deserves to win the race that measures speed. The slower runner has an equal "legal" opportunity to enter the race but a very much lower probability of winning. Of course, the race is not natural in the same sense as the sprinter's ability. It is brought into being through a collective decision, as is the prize or entitlement created by victory. Thus, it is quite possible to exclude certain activities altogether from organized competition or to alter the perquisites of victory. Duelling and gladiatorial combat are now outlawed. We readily grant that the consistent winner of 100-yard dashes is entitled to be called the world's fastest human. We grant (up to a point) the legitimacy of monetary rewards. But we would resist exempting this winner from obeying laws we must obey or giving the individual some political control over our lives, merely on account of the victory. More generally: EO does not contain criteria that determine the range of its application. This decision must be made on the basis of other considerations. For example, we no longer believe that entitlement to basic necessities arises solely from the ability to compete successfully for them in the economic sphere, however justly that sphere may be organized. Even those who can contribute nothing deserve sustenance. Under circumstances of extreme stringency, however, this judgment might have to be revised. In addition, the decision to open up certain tasks to competition based on ability does not entail awarding any particular prize to the able beyond entitlement to perform those tasks. EO declares that those best suited to be doctors ought to be selected; it does not say that doctors are entitled to $70,000 a year, or whatever they can gouge from an uninformed and terrified public.

The foregoing considerations help us to clarify the question that concerns Schaar most deeply—the relation between EO and democracy. First, the fact that antidemocratic thinkers and leaders have defended EO does not mean that it is incompatible with democracy but only that it is not specific to democracy. This is what we would expect if, as I have contended, EO must be understood primarily as an instrumental rather than as a self-sufficient principle. Second, EO sanctions vast inequalities of income and wealth—threatening to democracy—only if it is assumed that economic status ought to be determined by a competitive struggle that rewards those proficient in the art of moneymaking *and* if this proficiency is very unequally distributed.[82] But, as we have seen, there is nothing intrinsic to EO that makes mandatory its unfettered application to any particular sphere of human endeavor.

Most important, Schaar calls into question the relation between knowledge and authority. His distinction between specialization and hierarchy is valid, as is his claim that the former does not entail or justify the latter. But two qualifications are necessary. First, as Aristotle pointed out, there may be an inherent hierarchical relation among specialized functions: the architect guides the work of the bricklayer and the plasterer.[83] Second, if members of a group have agreed on a particular goal, specialized knowledge that conduces to the attainment of that goal does provide a basis for hierarchy. For example, if everyone wishes to cross an ocean and arrive at a common destination, then the individual who happens to be a skilled navigator has a rational claim to give orders. Failure to acknowledge this claim means either that the other members of the group did not understand the logical consequence of their original decision or that they silently ascribed a higher priority to other goals. But the navigator's rational authority is limited in both extent and time: it does not regulate the group's nonnavigational activities, and it vanishes when the destination has been reached.

Schaar's most fundamental argument runs roughly as follows: EO encourages the development of, and distributes rewards on the basis of, differing levels of technical competence. But, first, no valid claims to political authority can be based on technical competence. Further, no combination of knowledge and skill produces a distinctively political competence that provides a claim to authority. Thus, EO is incompatible, not only with democracy, but with the nature of politics. When the facts are properly understood, it becomes clear that politics must be nonhierarchical—democratic, participatory—and based on an equality of being and belonging.

It is easy to grant that technical competence does not by itself confer political authority. This is inherent in the fact that techniques are complexes of hypothetical imperatives while politics requires authoritative determinations. But even if EO were limited to technique, it would follow only that it is inapplicable to the political sphere, not that it is incompatible with it. Moreover, there is no reason to suppose either that EO is inherently limited to technical competence or that it is inevitably inegalitarian. If there are no significant inequalities along the dimensions relevant to a particular sphere of activity, then the application of EO leads to equality of result. Finally, the premise underlying Schaar's argument is simply wrong. There is distinctively political excellence or merit; its dimensions can be specified; it does constitute a claim to authority, though not the only one; and it is necessary for the success of all political orders, democracies included.

To support this claim, let me simply enumerate, quickly and with broad brush strokes, the major components of political excellence. These may be divided into three categories: virtues of mind, of character, and of self-presentation. Virtues of mind include: analytical intelligence; a clear grasp of desirable goals; the ability to determine the best available course of action; the instrumental knowledge needed to carry out this course of action; insight into individual character; an understanding of popular or collective desires, priorities, and beliefs; a recognition of the complexity of politics, carrying with it a willingness to gather information and to seek advice; and a sense of the boundaries of politics—the aspects of nature, inanimate and human, that resist it, and the human activities and aspirations that transcend it. Virtues of character include: strength of purpose, once determined; the self-confidence that prevents the political actor from being unduly sensitive to criticism or discouraged by unexpected difficulties; flexibility, limited only by a sense of which means are questionable, inappropriate, or forbidden; willingness to admit error; the largeness of soul that makes possible some intuitive knowledge of and sympathy with a wide variety of characters and ways of life; charity and generosity—the absence of the spirit of bitterness and revenge; and a sense of humor. Virtues of self-presentation include the impressiveness and dignity of bearing that command respect and the clarity and eloquence of speech that make possible informed, willing consent.

These virtues are the basis of an important claim to authority because they contribute to cooperation and the achievement of shared purposes. Without them, a political community will at some point lose both its bearings and its self-confidence. It would be very fortunate if these virtues were widely distributed; their incidence is subject to variation, influenced by factors largely beyond our control. It seems safe to say that the number of individuals possessing them to any significant degree at any time within a given community will be relatively small.

This does not mean that democracy is based on a mistake, moral or empirical. As Jefferson saw, the problem of democracy is to achieve some convergence of participation, consent, and excellence. It is thus a grave mistake to exclude EO from either the analysis or the operation of the political sphere. Whatever theorists may want, of course, politics is not likely to be purged of competition. But the attributes a system rewards may not be the ones it needs, especially over the long term. The distinction between the electoral coalition and the governing coalition has its analogue on the level of individual character.[84]

5.6.c. Robert Nozick: Equality of opportunity as an unjustifiable pattern of outcomes

Nozick offers four arguments against EO.

1. While Schaar criticizes EO for overemphasizing competition and fostering it excessively, Nozick attacks the principle from the opposite direction. EO falsely understates the individualistic, competitive character of human existence. Life is not a race with a starting line, a finish line, a central judge, and some complex of attributes to be measured. Rather, there are only individuals, agreeing to give and receive on an infinite variety of bases.

2. In making these exchanges, individuals care about what they get, not what others deserve or the handicaps under which they may have labored.

3. If someone chooses A over B as a marriage partner because of A's exemplary qualities, B cannot claim any right to the resources of A or of anyone else that would facilitate the acquisition of comparably admirable qualities. There is no decisive difference between this example and the more general claims made for EO.

4. The transfers demanded by EO conflict with the primary relation of entitlement that exists between the individual and whatever that person has justly acquired. There are no general rights, only particular rights to particular things.

To begin with, Nozick has overstated the case against the "race" metaphor. Certain kinds of abilities are generally prized within a community, and being excluded from an equal chance to develop them means that one is unlikely to have much of value to exchange with others: consider the problem of hard-core unemployment when demand for unskilled labor is declining. There is more than one race, but the number is limited. In a society in which rising educational credentials are demanded for even routine tasks, exclusion from the competition for education, or inclusion on terms that amount to a handicap, will make it very difficult even to enter the system of exchange. Nozick is aware of this problem. His "utopia" is designed to overcome it by providing a framework within which no limited range of talents can be uniquely prized and every human characteristic can be developed, evaluated, and exchanged in a variety of ways.[85]

But there are two objections to this solution. First, it is not clear that it is possible. Nozick concedes that the maintenance of the framework requires a permanent central authority that would have to adjudicate disputes, giving different communities and individuals a strong incentive to compete for control over it, and would in addition tend to aggrandize itself.[86] This community, like every one that has ever existed, would acquire a characteristic bias. Second, even if Nozick were right about utopia, existing conditions are very different: each political community allows a limited number of tracks for the development of a limited range of valued abilities or attributes, and individuals are not free to move from one community to another. The "race" metaphor captures the salient features of this situation, and EO is a reasonable way of dealing with it. No utopian theory can afford to assume that the principles governing the best case can be transferred, unamended, to imperfect actuality.

Nozick's claim that considerations of handicap and desert do not enter into the process of individual exchange is empirically false. For instance, many people deliberately patronize concerns employing handicapped workers; others favor local merchants and industries, even if they must pay higher prices. These choices cannot continue indefinitely. At some point each individual will conclude that the choice costs too much. But my argument is only that handicap and desert are one kind of consideration in exchange, not that they are the sole or even dominant consideration. But even if Nozick's claim were empirically true, what would follow from it? If handicap and desert ought to be taken into account, the fact that they are not in no way affects the obligation. The features of just exchanges cannot simply be read off existing practices, especially since there is reason to believe that these practices are not reflections of immutable human nature but vary widely, historically and geographically.

Various considerations suggest that Nozick's use of the marriage example is not justifiable. a) Certain types of activities, for which love or mutual attraction furnishes a paradigm, are usually thought to be outside the domain in which considerations of fairness or entitlement are operative. Love is thought to be private and not reducible to choice in any simple sense. Moreover, it is clearly ludicrous to try to develop general criteria of lovability that all mate selectors are rationally obliged to use. In all these respects, relations of love are distinguished from, for example, the employment market, in which job descriptions publicly establish criteria of selection the rationality of which can be discussed in the light of considerations such as the demands of the task and the needs of society. b) Relations of love cannot be systematically controlled through external intervention. All the rigors of the law cannot make us love or cease loving, and the more indirect efforts of parents, teachers, and religious authorities do not work very well either. In contrast, the behavior of opportunity grantors, such as schools and the employment market, can be regulated to a considerable degree. c) Nozick's example seems plausible because the notion that anyone is entitled to be loved by a particular person is so obviously ridiculous. But when the problem is generalized our intuitions cease to be as clear. Consider the following counterexample: A small fraction of the population is afflicted with a skin disease that renders the skin repellent to sight and touch but otherwise leaves the sufferers completely unaffected, able to earn a living and function normally. The only serious consequence is that no one, afflicted or healthy, can endure intimacy with the afflicted. The disease can be cured only by an expensive drug the cost of which is beyond the means of the wealthiest sufferer but the provision of which to all the afflicted would add only one dollar to each citizen's taxes. It is not ridiculous to suppose that the community as a whole would feel obliged to provide the drug, giving as justification the principle that as many citizens as possible should have the opportunity to enjoy a normal sexual and family life.

This and similar conclusions can be avoided only by invoking Nozick's final argument, that EO contradicts the morally primary substructure of particular rights to particular things. I have already shown that Nozick's arguments in favor of such particular rights are unconvincing. I would add that he is understandably uneasy about the purported inviolability of these rights, remarking, in a footnote, that the question of whether these side constraints are absolute, or whether they may be violated in order to avoid catastrophic moral horror, and if the latter, what the resulting structure [of moral theory] might look like, is one I hope largely to avoid.[87]

But the question cannot be avoided. When the crunch comes, Nozick contends that there is no right to life that justifies the involuntary transfer of justly acquired property.[88] As he makes clear, the "Lockean proviso" does not accomplish or justify this either.[89] Apparently, no catastrophe is severe enough to undermine or override prior entitlements.

This comes very close to self-refutation. Many moral theories tell us that there are things we must die for; very few, that we must die to maintain someone else inviolate in the possession of personal property. The ancient question, "Why be moral?" arises with special urgency in this case, and it is hard to think of a convincing answer. Moreover, since Nozick seems to believe that only existing persons have rights,[90] his position amounts to the claim that it is more serious to violate the rights of one individual than to annihilate, permanently and completely, the ability of another to enjoy rights.

These implausibilities stem from two errors, one particular, the other general. Nozick's hyper-Lockeanism forgets that Locke defended the right to life as natural and that for Locke "the natural right to property is a corollary of the fundamental right of self-preservation."[91] And he forgets that morality to a certain extent reflects the most important features of our existence and loses its bearings when severed from them. His emphasis on the separateness of our individual existences leads him to overlook the importance each of us ascribes to the continuation and improvement of personal existence and to depreciate the claims that arise out of this belief. The teleological component of morality cannot be expunged.

Thus, the fact that the application of EO will frequently contradict existing property rights does not mean that those rights should always take precedence. Temporal priority and moral priority are not coextensive. Nozick is right to insist that existing rights cannot be ignored or viewed simply as facts (hindrances to "rational" policy) with no independent moral weight. But these rights must be balanced against other sorts of rational claims.

5.6.d. Equality of opportunity: Further considerations

There are two different ways in which merit may be justified as a criterion of distribution. There are, first, activities whose chief purpose is to single out and recognize merit of various kinds (literary competitions, amateur athletics). In such cases, the employment of other criteria contradicts (some might say perverts) the activities themselves. Second, the merit criterion may be employed to select those who are best able to perform tasks that are generally valued. In such cases the employment of other criteria will, *ex hypothesi,* result in a loss of efficiency, a lower level of performance of the collectively valued tasks. Here, unlike the first case, the introduction of other criteria is not self-contradictory but reflects an interest in goals other than efficiency.

The sociopolitical employment of merit is nearly always of the second type, and this can give rise to intense disputes about the balance to be struck between efficiency and other considerations. Let us suppose, for example, that the imposition of racial or ethnic quotas on medical school admissions results in some loss of efficiency. (The case against this practice is much harder to make if this is not assumed.) Setting aside legal or constitutional questions, this fact in itself is not enough to invalidate the practice. It may be argued that the use of quotas is a way of reducing differences of income among different groups, of muting discord, of dealing with inequality of opportunity, or even of bringing about a situation in which the contradiction between efficiency and other goals disappears. The more serious the consequences of lowered efficiency, the weightier other considerations must be to override them. The trade-off for dermatologists would be different from that for brain surgeons.

An important kind of objection to EO is that it ignores ways in which individuals may benefit from performing certain tasks even if they are less competent to do so than others. One variant of this occurs in learning. If an apprentice carpenter is not permitted to perform the activities of carpentry, full competence cannot be attained. In this process the master carpenter must be willing to accept certain inefficiencies. Moreover, this argument has force even if the learner can never achieve the level of competence of the best practitioners of a task. The increase of knowledge, skill, and self-confidence that an ordinary person can experience when placed in a position of responsibility is an important reason to consider rotating such positions fairly widely.

In addition, EO is linked to specialization: efficient performance of a particular complex task is usually achievable only when an individual concentrates on mastering that task while ignoring most others. The human consequences of "one man, one job" may not be wholly desirable. Perhaps a part of our nostalgia, however ill-founded, for simpler, more rural existence stems from the sense that in such circumstances individuals were able to cope competently with a wide variety of tasks and demands and that this provided to existence a kind of wholeness, confidence, and satisfaction. Further, there is a relation between broad competence and independence, and between specialization and dependence. Dependence can be dangerous from the standpoint of both individual psychology and collective organization. For the individual, dependence can easily produce a sense of helplessness and oppression, extremes of rage, listlessness, suspicion, even paranoia. For the collectivity, dependence on specialization can give inordinate influence to small groups who can get their way by withholding or threatening to withhold a vital service that they alone can provide.

The conclusion that the criterion of merit ought to be employed in a specific situation leaves important questions unresolved. The content of merit may well be controversial. This difficulty goes deeper than the much-discussed lack of congruence between prized abilities and the indices used to ascertain their presence. For example, what is a good doctor? The prevailing view is technical: the good doctor is an individual capable of learning and using a wide variety of diagnostic and curative techniques. But it might be suggested that medical goodness has a moral component as well: the good doctor cares more about his patients' welfare than his own material advancement, gives great weight to need in distributing his services, never loses sight of the humanity of his clients. As soon as merit is viewed as multidimensional, trade-offs become unavoidable. What weight should be given to the likelihood—even the explicit promise—that a prospective doctor will provide health care to rural areas, ghettos, or other localities lacking adequate care? Conversely, should a system of assigned involuntary service for an extended period after medical school be instituted, would willingness to commit oneself to this be an important index of one's ability to become a good doctor? In these and similar cases, the content of merit is relative to our view of the *purposes* that functions or tasks ought to fulfill.

Finally, the decision to allocate a particular task on the basis of ability leaves a significant ambiguity about the resulting pattern of distribution. Most frequently ability is distributed continuously, while the distribution of tasks is discontinuous. If there are ten slots, the eleventh-most able applicant loses out entirely, even though that person may be only slightly inferior to the tenth-most able. Intuitively this seems unfair, or at least unfortunate and suboptimal: allocation should be *in proportion to* merit, not merely in accordance with it. In some cases, this difficulty may be ineliminable. But frequently, once this difficulty is accepted as significant, it will be found that mechanisms can be devised to reduce the discontinuity. A system of rotation may be feasible, in which the most able would perform the task for the longest period, the less able, for progressively shorter periods. Alternatively, a task involving several different operations can be subdivided in ways that promote both efficiency and equity: consider the various uses of paraprofessionals.

EO could be justified on utilitarian grounds if happiness or satisfaction consisted mainly in a rational fit between ability and activity. But there are two difficulties. First, the collective ability profile may not map neatly onto the profile of collectively required or permitted activities. This problem becomes acute in a small society that provides a relatively narrow range of alternatives. Second, the happiness derived from an activity is not directly proportional to our ability to perform it. We may want to do what we cannot do very well and derive more satisfaction from performing a higher task in a mediocre way than from a lower task done very well; conversely, we may not want to perform the most complex and demanding task, even if we are fully capable of doing so and it is highly valued by the collectivity.

There seem to be two opposed approaches. One—the "functionalist"—defines the range of available activities on the basis of collective requirements. The other—nameless?—would define that range on the basis of individual abilities and desires. The former is somewhat variable (what a collectivity needs to survive and flourish depends to a certain extent on how it defines its purposes) but has a hard core (provision of food, health, order, security). The latter is somewhat variable, through education/socialization, but also has limits set by the need to obtain and defend the collective material conditions for individual development and gratification.

6
The Nature of the Just Community

6.1. Introduction

At the beginning of this inquiry I stated that the evaluation of a human community was properly directed to the "way of life" enjoyed by the individuals comprising that community. We are now in a position to add some precision to this intuitive idea.

A *good community*, we may say, provides a way of life in which each individual realizes the human good to the greatest extent possible for that individual. In such a community, the only limitations on achievement of the good would be internal—genetically stunted capacities or psychological characteristics that interfere with self-development and the enjoyment of existence. The good community rests on three preconditions: nonscarcity; members who rationally respect one another's interests; and suitable relations with other communities.

The *just community* allocates the human good or the means to it in accordance with valid claims. The just community is distinguished from the good community in at least one of two respects: the existence of scarcity, or the presence of some individuals whose acts or qualities limit their valid claims to less than what is required for the greatest possible achievement of their good.

Clearly, neither of these two distinctions is simply a given or a fact of nature. The extent of scarcity is in part determined by the organization of an economic system. Any such system is subject to two kinds of constraints. First, the principles and institutions guiding the allocation of its products must take into account their effects on the overall level of production. In many circumstances, a decrease in the supply of human goods available for distribution is very unlikely to be counterbalanced by any other sorts of benefits. Second, the system of production must reflect the nature of the human good. Its products must be elements of or means to that good. The content of its productive processes and the division of its tasks must also be conducive to the human good or at least conflict with it as little as possible.

The community can to a certain extent influence the character of its members through education and training. This takes place in many ways: the family, formal educational institutions, occupational groups, and public rhetoric, to name but a few. Since rational principles of appropriate conduct are neither innate nor invariably comfortable, no community can safely forgo an organized attempt to impart them to its members.

Throughout this chapter I shall ignore the complexities stemming from *negative claims*—the acts or qualities of individuals that render them unworthy of attaining their greatest possible good. That is, I shall not be concerned with crime or with punitive justice. So constrained, distributive justice emerges from the interplay of scarcity and unequal claims. All claims are either zero or positive, and individuals may be denied objects of desire that would promote their good only if the claims of others are weightier.

Distributive justice is concerned with the allocation of a wide range of desired objects. They fall into four broad categories: economic goods, opportunities for development, political goods, and public honors. Each category has a distinctive basis of valid claims. In each case, the basis is composed of a number of different elements, each with some internal relation to what is to be distributed.

The application of allocative principles within a human community is subject to three constraints. First, the valid claims of members of other communities cannot be disregarded. These claims have two bases: urgent need (for the rudiments of survival and human development), and long-term increases in indigenous levels of production. Second, members of future generations would have a valid complaint if we employ resources in such a manner as to radically depress the quality of their lives. Making fair allowance for our needs, we must contribute to their well-being; we have no rational basis to give preference to our own existences at their expense. Third, we are not unfettered in dealing with members of other species. We may rationally give greater weight to our own existence, but we cannot inflict great harm or, a fortiori, extinction on them for the sake of some trifling comfort, amusement, or advantage.

For the most part, the following discussion of distributive justice will remain on the level of principles. I shall not directly ask what sorts of institutions are best suited to carry them into practice—not because this question is unimportant but rather because it presupposes complex empirical investigations that must be reserved for a later occasion. Knowledge of principles helps us to ask the most relevant empirical questions, but there is not likely to be a unique set of generally preferable institutions. As means to the realization of just principles, appropriate institutions will vary with circumstances. It may well be, however, that the range of institutions appropriate to what I have called the good community is quite restricted.[1]

Many of the principles I defend rest on judgments about characteristics of individuals. In this regard they run counter to Hume's injunction:

> It were better, no doubt, that every one were possessed of what is most suitable to him and proper for his use; but besides that this relation of fitness may be common to several at once, it is liable to so many controversies, and men are so partial and passionate in judging of these controversies that such a loose and uncertain rule would be absolutely incompatible with the peace of human society. . . . Justice, in her decisions, never regards the fitness or unfitness of objects to particular persons, but conducts herself by more extensive views. Whether a man be generous or a miser, he is equally well received by her, and obtains with the same facility a decision in his favour, even for what is entirely useless to him.[2]

Hume's argument has great practical force. But, I suggest, the search for desirable social and political institutions ought to proceed in two stages that Hume here tends to conflate. First, we should look for principles to which rational individuals determined to act justly would assent. Second, we should try to determine which institutions would most nearly produce outcomes conforming to these principles, given certain assumptions about human irrationality and moral imperfection. We may well be led to Humean conclusions. But how we justify such conclusions makes a difference. It is one thing to assert that we cannot make rational judgments based on individual characteristics; it is quite different to say that because granting institutions the power to make individual determinations opens up the possibility of grave abuses, we should deny them this power, forgoing the best outcome to foreclose the possibility of the worst. Hume's argument blurs the distinction between these contentions.

If the argument I advance in this book is correct, we can and must make principled judgments based on individual characteristics. In practice, we may want to limit the power of particular institutions to do so, because of possibilities of abuse, cost, or negative externalities. From this perspective, institutional design ought to be the constant effort to devise general structures and procedures the operation of which achieves the best fit circumstances permit with correct particular judgments. Debates over rules of arrest and evidence are paradigms of the kinds of concerns that should be at work as well in the sphere of distribution.

Although the discussion that follows is focused on principles, it does have a certain specificity. Many of the particular questions considered would arise only in communities with complex, cooperative systems of production and clearly delineated educational and political institutions. There are two reasons for this emphasis. First, the modern world is composed almost exclusively of such communities. To discuss them is to deal with the problems *we* face. Second, I assume that the human good can be fully realized only in such communities, whatever the virtues of simpler tribal organizations may be. This is not to say that complex communities are superior in every respect, but only that they alone are adequate to the full range of human possibilities.

This is not a historical or "progressive" thesis. Most of what I say could be applied without great distortion to the political life of classical Greece. And the distinction between the polis and the tribe was well known to Aristotle, who indeed conceptualized it along the lines I have just suggested.

6.2. Economic Justice

In the most general sense, an *economy* is a set of institutions and practices through which, first, labor, direct or mediated through human contrivances, is coordinated to provide services and to transform nature into objects that promote the human good and, second, such goods and services are exchanged.

So defined, *economy* is a normative concept. In practice, three kinds of goods and services are produced: the beneficial, the useless, and the harmful. In this context, economy may be viewed as a net product: the sum of the beneficial minus the sum of the harmful. The basis of this normative concept is provided by the theory of the human good. Products are either elements of the good or means to it. Different products promote the good in different ways and to different extents. Almost all are beneficial within certain limits, useless or harmful beyond those limits. The precise content of the beneficial will vary with circumstances.

The discussion of economic justice will concentrate on the economy as a system of production. I shall assume now, and later argue for, the claim that all voluntary exchanges among individuals whose income, property, and productive functions are regulated by principles of justice will themselves be just.

The fundamental problem, then, is to determine how the economic product is to be divided, within the constraints imposed by the effects of varying divisions on the overall level of that product. We note, first, a dual relation between the economic and political spheres, each in a sense providing the essential conditions for the other. On the one hand, production occurs within a framework of security and assurance provided by the political order. On the other, the political activities that lead to order—deliberation, coordination, regulation, enforcement—require resources provided by the system of production.

Second, relative to particular circumstances, some goods may be collective or public—nonexcludable and indivisible, obtainable only through collective action backed by threat of sanctions.[3]

Third, a community may decide that although other possibilities exist, certain goods, such as health care or transportation, are better provided through collective action than through systems of voluntary exchange.

Let us call the resources required for these three types of collective action *taxes* and the residuum (production minus taxes), *private resources*. For simplicity, assume that taxes are taken directly from the economic product prior to the division of private resources and that the enjoyment of the benefits of collective action does not require any transfer of private resources among individuals or from individuals to collective institutions.

For every individual, we may define an overall level of economic well-being as the sum of the benefits that individual derives from collective action plus benefits derived from his share of private resources plus the benefits derived from the performance of his productive function. We may further define the sum of benefits derived from collective action plus those derived from a share of private resources as income plus property, where income is understood as the sum of goods and services received directly plus recognized entitlements to them: money, food stamps, ration coupons, job-related perquisites.

Thus, the division of the economic product between public and private goods, market and nonmarket mechanisms, taxation and private resources, though of great complexity and practical importance, is theoretically subordinated to the following considerations within a given community: what is the level of overall economic well-being enjoyed by its members, how is this correlated with the different kinds and amounts of claims individuals can validly advance, and what is the most broadly beneficial way of rectifying any imbalance that may exist between holdings and claims?

We need, then, to investigate the claims to the three elements of economic well-being: income, property, and the organization and allocation of tasks.

6.2.a. Income
The principle of need

The primary basis of income distribution is *need*. As we have seen, the concept of need is neither obscure nor uselessly imprecise. Needs are divided into two categories: the means required for normal physical maturation and activity, and those required for intellectual, moral, and emotional development. Physical needs include food, clothing, shelter, healthful surroundings, medical care, and a system of public safety, order, and protection. Developmental needs include the family or, if necessary, some family substitute, institutions of training and education, and leisure—exemption from the process of production and securing of physical needs sufficient to allow the individual to profit from educational institutions and the life of the family.

The means without which needs cannot be satisfied must themselves be considered needs. Medical care is useless unless individuals have access to it. Thus, in communities where individuals live at considerable distances from one another, adequate systems of transportation and communication are included within the range of needs. Similarly, education and training may be impossible without some supplement to the child care provided by the family. If self-development stems in part from engaging in productive activities, then the means to those activities must be made available. The carpenter needs tools, the architect, drafting equipment, the scholar, books. As S. I. Benn and R. S. Peters point out, the determination of such "functional needs" rests on some agreement as to the nature and purpose of the activity in question, and this does not always exist.[4] But the fact that disputes about functional needs are constantly arising, frequently in the context of tax cases, does not mean that a core consensus does not exist.[5]

Within the sphere of physical needs, a meaningful distinction may be drawn between true needs and what is desirable. For example, a varied diet with occasional delicacies may be desirable, but it cannot be defended as a need. The needed diet provides enough calories and a full range of biologically necessary vitamins, minerals, and trace elements. Similarly, necessary clothing must provide adequate freedom of movement and protection against natural conditions and occupational hazards. No one needs a closet full of clothes in the latest style, produced from expensive and visually attractive materials. Social norms exist, to be sure, but they are indefensible if they obstruct the fulfillment of needs: bound feet and tight corsets are two of the more notorious examples. Again, it may be thought desirable to deal with the physician of one's choice, but unless this is significantly related to the level of public health, it can hardly be viewed as a need.

A similar distinction may be drawn in the sphere of developmental needs. Although adequate education and training are needs, it is not necessary that they be free gifts of the community to beneficiaries. Thus, if the outside work a student can do without impeding training is insufficient to cover the costs of training, some system of supplementary support is necessary. But it is not necessary that this come in the form of outright gifts or grants; from the standpoint of individual needs, a loan program is sufficient if repayment will not compel individuals to forgo the satisfaction of needs.

We must distinguish between need and dependence, psychological or physiological. It is, for example, absurd to view television as a need and to exclude television sets from bankruptcy proceedings or to include them in welfare programs, at least on that basis. Similarly, it would not be justified to include cigarettes within the sphere of need, even if 95 percent of a given population were addicted to them.

A rank-ordering of urgency exists among needs. In times of scarcity, physical needs must be satisfied first. If a choice cannot be avoided, resources must be diverted from leisure and training to the provision of those things necessary to sustain life. Nothing can justify the physical privation or death of an innocent person except the avoidance of such evils for a larger number of individuals.

The priority of need in the determination of income distribution is far from self-evident. The difficulty stems from the ambiguous status of the economic sphere. On the one hand, goods and services are instruments the worth of which is determined by the extent to which they promote the human good. From this standpoint, the instrumental considerations embodied in need-claims stand in the closest possible relation to income. On the other hand, as Nozick and many others before him have observed, economic goods do not appear like manna from heaven. They emerge out of a complex process of production and exchange, a process that generates its own characteristic claims. When someone says, "I'm entitled to this because I made it," or "I'm entitled to this because I obtained it through a voluntary exchange executed in fair circumstances," we cannot dismiss these claims as irrelevant, even if we come to feel that in some circumstances they must be subordinated to others. Intuitively, then, a theory of income distribution must attempt to take into account and systematize the moral force of both need- and desert-claims.

No rigorous or conclusive arguments can be adduced to support the priority of need-claims. There are, however, a number of considerations that point in that direction.

First, as I have argued, the primary purpose of collective political organization is the promotion of the human good for individuals. Need is defined relative to the human good—in particular, to the elements of the good (preservation and development) to which we accord the highest priority. A community in which large numbers of individuals do not have access to means of preservation and development must be judged undesirable, whatever its other strengths or virtues may be. (It is not only humanly but also morally undesirable if this deprivation results from human contrivance rather than uncontrollable natural or historical forces.)

Second, as we shall see, desert as a principle of claims to income is activated through participation in a system of production. But the purpose of that system is to promote individual well-being; desert-claims are constrained by the character of the activity through which they emerge. Further, in practice, a system of production will not function stably and desert-claims will not be recognized as binding if large numbers of individuals are left with unsatisfied needs. Deontological desert-claims, that is, are dependent on a set of activities the maintenance and perceived legitimacy of which rest on teleological requirements.

Third, except in circumstances of extreme stringency, we act so as to take into account the needs of those who cannot participate in the system of production. That is, in conditions of relative abundance, we believe that individual existence generates a binding need-claim, except when an individual acts so as to invalidate it, wholly or in part. Criminal behavior is widely thought to constitute invalidation. An intermediate case is suggested by the old distinction between "deserving" and "undeserving" poor, the former unable to work, the latter unwilling to. But one may concede that the need-claims of shirkers are weakened without denying the priority of the need-claims that most individuals can advance. That is what one would expect if, as I have suggested, need and desert are two species of entitlement, lying along a moral and conceptual continuum.

Fourth, the priority of need-claims rests in part on their concreteness. To leave needs unfulfilled is to inflict direct harm on individuals. Breaching a desert-claim, on the other hand, disrupts a moral relation without necessarily harming an individual whose claims have been overridden. And if direct harm does occur, it involves, *ex hypothesi*, deprivation of some good other than what is required for preservation and development, the most urgent elements of well-being. I do not mean to suggest that the disruption of a moral relation is a trivial matter, but only that when it is disrupted in the name of some concrete benefit for another individual, the good exceeds the harm. Many of our beliefs and practices reflect this. If a starving man steals a loaf of bread that someone else has baked for his own amusement, the urgency of

need overrides productive claims. In most communities, property relations are suspended or qualified during times of emergency or catastrophe, revealing that the practical validity of desert-claims tacitly
presupposes a context in which the needs of fellow members of the
community have been satisfied.

From a practical standpoint, one may object that giving priority to
need leaves inadequate scope for desert-claims and decreases initiative.
There are three kinds of responses to this objection. First, the content of
need as I have defined it is relatively spartan. A substantial percentage
of goods and services enjoyed by residents of advanced industrial
societies falls outside its boundaries, leaving significant scope for
desert-claims. Second, the fact that desert-claims are restricted in the
sphere of income distribution does not mean that they are similarly
restricted in other areas. In fact, the burden of my argument is to
suggest that many desert-claims are perverted when deflected into the
economic sphere and may be redeployed into more appropriate
areas—opportunities for development, political leadership, public
honor—to the advantage of both claimants and other members of the
community. Third, as I shall argue, it is empirically questionable to
believe that the incentive to participate in the system of production is
gravely diminished if desert-claims are restricted. Those whose formerly ignored need-claims are now honored will participate more en-
thusiastically and efficiently, and those whose income is decreased will
not become disaffected if they can be persuaded that the system as a
whole is being guided by equitable principles. For example, recent
surveys suggest that relatively few Americans question the principle of
substantial welfare payments to those who cannot contribute to production. Rather, recent protests have been directed against what many
see, rightly or wrongly, as subsidies to those who can work but do not
wish to, and to middlemen-bureaucrats who manage to achieve far
greater prosperity than average taxpayers by administering the claims
of the poor.

Finally, it should be understood that I am not arguing for the priority
of need in the strict Rawlsian or "lexical" sense. A system that evinces a
strong tendency to give priority to need in the great majority of cases is
in this respect just. In some cases it may be proper to honor the desert-
claims of those making extraordinary contributions, even at the expense
of the needs of others. Moreover, there is an order of priority within
needs, corresponding in part to the priority of existence over development. As needs become less urgent, the case for honoring desert-claims
is relatively strengthened. The priority of need expresses a first approximation or rebuttable presumption, not an inflexible rule. It is a
framework for analysis, not a universal answer to complex practical
problems.

The principle of contribution

Once needs have been satisfied, claims to income based on desert are activated. These claims, I argue, are based on individual contribution to the process of production, for three reasons.

First, there is a prima facie relation between contribution to production and income, since aggregate income is determined by production. Second, there is a close relation between what we do and what we claim as our own. This emerges most clearly in cases of creative activity: consider the connections between parents and children, poets and poems, artisans and artifacts. Third, outside the realm of immediate natural duties to others, each individual has an overriding claim to personal talents and energies. The principle of contribution emerges when this moral premise is combined with a commonsense understanding of action: we give what is ours with the expectation of reasonable return. The philosophic analysis of contribution seeks to add precision to our intuitive notions of what is reasonable.

The principle of contribution implies that desirable human qualities unrelated to production cannot, taken by themselves, serve as bases for claims on income.[6]

There is a further consideration. If contribution to production is to be a criterion of entitlement to income, then all must have the opportunity to contribute what they are able. A system that, for example, kept 10 percent of its potential producers outside the productive system while employing contribution as a distributive criterion would be manifestly unfair.

Contribution to production has five major components: sacrifice, duration, effort, productivity, and quality.

Sacrifice is the abandonment of some human good, required by the task one performs. Some tasks involve the surrender of physical security (police, firemen), enormous risks to health (coal miners, asbestos workers) or restriction of the pleasures of youth (medical specialists who must endure ten years of advanced training). When a task entails sacrifice, the performer is thought to deserve "compensation." The reasoning is straightforward. Individuals undertake tasks to promote their well-being or good. Now assume that there is no relevant difference between A and B except that A's job entails a much greater sacrifice than B's. If A does not receive some compensatory treatment, the aggregate good flowing from his task will be lower than B's total, but, *ex hypothesi*, there is no reason that can be adduced to justify this difference.[7]

It may be thought that there is an incongruity between many kinds of sacrifice and compensation in the form of income. This is true to a certain extent; income does not seem wholly commensurate with death, pain, or disease. The difficulty is that frequently nothing better is available. It is better to transfer some good to sacrificing individuals than none at all. There is another consideration. In most cases individuals making sacrifices want to be known, recognized, and respected for doing so. Reasonably, they view the transfer of a real and widely valued good as a sign of recognition. Conversely, attempts by financially hard-pressed cities to place police and firemen on an equal footing with other workers is resented as unfair, indeed as a sign of nonrecognition or contempt. This issue emerges clearly in the following exchanges:

> Last month, Victor Gotbaum, the head of the largest union of city workers, said in a television broadcast:
> "No city worker is going to get more than any other. It isn't in the cards. The police haven't gotten a nickel more than anyone else in the last six or eight years."
> Mr. DeMilia's response was that "the police officer who puts his life on the line every day cannot be treated like a clerk."
> This sentiment was echoed yesterday by many police officers after the delegate assembly meeting. One complained that "we're always giving up more than every other city agency—the only time anybody feels sorry for us is when there is a flag over the wooden box."
> Another said: "If you treat me like a porter, you'll get the service of a porter. That's what causes frustration among cops, young and old."[8]

The fact that most sacrifice is nonmonetary makes it difficult to determine the appropriate level of compensation. The problem is not wholly indeterminate, however, First, relative compensation should correspond to the relative importance of the sacrificed good. Second, the importance of the good must be discounted by the likelihood that it will in fact be forgone. Police serving in areas with high levels of violent crime deserve more risk compensation than those in quiet country towns. Third, a sacrificed good that cannot be replaced should be compensated at a higher level than one that is only temporarily abandoned or for which a reasonable substitute exists. Fourth, the absolute level of compensation should bear a reasonable relation to the good forgone. As participants in civil cases know, the "reasonable" is eminently disputable. There is, though, a useful benchmark. In general, if a given level of compensation makes many individuals eager to undergo the corresponding privation, the compensation is excessive. If you are a lawyer well acquainted with prevailing injury settlements and, as another car careens toward yours, find yourself hoping that you get whiplash, then the prevailing practice is disproportionate. Similar considerations apply to medical malpractice suits.[9]

Not every loss of some good constitutes a sacrifice. If an individual does not have a valid claim to a particular good, then the withdrawal of that good does not generate grounds for compensation. Suppose that a foreman favors a particular worker over an extended period, permitting him to take a much longer lunch break than others performing the same task for the same pay. If a new foreman refuses to continue this practice, the favored worker loses a good but has no grounds for complaint. A similar principle applies in instances of nationalization or expropriation. For example, a regime proposing to nationalize a foreign-owned mine is entitled to ask whether the rental fees and royalties it has received over the years have been fair or whether the workers have been paid appropriately, and to reduce its proposed compensation by the amount of the shortfall. Even if true, the owners' standard claim that the host country and workers were better off with the capital investment than they would have been without it is inadequate. The owners have benefited as well; the question is how the proceeds of the cooperative venture are to be fairly shared. Similarly, the expropriation of a class whose favored position depends on treating others unjustly does not require compensation for the full amount of the loss, although prudential considerations may require such compensation. Prior to the Civil War, many of those who denied the legitimacy of slavery supported schemes for federally funded purchases of slaves from their owners as a politically feasible method of emancipation.

Finally, compensation should not be confused with incentive or inducement. Incentives may be needed to increase the supply of those willing to perform a particular kind of task. In principle, compensation is independent of willingness to perform tasks. Someone who says, "I'm proud to be a miner, as were my father and grandfather before me," is nevertheless entitled to compensation for the special rigors of that occupation. Again, individuals may be more willing to undertake arduous tasks during periods of economic stringency, but they are not less entitled to compensation than in times of greater choice. There may, of course, be an indirect reduction of entitlement if the total of income available for distribution is significantly reduced. In spite of this distinction, compensation serves as an inducement as well, at least negatively. If it is widely known that a task requires uncompensated sacrifice, recruitment will be more difficult.

The concept of *duration* is simpler. All other factors being roughly equal, those who work longer should receive more. More precisely, the component of income that reflects duration should be directly proportional to time worked, since, given these assumptions, the ratios of time worked will be equal to the ratios of contribution to the total product. As we have already noted, the operation of this principle is subject to an important condition: access to work time must be open and fair. If the aggregate desire to work among the pool of equivalent workers exceeds the number of man-hours required to complete the task, hours of work should be distributed in proportion to individual desires. It would be difficult to devise a system more blatantly unjust than maintaining a constant workweek and firing the number of workers needed to reduce total work hours to the required level. Laws or contractual arrangements that create incentives to fire in this fashion are unwise. It seems improbable that in principle it is significantly more efficient to fire some than to reduce hours for all. But if it were, it would be preferable to spread the work around and to reflect decreased efficiency through a reduction in hourly wage rates.

The criterion of *effort* presents difficulties of theory and application. Intuitively, effort is the ratio between the work one does and the work one could do, making best use of one's present physical and mental powers. It is possible to interpret "best use" in a more demanding manner, relative to the potential an individual possesses at birth. From this standpoint, best use at time x is measured against the baseline of the person one would be if one had made best use of one's powers at every significant stage of development. One's present powers, that is, are themselves in large measure the result of effort. The consistent application of the criterion of effort would, so the argument runs, compel us to measure the totality of what we have made of ourselves. David Miller puts this clearly:

> Certain of the skills and abilities which a man uses in his work are the products of *previous* voluntary actions—for example, the decision to attend training courses—and there is no reason to tie desert to present voluntary actions at the expense of earlier ones. Surely the voluntary decision to acquire a useful skill should be rewarded in the future when the skill is exercised.[10]

In reply, we may note that presumably the acquisition of skill leads to greater productivity. If, as I shall argue, productivity is a relevant desert basis for income distribution, then the acquired skills are indeed rewarded, though in accordance with a separate principle. Miller's implied reductio is thus avoided.

But what is gained by defining effort in terms of present capacities? The answer, I suggest, is greater moral realism. What we are now may well be the outcome of past acts, but this does not imply that we are wholly capable of undoing the effects of these acts. Our self-inflicted limits and atrophied potentialities become a nexus of powerful habits, a character or second nature in some ways as immutable and confining as our natural endowments. The Sartrean vision of man as radically free, capable of choosing to discard settled patterns of behavior, rests on an excessively sharp distinction between will and self or character. Thus, although it is reasonable to hold adults responsible for what they have become (who was it who declared that "at forty everyone has the face he or she deserves"?), it is equally necessary to give moral weight to what they do within the confines of what they have become. Effort in my narrower sense, relative to present possibilities, is one measure of this.

In addition, this approach is supported by our moral intuitions. Consider, for example, a youth who devotes himself to reckless and self-destructive pursuits, culminating in an incapacitating accident. Through a determined program of physical therapy he overcomes a portion of his handicaps, to the extent that he is able to take on a relatively undemanding job. Our moral response is complex. On the one hand, we cannot help comparing his limited present accomplishments with our memory of his early possibilities. On the other hand, we admire and respect him for utilizing a high proportion of his remaining powers in circumstances in which another individual might have been content to vegetate. Remembering his youth, we feel sadness and pity, but the vanished past has ceased to be a locus of moral interest or to influence his present claims.

A familiar objection to effort as a desert-basis is that, while the intuitive moral force of effort rests on the belief that it represents what is truly within our power, in fact it is the outcome of external forces, such as family training and opportunities, over which we have no control.[11] There are two responses. First, this objection presupposes an overall view of human action in which the factor of autonomy, freedom, or responsibility has been altogether eliminated. As Nozick points out, it is paradoxical when those who adopt this line simultaneously claim Kantian inspiration and seek to base a political theory on individual choice.[12] Moreover, those who reject effort seldom offer a systematic determinist argument. Rawls, for example, retreats to the contention that, since observed effort is influenced by external factors (a plausible contention), there is no way to discount for this, and the idea of rewarding effort is therefore impracticable.[13] Not only is this a far cry from his earlier contention that "the notion of desert seems not to apply to these cases,"[14] it is also a non sequitur. To say that the relative influence of external and internal factors cannot be precisely determined (a truism) is not to say that unusually high or low internal contributions cannot be recognized with some confidence. At most, this practical problem places the burden of proof on anyone claiming that a particular individual's effort deviates significantly enough from the norm to warrant differential treatment. The second line of reasoning has already been sketched:[15] desert-claims need not presuppose that the proposed desert-basis is some fact for which the individual is responsible. If this is so, the determinist critique misses the mark altogether.

The critic may grant the validity of effort as a desert-basis but proceed to deny that it is relevant to income distribution. The inept person who tries hard may contribute very little to the quantity of goods produced. If so, why should effort generate claims on the product?

There are two sorts of replies. First, there is no compelling reason to construe contribution narrowly, as restricted to marginal product. We say, quite naturally, that the person who tries hard "gives of himself." He expends his own good—energy or activity—the supply of which is limited and which stands in a particularly intimate relation to his own being. The giving, moreover, is not at random or directionless; it is shaped by, and oriented toward, the process of production. It is reasonable, then, that the ensuing claims be directed toward the same process.

Second, the person who tries hard, ineptly, may nevertheless contribute indirectly to the quantity of production. He incarnates a principle that, if generally adopted, would lead to increased production. In many instances, the perception of this embodied principle will lead other workers to do better. Something of this sort happens frequently in sports, where an obscure journeyman player who demonstrates "hustle" and "desire" can inspire his abler but more lethargic teammates. It is, of course, not uncommon for such individuals to be resented, but the resentment is founded largely on guilt. The others know that they can do better and that they ought to, but they have half-succeeded in repressing their awareness of this knowledge. The zealous individual reminds them of what they would rather forget. Usually, though, if he is not intimidated into conformity by the initial resentment, the others will become uncomfortable enough to begin to meet their obligations.

It may be objected, though, that trying harder can hardly be considered an obligation if the task itself is demeaning or if it is destructive of body or spirit. Granted. The theory of income distribution is valid only in conjunction with a theory of task allocation that gives due weight to the effects of occupations on those who perform them. At the same time, we should be very cautious about labeling tasks as demeaning. Nothing that promotes the human good is demeaning. The dignity of useful work stems more from the moral attitudes and self-perception of the worker than from the external characteristics of his task. Of course, it would be visionary to expect that ill-founded community attitudes toward particular occupations would not affect these self-perceptions.

We come, finally, to the criterion of *productivity*. This may be defined as output per hour within a given system of production. The contextual proviso is needed to avert gross inequities. If A has the use of more efficient equipment than B, a simple comparison of hourly output will reveal little about their relative efficiency as workers. Similarly, the direct comparison would be inappropriate if, for example, the equipment were easier for right-handed workers to operate than for left-handed.[16] Differences in systems of production will have an indirect effect on claims, since they are likely to be correlated with differences in the supply of goods available for distribution.

Miller offers two objections to the productivity criterion that, if justified, would undercut its utility as a distributive principle. First, to say that if A's output is twice that of B, A deserves twice the income is to presuppose that each man "has a right to the whole product of his labour." But in modern society, a worker's productivity depends upon "technique and skills which he has not discovered for himself."[17] This is a decisive objection to any theory that seeks to make productivity the sole distributive criterion. But it does not follow that productivity cannot serve as one component of valid claims. It is in this manner that I propose to employ it: A portion of total income should be proportional to productivity.

Second, Miller contends that in many circumstances it is not only practically but also theoretically impossible to determine individual productivity, and the criterion therefore leaves a vast indeterminacy. He asks us to consider the following case: A working alone moves 6 sacks an hour, and B, 8; when they are set to work together, they can cooperatively move 21 sacks. We cannot tell whether they should be paid equally; or they should receive what they would have, working alone, and divide the extra earned through cooperation equally; or they should be paid in such a way that their totals preserve the 6 : 8 ratio of their noncooperative shares.[18]

It seems to me that the bulk of the alleged indeterminacy arises because the example is unrealistically underspecified. Suppose, for example, that cooperation takes the form of dividing the moving of sacks into a series of discrete steps carried out by one worker or the other. If so, the productivity of A and B could be determined for each of the subtasks and the results summed to determine overall productivity. The aggregation would of course depend on the weight attached to the various steps, leaving some indeterminacy, but common sense would certainly confine appropriate possibilities to a narrow range. In addition, the outcome of this procedure is unlikely to diverge too widely from the original 6 : 8 ratio, since that reflected the aggregate result when A and B each performed all the subtasks. The variation would probably be greater if A did $n - 1$ of the n subtasks much more efficiently than B but was held back by ineptitude in the last than if the original inequality resulted from A's lower efficiency, distributed fairly evenly across the subtasks.

If, on the other hand, cooperation takes the form of joint action all along the way, then one might well say that the task has changed, rendering solitary productivity almost irrelevant. A is no longer moving sacks, but rather moving-sacks-with-B, and similarly for B. Taken by itself, this "seamlessness" would suggest the propriety of equal pay. But there is another consideration: Equal division means that A benefits nearly twice as much from cooperation as B, A's share rising from 6 to 10.5 while B's rises from 8 to 10.5. There is no reason to believe that this is justified by A's productivity; indeed, in the absence of evidence to the contrary, it would be much safer to assume that A's contribution remains lower than B's, although the seamlessness of their joint activity makes this, *ex hypothesi*, impossible to determine. These considerations strongly suggest that A and B should each receive their noncooperative earnings and that the benefits of cooperation should be divided equally.

This case is underspecified in another way as well: We are not told who originated the cooperative plan. If A and B devised it jointly, the argument in favor of an equal division of the benefits of cooperation would be strengthened. If devised primarily by A (or by B), the deviser has contributed more than his labor and deserves a larger share of the benefits. If devised by a third party, that individual is entitled to an entrepreneurial dividend, some portion of the cooperative benefits.

To be sure, these refinements do not wholly eliminate the indeterminacy of the productivity criterion. But Miller assumes, without argument, that any significant indeterminacy renders a criterion useless. This assumption is mistaken, for two reasons. First, the demarcation of a range of possibilities is important, theoretically and practically. In Miller's own example, the varying interpretations of the productivity criterion constrain A's share in the range 9.0–10.5 and B's in the range 10.5–12.0. Second, it is not necessarily the case that in every situation there is only one just (or "most just") solution. The best, most plausible, and most defensible principles may well pick out a range of solutions equally acceptable from the standpoint of justice. A choice among these solutions may then be made on any number of other bases—chance, bargaining, history, aesthetics, etc.[19]

Thus far we have treated productivity as a purely quantitative criterion. But *qualitative* considerations are clearly relevant. There are two general types of cases. First, in a system of production involving highly routinized tasks, quality of work is most plausibly defined in terms of defects or mistakes. A worker's net productivity would be, roughly, total units produced/hour *minus* the number/hour rejected through inspection. Thus, if A produces 10 units/hour with a 10 percent defect rate while B produces 9 units/hour with a 0 percent defect rate, their net productivity would be identical. Of course, it is frequently impossible or impractical to determine the origin of defects. In the absence of good evidence to the contrary, it is fairest to determine an average defect rate and assess it against each individual's total production. Informal mechanisms will usually reveal individuals who are "not pulling their weight," forcing others to subsidize them. Second, quality is much harder to define and measure in a nonroutinized productive system. In general, the quality of a product is relative to its purposes, and the measure of quality is the extent to which criteria stemming from these purposes are fulfilled. If A and B both construct beds in equal quantities/hour, but long experience has revealed that A's beds on average last twice as long as B's, then A's productivity is twice B's. The same conclusion would follow if, for example, the hammers A makes can drive and extract nails twice as fast as B's hammers. Other cases are, of course, more difficult. If cook A's creations are as nourishing as, but much tastier than, B's creations, then at best a rough measure of quality is attainable. Perhaps the most we can say is that the difference of quality would be relative both to the percentage of consumers who rank A above B and to the vehemence or enthusiasm with which they do so.

None of these criteria is very helpful, though, in dealing with the most fundamental problem of income distribution. Every economy is composed of a large number of qualitatively different functions or tasks. The criteria that enable us to make relative judgments *within* tasks tell us nothing about judgments *across* tasks. For example, what are the relative claims of the most productive doctor and the most productive carpenter?

In the most general sense, there does seem to be a basis of comparison. Our entire discussion has presupposed an economy the products of which are means to or parts of the human good. The relative claims of the doctor and the carpenter should be regarded as proportional to the contributions of their respective products to the human good.

But, as we have seen, the human good is composed of a number of heterogeneous elements, and it is very far from clear how they can be reduced to a common measure. The conjecture we explored in Chapter 3, that in circumstances of desperate scarcity we can establish a rank-ordering among the basic types of good, may tell us something about the perceived urgency of the various goods, but it surely is not an adequate index of their worth *simpliciter*. There is a further difficulty. Even if we could find a common measure, there could be no direct transition from the value of the good produced to the valid claims of the producer, because the production is mediated by the choice of a productive system. The number of individuals sharing in the production of the desired amount of a good may be varied, as may be the division of production into subtasks. For example, the supply of doctors can be expanded or contracted by various means, and some of the doctors' functions can be assigned to nurses and paraprofessionals.

The usual response to this difficulty is to accept demand for various goods and services as the best index of their worth or value. There are two objections to this approach. First, ignorance, bad training, or constricted alternatives can lead us to desire things that do not benefit us.[20] Second, aggregate demand presupposes some distribution of income among individuals. For our purposes, at least, this is a hopeless circularity, since we seek some independent measure of the worth of goods as a guide to income distribution. Nevertheless, the general idea of determination of worth through demand has intuitive appeal. In circumstances in which there are no rational principles to serve as external constraints, it is reasonable to suppose that individual desire or subjective satisfaction should serve as the determining factor. Our theory of the human good supports this conclusion. Further, the theory of the good was derived in large measure through an analysis of desire. It would be strange, perhaps even self-defeating, to refuse to give weight to desire at precisely the point at which no other benchmark seems plausible or useful. But can demand be employed in a manner that overcomes the powerful objections against it?

As a thought experiment, imagine a community of individuals, each of whom accepts, in general, the view of the human good I have advanced. They agree, that is, on the major components of the good. We then ask each of them to imagine a way of life in which his individual good has been completely achieved and to attach to each component of that realized good a weighting representing its perceived relative importance or contribution to the overall good of the individual, with the proviso that the sum of each individual's weights must be the same. For each component of the human good, the sum of the weights it receives from each individual, divided by total weights for all components, represents the relative social importance of an amount of that good that fulfills the requirements of one individual. For simplicity, let us call this amount a *unit*. We can now say that an individual's contribution is equal to the relative social importance/unit of the good he provides, multiplied by the number of units for which he is responsible. (For the number of units, see the previous discussion of average product.)

On this basis we can resolve, at least in general terms, our second difficulty. The members of the community will agree that the best system of production is one that maximizes the sum of individual contributions, subject to the constraints of human and material factors of production. From this agreement, given the necessary information or assumptions, they will be able to arrive at some determination of the number of individuals who ought to be involved in the provision of each component of the good and the organization of the process of production within each sector.

We arrive, then, at a general criterion of contribution: An individual's contribution is equal to the relative social importance/unit of the good he provides, multiplied by the number of units for which he is responsible, when his contribution takes place within a desirable system of production. Later we shall discuss a proviso: The opportunity to perform tasks or functions, to make particular kinds of contributions, must be allocated on a fair and reasonable basis.

One may object to this thought experiment on the grounds that participants are asked to evaluate the contribution different activities make to their good in circumstances of nonscarcity. But, it may be alleged, there is no reason to accept this as the measure; evolutions of relative contribution will vary with circumstances. Thus, as Hobbes remarked,

> An able conductor of soldiers, is of great price in time of war present, or imminent; but in peace not so. A learned and uncorrupt judge, is much worth in time of peace; but not so much in war.[21]

We readily concede that overall evaluations of activities will vary with circumstances. But this overall judgment has two components: instrumental (hence, variable and contingent) worth; and intrinsic worth. These can diverge widely. In wartime we accord a high instrumental rating to some activities that are distasteful or even horrifying. The question then becomes: How are we to give substance and definition to our intuitions of intrinsic worth? My suggestion is that they are likely to emerge more clearly when the distorting effects of scarcity are removed. Intrinsic worth, that is, can best be understood as a free and unforced judgment made relative to the kind of beings we are rather than to the conditions in which we happen to find ourselves. Recall also that the judgment of intrinsic worth is at most one component in the determination of income distribution. Many of the others reflect particular circumstances, so that the overall result will be sufficiently realistic, that is, sensitive to the broad variations of human conditions.

Up to this point our discussion of contribution has for the most part been focused rather narrowly on productive work. But clearly an economic system requires other kinds of contributions: capital, entrepreneurship, organizational and managerial skills, and inventions. Indeed, if current conditions are any guide, these contributions are widely believed to be so important as to warrant very high levels of reward. Against this we have Hobhouse's powerful objection:

> The organizer of industry who thinks that he has "made" himself and his business has found a whole social system ready to his hand in skilled workers, machinery, a market, peace, and order

211

—a vast apparatus and a pervasive atmosphere, the joint creation of millions of men and scores of generations. Take away the whole social factor and we have not Robinson Crusoe, with his salvage from the wreck and his acquired knowledge, but the naked savage living on roots, berries, and vermin. *Nudus intravi* should be the text over the bed of the successful man, and he might add *sine sociis nudus exirem*.[22]

The conclusion Hobhouse drew from this seems unavoidable: Any estimate of contribution must try to separate "social" from "personal" contributions to production. Once this is done, personal marginal contribution is likely to be judged very much smaller than it first appeared. But we must resist Feinberg's suggestion that personal marginal contribution is only the "tiniest percentage of the total contribution" and that therefore it may seem like "the meanest quibbling" to employ it as a basis of distinction among individuals.[23]

Without any pretense of adequacy, let us look briefly at these controversial factors of production, the first of which is *capital*. We may begin with a general principle: if an individual is not entitled to x, then he is not entitled to anything the valid claim to which rests on being entitled to x. Thus, if A robs B at gunpoint and then invests the proceeds in a business, A is not entitled to any of the goods or profits flowing from the business. Again, if A forces B to work at gunpoint, then takes B's product, sells it, and invests the proceeds, A is not entitled to any return.

This is not the place to develop a full theory of *legitimate capital*, but some indications are in order. There is one unquestionably legitimate source of capital: savings (forgone consumption) out of a justly received stream of income. A source possessing a strong presumption of legitimacy is the sale of justly held property within an economic system in which income is distributed with reasonable equity and all have the right to participate in transactions. Capital acquired through gift, inheritance, or chance may be accorded legitimacy on utilitarian grounds, but if changing circumstances lead to a collective determination that, for example, inheritance taxes ought to be set at 100 percent, no individual is deprived of any entitlement.[24]

To simplify matters, let us assume that we are considering a sum of legitimate capital. Now suppose that A has four ways of using that capital: purchase of nondurable goods; purchase of durable goods; savings; or investment. Suppose further that the overall economy has a 0 percent rate of inflation and that "savings" is merely retention for future use at a 0 percent rate of interest. We may ask: What is the difference between saving and investing? One standard answer is that investment involves risk and that there must accordingly be a risk premium to equalize returns between savings and investment. To correct for this variable, assume that every available investment opportunity is guaranteed by the full faith and credit of the government. Another frequent answer is that investment involves surrendering the opportunity to make alternate use of capital for extended periods. But many forms of investment are more liquid than many forms of savings. At any rate, we can correct for this variable by stipulating that the use of capital may be regained with equal facility from either. Given all these assumptions, the distinction between saving and investing collapses. If A is willing to forgo present consumption and save at 0 percent interest, he ought to be willing to invest on the same terms, that is, agree to recover at some future date what he invests now. Note that saving at 0 percent is perfectly rational in any system in which income is significantly related to work and in which individuals expect to live longer than they expect or want to work.

But now suppose that the amount of consumption A and all others similarly situated are willing to forgo is not sufficient to meet the capital requirements of the economic system. In these circumstances, there are two possibilities: threats and incentives. The community may institute a program of forced savings with substantial penalties for those who do not comply, or it may offer an increment beyond the amount saved or invested that individuals consider adequate compensation for forgone consumption. Clearly, the size of this increment will vary with both circumstances and attitudes. Demographic changes may reduce the need for new investment, and times of war or collective hardship may increase the moral incentive to defer consumption.

As we are employing the term, *capital requirements* has two components: the morally required provision for future generations (the "just savings" rate); and the amount, over and above just savings, needed to finance desirable increases in production. In a sense, the amount required for just savings does not really belong to any member of the current generation, so that it may be reclaimed, for example, through taxation, without either interest or compensation for principal. The second component, surplus investment, is in no sense a moral requirement, since within a broad range no morally proper balance between consumption and investment can be determined. Here, the rate of interest serves to bring into balance the schemes of entrepreneurs and the propensity to save.

But let us probe a little deeper. Capital will be demanded only when the demander believes that it can be deployed productively. Joan Robinson states the conditions clearly:

> By using labour and means of production in the present to produce equipment it is possible to make a permanent net increase per man in the future—that is to say, the excess of the output of a given number of men employed in the future when using the ad-

ditional equipment, over what it would have been without it, is sufficient to provide for the renewal of the equipment when it wears out and something extra as well.[25]

Now let us suppose that in a particular case the increase in output is enough to cover the costs of depreciation and to repay the initial loan, with something left over. Who is entitled to the surplus? Usually this surplus is seen as the source of interest, but, as Jan Pen points out, this is in no way necessary. That is, the distribution of the net product of capital need not be correlated with the initial source of capital; unlike interest, the net productivity of capital is characteristic of all forms of economic organization.[26]

Here Robinson's remarks are illuminating. She dismisses the familiar claim that interest can be understood as the "reward of waiting."

An individual who has lent to a safe debtor has merely to allow time to pass to gather in his agreed interest. Does this correspond to a technical productiveness of the passage of time? Where natural processes are at work, as in the maturing of wine or the growth of trees, production takes place through time, without any expenditure of labour. If all production were of this kind we should be in the land of Cockaigne. Generally production requires work to be done; work takes time, but time does not do work.[27]

Rather,

Present purchasing power is valuable partly because, under the capitalist rules of the game, it permits its owner (directly or by lending to a business concern) to employ labour and undertake production which will yield a surplus of receipts over costs. In an economy in which the rate of profit is expected to be positive, the rate of interest is positive.[28]

As Robinson seems to suggest, this merely pushes the problem back one step. The capital provider's contribution to the joint product (at least in circumstances of no risk and 0 percent inflation) is precisely equal to the amount of capital provided. *Ex hypothesi*, he contributes no inventions, no entrepreneurial schemes, no physical effort. Prima facie, it would seem appropriate to repay the capital provider out of the joint product and then to divide the residuum among inventor, entrepreneur, and worker. There should, in short, be no unclaimed profit out of which interest could be paid.

There is, I suspect, only one way of blocking this argument. The net productivity of capital implies that investment leads to an expansion of goods and services available for distribution and consumption. The question, then, is how this increase is to be divided. If the rate of interest is high enough, the capital provider may actually claim more than the amount of the increase, and someone else will be forced to accept an absolute decline in his standard of living. But if the rate is too low, the propensity to consume will dominate, the investment will not occur, and all will be worse off. Intuitively, then, the just interest rate is that range within which all participants in the productive process have a share in the benefits of investment. Put slightly differently: the just interest rate ought to be viewed as the outcome of a bargaining process in which the agreement of every participant is required. Since the capital provider contributes nothing except forgone consumption, the best outcome is one in which the rate of interest is barely sufficient to induce investment.

Clearly, the propensity to consume is not a fixed fact of human nature. In addition to personal variations, it is affected by memories, expectations, inducement, and persuasion. Political communities ought to use education and public rhetoric to establish reasonable norms for saving. A social and economic climate that encourages unrestrained consumption runs the risk of driving up the cost of capital and shifting a greater portion of the net product of capital away from producers.

It may be argued that to ignore risk is to eliminate the key to the explanation of interest. Within the context of my discussion, it is reasonable to deemphasize risk: Individuals agree, at least in general, about what they want, and incomes are determined primarily by rational standards rather than supply and demand for different kinds of ability and levels of skill. But even within a competitive capitalist economy, I would argue, risk as an independent variable adds little to the understanding or moral evaluation of interest.

Consider first a game of chance in which the odds of success and payout ratios of the different alternatives are known. Individuals are quite willing to make gambles in spite of the fact that the overall return on the gambles, taken together, is never more than—in fact usually less than—the sum of the gambles. That is, the "interest" associated with gambling is either zero or negative. Thus, although the possibility of gain must be present to induce individuals to take risks, it does not follow that there must be an overall gain. Transfers from losers to winners are sufficient to keep the system in motion.

Now consider a game in which the odds of success and the payout ratios are not fully known. The difference between this game and the preceding one corresponds closely to Frank Knight's classic distinction between risk and uncertainty,[29] and it mirrors the essential features of most actual investment situations. Now, as Knight points out, the calculus of decision is the same as in the first game. The difference is that in the second, our comparison of the various alternatives is preceded by a subjective estimate of the probability of various outcomes. From the standpoint of the capital provider, the economy as a whole may be regarded as a game of the second sort. The subjective estimates of the winning players are fulfilled or more than fulfilled by events, while the hopes of the losers go unfulfilled.

We may grant that the winners deserve something beyond their original investment. They have expended, not only forgone consumption, but also effort and intelligence to contrive a realistic vision of future events. Of course, they may simply have gotten lucky. This happens frequently in politics. A leader will embark on a policy venture for indistinct or flatly mistaken reasons and then will reap the rewards of purported wisdom and foresight when it happens to prosper. But it is difficult to be lucky for very long. Someone who succeeds repeatedly is almost sure to possess many of the elements of prudence.

It is not clear, though, why the move from risk to uncertainty means that the overall return on capital should go from zero to positive.

The component of interest derived from uncertainty will be positive in the aggregate only if investors as a whole attach excessively low estimates of success to the various alternatives with which they are confronted. That is to say, there is an inverse relation between interest and the level of confidence. If confidence, though always subject to change, fluctuated around the line representing aggregate results, the rate of interest required to compensate for uncertainty would be zero.

There is, however, an important difference between ordinary gambling and the economy game. In gambling, the winners are paid by the losers, and wealth is neither created nor destroyed. But one form of economic loss occurs when the imprudent investor induces others to use their labor and materials to build equipment that makes things no one wants (the Edsel). Real goods have been squandered and cannot be transferred to the prudent investor. Thus, the rewards of prudence must come from the net product of investment.

This analysis suggests that there are two components of investment: pure capital provision, and the evaluation of opportunities. The claims of the capital provider are limited to the minimum needed to balance the propensity to consume and to compensate for perceived risk. The evaluation of opportunities is one aspect of entrepreneurship—the bringing together of different factors of production to generate an increase in available goods. It is, to be sure, somewhat passive. Typically, the prospective investor will read a prospectus that others have prepared. Still, this is a real contribution; the tempering of enthusiasm with skepticism weeds out many dubious ideas. The evaluator thus has some claim on the net product of his investment. Pure capital provision, on the other hand, is exemplified by the decision of individuals to contribute a percentage of their incomes to a pool of capital from which investments will be made by others, for example, pension funds.

Second: One of the advantages of this analysis is that it furnishes a reasonably clear line between capital provision and *entrepreneurship*. For our purposes, the entrepreneur will be viewed as an individual furnishing his time, effort, experience, and intelligence to coordinate factors of production so as to increase net productivity. While granting Hobhouse's caveat, it seems arbitrary to deny that the entrepreneur contributes to the formation of the net product and has a reasonable claim to some portion of it. But how is the extent of the just claim to be determined?

We already know that the entrepreneur's claims are limited in three ways. First, he is but one participant in the production of the net product. He cannot claim so much that one or more of the other participants is worse off than in the absence of the cooperative endeavor. Second, although some substitutions are possible, the net product will require some capital investment. The entrepreneur cannot claim so much that potential investors are offered less than their minimal incentive. *Ex hypothesi*, simple self-interest would prevent the entrepreneur from making such a claim deliberately, or from holding to it once he discovered his error. Third, claims based on need have priority over those based on desert, of which the principle of contribution forms a part. Thus, the entrepreneur can legitimately claim, not the whole of the net product minus the cost of capital, but only the residuum after provision for the needs of all involved in the productive process.

We may go further. Suppose someone invents an exciting new device, and two aspiring entrepreneurs, A and B, come up with competing schemes for producing it. Assume that A's has a net product of x, greater than B's y. If A's scheme is put into practice, A cannot claim to have contributed, or to be responsible for x, but only $x - y$. Conversely, the adoption of B's scheme (through nepotism, say) would actually cost the participants $x - y$; B's contribution is negative, since in effect he has led the collectivity to forgo advantages it could reasonably have hoped to procure for itself.

Third: The same principle may be applied to *management and organization*. It may be better to have the owner's son as vice-president than no one at all, but the son is making a negative contribution if there are other feasible candidates who could do the job more competently. Defining the set of feasible alternatives against which individual contributions can be measured is necessarily imprecise. In general, though,

if the costs of the search procedure appear low in relation to the esti-
mated benefits of more competent performance, the set of alternatives
has been unwisely restricted.

Finally, it seems counterintuitive that the claims of entrepreneurs and
managers should be proportional to total net contribution. Suppose that
the manager of a large firm devises a more efficient system of production, raising output from 100 to 105 units, while the manager of a small
firm succeeds in raising output from 10 to 11 units. The second manager
has contributed more, has had a better idea; the total effects of the first
manager's mediocre scheme have been magnified by the circumstances
of its implementation, and it is difficult to see why he should receive
any credit for these circumstances. Similar considerations apply within
firms. Suppose that a manager finds a way of reorganizing production,
raising output from 100 to 105 units, while an individual worker finds a
way of increasing his own from 1 to 1.1 units. The manager's position of
authority makes it possible for him to magnify the effects of his idea,
but "positional magnification" seems irrelevant to questions of contribution or desert. From this standpoint, it would be fairest to have a
box marked "Production Innovations" into which ideas are dropped
anonymously, with some system for subsequently matching ideas with
contributors. At the end of a reasonable period, the ideas would be
evaluated, the best implemented, and the contributors rewarded in line
with their relative contribution, whatever their official position.

Fourth: As I shall use the term, *invention* denotes an idea that contributes to the human good by either creating new kinds of means or
increasing the supply of existing means. Obviously, no hard-and-fast
line can be drawn between invention and management, although there
are clear cases. It is customary to view the innovative idea as the inventor's property; for some fixed period, all other individuals are debarred from making use of the idea without the inventor's consent. This
practice rests, it would seem, on the imperfect benevolence of most of
us. If contribution to human welfare were a sufficient reward, no inventor would hold his idea as property; he would accept only compensation for the time and effort he needed to perfect his idea. Analo-
gously, professors who cared only about advancing human knowledge
would demand neither copyrights nor footnoted acknowledgments.
Not only is perfect benevolence very rare, but also, the principle of
contribution gives the inventor a claim to a reasonable portion of the
benefits others may derive from his achievement. The inventor seeks to
realize this claim in one of two ways: by becoming an entrepreneur and
assembling labor and capital to produce copies of the idea; or by transferring the rights to his idea to an entrepreneur, in return for a fixed

sum or some percentage of the advantage the entrepreneur hopes to reap.

This gives rise to an apparent anomaly. If an idea promotes human well-being, it seems undesirable to restrict its use. If manufacturer A can employ an idea to produce a new good or more of an old one, then unless A can produce the full amount needed, all would be better off if B and C were allowed to employ it as well. The problem, of course, is that what is a gain from the standpoint of consumers is not necessarily one for producers. In a capitalist economy, at least, A benefits by lowering costs or increasing market share; but if B and C have access to the idea, no producer benefits. Indeed, under many investment circumstances, all three will lose. But if so, no one will have any incentive to make use of the idea, and consumers will be worse off than if A had exclusive rights to it. Usually, proponents of capitalism go on to claim that the comparison of the package, innovative A plus stodgy B and C, with the ideal "socialist" package of equally diffused innovation is misleading in two ways. First, innovative A is likely, if unchecked, to drive B and C out of business, diffusing the benefits of the innovation through market expansion. But second, B and C have every reason to seek to avert this catastrophe and, unless A chooses not to exploit his advantage, the only reliable means is to come up with superior innovations of their own. The system of exclusive rights thus leads to technological leap-frogging, increasing the overall pace of innovation and benefiting everyone. Clearly, though, there is a balance to be struck. If, to take an extreme example, exclusive rights were perpetual and further innovation hard to come by, the economy as a whole would be the poorer, by the amount of production forgone during the time it took A to wipe out competitors.

Thus, we may see patents—transferable exclusive rights of inventors—as the outcome of two different considerations. They provide the inventor with a way of bargaining for a reasonable share of the contribution he makes. At the same time, they provide the entrepreneur with something to bargain for. Even if inventors had the right to transfer their patents nonexclusively, they would quickly discover that in most circumstances no one would be willing to bid for them on that basis.

In determining the inventor's contribution, net product is a reasonable point of departure. Consider a new machine with the following characteristics: It can raise the output of some good from 100 to 105 units per year; it will last one year before needing replacement; and the labor and materials needed to produce the machine would be sufficient to produce 5 units per year of the good in question. Given these assumptions, we may conclude that the net contribution of the machine is zero.

Moreover, when a net contribution exists, it is necessary to consider the claims of those other than the successful inventor. Suppose that A and B have been working, independently of one another, on very similar projects for ten years and that A achieves success one month before B. From the standpoint of equity, it seems wrong to give A exclusive rights to the invention, since this would nullify B's efforts altogether. If B were on the wrong track, or so far behind A that it could not be determined whether he would ever succeed, then B's efforts need not be taken into account. In practice, of course, there will frequently be no alternative to the recognition of A's exclusive claims, but it is very hard to defend the theoretical proposition that the first to complete the technological race should win the entire prize.

A difficulty with the purely competitive determination of contribution is that it may not correspond with net contribution. Suppose that after an extended period of technological stagnation, A achieves a breakthrough that enables production to double from 50 to 100 units. After a brief lag, A's device sweeps the field. A year later, B comes up with a new approach that increases production from 100 to 110. One firm breaks rank and buys B's device; the rest are compelled to follow suit. If, as frequently happens, the price of A's device cannot be lowered enough to make it competitive, A ceases to get any royalties at all; and B is treated as though he has made a net contribution of 110 units rather than the actual 10. Thus, the rewards of innovation in a competitive system are much more closely tied to the pace of change than to the increment of change per stage.[30] Winner-take-all seems especially objectionable when an innovator builds on the efforts of those who have gone before.

The exclusiveness of the inventor's right presents another kind of difficulty. Suppose that A is granted such a right for his device and then decides, mistakenly, that its production would decrease human welfare. Until someone else comes forward with an equivalent or better idea, all—with the possible exception of A—pay a penalty. This seems absurd. The inventor has a claim to a share of what he contributes, but the patent is merely a technique for harnessing the individual's claim to the public benefit. In A's case, the reasons underlying the initial grant of control may justify withdrawing it, although it may be judged that the general benefits of the system are large enough so that the gains derived from making exceptions are not worth the risk of reducing confidence in the system as a whole.

All these difficulties may suggest to some that the entire notion of invention as personal property, linked in some fashion with net product, is a basic mistake. Consider the most plausible alternative: The political community constructs an "Inventors' Center" and provides its self-selected denizens with basic needs, leisure, raw materials, and equipment. Inventors are rewarded on a piecework basis: every invention that contributes a net product is credited to the individual's account, and some formal indices of importance are employed. The average inventor, generating one or two useful ideas every year, is able to live considerably better than the average inhabitant of the community, but by present standards the difference is quite modest. We may define the net contribution of the inventors as the difference between their net product and the rewards they reap.

Now, net contribution, so defined, may be determined, at least approximately, for competitive as well as collectivized systems. In comparing different forms of economic organization, it is not enough to compare observed rates of technological change. The aggregate costs of this change must be considered as well. It seems intuitively probable that the invention rate of the collectivized system will be notably lower than that of the more competitive. But if, beyond some point, the inventor's marginal reward exceeds the marginal product that it evokes, then the higher rate of change as well as the inventor are being counterproductively and unjustifiably subsidized by others—usually by those engaged in production rather than by the entrepreneur or the capital provider.

Incentives

The final determinant of income distribution is the system of selective incentives needed to bring about the performance of useful functions. As we noted earlier, incentives should not be confused with compensations. Compensation is determined relative to the level of real good sacrificed during the performance of a task, even if the worker does not perceive the sacrifice, while incentives are relative to individual attitudes towards particular tasks. Thus, incentive levels are highly sensitive to differences in education, moral belief, and patterns of respect and contempt. If a regime succeeds in persuading its citizens that the performance of certain unpleasant tasks is a moral duty, it can significantly decrease its reliance on material incentives. Similarly, an increase in the prestige or respect accorded a task will usually increase the "psychic income" derived from it, making possible a reduced reliance on material incentives. Of course, this would not occur in a community in which the prestige of tasks was directly proportional to the personal income associated with them.

Although I cannot prove it, it seems likely that there is a natural hierarchy of respect and prestige, independent of training and income, partly correlated with judgments of intrinsic worth of activities. Tasks involving scarce traits of mind and character or the ability to direct the activities of others successfully are widely prized by both those performing them and others. If true, this strongly suggests that the higher income generally associated with such tasks cannot be justified as an incentive. One suspects, that is, that in moments of candor most business executives, doctors, generals, and college professors would admit that they would want to continue their activities even at considerably lower income levels.[31]

Intuitively, incentives are just only in the context of a system of production judged from other standpoints to be just. Consider, for example, a young person who excels as both a scientist and an athlete. In a system in which the income of professional athletes has reached absurd levels, the income incentive required to induce this person to undertake a scientific career would be very considerable. It seems far more reasonable to conclude that the context within which such an incentive becomes necessary is unjust than to concede the justice of the incentive. To be sure, others may benefit enough from the incentive that there is a good reason to provide it; but justice in the full sense requires that incentives be determined relative to incomes that are fair and proportionate in other respects.

In addition, a given incentive level is unjustified unless all individuals capable of performing the task are taken into account. The fact that A requires an incentive of x to do the work in itself means nothing, for we need to know what incentives would be demanded by all other individuals as competent as A. Clearly, it is best to find the individual willing to accept the lowest incentive, since, *ex hypothesi*, the only justification for incentives is to promote the performance of useful functions. This is not to say that incomes as a whole should be determined by the lowest bids, but only the component of incomes constituted by incentives.

A general theory of income distribution

This completes our review of the principles that bear on income distribution. The problem that now confronts us is to combine them into a coherent theory.

A system of production is a way of organizing human beings and natural objects to produce the human good or means to it. Income is a claim on these products. It may take the form of a specific claim (food stamps, ration coupons) or a general claim (money). The total income of those involved in production cannot justly equal total production. At least some nonproducers, for example, children, must be provided for, and portions of the product must be set aside to cover depreciation and the real though unpresented claims of future generations.

At first glance it might appear that the most desirable distribution of income is the one that maximizes net production, the difference between total production and depreciation. (Depreciation is here used to include depletion of natural resources as well as the aging of plant and equipment.) But this is to forget that the means to the good does not produce human good unless it is attached to individuals. Principles of justice are principles of attachment or linkage. In the sphere of income distribution, they operate in two ways. First, the same means may do more to promote A's good than B's. The principle of need, supplemented by a rank-order of urgency among needs, reflects this fact and delimits the sphere within which it is decisive. Second, justice is concerned in part with a relational good—the appropriateness of A's having some good thing, A's "desert." The principle of contribution or participation reflects this. Most means to the good do not fall to the ground for instant appropriation like manna; they must be produced. Ceteris paribus, contributing to production increases desert, in proportion to the extent of the contribution. The most desirable distribution of income, then, maximizes net production, subject to two constraints: the gratification of needs, and the recognition of contribution.

As we have noted before, the first of these is a *prior* constraint. If the sum of needs is precisely equal to net production, the prima facie case for devoting all resources to their satisfaction is very strong. Individual needs cannot be lightly sacrificed.

There are two common objections to this position. First, assigning priority to the satisfaction of needs decreases the incentive to contribute to production, raising the possibility that everyone will be worse off. This problem, though real, is not as serious as it might appear. Moral or civic education can go a long way toward replacing the efficacy of the threat, "If you don't work, you won't eat." Within families, at least, the moral worth of contributing what one is able can be taught very effectively. This principle can also provide a basis for selective moral sanctions; the noncontributor who receives the scorn or disapproval of the other members of his group will usually shape up quickly. But, also, there is no good reason to believe that making a contribution, participating in a common endeavor must be forced on human beings against their inclinations, that is, that they are naturally lazy and shameless. On the contrary, there is a general though not universal propensity to contribute. This can be understood as both absolute—as a natural pleasure in organized activity—and as relative, as the natural belief that elementary reciprocity is violated by a regular policy of taking from others, decreasing their well-being, without giving what one can in return. This natural propensity can be weakened by disgust at the small minority of free riders and by the intrinsic unpleasantness of the contribution one is asked to make. The force of disgust can be reduced by the application of moral sanctions; at least the contributors will know that the free riders "aren't getting away with it." The unpleasantness of the contribution can be reduced by the belief that the productive system as a whole is fair and by a coordinated effort to strive for the best possible fit between the characteristics of specific productive tasks and the abilities and propensities of those asked to perform them.

Second, it is sometimes alleged that the needs of some individuals may justly go unfulfilled if this policy increases the well-being of future generations. To evaluate this allegation, we must look at specific cases. Suppose we are dealing with a steady-state economy, producing only enough so that if its members consume what they need and save the rest, future generations will be able to do so as well, but no progress will ever take place. The members of the earlier generation are in no way obligated to reduce their level of consumption; although they may choose to do so, it would be unjust to force them to. But if the steady state is well below the level of need gratification, then some additional measure of deprivation may be necessary and appropriate, and it may not be possible to carry out this policy through persuasion. Here, needs are denied in the name of other needs. This is compatible with the principle of the priority of needs. Of course, specific policies of development may allocate the burdens of deprivation unreasonably. The notion of relative urgency comes into play here. If some deprivation cannot be avoided, then the most urgent physical needs of everyone must be given priority. In general, if N_2 is less urgent than N_1, no one's N_2 should be satisfied until everyone's N_1 has been attended to. As we have seen, in circumstances of extreme scarcity some sort of lottery may be unavoidable, since otherwise equal satisfaction of needs will lead to the death of all.

But suppose that an economic system generates more than enough to satisfy needs.[32] The problem then is to allocate the surplus between the recognition of contribution and incentives to increase production.

The first step is to determine how the surplus would be distributed among individuals if all of it were determined by the contribution principle, that is, if none were used for incentives. I suggest that the use of incentives be subject to the constraint that no one receive less under an incentive system than he would have in the "baseline" system operating without incentive payments. Clearly, this is possible only if the production increase generated by the incentives is greater than or equal to the sum of the incentives. If not, some will be subsidizing the incentives of others.

This condition is intuitively plausible. Incentives are self-contradictory if their marginal product is less than their costs; the point is to increase production for the benefit of all, not only of the recipient of the incentive. It is of some theoretical interest to consider the case in which increased production is exactly equal to the incentive. On the one hand, the recipients of the incentive are better off and no one else is worse off. From the standpoint of individual well-being, this outcome seems clearly preferable to the situation that would prevail with no incentives. On the other hand, nonrecipients are likely to regard it as unfair that recipients have improved their position, absolutely and relatively, through an institution unrelated to personal desert and justified only on grounds of general utility.

These considerations suggest that to be socially effective and accepted, a system of incentives must be fair, especially in the cases in which the increase of production is known in advance to be equal to the amount of the incentive. Suppose, for example, that a tenant farmer is allowed to keep for himself all of what he grows above a certain quota. It would be not only unproductive but arbitrary to deny this same incentive to all other farmers similarly situated.

Distribution of the incentive surplus is somewhat indeterminate theoretically. If contribution is understood as relative, then the distribution of the surplus ought to be done in such a way as to leave the relative shares of all contributors unaffected. If contribution is viewed as absolute, then after all contribution claims have been satisfied, the residuum is an unclaimed collective asset, to be used in accordance with a collective determination. Since the possibility of production in excess of total contribution stems from the fact that the natural materials on which man works are not, in the last analysis, a human contribution, it might be most prudent to regard the residuum as a depletion allowance. But this is neither necessary nor obligatory.

6.2.b. Property

Property is an elliptical term, and its employment as an unadorned noun is at best indistinct. Hobhouse plausibly argued that to have property in x is to have a "recognized power of control" over x.[33] As he noted, control is multidimensional. It is necessary, then, to specify the respects in which control is recognized. To have absolute property in x is to have absolute control over the disposition of x in all conceivable respects— that is, regardless of situation or purpose.

6. The Nature of the Just Community

It is wholly sensible to speak of collective property. Such property arises when two or more individuals are recognized as having joint control over something. Joint control does not imply equal control, though it is compatible with it. Collective property may be conjoined with the full range of decisionmaking procedures.

Private and collective property are simply two different forms of control. The antithesis of property is a situation in which no control over things is generally recognized. This is likely to be tolerable only when the good in question is unlimited and easily obtained. In circumstances of scarcity, the absence of recognized control will lead to disputes, frequently of the violent and bloody variety. The struggles of very young children over toys give us a glimpse of this world.

In one sense, property appears to be superfluous to a theory of justice. Just property is nothing but rationally warranted control. In a community in which all share and recognize the same rational principles, no independent theory of property would be necessary or possible. To say that x is A's property would be a kind of shorthand for: A's control over x in the respects in question is rationally warranted. From this standpoint, property is nothing but the crystallization of shared judgments, coupled with the reminder that harm may legitimately be inflicted on anyone who disregards them.

In another sense, though, the theory of property is a distinctive division of an overall theory of justice. Generally, though not invariably, property is thought of as composed of objects that endure for a considerable time. This reflects a general distinction between objects that are consumed and objects that are used. A consumption-object benefits us only by being used up, ingested, transformed, or destroyed. A use-object confers benefits while remaining what it was, separable and unchanged. Of course, use-objects wear out. But this is because they are formed matter, hence transitory. The ideal or perfect use-object would never wear out; a consumption item that did not change would be worthless. Indigestible food is precisely that which our metabolic processes cannot transform appropriately, that which resists alteration.[34]

Property, then, is a beneficial durable good—as Aristotle put it, a tool or instrument, separable from its possessor, and useful for the purposes of living.[35] Property-claims are attempts to establish control in the present over means to some future good. It is the attempt to bind the future that makes property-claims so disputable. There is very little uncertainty, assuming good information, when someone asks for food now to stave off imminent starvation. But when someone lays claim to a tool, house, or plot of land on the basis of present facts or present estimates of future facts, a latent tension is built into the relation between man and thing. On the one hand, if property-claims must be endlessly reassessed in the light of changing conditions, individuals cannot plan for the future, since they do not know whether they will control the means required for a contemplated course of action. On the other hand, if property-claims are not open to reassessment, they will at some point lose their rational warrant and come to rest either on direct coercion or tacitly coercive tradition. This is the case for *any* theory of property offering as bases for just holdings reasons that extend to facts or circumstances other than those prevailing at the instant of acquisition. Nozick concedes that property justly held at time t_0 may become illegitimate or restricted at t_1 because of changes over which the owner had no control. Some of your rights disappear if every water hole except yours dries up.[36]

As Hobhouse noted, the question of whether property should be private or collective cannot be answered in a blanket or a priori manner. Our view will be affected, not only by the functions or purposes of different kinds of property, but also by changes of circumstance— famine, war, depression. Nevertheless, arguments familiar since Aristotle's critique of Plato's *Republic* support the conclusion that a significant fraction of property ought to be held privately. First, private ownership is a source of pleasure, since it is an outgrowth of the natural and ineradicable love we bear toward ourselves. Private and civic education must seek to moderate self-love, but it is visionary to build social policy on the hope that citizens can be led to care for others as much as they care for themselves. A system that allows for no private property would lead to permanent dissatisfaction. Second, we are individuals, not only separate but also different. Social policy must seek to harmonize these differences, since it would be neither beneficial nor possible to eliminate them. Each of us uses property to express and minister to his individuality with a precision and sensitivity that no collective mechanism could duplicate, even if it sincerely wished to do so. By choosing and arranging objects, each of us creates an environment within which his tasks can be comfortably performed and individual projects undertaken with the least possible obstruction. The reduction of our ability to create some congruence between ourselves and our immediate world is such a significant loss that it is unlikely to be counterbalanced by any other benefits. Even during the inevitable "deprivatization" that occurs in military service, soldiers insist on the right to deploy various personal effects to express their origins, desires, and hopes and to create a reflection, however pale, of home. Third, it is natural to care more for what is wholly one's own, as an extension of oneself. This leads to conservation and decreased depreciation. We are lavish in spending time and effort to keep up the house we have struggled to buy; if placed in a public housing project, we tend to be less scrupulous about maintaining it. And even if we care about common property, there is a temptation to hope that others will relieve us of the burden of caring for it and that our own shirking will not have noticeable effects. The number of free riders multiplies and the property deteriorates. Fourth, private property tends to lead to greater production, for two reasons: individuals work harder when they are working for themselves (productivity on the small private plots of Russian peasants is enormously higher than on collective farms with identical soil and climate); and collective ownership can lead to time-consuming disputes and bitterness if some feel that they are making a greater than average contribution without being commensurately rewarded.

On what may valid claims to property be based? The most illuminating point of departure is the Lockean state of nature. If we suppose that raw materials are plentiful and accessible to all, then an individual's claim to x stems from his having "mixed his labor" with x. Suppose that A, alone in a vast forest, chops down trees and builds a cabin. If B comes along and demands the cabin, A may reasonably reply that nothing is preventing B from building his own. Cabins come into being only through labor; B's demand amounts to the claim that A should labor *for him*. In the absence of other considerations, this claim is groundless. Moreover, A's labor is a portion of his overall activity, and there is an intimate connection between activity and existence or identity. What we are is in large measure what we do. As crystallized or reified labor, the cabin is in part an extension of A's being. It is his *own* to the extent that anything is. Indeed, there is no distinction between A's cabin and A's body, since physical survival requires the continual appropriation and transformation of natural materials. A's labor is not creation *ex nihilo*; the cabin that embodies labor is not wholly the product of labor. But there is no way of separating these components, any more than Shylock could take flesh without blood. Thus, B cannot expropriate the cabin, somehow leaving behind A's labor. Even if he could, he would not, for then the expropriation would lose its point. The residue would be nothing but the raw material to which B already has easy access.

As Locke noted, appropriation through labor is limited even in circumstances of nonscarcity. We must be able to *use* the products of our labor to some advantage before they spoil or decay. If A chops down ten acres of trees and uses one tenth of them to build his cabin, leaving the other nine tenths rotting on the ground, the remainder is not his, even though he mixed his labor with it. When we are dealing with natural objects, unmediated by permanent stores of value, our appropriation must make sense, must promote our good.

Locke's nonscarcity proviso is two-sided. Positively, it rests on the plausible principle that any act that benefits some without harming anyone is desirable and permissible. Negatively, it prohibits acts of appropriation that harm anyone, whatever benefits may accrue to the appropriator. This seems more controversial. If trees are in short supply, why may *A* not use them to build a shelter even if this prevents *B* from adding a ballroom to his existing shelter? It is impossible to be sure, but I suggest that Locke saw the nonscarcity proviso—and indeed the entire question of "original acquisition" of unowned objects—as operating in the context in which individuals are striving to fulfill urgent needs. Certainly the examples he gave—centering as they do on food and clothing—support this interpretation. Further, he explicitly argued (on empirical grounds) that if acquisition is restricted to what we can use to further our good, the prohibition against harm will never be violated:

> This I dare boldly affirm—that the same rule of property, viz., that every man should have as much as he could make use of, would hold still in the world without straitening anybody, . . . had not the invention of money and the tacit agreement of men to put a value on it introduced—by consent—larger possessions and a right to them.[37]

And, finally, he suggested that the abrogation of the use criterion and the legitimation of acquisition in times of scarcity, brought about by the invention of money, are consistent with the prohibition against harm, *if* harm is interpreted to mean "deprivation of means to the human good." The increased productivity made possible by the liberation of acquisition redounds to the benefit of everyone: "A king of a large and fruitful territory [in America] feeds, lodges, and is clad worse than a day-laborer in England."[38] Everyone consents to the invention of money, for everyone benefits from it. It is hardly accidental that limitations on unrestricted property rights began to emerge in the wake of the early Industrial Revolution; the English "day-laborer" began to wonder, with considerable justice, whether he was better off than the pre-Columbian denizens of America—let alone his own father and grandfather.

Locke's attempt to fix a "baseline"[39] in terms of need-satisfaction seems unsatisfactory. The way of life of the laborer includes, not only what he receives in wages, but also what he must do to obtain them. The worth of the way of life is equal to the worth of the wages *minus* the effort, sacrifice, and pain of labor. Thus, if subsistence "in America" requires less effort to obtain than the wages needed to purchase an equivalent standard of living in England, the English laborer may be worse off, even if his basket of available goods is larger than the American's. The question then arises: What quantity of material goods constitutes adequate compensation, such that the laborer is not made worse off by the system within which he toils? To the extent that a determinate answer is possible, it surely depends on a much fuller theory of the human good than Locke presented. One might try to take, as a proxy for such a theory, the wages the laborer would accept if confronted with a choice between life in England and in America. But the choice situation must be carefully defined. It is one thing if peasants leave the land for the city in search of better opportunities, quite another if they are expelled at gunpoint. If a large percentage of the urban labor force is present involuntarily, prevailing wage rates prove little about the relative desirability of the different ways of life.

Nozick's failure to ask why Locke introduced the nonscarcity proviso makes it difficult for him to deal sensibly with cases that fall outside the letter of the proviso. He insists, for example, that a researcher who synthesizes a lifesaving drug out of plentiful raw materials is under no obligation to share it with others except on the terms he finds agreeable.[40] If A, suffering from a curable disease, does not have the amount of money that the researcher demands, the researcher is not obliged, hence cannot be forced, to save him from dying. But since the point of the nonscarcity proviso is to ensure that no one is prevented from fulfilling basic needs as the result of another's action, the researcher is as culpable as the person who appropriates the last water hole and refuses to share it.

Another line of argument leads to the same conclusion. Nozick argues that property, once justly acquired, can be transferred only through voluntary transactions. Let us set aside other objections and ask: What is a voluntary transaction? If a robber puts a gun to your head and says, "Your money or your life," we are somewhat reluctant to describe the ensuing transfer of funds as a voluntary transaction, even though in the strict sense you chose to do so, could have done otherwise. But the researcher is telling you exactly what the robber did. There is, of course, the difference that, whereas the robber threatens to inflict harm on you that you otherwise would not have undergone, the researcher threatens to withhold a good, allowing you to undergo the harm that would have been your lot without him. I do not wish to deny that the obligation not to harm others is considerably broader than the obligation to benefit them. But this is irrelevant, given Nozick's argument, in situations that inherently obstruct the possibility of voluntary agreement. It would be going too far to stipulate that voluntary transactions can occur only between individuals who enjoy near parity in bargaining power. But if, for all practical purposes, A cannot do without some good that only B can provide, then no real bargaining can occur: A is at B's mercy, and B can extract whatever he chooses from A. Thus, those who considered a situation unjust in which individual workers confronted a corporate employer were not necessarily questioning the principle of voluntary transactions, but only denying that real bargaining and voluntary agreement were possible under such circumstances.

In the course of an argument against Henry George, John Ryan brings to light an important ambiguity in Locke's theory of original acquisition. Consider any plentiful, unowned natural resource. By mixing our labor with it, we transform it in some significant respect: spatially, as when we carry water from a common well; or formally, as when we use trees to build a cabin. "Mixing" is not instantaneous, however, but rather a temporal process with a definite beginning. The process cannot begin at all unless we appropriate something that we have not yet transformed. This appropriation occurs through *occupation* of the unowned or, more generally, by *laying claim* to it.[41] Thus, Locke was right to say that "it is the taking any part of what is common and removing it out of the state nature leaves it in which begins property."[42] But he was mistaken in insisting that labor was the sole or even primary mode of removal.

The distinction between labor and occupation as titles to property seems warranted theoretically. There are, however, reasons to believe that the differences are not as great as they might appear. First, as Ryan notes, the limits of just occupation are established by the extent of what we can use. In practice, then, occupation does not increase the total of an individual's just claims, since the occupation limit is the same as the labor limit. Second, occupation is in many respects a provisional claim. If we, for example, occupy a plot of land but never live on it or make any effort to improve it, our title becomes suspect. Many states give individuals an opportunity to acquire title to public land through occupation, with the proviso that they improve the property to a certain degree. Occupation gives us the right to use, but if we do not exercise that right, it atrophies. Third, it is difficult to establish a clear line between "occupying x" and "mixing one's labor with x." Usually, the establishment of occupation requires physical proximity and some specific gesture or sign: we must drive the stake, build the fence, raise the flag. If this were not so, each of us could lay claim to the universe with equal legitimacy.[43] As ordinarily understood, then, occupation requires a certain degree of transformative effort. Conversely, labor never transforms the raw material completely. Some of it is left untouched, and the rest is unchanged in many respects.

This discussion has provided us with the elements we need for a general theory of just property. Claims to unowned materials are

6. The Nature of the Just Community

founded on labor or occupation. But the extent of these claims is limited by the needs of others. As we saw, this was the most sensible interpretation of Locke's nonscarcity proviso. Our just claims are also limited by our ability to make use of what we appropriate. We are not entitled to huge tracts of fallow land or heaps of rotting fruit. The criterion of use points in another direction as well. If we can in principle use x for our benefit but actually use it to harm ourselves or others, our property-claim is weakened. If A strongly suspects that B is about to use B's gun to commit murder, A may justifiably restrict B's control over the gun by hiding it, locking it up, refusing to return it. If B is about to commit suicide, the argument tends in the same direction, though with more room for dispute. In general, whenever A is justified in preventing B from doing harm to himself, A is justified in depriving B of the means without which the harm cannot be inflicted. This amounts to a restriction of property-claims, since, as we saw at the outset, property is best understood as warranted control.

What then of the famous story in which Xenophon represented the young Cyrus as approving a large boy's forcible exchange of his small coat for the large coat of a small boy? Cyrus was certainly wrong to treat the fact of ownership as morally negligible. On the other hand, if we suppose that the small boy could make no use of the large coat, then Cyrus may well have been correct. And even if the small boy could use it to a certain extent, circumstances could arise in which the forcible transfer was justified. Suppose, for example, that the two boys are caught in a blizzard. The large boy knows that if the coats are exchanged, both boys will survive; if not, both will die of exposure. If the small boy does not know this, would a forcible exchange be wrong? And if neither knows it, would a third party be wrong to carry it out?

Hume's discussion of this story raises the two most significant objections to my line of argument. First, in the long run the economic disruption and uncertainty produced by such forced exchanges will leave everyone worse off. Second, the utility of the forced exchange depends on the wisdom and fairness of the party applying the force, and it would be foolish to presuppose this in very many cases.[44] The first point seems empirically dubious, at least as a generalization. If members of a community understand in advance that they may from time to time be taxed to help other members who have been victimized by natural disasters, this uncertainty can be factored into their economic decisions. Even if some reduction of efficiency takes place, this may be a reasonable price to pay to avert catastrophic harm. The benevolent taxing power may even be able to convince them that in the long run the transfer is in their interest as well. If we suppose that, given adequate information and powers of understanding, participants in an involuntary exchange would consent, then the use of force ceases to be so distasteful. What are the moral claims of ignorance?

Hume's second point has great practical weight. The power of compulsion is very likely to be in the hands of the ignorant or unjust. If so, the results of legitimizing forcible transfers will be very bad, even in comparison with the not infrequent unfairness of a system of voluntary transfers. This may be a good reason not to invest a central authority with such powers unless there is ample ground to trust that authority. The Romans were able to make good use of the institution of temporary military dictatorships because the Republic produced trustworthy leaders whom they knew how to recognize. But it is not a good reason to abandon the external norm of beneficial property distribution altogether. From a political standpoint, the task is to find the combination of private and public authority that will best approximate it. These institutional arrangements will almost certainly be subject to alteration when circumstances change.

Under present conditions, the title to nearly all property arises through transfer rather than by original acquisition. This presents some complexities, but no special difficulties. If at a given time the distribution of both property and income is just or approximately so, and if everyone is free to participate in economic transactions, then any voluntary transfer or exchange made nonfraudulently and in reasonably full knowledge is prima facie just. The reasoning is simple. In such circumstances, individuals do not have claims against one another's property, and individuals entering into transactions will improve their own situation without harming anyone else. The posttransfer distribution is subject to the same constraints as was the original distribution, however. Personal and natural disasters can generate new need-based claims against holdings, and combinations of transfers can create monopolies that are impermissible even if inadvertent.[45]

6.2.c. Allocation and organization of tasks

Up to this point, we have confined our discussion to the allocation of the products of human endeavor and to natural objects insofar as they have been affected by human beings in some way. But productive activity has two dimensions: It affects not only the external world but also the producer. The second dimension was already under discussion in antiquity, usually in the context of the relation between kinds of occupation, moral development, and the possibility of political participation. At least since Marx, a split has developed between liberal and socialist thought. Liberals of all stripes have tended to focus on external production (lately, net rather than gross production) as the main gauge of human well-being and benchmark for economic policy. Critics of liberalism, frequently taking their inspiration from Marx's 1844 manuscripts, have insisted that the internal dimension must be given its due: If labor is "dehumanizing," the fact that real wages are rising and more goods and services are available for acquisition may not be decisive.

On the most general level, the critics of liberalism are clearly correct. From either a collective or an individual standpoint, the human worth of a task is determined by two factors: goods and services produced or received, and what human beings undergo in the course of working. This frequently emerges in the demands workers make. If a task is considered dangerous, boring, stultifying, frustrating, workers will shy away from it and insist on higher levels of external compensation. Thus, it is patently ridiculous to claim, as Rawls does,[46] that the internal effects of tasks do not fall within a theory of justice. If justice is concerned with the appropriate allocation of benefits and burdens, then internal effects are relevant, since they obviously can be beneficial or burdensome in crucial ways. Presumably, we are interested in comparing the overall well-being of whole individuals, not parts of parts. The level of each individual's well-being is determined by the totality of what he undergoes. This totality is genuine, existential, not a theoretical artifact, since it arises unavoidably from physical identity and the unity of consciousness. This is not to say that every component of well-being belongs to a theory of justice. But those components that can be significantly affected by human choice and endeavor may not be excluded.

To define the problem more precisely, imagine a community called on to be completely self-sufficient. From the external standpoint, the function of its economy is to produce the full range of items for consumption, items for use, and services needed for the realization of the good for all its members. From the internal standpoint, the problem is to arrange the process of production so as to promote the good of those engaged in it to the greatest extent possible. The tasks performed may impede the attainment of the good in three ways: by endangering life or health; by stunting or distorting the development of powers; and by thwarting inclinations, reducing subjective satisfaction.

We arrive, then, at the concept of the *social worth of tasks*. The social worth of a task may be defined as the sum of the internal effects on its performer and the net goods and services flowing from it. (Net goods and services equals gross production minus some suitable allocation of undesirable externalities.)

It might appear that the purpose of an economic system is to arrange its tasks so as to maximize the sum of their social worth. After all, both components of social worth are measured in the same terms: promotion of the human good—one directly, the other through the mediation of external objects and activities. To maximize social worth, then, is to maximize the attainment of the human good.

There, however, two objections to this approach. First, it overlooks distributive considerations. Intuitively, it seems highly questionable to maximize social worth by allocating to some minority of the population tasks that are profoundly destructive of their good, especially when these tasks, even taking compensation into account, are relatively poorly rewarded. Second, even though both components of social worth point toward the same end, they are not always easily commensurable. A rich country can give its coal miners comprehensive medical care but may not be able to save them from black lung disease. Increased reliance on coal production may in the long run reduce energy costs, freeing resources for other purposes, including medical services, but it is not easy to see on what basis an increment of production could be equated with an increment of injury or disease. Thus, if total social worth is increased by increasing both components simultaneously, the change is unquestionably desirable. But if the two components move in opposite directions, we do not seem to have an unequivocal basis for evaluating the policy that produces these changes.

If the two components should have a strong tendency to move in the same direction, the theoretical difficulty we have sketched would not be very serious. Unfortunately, there are both theoretical and empirical reasons to believe that this is not the case. Imagine a community with a fixed supply of productive workers. In general, external production will be maximized when the number of sick or disabled workers is kept at a low level and workers are assigned tasks on the basis of their efficiency. Efficiency is the outcome of two factors: the ability to perform a task, and the degree of subjective satisfaction derived from performing it. The most efficient worker will have the competence to do his job coupled with the willingness to do it to the limits of his competence. The willingness cannot be coerced but must arise out of the satisfaction provided by the job itself.

There is, then, some overlap between external and internal requirements. Maximization of production requires a significant level of physical well-being and subjective satisfaction; doing what we are best able to do not only promotes our satisfaction but develops some of our abilities to a high degree. But the areas of conflict are evident. The physical well-being we need to do our jobs may be far from genuine health and fitness. The repetition of a limited task develops a part of us but leaves the rest fallow. Indeed, it may overdevelop that part. We would not deliberately embark on a program of physical training that would at length give us one grotesquely bulging muscle, but repetition may have exactly that effect on our mind or character. Even worse, some productive activities may promote traits that are more analogous to tumors or disfiguring marks than to overdeveloped organs. Think, for instance, of Charlie Chaplin lurching off the assembly line in *Modern Times*, a wrench in each hand, uncontrollably twisting every round object in sight. The satisfaction we get from doing one thing well may blind us or make us indifferent to the ways in which we are not attaining the full good of which we are capable.

If we approach the problem from the other direction, with the object of making the internal effects of productive activity as salutary as possible, we are led to consider a wide variety of means. Conceptually simplest is the systematic elimination of the most harmful tasks. In some cases this might require the substitution of technology for human labor, a strategy employed successfully in the most modern steel mills. In other cases we may be required to replace some means to necessary ends with others. Suppose, for example, that a particular crop can be harvested only by hand with a tool that forces the farm worker into an unnatural stance, producing pain and untreatable spinal difficulties. Unless this crop provides some unique and needed sustenance for the members of the community, the human costs of producing it are prohibitive. Within a just system, this would in part be reflected in a level of wage compensation that would discourage consumption and encourage redeployment of productive efforts.

Even if the definition of tasks is held constant, various kinds of improvement are possible. In many cases, allowing individuals more flexibility to determine when they will work—which days, which hours during the day—will greatly increase the satisfaction of task performance. Some of the problems of overspecialization can be alleviated by allowing or encouraging individuals to perform a variety of tasks. Automobile producers now permit workers to become "utility men," reasonably adept at all the operations along the assembly line. Such workers are then able to fill in gaps as they choose, varying their work experience. The Postal Service is attempting to break up the most monotonous jobs by switching workers to other tasks for fifteen minutes out of every hour.[47]

It may well be the case that at a given level of technology many particularly onerous and dangerous tasks cannot be eliminated. In some instances their negative effect may be reduced by distributing them over a wide range of individuals rather than requiring some to spend their lives performing them. The military draft system is an instance of this; there is no reason why it could not be extended to civilian occupations, perhaps in the form of compulsory, universal national youth service between the ages, say, of eighteen and twenty-one. Such a scheme might have educational and political advantages as well. Even those who perform military service unwillingly come away with a more nuanced and sympathetic view of those who select it as a career. Similarly, direct experience of unpleasant tasks and working conditions may lead to more realistic analyses of the economic system and increased political support for just compensation.

Practical considerations point in both directions. On the one hand, dividing up the least desirable tasks may be not only fairer but also aggregatively beneficial whenever threshold effects exist. If thirty people perform an undesirable job for one year each, the sum of enduring negative physical and psychological effects may well be smaller than if one person performs it for thirty years. (If a tree is artificially bent toward the ground for a short period, it will return to the perpendicular when released. If the constraint is prolonged beyond a certain period, it will be permanently skewed.) On the other hand, certain rigors and dangers may be reduced by skill and familiarity. There is some evidence that the program of frequently rotating junior officers during the Vietnam war led to higher mortality rates for them and the men they commanded. One suspects that if coal mining or high-altitude construction work were done for short periods by novices, the overall death and accident rate would rise significantly.

All the allocative techniques discussed so far have presupposed invariant task definitions. Clearly, an economic system would be altered more radically by reorganizing the ways in which basic functions are carried out. In some cases it may be possible and desirable to redraw the boundaries of specialization. For example, nurses could well be given more responsibility for tasks now performed by doctors, especially in areas in which judgment, experience, and sensitivity to the needs and histories of individuals are more significant determinants of the quality of health care than are high levels of technical training. Such changes would lead to both a more efficient use of resources and a greater degree of satisfaction for nurses. Similar possibilities exist in other professions. They are resisted by those whose income and authority would be reduced, although these considerations are usually masked by rhetorical expressions of concern for the public good.

It is also possible to reorganize the process of production around completed products rather than discrete tasks. At some automobile plants, groups of workers collectively produce automobiles, performing the required operations sequentially in the group's own area rather than along an assembly line. This achieves some of the same purposes as task rotation, but there is some evidence that it has other results as well—increased satisfaction in one's work, since the results are clearly visible in a separate product, and some reduction in the debilitating isolation stemming from the repetition of routine tasks performed without the need for conscious or willed cooperation.

Decisions about the content, organization, and allocation of tasks are an integral part of the productive process itself. The most fundamental questions arise in determining who is to make these decisions and in what manner. There are three major alternatives. Decisionmaking, or "management," may be viewed as a specialized function requiring a distinctive range of abilities, which ought to be performed only by the most able. If this is combined with the empirical premise that managerial ability is unevenly distributed, one is led to a hierarchical system of authority with a more or less permanent class of managers into which new young members are constantly recruited. If one views management as containing significant nontechnical components that require no extraordinary ability, then two other possibilities emerge: a hierarchical system in which the membership of the managerial class is steadily changed, for example, five-year terms with 20 percent replaced each year; and a system of collective decisionmaking in which, in effect, all are managers. It is, in addition, quite possible to concede that managerial ability is to an extent unequally distributed but nevertheless to prefer either of the latter alternatives to the first, if there are good reasons to believe that the benefits of participation—usually described as increased satisfaction and the development of aspects of mind and character—outweigh the loss of efficiency and production.

In recent years, many European countries—notably, Sweden, Denmark, West Germany, and the Netherlands—have put into effect plans to increase the participation of workers in management decisions. The results have been inconclusive. Anecdotal evidence suggests that the costs of collective decisionmaking in lost time, money, and production can be very high; this is the outcome that would be predicted on theoretical grounds. These costs would be appreciably lower in systems with rotating participation—periodic elections to boards of management. A less tractable difficulty is that inevitably those involved in the process of production will give much greater weight to the quality of their own work experience than to the needs of production. Changes in the work experience are immediate, palpable, and felt as highly significant, while the effects of lower production tend to be spread out over producers and consumers. In an economic system in which each worker may try to maximize the benefits derived from the work experience while shifting the burdens to others, the well-being of all may eventually be reduced. This danger is especially acute in systems in which collective mechanisms, for example, government support for highly inefficient firms, make it possible for producers to externalize the costs of inefficiency. The contemporary British economy has frequently been analyzed in these terms.

In the best of all possible worlds we would not have to concern ourselves with production. All our external, instrumental requirements would be fulfilled without effort, and we could choose our activities on the basis of their contribution to our development and satisfaction. Perhaps such a world will come about through continued technological progress. One may well doubt it. We need not only goods but also services, and it is difficult to imagine how technology could do away with the need for human judgment and personal relations during the provision of services. Besides, the technological paradise would have to be maintained by human effort and contrivance.

For the foreseeable future, then, and probably forever, we need to devise and participate in some system of production. We can imagine a second-order paradise in which there would be a perfect fit between the requirements of the productive system and the well-being of the individuals comprising it. No necessary activity would harm its performer, and the distribution of necessary activities would be congruent, quantitatively and qualitatively, with the distribution of abilities and preference.

In our world, of course, neither of these conditions is satisfied. To a certain extent, we can alleviate the distributional problem through technology, training, and a system of incentives designed to close the gap between our productive needs and our personal preferences. The existence of necessary but harmful tasks is both more troubling and less tractable.

As we have seen, this tension between the valuable outputs of the productive system and its harmful effects on producers gives rise to two fundamental problems: how to strike an appropriate balance between internal and external goods, and how to distribute unavoidable harm among producers. Neither can be precisely resolved, but the foregoing discussion has provided us with the elements needed for a general solution.

1. *The problem of balancing.* There are strong reasons to give priority to the internal good of producers. First, to a large extent we are what we do. Our activity defines and shapes us directly, and the quality of our activity determines the quality of our existence. Second, the improvement of our existence is the purpose of all our activity. The goods we produce are merely means to this end, and good only insofar as they are means. On the other hand, of course, we cannot do without external goods, since without a certain quantity of them our good is meaningless or unattainable.

Since our productive activity is part of our existence and its improvement a part of the improvement of our existence, the relations of priority and urgency among the elements of the human good come into play. We must then attach the greatest urgency to overcoming obstacles to physical existence and well-being, next to the development of our capacities and character, and finally to the attainment of satisfaction.

It follows, then, that the goods we produce must promote the human good at a level of urgency equal to or higher than the good producers must sacrifice. If food can be produced only through a labor system that cripples farm workers, the harm must be accepted, since the only alternative is forgoing an even more urgent good. At the other extreme we would find workers suffering and dying to produce diamonds for the adornment and enrichment of a few.

It follows, further, that we must seek to use our resources to find substitutes for harmful activities up to the point at which the goods of production we invest or do without deprive us of a human good equal in urgency and quantity to the good it achieves. Thus, assuming adequate quantitative measures, expenditures to improve health and safety within factories are necessary and appropriate up to the point at which they entail reductions of equal consequence in expenditures for, for example, public safety or medical care.

I do not mean to suggest that it is irrational to sacrifice one's urgent good to promote the less urgent good of others, as in the case of immigrant parents ruining their health through excessive and debilitating work to provide their children with cultural and educational opportunities. But the rationality of this behavior rests on special conditions not often satisfied within the economic sphere. The bonds between parents and children are so close that the parents view the advancement of their children's interests as advancing their own. Further, the sacrifice is voluntary. Although we admire those who make it, it is not obligatory. It would then be wrong to force them to make it, legally or through the structure of the productive system. Finally, for some individuals voluntary sacrifice brings about a kind of character development and satisfaction that cannot be attained through direct self-promotion. These benefits are unlikely to result from involuntary sacrifice, which usually breeds either crushed resignation or disfiguring resentment.[48]

2. *Distribution of harm.* Harm incurred during productive activity is a problem because of the imperfections of compensation and rectification. If the effects of debilitating activities could be fully overcome through better medical services or technological advances, just distribution would be simple: compensation and capital investment, guided by the principles set forth in previous discussions. In present circumstances this solution is not feasible.

One possibility would be to arrange and allocate tasks so as to minimize aggregate harm. To do so, we would have to consider threshold effects as well as the differential effects of activities on different individuals. Potentially harmful tasks would be assigned to those with the skill to anticipate and ward off danger or the physical and mental strength to endure adversity. Dividing exposure to harm would make sense for activities with clear-cut threshold effects—for example, those involving proximity to radiation. For those without such effects, dividing exposure to harm would probably increase the total, since the average level of skill and experience would be much lower.

As one might expect, the minimization principle runs into difficulties. Some individuals would be compelled to run large risks for extended periods while others were left unscathed. Experienced workers in dangerous occupations might not be allowed to retire when they wished, since early retirement would imply a larger number of harm-prone novices. These examples, which could easily be multiplied, strike us as problematic because we feel that, with the exception of those who demonstrate repeated lack of regard for the claims of others, all individuals are equally entitled to the goods of existence and development and thus that there is a presumption in favor of distributing impediments to these goods equally except in instances in which all would benefit from exempting an individual or class of individuals. This principle would dictate employing policies of, for examples, national service, task rotation, redefinition of tasks to equalize risks, and lotteries in cases in which risks are indivisible. But clearly it would be troubling if the implementation of such policies should lead to a significantly higher level of work-related death, accident, or physical or mental disorder.

At this point, having reached a version of the hoary equality-versus-maximization conundrum, it might seem tempting to murmur a few intuitionist platitudes and slink off. But we can, I suggest, avail ourselves of an auxiliary principle: The more serious the potential harm, the more appropriate it is to strive for equalization of risks. This seems clearest in the most extreme case. The only fair system of military conscription is one based on universal eligibility and selection by lot, with exemptions only in those cases in which an individual is either unfit to contribute or certain to contribute more to the military effort by doing something else. In addition, the risks of different occupations may be equalized by shortening the required period of exposure to harm for the most dangerous occupations. It is thus reasonable that those who undertake careers as soldiers, policemen, or firemen be enabled to retire relatively early.

Another principle seems appealing as well: The more voluntarily an individual assumes a risk, the less necessary it is to equalize his risk with that of someone who is not so inclined. One may suppose that every community contains some individuals for whom life and well-being lack savor unless they are endangered or jeopardized. To the extent that such individuals select dangerous occupations, the principle of harm-minimization may be preferred to that of harm-equalization. Of course, the plausibility of this claim rests on the choice being voluntary in a strong and rigorous sense. It must be made in reasonably full knowledge, not as the result of systematic socialization or indoctrination, with other alternatives truly open and available.

But individuals choose, not isolated activities, but packages of activities plus incentives. Suitable incentives can render almost any activity attractive to the requisite number of individuals. It is far from clear which activities should be allocated through incentives, which on the basis of laws backed by threats. Provisionally, one might suggest that the use of incentives becomes counterproductive when they interfere with the provision of goods at an equal or higher level of urgency. For example, the volunteer armed forces, conceived and launched during a period of prosperity, are now being called into question because the high level of required incentives is diverting scarce resources away from weapons procurement and research.

We arrive, then, at the following conclusions: The extent to which tasks can be freely chosen is determined both by the overall justice of the economic system and by the quantity of resources it can dispose of to meet urgent requirements. Within the voluntary sphere, the arrangement and allocation of tasks should be guided by the principle of harm-equalization and, if choices must be made, priority given to the equalization of the greatest harms—generally, those for which compensation is least possible.

We may combine these conclusions with the results of the previous discussion. The most desirable system of production arranges and allocates tasks so as to maximize the aggregate physical well-being, development of our powers, and satisfaction (in that order of priority) we derive directly from them, subject to two constraints: first, the maintenance of a level of production such that human goods of equal urgency and greater quantity are not sacrificed to achieve further improvement in the work experience; and second, the equalization of risk or harm associated with tasks not freely chosen, priority being given to the equalization of the greatest harms.

Let us now examine the allocation of tasks within such a system from the standpoint of individuals who seek to perform them. Setting to one side entitlements that may be generated by contractual obligations or seniority systems, there are three bases for claims to perform tasks. Individuals may make claims based on the ability to perform tasks, the development of powers resulting from their performance, or the satisfaction performing them will engender. Each of these would be decisive if the others were held constant. In practice, of course, they are not, but rather come into conflict.

As our earlier discussion of equality of opportunity indicated, claims based on ability are very powerful, especially in a system that permits and encourages all to become aware of and cultivate their powers. If tasks are done by the most able, the quantity and quality of human goods produced is likely to be maximized. There is, besides, a significant correlation between being able to do something well and deriving satisfaction from it. The imperfections of this correlation stem from beliefs about the different rank or worth of tasks. Some would prefer to do a higher task badly rather than a lower one well. Perhaps it is safest to assume that such individuals will be dissatisfied whichever task they end up with.

The most serious conflict is between the claims of ability and those of development. After a relatively short period, someone who easily does the job he is best able to do will probably cease to learn from or be changed by it. A less able person might well learn more, even if he will never perform it as well as the more able.

If the level of production of a particular good is at or above required levels, the claims of ability are weakened; the community can afford to allow individuals to develop themselves. Conversely, if some good is urgently needed and in short supply, the claims of ability must predominate.

In addition, we need to examine benefit and harm in individual cases. The benefits of development-claims accrue to those making them, while the costs are borne by others. Some costs are clearly unacceptable. The benefit that some incompetent might reap from shouldering the responsibilities of being, for example, a brain surgeon or a military leader is insignificant in comparison with the harm others will undergo. At the other extreme, it may well make sense to assign to the less able positions of limited responsibility, for example, committee chairmanships, middle management positions, if others thereby suffer only minor inconveniences. In intermediate cases, various devices may be employed to reflect the balance of claims: task rotation, with the more able performing the complex tasks a higher percentage of the time; or systems of supervision that allow the less able to learn on the job while screening out their most dangerous mistakes.

The system for the organization and allocation of tasks we have outlined is not, in the main, based on involuntary assignment of individuals to tasks. To be sure, just organization of tasks can arise only through conscious collective endeavor, and involuntary assignment may be necessary in special cases or stringent circumstances. But to a very large extent, the allocation of tasks within a just system may rely on individual choice. The reasons are clear. First, individual choice will occur in the context of incentives that reflect productive needs. Second, tasks voluntarily undertaken will tend to promote both individual satisfaction and productive needs. Third, the preference for higher tasks that individuals can perform less competently will be counteracted by declines in the productivity component of the incomes they receive. Fourth, in a system in which all have access to training and opportunity, the desire for tasks conducive to development will be widespread. But in the cases of individuals for whom this desire is swamped by other kinds of desires, for example, for immediate subjective satisfaction, compulsion is not likely to promote their development significantly. The purpose of a just economic system is to remove as many external obstacles as possible to the achievement of individual good and to encourage individuals to perform useful activities that promote their total good, not just a part. But no economic system can force individuals to make the best possible use of their opportunities.

At this point, let me summarize the role that the principle of subjective satisfaction plays in my theory. It may seem that need, which incorporates preservation and development, and the worth of rational action have virtually nullified the force of subjective satisfaction and that desert, a relational rather than individual good, is in principle indifferent to subjective satisfaction. This impression is mistaken, although of course subjective satisfaction cannot have the centrality for me that it does for classical utilitarians.

Subjective satisfaction affects distributive outcomes in at least five ways. First, it regulates exchanges among just holdings. Second, it is one of the elements that enters into the decision whether to exercise one's entitlements—to appropriate and use everything to which one has a valid claim. Third, as we have seen, it has an important impact on individuals' choice among productive tasks. Fourth, it affects the degree of effort an individual exerts, as well as the balance an individual seeks to achieve between production and leisure. Fifth, it determines the allocation of surpluses or windfalls—the excess of valued things over valid claims. I have suggested that in situations of this sort, classical utilitarian maximizing has great intuitive force.

6.2.d. Constraints on economic systems

Domestic production, allocation, and consumption are subject to three kinds of constraints: the valid claims of other communities, of future generations, and of other living species.

Other communities

Every political community claims the right to determine its membership by regulating immigration. (Other modes of regulation—

restrictions on citizenship and emigration—raise equally important issues but are not germane to my purpose here.) This right can easily be defended. Each community has a legitimate interest in preserving the way of life it has chosen, and a massive influx of individuals with different beliefs and expectations would make this much more difficult. Further, each community seeks to provide a satisfactory level of material well-being for its members, and in some circumstances immigration impedes the achievement of this objective. Finally, each community requires a degree of harmony, consensus, and coordination, while immigration can exacerbate differences and encourage divided loyalties.

These reasons do not however warrant the conclusion that the exclusionary rights of the community are absolute. In certain circumstances individuals may have strong claims against communities of which they are not members. The case of the European Jews in the 1930s is particularly clear-cut. It became evident to all impartial observers that the Jews faced increasing political persecution, economic deprivation, and physical danger in the countries of their birth. The difficulties that admitting them would have produced for host countries were far outweighed by the harm wrought by excluding them, and this would have been true a fortiori if the potential hosts had worked out a coordinated plan.

Mexican immigration into the United States poses more complex problems. The incentives are almost entirely economic. The number of actual immigrants is very large and of potential immigrants is even larger. American workers in the affected areas rightly fear that wages will be depressed; cities complain of the strain on social services; politicians fear loss of political control; and citizens are confronted with demands for bilingual education and other changes. Many complain that Mexico has not moved aggressively enough to increase employment opportunities and social services or to stem the flight of peasants from the countryside. On the other hand, it may be argued that the economic and social benefits to the potential immigrants far outweigh the burdens on the United States; this claim could be strengthened by a national policy that shared costs equitably rather than allowing them to fall disproportionately on certain socioeconomic groups in a few states. If hundreds of thousands of innocent victims of history and demography can quintuple their wages and liberate their children from malnutrition without significantly lowering the living standards of present American citizens, then a policy of exclusion goes beyond the limits of reasonable self-preference. We may add (adapting a Platonic argument) that no wall can be built between our treatment of others and of ourselves. If we apply the pure principle of collective selfishness in our dealings with the rest of the world, then the moral and psychological foundations of domestic cooperation are eroded.[49]

The broader question of redistributive transfers of income and resources among nations overlaps with, but is distinguishable from, the problem of just immigration policies.

The question of international economic justice has been much discussed in recent years, and extreme claims have been advanced. Some have claimed that communities are entitled to whatever they produce and that aid to other communities is a matter of charity or prudence rather than of justice. Others have suggested that justice requires near-equalization of incomes without regard to national boundaries. Those considering the issue more soberly have tended to speak in practical or ad hoc terms appropriate to specific situations without explicit regard to underlying principles.

One case seems clear-cut. If, given a just or nearly just initial situation, community A forcibly appropriates the income or wealth of B, some form of rectification or reparation is in order. The concept of war reparations is an extension of this. If A's unprovoked aggression forces B to devote lives and resources to its own defense, A has appropriated B's property, at least in the sense that B's freedom to make best use of its resources has been restricted. The fact that the victor routinely charges the vanquished with aggression and exacts reparations, whatever the facts of the case, does not mean that the practice lacks theoretical justification.

Redistributive claims among nations are frequently linked to the assertion that exploitation has occurred in the past and must be redressed. Exploitation is notoriously difficult to define. As a rough approximation, we can say it is somewhere between a fair bargain and forcible appropriation. Most would agree that if parties to a transaction have equal access to information and comparable ranges of alternatives, then voluntarily consent, the agreement is not unjust even if one party is pleasantly, the other unpleasantly, surprised by its consequences. On the other hand, the unprovoked use of force to seize the resources of others is under most circumstances patently unjust. Exploitation, then, occurs when some important asymmetry in the bargaining circumstances of the parties leaves one with no feasible alternative to an agreement the terms of which are unfair.

We can move closer to an operational definition by considering specific cases. It is not in principle exploitive to pay low prices for abundant products or to be compelled to pay more as demand increases or supply contracts. But suppose that one country falls victim to famine or epidemic while another controls sizable surpluses of wheat or medicine. The needy country may be ready to agree to terms that would imply a drastic reduction in living standards or permanent loss of control over natural resources or means of production. Nevertheless, the lucky country would not be justified in insisting on such terms. It is not in principle exploitive to transform a bargaining situation by entering into combinations with other buyers or sellers. But exploitation may occur if the combined parties seek to prevent those on the other side from joining forces as well. Thus, for example, OPEC would have no cause for complaint if the consuming nations joined together to coordinate bidding for oil and to restrict consumption, and it would be exploitive to prevent this by threatening a renewed oil embargo. If one country supplies the capital another needs to create new industries, it is not exploitive to expect a substantial percentage of the profits in return. But it is exploitive not to offer the recipient nation a fair opportunity gradually to acquire a share in the means of production. Nor is it in principle exploitive to pay workers in the country receiving the investments less than those in the country making them. But a wage rate may be exploitive even if the workers benefit somewhat from the new industry—that is, have higher real income with it than without it. This is the case when one or more of the following conditions is satisfied: wages reflect a deliberate effort to make permanent a lower standard of living for workers in one country than another; the wage level increases the income differential between workers and owners in the long run; the wage level produces profits that exceed the requirements of research and development and capital investment; or wages could be increased significantly without either significantly impairing the competitive position of the industry or stimulating the substitution of capital-intensive technology for workers.

All of these criteria are highly imprecise, and some involve the comparison of hypothetical alternatives. No doubt many ambiguous cases exist. Still, we may conclude that exploitation is a nonvacuous concept that can give rise to valid claims for redress. Under some circumstances, expropriation may be a justified response to systematic, long-term exploitation. It has the effect of penalizing those who are likely to have unfairly benefited in the past. Significant inequities will, however, occur. Consider the case of the long-term shareholder who sells his stock to someone else shortly before expropriation is decreed. Whether it benefits those who have borne the greatest burdens is more doubtful. Domestic ownership of the means of production does not necessarily imply a higher standard of living for workers. If the country's class structure is highly unjust or its need for investment capital great, real wages may actually decline.

Suppose that nation A is guilty of neither theft nor exploitation. What, if any, are B's claims against A? To begin with, the argument that

6. The Nature of the Just Community

B has contributed nothing to the product *A* has produced and so has no claim to a share is a non sequitur. Many individual members of *A* have contributed nothing but, as we have argued at length, have valid claims based on need. From this standpoint, there seems to be no distinction between members of *A* and members of *B*; if need is valid for the one, it ought to be for the other. It may be argued that communities are held together, indeed constituted, by shared loyalties or special bonds of mutual responsibility. If so, it cannot be the case that the claims of nonmembers are equal to those of members. This is true in one respect. If your child and someone else's are drowning simultaneously and you can save only one, you are not morally required to be impartial. Similarly, if communities are forced to choose between the needs of members and of nonmembers, the former may be given precedence, in fact must be if the community is to survive as a collective venture. But follow out the analogy. If your child stubs his toe while another child is drowning, it would be wrong to comfort yours rather than to save the other. Similarly, need is to be given priority, wherever it may occur. The provision of adequate food, medical care, clothing, shelter, and education is a weightier and more urgent good than is the enjoyment of the last increment of comfort a wealthy society can provide its members.[50]

This simple proposition is not very popular. In present circumstances, it would probably cost the developed nations about 10 percent of their gross national product.[51] By way of contrast, American foreign aid for 1978 amounts to about one-fourth of 1 percent of GNP, while the most generous donor, Sweden, allocates less than 1 percent.[52] The apparent political impossibility of thus redeploying resources in response to worldwide need indicates the extent to which current political communities are vehicles of collective selfishness. It will not do to argue that without the developed nations, the less developed nations would be even worse off. This is true but beside the point; the issue here is not exploitation but rather obligation.

The problem becomes more complex when the situation that gives rise to redistributive claims is a product, not of natural or historical accidents, but of political decisions. Suppose, for example, that a community is plunged into famine by a reorganization of agricultural production that will depress output as long as the new system is retained. Perhaps the best course is to relieve the first effects of the policy while making it clear that self-destructive folly will not be indefinitely underwritten. Of course, this recommendation rests on the premise that no government can very long afford to ignore the misery of a large fraction of its population. If a government coercively imposes and can forcibly maintain a destructive policy, then the morality of refusing to aid the

248

innocent victims becomes more dubious. Or suppose that misery and suffering results, not from inadequate per capita income, but from a highly inequitable distribution within a community. In these circumstances, external contributions may well have the effect of subsidizing the income of the upper classes.

Charles Beitz and Brian Barry have recently offered appealing arguments in favor of equal access to natural resources as an important principle of international distribution. They contend that the right of nations to dispose of resources within their borders cannot be considered absolute but rather requires justification in light of competing claims. After all, justice must concern itself with initial holdings as well as the patterns of rational cooperation that flow from them. And surely the existing distribution of resources, arrived at through force and accident, is "arbitrary from a moral point of view" if anything is. Unlike natural talents, natural resources are separable from individuals, and no one stands in a naturally privileged relation to them. There is therefore a strong presumption in favor of equality of opportunity to make use of such resources.[53]

These arguments have the virtue of reminding us that, as presently understood, national boundaries imply collective claims to property. It seems plausible to suppose, then, that the moral restraints on individual acquisition can be invoked against them as well. As I have argued, though, individual acquisition of unowned resources is limited primarily by the needs of others. If so, fair access to resources is not an independent criterion at all, as it could be invoked only under circumstances in which, and only to the extent that, claims based upon need come into play.

There is another reason to believe that equal access to resources is not a fundamental consideration. I have argued that the benchmark of justice is the way of life enjoyed by individuals and that the best measure of this is the extent to which they achieve certain end-states. From this standpoint, access to resources becomes important only to the extent that it impinges on the ability of individuals to attain their good. An equal share of natural resources is not, however, a necessary condition of prosperity—consider the cases of Japan, South Korea, and Singapore. Organized human endeavor, not natural resources, is the major determinant of per capita wealth in many cases, at least within the context of modern economies.

Finally, the notion of access is ambiguous. An individual may have access to resources in two ways—through direct possession and through exchange. What matters is total access, not either of the elements considered in isolation. This suggests two points. First, there is a crucial distinction between seeking to exchange one's holdings of a natural resource on favorable terms and withholding it from the market altogether, especially when potential buyers cannot find other sources or cannot substitute other kinds of resources for what you have withheld. Second, it is undeniable that initial holdings of resources affect terms of exchange. As a result, A may have to work harder than B to enjoy the same level of well-being. We should, however, resist the conclusion that this is ipso facto unjust. After all, differences of natural talent or of entitlements stemming from past efforts can also bring about this kind of inequality without generating a moral requirement to redress it.

Redistribution across national boundaries encounters well-known practical difficulties that affect both its scope and its means. For example, under some circumstances it would probably have a negative impact on production. At a certain point, expansion of aid would become counterproductive, creating more need than it fulfilled. Clearly, there can be no requirement to reach this point. Of greater practical importance is the fact that, while aid is here being justified as a response to individual need, the aid rarely finds its way to the individuals in need, since it must be filtered through the government, bureaucracy, and class structure of the recipient nations of which these individuals are members.[54] The conclusion is obvious. Since the obligation is to individuals rather than to communities, there is no obligation to aid communities that do not transfer the aid to their members on the basis of need. In such circumstances, however, the obligation to aid does not cease. Rather, the aid must be channeled directly to those who need it. Otherwise, needy individuals would be made to suffer for the injustice of their communities. The argument is symmetrical. While need-claims are not responsive to differences of sovereignty, neither are the modes of requiting them.

There are some considerations suggesting that from the standpoint of redistribution, unrestricted immigration might be both fairer and more effective than direct transfers of resources. Immigration allows individuals to determine the extent of their own needs and to improve their own economic position directly rather than through a distorting governmental mechanism that deflects benefits to the undeserving. Immigration also increases the element of reciprocity: the immigrant seeks to exchange labor for income, to cooperate in the production of the output, of which the worker claims a share. The argument that immigration purchases more effective redistribution at the cost of unfair social and cultural dislocation is not compelling. Appropriate policies enable immigrants to preserve important elements of their national identity and impose some significant changes on the population of the host country as well.

There are two basic forms of aid: helping others directly and helping them to help themselves. The latter is preferable for many reasons. Overall well-being is increased rather than a constant sum redistributed; the political unpopularity of, on the one hand, significant sacrifice of material well-being and, on the other, significant abrogation of sovereignty, is minimized; and the complex psychological dangers of enduring obligation and dependence are reduced.

Helping others to help themselves is a form of capital investment, human and material, designed to spare them the full horror of primitive accumulation. This aid must be guided by three principles. First, the direction of aid should correspond to the priority of need. If a community cannot feed itself, the first object of aid is to increase either agricultural production or the production of goods that can readily and reliably be exchanged for agricultural products. Second, capital investment is no substitute for direct aid. A starving peasant will not be comforted by the assurance that his great-grandchildren will reap the rewards of farsighted policies. This raises complex questions. If resources are scarce, there may be a stark choice between the present and the future. We will explore this later, in our discussion of just savings. For now, we state dogmatically that, while individuals may be asked to live poorly for the sake of the comfort and development of future generations, they cannot be required to undergo extreme physical pain, deformation, or death to achieve these purposes. Third, the aid must be so administered as to maximize the speed at which its recipients can fend for themselves. If, as is usually the case, the core of investment is a body of knowledge and technology, recipients must be encouraged to acquire the requisite practical and theoretical understanding. The alternative is permanent dependence. A similar issue arises in the evaluation of colonialism. While the intentions of colonial powers were in no case benevolent, some colonial policies left behind a significant group of individuals with bureaucratic, economic, or military competence, while others forced newly independent countries to make an unpleasant choice between, on the one hand, chaos and suffering, and, on the other, long-term dependence on either the former colonial power or a self-interested third party.

Future generations

Two questions arise when we confront the claims of future generations: Are relations between the living and the unborn moral relations—more specifically, relations of justice? If so, what is the extent of the valid claims the unborn have against the living?

Rawls and most others dealing with this issue have simply assumed a positive answer to the first question. Recently, however, Thomas Schwartz has forcefully dissented. His negative argument runs roughly as follows: All long-run social policies affect the composition of the population to such an extent that after a relatively small number of generations (six to eight) the chances are infinitesimal that any individual who exists under the regime of a long-run policy would have existed if the policy had not been adopted, and conversely. We cannot then say that any individual would have been better or worse off, given different policies, since the policy populations have no members in common. But if no one is benefited or harmed, then the future state of the community is irrelevant to the evaluation of public policy, and future generations cannot reproach us for what we have done.[55]

Let us concede the factual premise. We stipulate, further, that we know nothing about the composition of remote future generations except that they will be composed of beings very much like ourselves, with the same mix of claims and similar conceptions of the human good. Now, assuming that we can reach agreement among ourselves about the remote outcomes of presently available policies, we can agree that the state of the world would be better under A than B and that, say, under A there will be more of the means to the human good, more justly distributed. Given my assumption, this evaluation does not depend on the specific membership of the policy population. From the standpoint of justice, what matters is the extent to which valid claims are requited, not the identities of those advancing them. States of the world, then, can be evaluated and rank-ordered even if their hypothetical populations are entirely disjoint.

Suppose that in the face of this we adopt policy B, where B is, for example, a program of nuclear testing that increases mutations and birth defects and leaves large portions of the earth's surface unfit for cultivation or habitation. The reflective denizen of the B-world will say: "If not for B, I would not be here. Since I attach a positive value to my existence, in spite of its depressing circumstances, I personally have no basis for complaint. But under A, the individual who would be here in my place would enjoy a more satisfactory existence than I do. Neither he nor I had any prior right to exist. But the essence of morality is to attach the same moral weight to the interests of others as to one's own. Thus, although I value my existence, I must say that it would have been preferable had the policy that implied my nonexistence been adopted."

I shall spare the reader a dramatization of an A-world member's position. The point is clear: Members of the present world, the A-world, and the B-world will agree that the A-world is preferable to the B. If it were the case that there are no significant differences between the two policies except that the outcome of A is unequivocally preferable to that of B, then members of the present world would have a conclusive reason to choose A, even if (and I concede this only for the sake of brevity) it would be wrong to say that anyone would be harmed, or have just cause for complaint, if B were chosen.

Of course, there will almost always be significant differences between A and B. Specifically, choosing A will usually require members of the present world to sacrifice a portion of their own well-being by accepting restrictions on various activities (procreation, production dependent on nuclear-generated power) or on the consumption of what they have produced or of the bounties of nature. In itself, this is hardly a decisive objection to A, since under all but the most fortunate circumstances justice will require some members of the present world to sacrifice a portion of their well-being to further that of other members. The question is, rather, whether the present nonexistence of potential beneficiaries means that the existence they would enjoy is of no moral weight whenever it would entail sacrifices by existing beings.

An example may bring out the full force of this question. Suppose that a young couple has good reasons to believe that they could conceive a healthy child and raise that child so that both he and others would regard his existence as desirable. Suppose further that this would entail significant sacrifices for the couple (they are not well-off and are not particularly inclined to enjoy the process of child-rearing) but that they correctly recognize it to be the case that the benefits their potential child would receive from existence far outweigh their sacrifices. Would it be morally wrong (unreasonably and culpably selfish) for them to decide not to have the child? (To forestall an irrelevant line of argument, suppose that they carry their decision into effect through sexual abstinence.)

On the one hand, it is clear in one sense that the claims of actual existence are stronger than those of potential existence. Having the baby and then killing it would be wrong except in the most extraordinary circumstances. An existing individual is a claim-bearer whose interests may not be disregarded. A potential individual is not a claim-bearer in the same sense. Note that the Catholic church is not opposed to abstinence—indeed, requires it in some cases—and that its opposition to abortion is based on the premise that the individual is actual rather than potential from the moment of conception.

On the other hand, the question involves, not only claims, but also alternative future states of the world. Suppose the couple believes that the continued existence of the human race is desirable; if they attach a positive value to their own existence, they would be hard pressed to deny this. Their refusal to have a child could well be interpreted as a refusal to assume their fair share of the costs of bringing this about.

6. The Nature of the Just Community

They could, of course, argue that their decision has a negligible effect on the overall outcome, since there will always be plenty of people who either have children unreflectively or consider the worth of their existence to be enhanced by having children.

Let us set aside the question of whether a defensible general principle of exemption can be constructed on this basis and explore the implications of varying the empirical premises. Suppose, for example, that in the aftermath of a nuclear holocaust the couple does not know whether anyone else has survived. If they value the continued existence of the species, they have no choice but to procreate, even if their own existence, already a source of weariness and disgust, would be rendered even less attractive. But suppose they do not value the species. Even so, they will be forced to consider the possibility that future generations might have a very different attitude and that their own decision here and now may permanently foreclose the opportunities others would otherwise enjoy. The fact that these others do not now exist as bearers of claims is irrelevant. The very fact that their existence is possible means that their possibility must be taken into account. The couple is not just deciding for itself, however much it may wish to pose the question in those terms.

This is an extreme case, but it reveals the core of the argument in favor of considering the interests of future generations as a moral responsibility, not just as a whim or preference we happen to have. What we do now affects the possibilities open to those who do not yet exist, indeed determines the possibility of their existence itself. Willy-nilly, we share in a responsibility for the human condition that cannot be reduced to the obligations toward, or claims of, specific and identifiable human beings. It is true that the human condition is nothing but the form of existence that individuals can enjoy. But it is a fallacy to argue from this moral individualism to the conclusion that moral evaluation is somehow interrupted when the identity of individuals is changed, by chance or choice.

There is another, less global argument against the claim that we are constrained only by the effects of our acts on actually existing individuals. Imagine a young woman who enjoys using a mind-altering drug that affects the process of conception in the following way: the sperm that would otherwise fertilize the ovum is killed on contact, and the genetic material of the next sperm is disturbed in such a way that the baby.is born defective. *Ex hypothesi*, the defective baby was not made worse off, since its defect is the condition of its existence. Nevertheless, the woman's act was wrong, and it was wrong because it harmed the baby. The claim that the act was wrong only because it contradicted the interests of the mother and imposed costs on others is inadequate, since the conditions of the example can easily be revised to rule these secondary effects out without decreasing our intuitive sense that the act was indefensible. The implications are clear. We act in a moral environment constituted, not just by the particular claims of particular individuals, but also by a general ideal of desirable existence or individual perfection. We harm or wrong those who, as a result of our actions, are restricted in their pursuit of a desirable existence. Our responsibility to future generations is, at the very least, not to create such restrictions.

Even if one accepts this general line of argument, it is difficult to move to a more precise specification of justice among generations. Rawls's conclusion that the problem is theoretically indeterminate seems plausible.[56] With no pretense to finality, let me suggest an approach.

On the one hand, numbers are significant in the evaluation of social policy. The fact that one policy reduces, in the aggregate and in the long run, human misery or promotes the human good to a greater extent than another is a powerful argument in its favor. On the other hand, we are separate beings. The Platonic effort to make us feel pleasure and pain or receive benefit and harm as one organism necessarily fails, as does the classical utilitarian attempt to evaluate our condition as though we were such an organism. The separateness of our being takes on particular significance in considering justice among generations, since in principle those who are asked to make sacrifices cannot subsequently benefit from them, except to the extent that their imaginative sympathy enables them to identify their interests with those of remote beneficiaries.

As Rescher suggests, these countervailing intuitions cannot be reconciled monistically.[57] In the case of justice among generations, the principle of constrained ideal average utility seems to work best. We are primarily interested in the extent to which the members of a community, considered as individuals, are able to enjoy a desirable way of life. At the same time, it is very questionable that some individuals or generations be required to make sacrifices beyond a certain point, simply to increase long-run average utility. Intuitively, then, we choose the policy that maximizes long-run average utility, with the constraint that no one enjoy a level of well-being below some fixed point if redistribution can raise that individual above that point without plunging someone else below it.

The problem, of course, is to determine the floor. One possibility would be to use the totality of need. This might be sensible in a community in which average utility is at or above the requirements of need. But since most communities—including the ones for which savings or investment is the most urgent social problem—are not so fortunate, the adoption of need as a standard would leave the problem almost entirely indeterminate. But recall that need has two components, physical and developmental, and that the claims of the former are prior to those of the latter. We may suggest, then, that physical need serve as the floor in all cases in which average utility is at or above its requirements. Individuals may be required to make great sacrifices, but no one can legitimately be required to undergo physical misery, sickness, or death to promote the higher good of others. As we have seen, some individuals may voluntarily undertake such sacrifices, but such decisions are supererogatory.

To engender a general principle of justice among generations, the utility floor must be combined with two other premises. First, the level of material well-being required for the full realization of the human good is finite or limited and determinable, at least approximately. This premise is amply supported by our previous discussion of the human good. Second, for purposes of planning and evaluation, the human species must be considered to have an unlimited temporal existence. Obviously, we cannot know whether this is true. But in the absence of evidence to the contrary, it seems safer and more sensible to assume that it is. Even setting scientific arguments to one side, clearly the consequences of incorrectly assuming the eternity of the human species are less catastrophic than those of incorrectly assuming that the world is coming to an end and consuming resources on that basis.

Given these assumptions, the problem of intergenerational justice becomes tractable, as indicated in Figure 2. Policies A (living off capital), B (the generation of a catastrophe), C (replenishment), and F (excessive sacrifice) are excluded prima facie. The choice between D (lesser initial sacrifice, more gradual progress) and E (greater initial sacrifice, more rapid progress) is made by comparing the areas of I and II. If I is greater than II, D is preferable; if the reverse, E. This "deductive" decision procedure is intuitively plausible as well. We are interested in the marginal productivity of sacrifice. This cannot be determined simply by comparing the rates of progress experienced under different policies—the slopes of the lines. The starting point—the level of deprivation the initial generation will undergo—and the length of time that deprivation will be greater than under alternate policies are also crucial evaluative foci. Note, finally, that if we reject the possibility of satiation, then all that matters is the slope of the line, with the utility floor as a constraint on starting points. If we reject the floor as well, then we need examine only the slope. Stalin understood this perfectly, as did the early capitalists.

It is not possible here to enter into a full discussion of the principle of average utility. But we must confront a powerful argument against it.

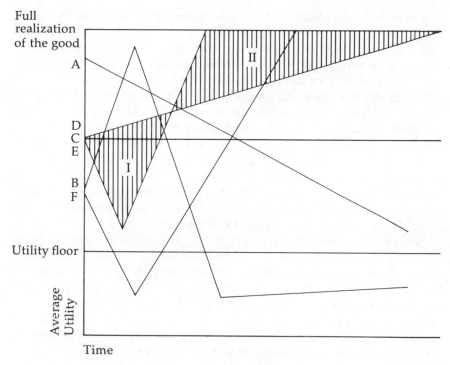

Figure 2. Intergenerational justice: policy alternatives

Average utility, it is contended, has a "fatal flaw": it conflicts with Pareto optimality. Consider two policies, *A* and *B*. Under *A*, a group of individuals would enjoy a certain average utility. Under *B*, that group would enjoy a slightly higher average utility, while another group, which would not have existed under *A*, enjoys a level of utility that is positive but low enough to reduce the average of the two groups below the average prevailing under *A*. The principle of average utility directs us to select *A*, while Pareto optimality mandates *B*, since all the members of both groups are better off than they would be under *A*.[58]

The conflict between the two principles is clear. What is not so clear, however, is why the conflict works to the disadvantage of average utility. Let us flesh out the example as follows: Under *B*, the group decides to have children and to hold them in perpetuity as slave laborers. The parents benefit through a higher level of material well-being and increased leisure, and the enslaved children, though bitterly discontented with their lot, do not prefer death to their mode of existence. Is it the case that this world is preferable to one in which the initial group had decided not to have any children? I think not. The reason is that there is a difference between comparing the preferences or well-being of actually existing individuals and comparing existence with nonexistence. From the fact that an individual, once brought into existence, prefers a bad life to no life at all, it does not follow that it is desirable, let alone required, to bring that individual into existence. It does follow, however, that it would be wrong to kill that individual, once alive.

This example suggests a more general point. Whenever at least one of the alternatives among which we are asked to choose differs by the addition or deletion of at least one member from the reference groups of the other alternatives, the criterion of Pareto optimality cannot be applied at all. If an individual does not exist under alternative A, then it is meaningless to say that that individual is better off under B than under A. "Better off" is a judgment arrived at by comparing states of existence predicated of existing individuals; if someone does not now exist, there is no possible basis of comparison.[59]

But even if average utility is acceptable in the abstract, one may well object to its application to the problem of justice among generations. Suppose we temporarily occupy a public campsite. When we leave, we are asked to restore it to the status quo ante by cleaning it up and repairing any damage we may have caused. But we are not asked to improve it by building tables or fireplaces that were not there when we came. The guiding principle is a negative one: No one's opportunity should be decreased by the position he happens to occupy on the temporal continuum, if such decrease can be avoided through human effort. If someone fulfills this obligation and goes beyond it, latecomers benefit from and ought to be grateful for the act. But they could not claim it as their due, and no one could be required to perform it. It was an act of benevolence, not justice. Similarly, one might argue, our overall responsibility to future generations is not to use our opportunities so as to decrease theirs. We must avoid the destruction of resources, for example, through the long-term contamination of land and sea by radioactive wastes. We must set aside enough of what we produce to provide for the depreciation of instruments of production, and we must either halt the depletion of natural resources by replacing them as we use them (reforestation), or, when this is impossible, set aside enough resources to discover adequate substitutes for them (investment in solar energy). But beyond this, we have no obligation to provide future generations with a better way of life than the one we enjoy, and we do not behave unjustly if we choose not to make sacrifices on their behalf.

There is, I suspect, no conclusive response to this line of argument. But imagine a world that shared our concept of the good but lacked the concept of claim. If we assume, as we have throughout, that in all our acts we pursue the good and that the best act is the one that promotes the good to the greatest extent, then in the claimless world the best acts would simply be maximizing acts. As we have presented it, the theory of justice is a set of claim-based constraints on simple maximization. These claims are of two sorts: those arising from the brute fact of our separate existences as individuals, and those arising from specific qualities of our existence that distinguish one individual from another. If this general view of justice is correct, and if we may assume that no other kinds of rational constraints exist, then justice itself implies that rational action is maximizing action except when maximizing conflicts with those claims specific to justice.

Given our empirical assumptions, savings beyond what is required for the maintenance of the status quo is maximizing action except when the status quo contains everything needed for the attainment of the human good. The question, then, is whether there are claims of the present generation that constitute constraints on maximization of the good over time. We have already discussed one such constraint—the utility floor. But unless we live in truly wretched circumstances, this will not rule out all saving. A broader constraint might be based on the principle of production: Each generation is entitled to dispose as it wishes of what it has brought into being through its collective efforts. But even if this were granted, the fact remains that only a small percentage of our total product is directly attributable to our own efforts. The greater part we owe either to nature or to the accumulated efforts of past generations. We are not so much the owners as we are the trustees of these inestimable benefits.

We may support this with an argument based on moral psychology. Suppose we believe that a lifetime of effort will make us no richer, wiser, or more contented than we are now. Under these circumstances, I suggest, it would be very difficult to act at all. Hope—belief in the possibility of significant improvement—is a precondition for ascribing meaning to our lives, unless we are fortunate enough to have everything we need and want. Kant suggested that this is true a fortiori for our existence as a species.

> It is a sight fit for a god to watch a virtuous man grappling with adversity and evil temptations and yet managing to hold out against them. But it is a sight quite unfit not so much for a god, but even for the most ordinary, though right-thinking man, to see the human race advancing over a period of time toward virtue, and then quickly relapsing the whole way back into vice and misery. It may perhaps be moving and instructive to watch such a drama for a while; but the curtain must eventually descend. For in the long run it becomes a farce.[60]

But progress is in part within our power to control. By sacrificing for the future, we make it more likely that those who come after us will enjoy a better existence. By saving, then, we help to transform a farce into a meaningful drama. If we do this, we may well enjoy more satisfaction than we could derive from the heedless consumption of everything within our grasp.[61]

Other species

I have already discussed at length the philosophical basis of the argument that other species of animals have valid claims that we are not free to ignore. Animals are not simply material objects to be used as we wish. All animals have interests—specific goods toward which they tend to strive, the absence of which is felt as deprivation or lack. In cases of conflict, we may give preference to the interests of our own species, but only when the good we obtain is clearly more significant than the harm animals undergo.

The interests of animals are divided into two broad categories: existence and developed existence. The interest of existence has a number of important implications for human policy. We are not free to annihilate entire species unless the existence of our own species is at stake. Thus, for example, it would be wrong to wipe out a species just to be able to generate electric power a bit more cheaply. We are not free to engage in wanton killing of individual animals—hunting for sport. If, however, there is evidence that natural ecological forces will lead to the death of significant numbers of animals, we may kill a smaller number to prevent this. We may kill animals for food only to preserve ourselves, when no morally preferable alternative is available. And we may kill animals during experimentation only when it is reasonable to suppose that some greater good—exemption from death or prevention of serious disease for ourselves or other species—will be secured thereby. The mere satisfaction of human curiosity about the pain thresholds of other species or their response to extreme situations is a patently inadequate justification.

The interest of development requires us to provide animals dependent on us with what they need for full physical development and enjoyment of their natural mode of existence. We are not justified in subjecting them to growth-stunting malnutrition or depriving them of space and freedom to exercise. Nor is it appropriate to alter animals, physically or behaviorally, merely for our own amusement and gratification.

As Nozick notes, introducing the notion of "natural" or "nondegraded" existence raises a tangle of difficulties, since it calls into question practices such as breeding animals for domestication. This issue would not be difficult if it were clear that domestication benefited the animals in question as well as human beings. Aristotle made exactly this claim. Not only is the rule of reason over nonreason natural, so that tame animals are by nature better than wild, but also human rule over animals conduces to their safety or preservation.[62] Each of these assertions is questionable. The first rests on an inference from the appropriate relation between parts of the soul within one organism to relations between organisms. But this is invalid, especially if each organism has a particular kind of good that it seeks in its own way. Thus, our ordinary judgments by no means unequivocally favor tame animals. We find tame animals more useful for our purposes, but we frequently find wild animals more interesting, exciting, or even admirable. Consider our response to an animal that refuses to accept captivity and struggles to the death to regain its freedom.

Aristotle's second argument is no more persuasive. The rule of humans conduces to the preservation of animals primarily when we have deliberately rendered them dependent on us. In circumstances of natural freedom, they care for themselves quite successfully, and they frequently languish when we abruptly substitute our contrived practices for their spontaneous instincts. Besides, the claim that human rule is good because it preserves animals coexists very uneasily with the contention that nature intends animals to be eaten by man.[63]

6.3. The Allocation of Opportunities for Development

All activities have two dimensions: external effects on nature and other beings, and internal effects on the agent. Internal effects are of two kinds: alterations in the agent's state of satisfaction, and contributions or obstacles to the agent's development. Activities that offer the possibility of significant contributions may be called opportunities for development. As we have seen, some productive activities provide this benefit as well. But many developmental activities make little or no contribution to the production of goods and services.

Opportunities for development stand in a complex relation to the system of production. They are, to begin with, dependent on it. They require resources drawn from production, and those participating in them must be exempted, temporarily or permanently, from productive activities. Development requires leisure. It follows, then, that at least some developmental activities are dictated by and subordinated to the needs of production. Without certain kinds of trained abilities, the level of production will drop, reducing the quantity of resources that can be devoted to human development.

But intrinsically production is subordinated to development. Goods and services are means; development is an end, one of the fundamental elements of the human good. The partial and limited subordination of development to production is justified only by physical needs and by the material preconditions of development itself. Thus, a fundamental perversion occurs when the subordination of development to production continues beyond that point. A wealthy community that determines the worth of all activities by the extent to which they add to its wealth has forgotten what wealth is for. A system of training, education, and culture wholly subservient to the system of production denies the humanity of its participants, no matter how clever and sophisticated it may appear.

The appropriate balance between what we may call "technical" and "liberal" development cannot be determined abstractly, but only in relation to the overall material circumstances of the community. A very poor community may well devote all the scarce resources at its disposal to the cultivation of abilities that increase production. Indeed, to do otherwise would be unjust to those whose physical needs are not fully provided for. In an extraordinarily wealthy community, each individual would have as much leisure as he could use, coupled with a broad variety of developmental opportunities. Here, limitations on development would be exclusively internal, and each individual would progress as far as his desire and innate ability would carry him.

Let us consider the intermediate case of a community that has some surplus beyond the requirements of physical need and technical development to devote to liberal development, but far less than what would be necessary to eliminate all external limits on development. In this situation of partial scarcity, two related problems emerge: the general design of a developmental system, and the allocation of opportunities within that system.

In general terms, claims on developmental opportunities are based on an individual's ability to profit from them. If I have no innate talent in a particular area, it is unjust for me to exclude someone with that talent and the desire to develop it from the opportunity to do so. Unfortunately, this general principle does not take us very far toward the resolution of the allocative problem, even though it rules out many flagrant abuses. We need, in addition, answers to two questions.

First, how do we compare the importance or moral weight of the benefits derived from radically different *kinds* of opportunities? Consider an extreme example: Suppose that the same amount of resources will enable a congenitally retarded person to learn the rudiments of speech and motor coordination or an immensely talented person to become a brilliant mathematician. (To rule out irrelevant complications, let us stipulate that the net external effects will be equal.) Each person has reached the limit of which he is capable. But is the full development of every individual of equal weight, whatever the differences of natural endowment?

We discussed this question previously, in the context of income distribution. Our conclusions are applicable here. There is a distinction between the intrinsic worth of a human characteristic and its claim-generating properties. Ceteris paribus, we would prefer a world in which everyone's innate capacities were more extensive to our present world, and we would choose to be mathematically talented rather than congenitally retarded. Accordingly, we would prefer *for ourselves* the full development of more extensive capacities to the full development of lesser ones. But it does not follow from this that whenever the developmental interests of different individuals come into conflict, the development of higher or more extensive capacities is to be given priority. A policy that simply maximizes the sum of intrinsic worth treats the characteristics of separate individuals as an artificial, disembodied unity, forgetting precisely that they have no existence apart from the individuals in whom they inhere.

It may be argued, nonetheless, that there is something more horrible about the incomplete development of great capacities than the waste of lesser gifts. This objection has an intuitive appeal, but one might say with equal justice that it is more horrible for someone who can be taught to speak to be condemned to a life of inarticulate quasi-animality than for someone who could have been a great mathematician to lead an ordinary life. Perhaps the most we can say is that our intuitions about the relative desirability of the best cases are more or less counterbalanced by the relative unacceptability of the worst cases.

This position is midway between the principle of perfection that Rawls castigates and the Difference Principle that he advocates.[64] On the one hand, there is no intrinsic reason why the claims of those with higher capacities should be given greater weight in the allocation of developmental opportunities. On the other hand, it is both arbitrary and counterintuitive to give priority to the least favored. Nozick's objection is decisive: If it is not self-evidently right for families to skew the expenditure of educational resources toward their least talented children, then how can this bias be appropriate as a matter of public policy?[65]

In circumstances of scarcity, however, there are usually good reasons to give greater weight to the more favored. Their abilities, once developed, can be used to benefit others as well, while frequently the development of the less gifted benefits no one except themselves. Thus, for example, it would make sense for a poor rural village to use all of its developmental resources to provide higher education to its most talented young person, with the understanding that the educated person would return to operate a primary school that all could attend. The policy of concentrating resources would be much harder to defend if the young person could not reasonably be expected to return.

The second question considers not only different kinds of development, but also different degrees. Imagine a small community with 15 students, 5 of whom can derive benefit from 5 years of education, 5 from 10, and 5 from 15. (For simplicity, suppose that the cost of education per year per pupil is the same, regardless of level.) There is no difficulty if the community can afford 150 pupil-years of education; each student could be educated to the limits of his capacity. But if the community can spend only half that amount on education, various alternatives emerge. Each student could be given a basic 5-year education; each could be given the same fraction (one half) of what he can use with profit; each of the most talented could be given a full 15-year education.

Ceteris paribus, the answer depends on the shape of the learning curve. If learning is "front-loaded," for example, if the first group does 100 percent of its learning in the first 5 years, the second 80 percent, and the third 60 percent, the case for giving everyone a basic 5-year education is strengthened. If learning were perfectly linear, the equal-fraction alternative would become more attractive. Underlying our intuitions is the principle that valid claims should be proportionately requited. Resources should be allocated so that each individual is enabled to develop his innate abilities to roughly the same degree.

Two lines of argument suggest that the basic education solution is preferable. The first is our intuition that the greatest development does occur during the earliest years of formal training. The world is opened up to us, and we learn how to learn for ourselves. If we can read accurately and imaginatively, think logically, and perform simple mathematical operations, we can continue to progress through our own efforts. For those of more limited ability or ambition, basic education is the difference between a degree of openness and self-determination on the one hand, or a life closed in on itself, bounded by the narrowness of direct experience and traditional authority.

The second line of argument is that in practice the conditions of our example are unrealistic. We cannot know at the outset the degree to which different individuals can profit from education and training. With rare exceptions, these judgments can be made responsibly only after individual differences have manifested themselves during the process of education itself. The prolonged and acrimonious debate about the British 11+ examination system suggests that five or six years of primary education are an insufficient basis for the allocation of further opportunities. Thus, a system that provides extensive opportunities for a few while excluding most others from any share is almost certain to allocate those opportunities arbitrarily, on the basis of status, wealth, or family background rather than on the ability to profit from them.

Of course, a poor community may not be able to adopt the norm of universal basic education as an immediate policy. The needs of production and governance may dictate a crash program of developing a small, highly trained technical and intellectual elite. But such a program can in the long run be justified only by the increased opportunities that the others, temporarily excluded, come to enjoy as a result. All too often, the elite forgets that it is only an instrument for community development and comes to think of its knowledge as a mark of innate superiority and its privileges as the just reward of that superiority. All developing countries face this antinomy in one form or another: knowledge and skill are at once indispensable and, as a kind of power, profoundly dangerous. The only solution that goes to the roots of the problem is moral education that instructs the able in the duties that accompany their opportunities. The Chinese appear to have recognized this, only to run up against a new difficulty: Those most dedicated to the community are not necessarily those with the talents needed to promote the community's well-being.

6.4. The Allocation of Political Goods

The two main classes of political goods have been well established since Aristotle's analysis—citizenship and positions of public trust and responsibility.

6.4.a. Citizenship

We may define the citizen of a community as someone who: may fully participate in judging that community's public policy and the performance of its leaders; is eligible for positions of leadership on equal terms with all others; and is entitled to the full protection of the laws and the use of common resources for physical and material support on equal terms with all others.

Citizenship, then, is a sphere of equality. Citizens will vary in competence and influence, but all are equally permitted to bring whatever qualities of will and intellect they possess to bear on the determination of public affairs. The equality of citizens is linked to the formal characteristic of the claims on citizenship. To have a valid claim on citizenship in a community is to meet all the necessary conditions for citizenship. All who meet them have an equal claim, are equally "qualified."[66] Just allocation of citizenship is its allocation to all qualified individuals, and the theory of citizenship is the enumeration of its necessary conditions.

First, the citizen must be able to act independently and to assume responsibility for his acts. This condition usually takes the form of a requirement that full participation be limited to those who have reached the age of maturity. The defects of this requirement are well known: There is no guarantee that chronological and psychological maturity will be correlated. But the requirement expresses a statistical tendency, combined with the conceptual and practical difficulties inherent in any attempt to make a case-by-case determination.

Many have observed that independence has a socioeconomic as well as psychological component. Rousseau feared that the poor would sell their votes for bread. This has come to pass in big-city political machines, industrial company towns, and in rural areas where a few rich landowners can control the lives and livelihoods of tenant farmers.[67] Kant drew a distinction between independent and servile occupations: In independent occupations one sells or exchanges one's skill or the products of that skill, while in the servile, other individuals direct the use of one's labor power.[68] More recently, various critics have suggested that the economic inequalities permitted by Rawls's Difference Principle tend to undercut the equality of citizenship on which he insists.[69]

These are reasonable qualifications. I believe, however, that they are superfluous in the context of the just economy I have just described. If the fulfillment of needs is given priority, the principle of contribution recognized, and tasks organized with an eye toward the development of individual producers, then participating individuals will view themselves and be viewed by others as substantially independent.

Second, the citizen must be able to articulate his interests and to evaluate the effects of present and proposed policies on them. This is less stringent than it may appear. All those who can speak intelligibly, think—however slowly and haltingly, remember and imagine with some accuracy, and perceive themselves and their environment without excessive distortion, may be presumed to fulfill this requirement. Two kinds of individual are, however, excluded: those whose innate intelligence is so low that speech and reasonable self-regard are not possible, and those, whatever their intelligence, whose sense of themselves and of their world has become seriously warped. Without care and guidance, such individuals tend to harm rather than benefit themselves. They are entitled to the protection of the laws and the care of the community, but in crucial respects others must make decisions for them, on their behalf.

As recent events have shown, these requirements may be abused. To preserve itself from critical scrutiny and change, a community may label as disturbed or disordered someone whose views differ sharply from prevailing opinions, who perceives injustice more clearly and responds to it more intensely and courageously than do "normal" individuals. But the existence of such abuses does not mean that all mental illness can be analyzed as moral dissent or, *pace* Laing, as a "rational" response to contradictory imperatives. At most, it indicates the need for careful prodecures, exempt from political pressures, to determine instances of mental illness, and for standards of normality that give the benefit of the doubt to aberrant individuals and that have been rigorously scrutinized for subtle social and political biases. The belief that mental illness is political, that it merely represents the boundary of what a particular community is willing to accept, is gaining ground as one of the intellectual pieties of our age. It is as one-sided and dangerous as the complacent, unselfconscious, or repressive concepts of normality it seeks to overthrow.

Third, the citizen must recognize and take into account the interests and claims of others. In the best case, all would accept and act on the principles of justice. But if perfect justice were a criterion of citizenship, there would be few if any citizens. Rather, the citizen's self-preference, his inner tendency toward injustice, must be limited by a sense of reciprocity, rudimentary fairness, and shame. This requirement, then, excludes those who through a sequence of acts have manifested a settled determination to ignore the claims of others. Such acts include serious crime—theft, assault, murder—when they are committed for private gain rather than as part of an effort to ameliorate or overthrow unjust institutions. Equally culpable are those who cling stubbornly to blatantly unjustified privileges, maintained at the expense of others. After a political upheaval, the formerly oppressed may allow their former oppressors to retain citizenship for practical reasons or as a gesture of reconciliation, but they need not do so as a matter of justice.

Fourth, the citizen must have a basic understanding of the language, beliefs, history, and institutions of his community. They are the community's common experience, on the basis of which sharing, joint action, and what Aristotle called "concord" or "civic friendship" can exist.[70] An individual who wishes to participate with others in determining or judging public affairs must be able to speak directly to them and to understand the meaning or significance of facts, events, and proposals. But meaning is both contextual and historical. For example, to understand a state of affairs, we must know whether it represents progress or regress from previous conditions and how it is perceived and evaluated by our fellow citizens. To understand the reaction to a proposal, we must know something about how its constitutive terms and principles have been employed in the past, and to what effect.

I do not mean to suggest that this shared experience is harmonious or homogeneous, for this is never the case. Indeed, it is the partial discordance or even contradiction within this experience that provides the profoundest political opportunities. A crucial element of political skill and efficacy is the ability to use the admirable elements of a tradition as weapons against its less admirable beliefs and practices. We must, as Oakeshott suggests, pursue the "intimations" of our tradition. But equally, we must choose *which* of its intimations to pursue, and tradition cannot make this choice for us. Our shared experience gives us a political vocabulary and grammar, not a script.

Clearly, this requirement is fraught with peril. Goethe was not alone in arguing that Jews could not be full citizens of any European nation because they did not participate in Christianity, the most fundamental element of the shared European experience. Thus, some Jews sought to become citizens through conversion. Others strove to overcome their disability by working to increase the importance of the secular, universal component of the European experience at the expense of Christianity, or, less honestly and realistically, by convincing themselves that this change had occurred or would inevitably and automatically occur. In the event, of course, Goethe was right. The problem of Jewish citizenship was resolved only by the creation of a community at the core of which stood the shared Jewish experience and by emigration to communities whose self-definition was much more strongly secular.

There is no sure or mechanical way to distinguish the fundamental from the peripheral or to guarantee that shared experience will not be used as an excuse to block change and perpetuate injustice. Nevertheless, shared experience cannot be ignored as a criterion of citizenship. Not only is it a brute fact, but also the sharing that its determinate particularity makes possible is the basis of much of what is beneficial and satisfying in our collective existence.

Fifth and finally, a citizen must be loyal to his community. Loyalty consists in two related elements: a deep and enduring bond of attachment to the community, and the settled determination to give preference to the interests of that community, to the extent that justice permits. Thus, loyalty is to the community as love is to the family. To love one's parents is not to believe that they are without flaws or to accept them as they are but rather to acknowledge profound obligations and similarities. These obligations are not unbounded. If a parent has committed a horrible crime, the child is not required to conceal it or to obstruct the course of justice. But it would be strange not to accept small misdemeanors and to swear out a complaint as one would against a stranger. If resources are limited, it would be wrong to be impartial between the claims of one's family and of others.[71]

Similarly, loyalty to one's community does not mean unquestioning acceptance of all its beliefs and practices but, rather, acknowledgment of the benefits one has received coupled with endorsement of its basic principles. We cannot, then, be expected to be loyal to a community that deliberately inflicts harm on us or that rests on a foundation of grave injustice. At most, loyalty requires that we be predisposed in favor of our community and that we place the burden of proof on those who accuse and attack it. A sign of loyalty is that, when we are forced to oppose our community, we do so with regret rather than with zealous and joyful hate. Loyalty is not conformity, but it limits both the content and the manner of our dissent.

The criterion of loyalty is always controversial to a certain extent because, as we observed before, there is no simple way of distinguishing basic principles from peripheral practices. At some level of generality, everything is the same, and communism becomes "twentieth-century Americanism." In practice, though, we can usually distinguish among policies, institutions, and principles. Loyalty permits us to attack policies and institutions in the name of principles, as long as our method of opposition is not such as to subvert those principles.

There is, then, an important difference between citizen loyalty and family love. The object of love is individuals, not the arrangement of or the relations among them. Our obligation to our parents does not cease if they become divorced. The object of loyalty, on the other hand, is dual. It consists in individuals, the fellow members of our community, and in the underlying ordering of individuals that determines our collective purposes and deliberative practices. We are asked to be loyal, then, to both the form and the matter of our collective existence. A person who in all sincerity tries to overthrow the government with the aim of benefiting the members of his community may fairly claim to be benevolent but cannot be considered loyal. A person who is impartial among all communities espousing the same principles as his own is not loyal in the full sense, although he is closer to being so than the benevolent revolutionary.

If we acknowledge these five requirements as necessary conditions, it follows directly that communities may deprive members who do not—or cease to—fulfill them of citizenship, and they may on the same basis deny citizenship to nonmembers. A more interesting question is whether these requirements, considered together, should be construed as sufficient conditions. If so, justice would demand that a community admit into full citizenship all individuals who both fulfilled them and indicated a desire to join. There can, I suggest, be only one objection—the possibility that admitting large numbers of new citizens will significantly reduce the per capita income of present citizens. This may be dealt with quite simply on the basis of our previous discussions. If a community has fully discharged its obligations of economic justice toward other communities, and if there are strong reasons to believe that the admission of new citizens will further decrease per capita income, then it does not behave unjustly in excluding them. If a community has not discharged its economic obligations, it has no basis for exclusion even if admission will reduce per capita income, since it does not have a valid claim to the level of prosperity it presently enjoys. In present circumstances, the restrictive immigration policies adopted by most of the wealthier nations can be viewed only as wholly unwarranted acts of collective selfishness.

These considerations do not affect the problem of emigration policy, which is much more complex. On the one hand, the desire to emigrate may be construed as a breach of loyalty. It may also constitute a failure of reciprocity: the individual has benefited in various ways from membership in the community, which has invested its resources to provide him with productive skills in the expectation that all will profit from them. The would-be emigrant must consider the possibility that his departure will make the situation of others even less tolerable. From the most general standpoint, it may be the case that a universal policy of unrestricted emigration would leave the vast majority worse off, since the most talented and ambitious would lack incentive to work for the amelioration of economic and political imperfections in their native communities.[72] On the other hand, individuals may have accepted benefits from the community involuntarily, in the belief that they would never have an alternative to life in that community. This is especially likely to be the case when these individuals are members of groups treated unjustly or persecuted by the community's dominant groups, since, as we argued previously, a community that harms particular individuals has no claim to loyalty from them. Finally, the imperative to remain and fight is weakened if there are good reasons to believe that one's own efforts, even when combined with all others of like mind, are not likely to make the community's policies more just or its way of life more tolerable.

We arrive at the following broad conclusions: If a community has treated would-be emigrants justly, then it is reasonable for it to require compensation for its investment in them, either from the emigrants themselves or from the community that will benefit from their skills without having underwritten their development. A just community may also restrict emigration as it sees fit, since most of those wishing to leave are motivated by hope of economic gain, which they place above loyalty to the community that has treated them well. Without restrictive emigration, it would be very difficult for poor communities to improve themselves through a program of internal development. But if a community has treated would-be emigrants unjustly, it does not have a valid claim to compensation for skills they may have acquired, since they have already paid for them many times over in the course of being denied their fair share of economic or political goods. Further, an unjust community has no excuse whatever to restrict the migration of those it mistreats. Not only does injustice sever the obligation of loyalty, but also it means that the community refuses to consider its recipients as full and equal members. From a moral standpoint, it is a simple contradiction simultaneously to deny certain individuals the privileges of full citizenship while insisting that they remain to bear its full burdens. From the standpoint of a cynical national policy—the benefits of exploitation, joys of persecution, or requirements of national unity and prestige—this moral contradiction may of course make perfect sense.

6.4.b. Political leadership

In considering the question of political leadership, Aristotle's distinction between making and judging furnishes a useful point of departure. We are in need of shoes and, therefore, of shoemakers. But we do not need to be shoemakers or to possess their skills in order to judge their products. Sound judgment requires only common sense and an awareness of our own desires and interests. Other experts may from time to time contribute to the process of judging, as when podiatrists inform us that certain shoes that look and feel good may in the long run cause foot problems. At most, though, these experts provide facts or statistical relations, while we as users furnish the general criteria of worth within which their testimony attains significance. And, finally, it is *our* experience of the product, its actual effect on our well being, that constitutes the focus of judgment.

There is, to a certain extent, an analogy between politics and technical activities. As we have defined it, citizenship involves the capacity for judging policies, a capacity well within the competence of normal human beings if they are allowed to develop and exercise it appropriately. But the ability to judge does not necessarily imply the ability to make. Policy in the broad sense, the political "product," has three major components: the formulation of proposals in response to problems or opportunities; the justification of proposals by linking them to and articulating the shared experiences of the community; and the execution of proposals, once adopted, in light of particular circumstances. If all citizens can fulfill these functions with equal ability, then all should do so, simultaneously or sequentially. But if there are differences of ability, claims to perform these functions would seem to be unequal as well. After all, the purpose of public policy is the well-being of the community. If the more able make it, or have a greater voice than others, the well-being of all citizens will be promoted to a greater extent.

Even if the ability to make policy were equally distributed, a further consideration suggests the need for some institutional distinction between making and judging. Experience shows that, considered collectively, a large group of individuals is more able to judge the merits of a proposal than to devise one. Even relatively small groups find it expedient to deputize a few of their members to formulate proposals in a designated area and to report back to the full group. This is the case even when the deputies are not thought to be more able or concerned than are the other members. Similar considerations underlie the traditional desire for a strong executive. The fact that this strength can and will be abused does not mean that the community can do without it entirely.

In discussing Schaar's views, I have already argued that there is a distinctive political skill, consisting in specific characteristics of mind, character, and self-presentation, and that it is unequally distributed. I shall not repeat this argument here. It is, I believe, amply confirmed by our everyday experience of politics, where the distinction between competence and incompetence emerges with brutal clarity. But we may now add a crucial element: Political excellence in the full sense has two components, skill and the settled determination to act justly, informed by an understanding of the requirements of justice. In isolation, each component may harm the community. But there is no greater blessing than the presence of individuals in whom they are conjoined. It is political excellence in this sense that provides the amplest claim to positions of responsibility and trust.

There are two qualifications. First, the fact that political excellence is unequally distributed does not mean that the citizen body is divided into those who fully possess it and those who lack it entirely. There is, rather, a continuum, and only rarely is some individual absolutely preeminent. A system that seeks to allocate positions of leadership justly must therefore seek to disperse leadership, functionally or temporally, so that all those with a significant claim may participate in proportion to that claim. The existence of local and regional as well as national offices may in part serve this function, as may other sorts of decentralization. Obviously, the employment of the procedure is constrained somewhat by the need for dispatch and coordination. It is also possible to restrict the length of time that any one individual may occupy a particular position of leadership. The more equally excellence is distributed and the easier it is to make good the loss of experience, the greater the net benefits of this policy.

Second, to the extent that political skill is an element of individual development and comes into being through the exercise of responsibility, a broader dispersion of leadership is desirable than would be dictated by the distribution of skill at any given time. As is the case in technical activities, the problem is to balance the internal against the external effects. Clearly, the claims of individual development are strengthened as the potential harm stemming from the misuse of responsibility diminishes. President Kennedy's famous jest on appointing his brother Attorney General, that he wanted to give him some experience before he went out to practice law, would have been monumentally irresponsible if it had been intended seriously. But the underlying argument may be sensible in cases in which the content of authority is less important, its scope more restricted, or its exercise more subject to supervision and review.

Describing in general terms the bases of valid claims to political leadership is very far from specifying a mechanism that will select individuals in accordance with these claims. All of the traditional alternatives—hereditary monarchy or aristocracy, elite training, advancement through a dominant party or organization, election, lot—are imperfect procedures in Rawls's sense, and each has its characteristic difficulties. There probably is no best alternative, valid for all times and circumstances. In every situation, then, the prime task is to diagnose and to prescribe for the specific structural defects revealed by experience. For example, citizens of the United States should ask whether the existing format of presidential and congressional elections tends to select for certain individual characteristics and, if so, whether the degree of overlap between these characteristics and political excellence is the highest achievable within the range of available electoral procedures. Clearly, this question must be posed far more precisely, and rigorous empirical studies are required. There is, however, a growing body of anecdotal evidence suggesting that individuals of honor and ability have become increasingly discouraged by the rigors—some remediable—of the electoral gauntlet, and that the qualities of persistence, determination, organization, and obfuscation needed to win elections at the national level stand at some considerable remove from the excellence successful policymaking requires.

6.5. Public Honor

We may define public honor as praise and recognition bestowed, spontaneously or through collective decision, by the community on individuals who are usually though not invariably members of that community. Public honor may take many forms: medals, titles, admission to honorary societies, encomia, ceremonies, to name but a few. Its purpose is to single out particular kinds of individuals for admiration and emulation. There are, then, only two valid claims to public honor: individual excellence, and acts that greatly benefit the community.

It is clear that honor falls within the purview of justice, since we believe that it can be misallocated. We frequently say that A did not deserve his recognition or that B, whose acts or qualities are far superior, has been "unjustly neglected." And we may feel that prevailing standards of public honor are inappropriate, even if A and B have been treated with formal fairness.

In every community some individuals are honored to a greater extent than others. Frequently, though, they are honored for acts and qualities unrelated to the real needs and advantage of the community and even antithetical to the virtues it claims to admire. A system of public honor tends to close the gap between private and official belief, reducing hypocrisy and increasing the unity and integrity of the community.

Since honor is very widely prized and sought, it strongly tends to encourage the development of those qualities and the performance of those acts to which it is known to be linked. It is both an incentive and a reward. Considered as an incentive, it is in one sense intrinsically scarce. If all are equally honored, no one is really honored. Honor is selective, a mark of distinction, and it depreciates as it is multiplied. In another sense, honor is plentiful. It does not require the diversion of material resources, and it may be added without cost to the armory of incentives a community has at its disposal. It is, then, equally available to rich and poor communities. Indeed, poor communities have reasons to give it great weight. They have little choice, since material resources that can be deployed as incentives are limited. And, in the absence of other incentives, honor is likely to be more than ordinarily effective.

Honor also has advantages as a reward. In many cases it seems far more appropriate than material rewards. There is, for example, a gross disproportion between money and exemplary courage, while public recognition (the Congressional Medal of Honor) is closer to payment in moral currency. Further, honor does not pervert virtue or excellence as readily as does material reward. An act performed for money may be highly useful, but it loses all tincture of virtue. As Aristotle noted, there is, if not identity, a kind of harmony and congruence between virtue and honor:

> Men seem to pursue honor to assure themselves of their own worth; at any rate, they seek to be honored by sensible men and by those who know them, and they want to be honored on the basis of their virtue or excellence.[73]

We seek honor as a remedy for the intrinsic imperfections of self-knowledge. Thus, honor is worthless, or worse than worthless, if its public justification contradicts what we know to be true about ourselves. Love of honor would be the "last infirmity of noble minds" only if we could attain full self-knowledge. It becomes a perversion only when the proper balance between internal and external criteria is upset and we frantically seek from others what we can only give to ourselves.

Communities, then, would be well advised to substitute honor for material incentives to the greatest possible extent. This would not only reduce the importance of the component of income least related to personal merit or claims but would also be conducive to the habits of mind and character the development of which is one of the major aims of the community.[74]

7

Conclusion

In this concluding chapter I want to develop, very briefly, some of the implications of my analysis of justice.

7.1. Justice and Democracy

We employ principles of justice to evaluate the operation of political institutions and procedures. However desirable they may appear in other respects, particular institutions and procedures cannot be considered just unless they tend strongly to lead to just outcomes.

If all or nearly all members of a community were just, institutions would not make much difference. Disagreements would be limited to matters of fact or projected future consequences of available alternatives. Everyone would trust everyone else to act correctly, giving due weight to every interest. Checks and balances would be unnecessary. Indeed, it would be wholly reasonable to delegate the most skillful and farsighted individuals to act for the community, subject only to the restriction that others may benefit from a more limited opportunity to serve in some political capacity. Institutions would be devised to promote, as efficiently as possible, certain technical objectives: collection, organization, and dissemination of information; full deliberation and unambiguous decisions; effective coordination of individuals in pursuit of shared goals; and supervision and evaluation of policies, once undertaken.

Within a theory of justice, a more extensive problem of institutions arises for two reasons. First, individuals have neither a well-developed innate understanding of justice nor an innate propensity to act justly. Political institutions are required in order to promulgate an understanding of justice and to render it effective through civic and moral education. Second, not all human beings can be made just through education. Of those open to moral education, some can be improved to a much greater extent than others; some are or become wholly impervious and can be influenced only by external rewards and punishments.

The devisers of fundamental institutions are therefore compelled to ask whether human beings can be organized so as to dampen the effects of their unjust *intentions* in the determination of their collective *acts*. In this connection, some have argued that the closest possible approximation to justice would flow from the most perfectly democratic institutions and that existing injustices, insofar as they are remediable at all, can be ameliorated by moving toward a more perfect democracy.

In the abstract, this thesis is implausible. If within a given community some are more just than others, it would seem that results more in accordance with justice could be obtained by giving the more just a greater say in the determination of collective decisions. But, the democrat will reply, this "aristocratic" proposal, however appealing, has already transcended the institutional plane. There is no way to guarantee that, once the aristocratic principle is adopted, those who are more just will in fact end up occupying positions of greater authority. Indeed, there are reasons to believe that the less just will strive more effectively, if less scrupulously, to obtain them. If the rule of the best is best, the rule of the worst is worst. All institutions that strive for the former leave open the possibility of the latter. Since the latter is very terrible, it is unreasonable to run a significant risk of permitting it to come about. Democracy therefore forgoes any direct attempt to place the best in positions of authority, though it may seek to create a tendency in that direction through auxiliary devices, in order to preclude the possibility that the worst will obtain great or unlimited power.

We cannot enter into a full evaluation of the democrat's claim to comparative institutional superiority or of the appropriateness of his use of the maximin criterion. But we can at least clarify the problem by examining the impact of democratic institutions on different distributive sectors.

If democracy is viewed simply as a decisionmaking procedure, the problem becomes indeterminate, since democratic procedures are compatible with a very broad range of institutional structures. The College of Cardinals elects the Pope; the Politburo resolves some policy and personnel questions by majority vote. But neither the Catholic church nor the Soviet Union is customarily considered to be a democracy. At least since Aristotle's analysis, democracy has been associated not only with a specific kind of decisionmaking procedure but also with a system in which a high proportion of the individuals comprising the community have the opportunity to participate in that procedure.

If we view democracy in this manner, we can say from the outset that in one respect democracy is clearly more just than other alternatives: the distribution of citizenship. Our analysis of citizenship produced a set of criteria that most members of the community are likely to satisfy. Any system that excludes a large proportion of its population from full citizenship through racial, economic, or sexual restrictions or through a dominant political party that in effect divides the community into participants and nonparticipants, is almost certainly unjust in that respect and probably in others as well. It is not accidental that when Aristotle examined citizenship, the definition he arrived at was, as he noted, democratic.[1]

On the other hand, there does not seem to be a close relation between democracy and wise allocation of leadership. Even in cases in which it is meaningful to speak of "the majority," the need to obtain and retain its support is compatible with good leadership only when the majority wants what is right and achievable without short-term sacrifice. Democracy does, however, have some advantages. It tends to broaden the pool of ideas and information from which leaders may draw. It alerts leaders to situations in which the efficacy of public policy will be undermined by popular resistance. And it places obstacles in the path of those who wish to rule only for their own advantage, disregarding the interests of the other members of the community.

Recent work suggests that in certain kinds of situations there is no one majority, but rather groups of minorities that can be combined in various ways to produce a large number of potential majorities. This would seem to offer the just leader who is also politically skillful some important opportunities within a democratic context. Far from passively accepting the dictates of a preformed majority, he may seek to define issues in such a way as to form a majority coalition of those whose views and intentions are most nearly just. American history offers many examples of this strategy, of which Lincoln's efforts during the 1850s are perhaps the most striking.

But this opportunity implies a countervailing disadvantage. Whenever one potential majority has been actualized, other possible majorities may be opposed to it by self-interested leaders appealing to the interests of those excluded from the prevailing majority. Thus, a just leader who is not supported by a stable majority that cares fairly intensely about his policies will always be vulnerable to successful attacks. In such circumstances, the just leader will be faced with a choice between losing power and tampering with democratic procedures.

This problem is particularly acute in the context of economic issues. It has been shown that there is no determinate solution to the problem of dividing resources by majority vote once we assume that each voter is interested in obtaining as large a share as possible for himself. Every proposed division can be defeated by another proposal, resulting in a voting cycle that must be arbitrarily—that is, nondemocratically—terminated. Worse, the range of possible proposals is very wide, and there is no tendency *stemming from democratic procedures* to move toward any particular pattern or outcome, egalitarian or otherwise.[2]

An important result follows. Many have quite properly criticized the "market" (the sphere of voluntary transactions) from the standpoint of economic justice as an imperfect procedure. Frequently, such critics seek to transfer allocative authority to the political sphere. But democratic voting is also a highly imperfect procedure. There is no way of determining a priori whether market mechanisms or political procedures are more conducive to the attainment of justice. As Aristotle observed, in the context of class war democratic politics can be the politics of expropriation.

In practice, one may suggest, the worst excesses will probably be avoided in a system in which the market and political institutions compete for jurisdiction over economic policy, each affecting but not dominating the other. In a rough way, the market tends to honor claims based on productivity or contribution, while democratic institutions allow those excluded from or mistreated by the system of production to press claims based on need.

In the last analysis, one must agree with Rawls that the quest for a purely institutional or procedural solution to the practical problem of obtaining justice is futile. Every community, whether democratic or not, must rely on a rudimentary sense of fairness and equity among its members.[3] This sense is not innate, but must rather be fostered through some system of education. The traditional American penchant for political engineering or institutional tinkering is thus profoundly one-sided; democratic procedures are almost vacuous in the absence of collectively held moral convictions.

Fortunately, there is some connection between democratic procedures and salutary beliefs. As events have shown, it is very difficult to proclaim one's adherence to democracy while seeking to exclude, for reasons of self-interest, groups of individuals from citizenship; the rational basis of democratic citizenship implies that most are eligible to enjoy it. Once someone is a fellow citizen, publicly visible and as entitled to press his claims as you are to press yours, it is very difficult to believe that his interests do not have to be taken into account. That is, any attempt to *justify* democratic procedures will rest on a set of principles, prudential and moral, that constrain the range of permissible decisions.

7.2. The Worth of Justice

Since the time of the Sophists, justice has been viewed as the most problematic virtue. It is easy to see how courage and wisdom are beneficial, but justice frequently demands sacrifices that do not seem to be to our advantage. What, then, can be our motive to act justly? What confers on justice the worth that should induce us to prefer it to injustice?

The Hobbesian answer, that in a system in which all act justly all are better off and that the "fool" who breaks rank will necessarily suffer a loss, is unpersuasive. It may hold true for ordinary injustice, but it overlooks the worry about single-minded, self-concealing, tyrannical injustice that motivates the argument of the *Republic*.

The Platonic answer turns on the meaning of *advantage*. The *Republic* culminates in the contention that the human good consists in the right ordering of the individual soul, with reason ruling, spiritedness a submissive ally, appetitiveness a chastened slave. But, we learn, justice is precisely this ordering. In choosing it, then, we choose the greatest advantage for ourselves; the problem of the motive dissolves.

Now—setting aside the doubts we may have about this as moral psychology—there is an obvious difficulty. The internal, psychological definition of justice is individualistic and egoistic. By itself, without the addition of other premises, it cannot lead to determinate judgments about states of affairs that, as we saw at the outset, are the primary focus of political justice. And it cannot tell us how, or why, to take the good of others into account when it conflicts with our own. The *Republic* purports to show that the greatest political advantage can be secured only through the rule of the wise. But the wise, it turns out, see the right ordering of their souls as secured more reliably through contemplative activities than through rule. Hence, they do not wish to rule and, given the premises already conceded, it is difficult to see what kinds of argument could be deployed to persuade them. As Plato indicated, the gulf between psychological and political justice can be bridged only by force—a distressingly paradoxical result.

The Platonic answer is not wrong in principle, but merely incomplete. Justice, I have argued, is a subset of rational activity. Thus, the worth of justice is a consequence of the worth we ascribe to rational activity. Justice is concerned with possessive relations. Individuals are morally linked to their possessions through claims—reasons that seek to justify the possessive relation. But reasons are, as we have seen, inherently and unavoidably generalizable. To espouse rationality is to grant that the weight of your claim is no more than equal to that of all others that can appeal to the same grounds, to the same degree. Although, as Plato saw, the worth of justice is rooted in a commitment to the rational life, justice moves from the internal life to the external world and from the individual to the collectivity, when we examine the logical entailments of rationality applied to the practices that constitute the domain of justice.

To say that justice is not an ought or commandment but rather an aspect of our human good is not to say that the practice of justice is easy or comfortable. Frequently, reason will not permit us to claim something that would serve one of our important interests: physical security, development, satisfaction. The knowledge that our renunciation has promoted our higher good and preserved our self-respect is never wholly unmixed with regret for advantages forgone. Perhaps we may dream of a harmonious world in which, as Marx said, the free development of each is the condition for the free development of all. Probably some conflict is ineradicable. If so, justice requires us to accept our share of the limitations fate has imposed on our species.

Aristotle confronted this difficulty at the end of the *Politics*. The full realization of the human good involves citizenship, which requires leisure for its mastery and exercise. Citizenship, then, is incompatible with a life devoted to the exigencies of economic production or exchange.[4] Citizens must have the use of property for which they are not required to work. Thus, the population of the community is to be divided into two categories: *integral parts*—citizens who do not work; and *necessary conditions*—workers who are debarred from citizenship. This is not necessarily disturbing if, as Aristotle argued, not all are capable of sharing in the developmental goods afforded by citizenship: "Some may share in it fully, but others can only share in it partially or cannot even share at all."[5] But Aristotle never argued that those excluded cannot benefit from participation. On the contrary, having given reasons why all noncitizens ought to be slaves, he observed that "it is wise to offer all slaves the eventual reward of emancipation."[6] If so, then slavery can hardly reflect natural incapacity.

Why did Aristotle prefer a situation in which some are wholly satisfied, others wholly deprived, to the other available alternative—universally shared partial deprivation? I suggest that he saw a world in which, for example, all would work for six hours a day as composed of lives not radically distinguished from simple slavery. Those who would have been leisured citizens suffer a great loss, while those who would have been slaves make only a marginal gain. Thus, aggregate human good is greatly reduced. On this interpretation, Aristotle was an ideal utilitarian, taking the human good as his maximand. The difficulty, of course, is that ideal utilitarianism so conceived is incompatible with the principle of proportionality—a principle Aristotle unequivocally reaffirmed at this very juncture in the *Politics*.[7] A choice needed to be made, but Aristotle does not appear to have made it.

This outcome may lead some readers to wonder whether there may not be more of a case for ideal utilitarianism than I have provided. Perhaps. I suggest, however, that it reveals the strength and plausibility of the proportionality principle, for which I have contended throughout this book. Proportionality reflects the determination to bring within the purview of reason our individual differences and collective limitations, without either denying or capitulating to them.

7.3. The Limits of Justice

The passion for justice is indispensable but dangerous, all too often shading over into destructive fanaticism. This excess is likely to occur when justice is identified with perfection or expanded to cover the totality of human experience. Thus, I end this discussion on a cautionary note by enumerating the limits of justice.

First, if justice is, as I have argued, more than voluntary agreement, it is less than perfect community. It allows us to retain our separate existences and our self-regard; it does not ask us to share the pleasures, pains, and sentiments of others. Justice is intelligent self-regard, modified by the requirements of rational consistency. To view one's own claims impartially is not to identify oneself with others.

As a set of rational principles, justice is preeminently a virtue of the public sphere, flanked on the one side by pursuit of private gain, on the other by the partial annihilation of separateness and self-regard that we call friendship or love. No doubt, as Aristotle said, "When people are friends, they have no need of justice, but when they are just, they need friendship in addition."[8] But friendship is not, strictly speaking, a part of justice. For the most part, it is self-defeating to seek the comprehensive satisfactions of friendship within the sphere regulated by justice or, as Sartre and others have done, to use the rare and fleeting moments of greatest collective unity as the standard by which normal politics is judged and found wanting.

By the same token, justice cannot be said to regulate the sphere of private sentiments and attachments. We cannot be obliged to love, except when our acts and promises have created a situation within which love may be presumed. In the sphere of love, needs and merits may have an effect on our sentiments, but they are not claims that we must honor. In part this is because we cannot fully control the direction and intensity of our sentiments, in part because universal standards are somehow out of place. Still, the intrusion of justice sometimes occurs, with disastrous effects. Nothing is more heartbreaking than someone "worthy" of our love whom we cannot love; nothing is more annoying than someone whose needs press on us an unrequitable demand for love.

Second, justice establishes our right relation to the external world of natural objects, other individuals, and opportunities for acting. Thus, aspects of individual perfection that deal with our relation to ourselves are outside the realm of justice. It is a mistake to suggest, as Hobbes did, that all virtues can somehow be derived from the requirements of sociality. Some private virtues may even stand in tension with the requirements of collective existence, without thereby ceasing to be desirable.

Third, not only is justice restricted to external relations—it is not even the sole regulator of such relations. Beyond distributive justice stands supererogatory benevolence; beyond retributive or punitive justice stands mercy. We are permitted to do no less than justice; we are allowed and even encouraged to do more. It seems impossible to reduce these very different springs of action to a common measure.

Fourth, as we have seen, a philosophical theory of justice is not, considered by itself, an adequate or comprehensive guide to political practice. For the first point, the theory of justice is a theory of *ends,* not of institutions. To be sure, it excludes certain kinds of institutions. But for the most part, institutions are means, and appropriate means vary with circumstances. Thus, even the perfect realization of justice will permit a wide range of institutions, in the same way that the good marksman can continue to hit the bull's-eye by adjusting his sights in accordance with wind and distance.

For the second, the theory of justice may give us a view of the best community. But we cannot in any neat and logical way derive from this view a set of subsidiary principles that will allow us to judge the relative worth of highly imperfect sets of institutions. Justice is multidimensional, not monistic; the priorities and weights that obtain in the best case may not be appropriate to nasty actualities. Thus, it is perfectly possible for individuals who agree completely about the best case to disagree, for example, about whether a particular community has been improved or made worse by a revolutionary upheaval.

In practice, then, a theory of justice cannot be a science of justice. Its wise application, always controversial to an extent, requires extensive, detailed knowledge, an ability to surmise what is possible or probable within a given situation, and prudence in the broadest sense—a feel for what might be called the human and moral center of gravity.

Fifth among the limits of justice, as we have defined and discussed it, is the fact that justice is linked to the sphere of collective existence or politics, as its chief though not sole virtue. Justice, then, would be unlimited if politics comprised or properly regulated the totality of human experience and endeavor. But this is not the case. We have already seen that there is an autonomous sphere of private sentiments and affections. Some may feel that, in cases of conflict, this sphere ought to be subordinated to the public sphere, even at the cost of individual suffering: Creon's case against Antigone is not insubstantial, and E. M. Forster's publicly stated desire for the courage to betray his country in the name of friendship may seem self-indulgent.

But politics is bounded in other ways that make this case harder to sustain. There is, as Hegel suggested, a realm of *absolute spirit*—art, religion, and philosophy. Each of these, while affecting and drawing sustenance from the political sphere, in part escapes and transcends it. A sign of this is what happens when the community attempts to extend total control over them: bombastic poetry, sculpture, and architecture; lifeless ceremony and false piety; Lysenkoist biology pretending to be science, and servile ideology cloaking itself in the proud robe of autonomous reason.

These perversions would not be so dismaying if the perverted activities were not so humanly important. We cannot but feel that politics, a means for procuring the good life as well as life, must somehow bend its knee before these manifestations of the striving for excellence and transcendence. This does not mean that in practice the claims of the community must always give way. But it does mean that these claims must always be interpreted in the light of their incompleteness. Unmitigated by this saving awareness, the passion for justice leads us to forget the full range of human possibilities and to lose the precious vantage point beyond politics that simultaneously allows us to define the worthy ends that politics can achieve and to mitigate the tragic seriousness with which we would otherwise be forced to view the daily disasters and imperfections of political life.

Notes

Chapter One

1. John Rawls, *A Theory of Justice*, p. 103.
2. *Force of Circumstance*, trans. Richard Howard, pp. 34–35.
3. *Theory of Justice*, p. 114.
4. *Ibid.*, p. 12.
5. "Nature and Soundness of the Contract and Coherence Arguments," Norman Daniels, ed., *Reading Rawls*, p. 158. See also Thomas Nagel, "Rawls on Justice," *Reading Rawls*, p. 5.
6. *Nicomachean Ethics* 5. 6. 1134a26–30.
7. *Anarchy, State, and Utopia*, p. 183.
8. "The Original Position," in *Reading Rawls*, p. 51.
9. *Theory of Justice*, sec. 50.
10. See *Politics* 3. 9 and 5. 1.
11. For a consideration of some of these issues, see Peter Singer, "Famine, Affluence, and Morality," *Philosophy and Public Affairs* 1, 3 (Spring 1972): 229–43.
12. *Communication and the Evolution of Society*, p. 201.
13. *Natural Right and History*, p. 7.
14. *Theory of Justice*, p. 51.
15. *Ibid.*, p. 252.
16. For a sensible and well-informed preliminary analysis, see David L. Hull, *Philosophy of Biological Science*, chap. 4.

Chapter Two

1. See John Rawls, *A Theory of Justice*, pp. 8–9, 145, 241, 245–46, 303, 351, 391, 587.
2. See James Miller, "Some Implications of Nietzsche's Thought for Marxism," *Telos* 37 (Fall 1978): 22–24.
3. For a broader and more historically sensitive account of utopian thought, see Frank E. and Fritzie P. Manuel, *Utopian Thought in the Western World*, pp. 1–29.
4. For a brief discussion, see Alan Gewirth, *Reason and Morality*, pp. 36–37. For a more elaborate version, see Joseph M. Boyle, Jr., Germain Grisez, and Olaf Tollefsen, *Free Choice: A Self-Referential Argument*.
5. *Gorgias* 494D–499B.
6. *Of Grammatology*, trans. Gayatri Chakravorty Spivak, pp. 49–50.

7. Ludwig Wittgenstein, *Philosophical Investigations* 1, 1–45.

8. *On Interpretation* 16a.

9. *On the Soul* 431b21.

10. *The Disputed Questions On Truth,* q. 1.

11. Immanuel Kant, *Critique of Pure Reason,* B xvi.

12. René Descartes, *Discourse on Method,* trans. Arthur Wollaston, p. 53.

13. *Moral Reasoning,* chap. 3–5.

14. Quoted *ibid.,* p. 123.

15. *Ibid.,* pp. 126–29.

16. *Ibid.,* pp. 106–8.

17. *Ibid.,* p. 44.

18. One could imagine a Wittgensteinian defense of the first of these along the following lines: a) By "form of life" one means, not a particular community, but rather a particular kind of activity, one that may be carried on in many different communities. Morality is in fact a distinctive activity, the general features of which make it very unlikely that any community could exist without it. b) These general features correspond to certain general facts of nature that may be assumed to affect all communities in a roughly comparable fashion. For a discussion of the role of "general facts of nature" in Wittgenstein's thought, see Richard Flathman, ed., *Concepts in Social and Political Philosophy,* pp. 20–30.

19. See especially the *Encyclopedia,* secs. 6 and 142.

20. *Ethics* 2. 1. 1103a14–26.

21. *Politics* 1. 2. 1253a30–31.

22. *Physics* 2. 2. 194a28–32.

23. *Ethics* 1. 13. 1102a26–1103a2.

24. See Shirley Robin Letwin, "Nature, History and Morality," in R. S. Peters, ed., *Nature and Conduct,* pp. 232–33.

25. See James D. Wallace, *Virtues and Vices,* pp. 18–25.

26. This is a summary of the critique Oakeshott propounds in *Rationalism in Politics.*

27. See *The Human Condition,* pp. 175–236. I do not mean to suggest that this is Arendt's only (or last) word on the problem of utopia.

28. *Ibid.,* pp. 205–6.

29. *The Prince,* chap. 15.

30. For a brief discussion, see Nicholas Rescher, *Distributive Justice,* pp. 120–21. George Kateb's *Utopia and Its Enemies,* chaps. 1–3, offers a comprehensive survey of this question. The essays by Kai Nielsen, "On the Choice Between Reform and Revolution," and Peter Caws, "Reform and Revolution," in Virginia Held, Kai Nielsen, and Charles Parsons, eds., *Philosophy and Political Action,* deal thoughtfully with the moral problems of revolutionary force and violence.

31. For the purposes of this discussion, we are intentionally overlooking an important consequence of the temporality of M—the tendency of M to carry over into, and pervert, B. Or, for simplicity, we may assume that the historical externalities of M are already incorporated into our view of B.

32. See *Politics* 2. 8. 1268b22–1269b28.

33. *Critique of Pure Reason,* A597–B625, note.

34. *Ibid.,* A317–B374.

35. Quoted in Jonathan Benthall, ed., *The Limits of Human Nature,* p. ix.

36. For a particularly horrifying and ludicrous example, see the views of Sir Hans Krebs, discussed by Robert Young, "The Human Limits of Nature," in

Benthall, ed., *The Limits of Human Nature*, pp. 247–49.

37. *Ethics* 9. 8. 1168a28–1169b1.

38. As background for these necessarily too-brief reflections, consider Benthall, ed., *The Limits of Human Nature*, and the essays by Renford Bambrough, Anthony Quinton, Christopher Cherry, Roger Scruton, and Shirley Robin Letwin in Peters, ed., *Nature and Conduct*.

39. On the question of metaethics, see Gewirth, *Reason and Morality*, p. 362, and the articles cited on p. 379n22.

40. See especially Agnes Heller, "Towards a Marxist Theory of Value," *Kinesis* 5, 1 (Fall 1972) and György Márkus, "Human Essence and History," *International Journal of Sociology* 4, 1 (Spring 1974). Habermas's most sustained reflections on this question are in Theodor W. Adorno et al., *The Positivist Dispute in German Sociology*, pp. 131–62, 199–225. See also his *Theory and Practice*, chaps. 1 and 7, and *Legitimation Crisis*, Part 3, chaps. 2–5.

41. *Nature and Conduct*, p. vii.

42. See especially *Freedom and Reason*.

43. See his "Descriptivism," in W. D. Hudson, ed., *The Is–Ought Question*, pp. 254–57.

44. *Theory of Justice*, pp. 46–53, 577–87. See also "Outline of a Decision Procedure for Ethics," *Philosophical Review* 60, 2 (April 1951): 177–97.

45. See *Theory of Justice*, pp. 19–20, 319, 579–80. Ronald Dworkin responds to this ambiguity, which he characterizes as a conflict between "constructive" and "natural" interpretations of reflective equilibrium, by arguing that only the former is consistent with Rawls's insistence on two-way revisability. This is true. But Dworkin's resolution seems to ignore altogether Rawls's equal insistence on fixed points. Thus, Dworkin's objection to Hare's claim that Rawls is an intuitionist is not persuasive. See Norman Daniels, *Reading Rawls*, pp. 26–37 and 81–85.

46. This assumes, as Rawls usually does, that *some* equilibrium is always attainable. This may be a strong and unwarranted assumption. See Robert Nozick, *Anarchy, State, and Utopia*, pp. 277–79.

47. For a subtle and wide-ranging discussion of these issues, see Norman Daniels, "Wide Reflective Equilibrium and Theory Acceptance in Ethics," *The Journal of Philosophy* 76, 5 (May 1979): 256–82.

48. See Patrick Riley, "On the 'Kantian' Foundations of Robert Paul Wolff's Anarchism," in J. Roland Pennock and John W. Chapman, eds., *Nomos 19: Anarchism*, pp. 302–9; Hardy Jones, *Kant's Principle of Personality*; Jeffrie Murphy, *Kant: The Philosophy of Right*, chaps. 2 and 3; Keith Ward, "Kant's Teleological Ethics," *The Philosophical Quarterly* 21, 85 (October 1971): 337–51.

49. "Objective Ends in Kant's Ethics," *Archiv für Geschichte der Philosophie* 56, 2 (1974): 156–71. For related positions, see Barbara Herman, "Morality as Rationality: A Study of Kant's Ethics" (Ph.D. dissertation, Harvard University, 1976), pp. 25–78; Mary Gregor, *The Laws of Freedom*.

50. "Objective Ends in Kant's Ethics," pp. 166–67.

51. *Ibid.*, pp. 168–69.

52. *Knowledge and Human Interests*, p. 314.

53. "A Theory of Communicative Competence," *Philosophy of the Social Sciences* 3, 2 (June 1973): 153–54.

54. "Towards a Theory of Communicative Competence," *Inquiry* 13, 4 (1970): 372.

55. See Glaucon's speech in *Republic* 358E–362C.

56. Quoted in McCarthy, "A Theory of Communicative Competence," p. 140.

57. *Ibid.*, p. 151.

58. *Ibid.*, p. 154.

59. For further reflections on these themes, see Thomas McCarthy, *The Critical Theory of Jürgen Habermas*, pp. 310–33.

60. "Nature and Convention," in *Ethics and Action*, pp. 61–62.

61. *Ibid.*, pp. 67–68.

62. Hobbes, *Leviathan*, chap. 4.

63. "Nature and Convention," pp. 59–60.

64. *Ibid.*, p. 69.

65. *Leviathan*, chap. 11.

66. "Nature and Convention," p. 70.

67. *Ibid.*, p. 71.

68. *Reason and Morality*, p. 171.

69. *Ibid.*, pp. 42–47.

70. *Ibid.*, pp. 23, 156, 159.

71. *Ibid.*, p. 53.

72. *Ibid.*, p. 137.

73. *Ibid.*, p. 67.

74. *Ibid.*, pp. 71, 89–95, 146–47.

75. See especially G. E. M. Anscombe, "Modern Moral Philosophy," in Hudson, ed., *The Is–Ought Question*, pp. 175–95; Philippa Foot, *Virtues and Vices and Other Essays in Moral Philosophy*; Wallace, *Virtues and Vices*; John Casey, "Human Virtue and Human Nature," in Benthall, ed., *The Limits of Human Nature*, pp. 74–91.

76. See *The Is–Ought Question*, Part 4; W. D. Hudson, *Modern Moral Philosophy*, pp. 264–81, 294–320; Beardsmore, *Moral Reasoning*, chaps. 1–4.

77. "Moral Beliefs," *Virtues and Vices*, pp. 114–20.

78. See Hudson, *Modern Moral Philosophy*, pp. 303–4.

79. "Moral Beliefs," p. 122.

80. D. Z. Phillips and H. O. Mounce, "On Morality's Having a Point," in *The Is–Ought Question*, p. 237.

81. "Moral Beliefs," p. 123.

82. *Ibid.*, pp. 123–25.

83. *Ibid.*, p. 125.

84. *Ibid.*, pp. 128–29; compare Hobbes, *Leviathan*, chap. 15, section entitled "Justice Not Contrary to Reason."

85. It is hardly accidental that in a recently added note, Foot abandons the attempt to justify justice on the basis of individual advantage or rational choice and asserts that "the reasons men have for acting justly . . . depend on contingent human attitudes" (*ibid.*, pp. 130–31). I shall argue that this strategic retreat is unnecessary, that it rests on too narrow a conception of individual advantage.

Chapter Three

1. See *Republic* 335E.

2. For important critical remarks on the centrality frequently accorded to preference, see T. M. Scanlon, "Preference and Urgency," *Journal of Philosophy* 72, 19 (6 November 1975): 655–69, and Charles Fried, "Difficulties in the Economic Analysis of Rights," in Gerald Dworkin, Gordon Bermant, and Peter G. Brown,

eds., *Markets and Morals,* pp. 175–95.

3. See Robert Paul Wolff, *Understanding Rawls,* pp. 106–11. As Isaiah Berlin has contended, "We seem to distinguish subjective from objective appraisal by the degree to which the central values conveyed are those which are common to human beings as such, that is, for practical purposes, to the great majority of men in most places and times. This is clearly not an absolute or rigid criterion; there is variation, there are virtually unnoticeable (as well as glaring) national, local, and historical peculiarities, prejudices, superstitions, rationalizations and their irrational influence. But neither is this criterion wholly relative or subjective, otherwise the concept of man would become too indeterminate, and men or societies, divided by unbridgeable normative differences, would be wholly unable to communicate across great distances in space and time and culture. Objectivity of moral judgment seems to depend on (almost to consist in) the degree of constancy in human responses. This notion cannot in principle be made sharp and unalterable. Its edges remain blurred. Moral categories— and categories of value in general—are nothing like as firm and ineradicable as those of, say, the perception of the material world, but neither are they as relative or as fluid as some writers have too easily, in their reaction against the dogmatism of the classical objectivists, tended to assume." *Four Essays on Liberty,* p. xxxii. For a similar view, persuasively defended, see Michael Walzer, *Just and Unjust Wars,* pp. 3–20.

4. *Ethics* 9. 9. 1170a25–b2.

5. *Ethics* 9. 9. 1170a24; consider also 1. 5. 1096a1.

6. *Ethics* 9. 4. 1166b12–13.

7. *Ethics* 10. 2. 1172b35–1173a5.

8. For a further discussion, see William Galston, *Kant and the Problem of History,* pp. 193–94, 257.

9. For a useful summary discussion of the issues raised by the theological premise, see Paul Edwards, "Life, Meaning and Value of," in Paul Edwards, ed., *The Encyclopedia of Philosophy,* 4:467–77.

10. For seminal expositions of these and related points, see especially Rousseau, *First and Second Discourses,* and Nietzsche, *Birth of Tragedy* and *Use and Abuse of History.*

11. I am indebted to Harrison Wagner for the suggestion that, while friendship may render justice unnecessary as a *motive,* it may still require some aspects of justice as a *standard.* Friends do not automatically know what to do for one another. If this is so, my general thesis is strengthened.

12. *Leviathan,* chap. 6.

13. See *Social Contract,* 1:8.

14. See *Ethics* 10. 8. 1178b33–1179a17.

15. For a lucid discussion of this distinction, see John M. Cooper, *Reason and Human Good in Aristotle,* pp. 89–180.

16. See *ibid.,* pp. 155–68.

17. For a sensible description and defense of continuous orderings, see Brian Barry, *Political Argument,* pp. 3–8. Aristotle's critique of Plato's theory of the good, coupled with his claim that the political good, that is, the ground of entitlement, is composed of heterogeneous elements, leads in practice to a similar position. See *Ethics* 1. 6, *Politics* 3. 12–13, and Harry Jaffa, "Aristotle," in Leo Strauss and Joseph Cropsey, eds., *History of Political Philosophy,* pp. 108–16.

18. See *Ethics* 10. 4. 1175a3–10.

19. *Gorgias* 492B.

20. *Leviathan,* chap. 11.
21. *Being and Nothingness,* p. 178.
22. *Ibid.,* p. 174.
23. *Ibid.,* p. 63.
24. *Ibid.,* pp. 77–78.
25. On this question Hegel's position is much more plausible. Hegel argued that animal existence is characterized by "the feeling of lack (*Mangel*)." Lack arises from the requirements of life, that is, a pregiven organic totality. Animals have an innate "urge" to overcome lack.

Thus, Hegel was able to do what Sartre has failed to do—distinguish between lack and desire (*Begierde*). The former requires only prereflexive consciousness or sensitivity; the latter comes into existence only with self-consciousness. Compare *Encyclopedia,* sec. 359, with *The Phenomenology of Mind,* trans. J. B. Baillie, pp. 220–26.

The basis of this distinction is the simple observation, the theoretical expression of which goes back at least to Aristotle's *On the Soul,* that perception and sensitivity can exist independent of self-consciousness. Sartre cannot consistently acknowledge this fact. To do so would be to concede a form of existence intermediate between the dualism of for-itself and in-itself.

26. *Symposium* 199B–204C.
27. *Being and Nothingness,* p. 152.
28. See also Wilfred Desan, *The Tragic Finale,* pp. 140–44.
29. *Being and Nothingness,* pp. 64, 151.
30. At one point Sartre does claim that all internal negation is based on lack, which is the "original internal negation." But this is merely asserted, without either proof or any attempt to reconcile it with his own opposing claims. See *ibid.,* p. 64n10.
31. *Symposium* 193A.
32. *Ibid.,* 206A.
33. *Being and Nothingness,* p. 66.
34. *Ibid.,* p. 516.
35. *Ibid.,* p. 194.
36. See *ibid.,* pp. xlv–l.
37. *Ibid.,* p. 66.
38. *Ibid.,* p. 517.
39. *Symposium* 207A–212B.
40. For a more thorough discussion, see Galston, *Kant and the Problem of History,* pp. 180–83, 251–55.
41. *Critique of Practical Reason,* p. 132.
42. *Foundations of the Metaphysics of Morals,* p. 12.
43. For related considerations, see W. D. Ross, *The Right and the Good,* pp. 135–36.
44. On this point, see also p. 101.
45. For a seminal statement of the publicity requirement, see Kant, "Perpetual Peace," in Hans Reiss, ed., *Kant's Political Writings,* pp. 125–30. For recent restatements, see William Frankena, *Ethics,* pp. 5–6, 16–18, and Brian Medlin, "Ultimate Principles and Ethical Egoism," in David Gauthier, ed., *Morality and Rational Self-Interest,* pp. 59–63. For what is I believe a decisive defense of the position I have taken, see Jesse Kalin, "In Defense of Egoism," in *Morality and Rational Self-Interest,* pp. 80–87.
46. For a strong statement of the case against egoism, see Medlin, "Ultimate

Principles and Ethical Egoism," pp. 60–63. For the response on which my brief remarks are based, see Kalin, "In Defense of Egoism," pp. 72–80, and also Virginia Held, "Rationality and Reasonable Cooperation," in *Social Research* 44, 4 (Winter 1977): 708–17.

47. *Reason and Morality*, p. 87.

48. *Ibid.*, pp. 87–88.

49. John Locke, *The Second Treatise of Government*, sec. 11.

50. I am not arguing that reason and force are antithetical, that is, that force is always unreasonable, but only that the rejection of justification leaves no alternative to force in its various modes in the resolution of conflict. For an interesting and spirited debate on this question, see Stephan Körner, ed., *Practical Reason*, pp. 113–88.

51. Karl Popper's claim that the commitment to rationality is necessarily based on faith—and is the sole article of faith rationality allows—has sparked a vigorous debate. In *The Retreat to Commitment*, W. W. Bartley has tried to show that this dogmatic element can be eliminated and that rationality, appropriately defined, can be viewed as self-grounding. J. W. N. Watkins argues that Bartley's attempt fails, for reasons that doom any effort to present reason as self-grounding. See "Comprehensively Critical Rationalism," *Philosophy* 44, 167 (January 1969): 57–62. Various critiques of this argument, together with Watkins's reply, are found in *Philosophy* 46, 175 (January 1971): 43–61. Another important analysis of self-grounding is offered by Gerard Radnitzky, *Contemporary Schools of Metascience*, pp. 174–83. In *A Justification of Rationality*, John Kekes tries to ground rationality in problem-solving, arguing that we face certain unavoidable practical problems as part of the human condition and that without rationality we cannot hope to solve them. His argument, though plausible, is weakened by his failure to deal with the claim that from certain standpoints rationality can itself *be* a problem. In addition, he assumes that rationality and the pursuit of self-interest are substantially identical. In the sphere of practical rationality, this is much more obviously true of internal than of external rationality.

52. For a discussion of these two criteria, see Scanlon, "Preference and Urgency."

53. See *Theory of Justice*, sec. 82. For a general discussion of the "nonbasic" character of all monistic social choice principles, see Amartya K. Sen, *Collective Choice and Social Welfare*, pp. 198–200.

54. "Negative and Positive Freedom," in Flathman, ed., *Concepts in Social and Political Philosophy*, p. 296.

55. Rawls, accepting the triadic analysis, is consistent enough to defend freedom as a primary good—as a universally valuable means. But he goes on to offer the sensible, conventional case for paternalism (*Theory of Justice*, pp. 248–50). It seems that freedom is always good . . . except when it isn't!

56. *On Being Free*, p. 37.

57. *Ibid.*, p. 99.

58. See *Taking Rights Seriously*, pp. 268–72; "Liberalism," in Stuart Hampshire, ed., *Public and Private Morality*, pp. 123–25.

59. *Laws of Freedom*, p. xii.

Chapter Four

1. *Social Justice*, pp. 17–18.

2. For discussions of these and related points, see Gregory Vlastos, "Justice and Happiness in the *Republic*," in *Platonic Studies*, pp. 111–39, and Allan Bloom, *The Republic of Plato*, pp. 373–79.

3. This conjecture may be traced back to Aristotle's four-term, geometrical account of distributive justice; see *Ethics* 5. 3. Miller's remarks in *Social Justice*, pp. 18–19, are representative of how this is translated into a contemporary idiom.

4. For a clear distinction between the comparative and noncomparative elements of justice, see Joel Feinberg, *Social Philosophy*, pp. 98–99.

5. *Ethics* 5. 2. 1130a15–b5.

6. See especially *Ethics* 8. 7. 1159a10–13.

7. *Ethics* 5. 4. 1132b10–15.

8. For an examination of the significance of and relations between these definitions, see Giorgio del Vecchio, *Justice*, pp. 51–76.

9. Note that Locke did not hesitate to describe a man's life as part of his property. *Second Treatise of Government*, sec. 123–24.

10. We are thus led to question the conclusion of the discussion between Socrates and Polemarchus, that it can never be just to promote the moral deterioration of anyone (*Republic* 335B–E). This maxim focuses entirely on consequences, or the future, while ignoring the implications of the present. It is quite sensible to say that in certain circumstances someone may not deserve to be good and may have no cause for complaint if we fail to facilitate his becoming so. We are more inclined to affirm this if we believe that the person in question has deliberately and freely selected an evil life, in full knowledge of the alternatives. Thus, Socrates' maxim is implicitly linked to his more famous teaching that no one knowingly selects evil over good.

11. See Ross, *The Right and the Good*, p. 138.

12. This is roughly the way Nicholas Rescher poses the problem in *Distributive Justice*. The outlines of this approach are found in Aristotle's *Ethics* 5. 3. and *Politics* 3. 9.

13. Compare *Theory of Justice*, pp. 3–4, with pp. 6, 9–10.

14. *The Right and the Good*, pp. 16–34.

15. *Ibid.*, p. 19.

16. Brian Barry's use of indifference curves is appropriate to this kind of situation. See *Political Argument*, pp. 3–8.

17. For related remarks, see Miller, *Social Justice*, pp. 18–19.

18. David Hume, *A Treatise of Human Nature*, ed. L. A. Selby-Bigge, book 3, part 1, chap. 2, pp. 487–88.

19. *Ibid.*, p. 494.

20. *Theory of Justice*, p. 62.

21. *An Inquiry Concerning the Principles of Morals*, ed. Charles Hendel, p. 25.

22. See *Theory of Justice*, pp. 62, 93, 433–34.

23. *Ibid.*, pp. 440–42.

24. *Ibid.*, pp. 326–29, 442.

25. See Brian Barry, *The Liberal Theory of Justice*, pp. 59–65.

26. *Ibid.*, pp. 55–56.

27. *Ibid.*, pp. 116–17.

28. *Theory of Justice*, pp. 223–24.

29. See *Politics* 3. 11.

30. Hume, *Inquiry*, pp. 15–18; see also *Theory of Justice*, pp. 126–28.

31. *Inquiry*, p. 17.

32. For another discussion of these issues, which arrives at similar conclusions, see Brian Barry, "Circumstances of Justice and Future Generations," in R. I. Sikora and Brian Barry, eds., *Obligations to Future Generations*, pp. 210–15.

33. *Theory of Justice*, pp. 63, 152, 247, 542–43.

34. For an excellent analysis, see Barry, *Liberal Theory of Justice*, chap. 7.

35. Rawls never lays this out very clearly, but it is strongly suggested by his characterization of excessive wealth as "a positive hindrance, a meaningless distraction at best if not a temptation to indulgence and emptiness" (*Theory of Justice*, p. 290). Barry's description of this as "puritanism" misses the point, although he is quite right to suggest that it is incompatible with the assertion that wealth is a primary good. (*Liberal Theory of Justice*, p. 120.)

36. For a consideration of this and related questions, see Habermas, *Legitimation Crisis*.

37. See especially *Social Contract*, 3:15.

38. *Distributive Justice*, pp. 87–112.

39. For additional remarks on these questions, see Norman Bowie and Robert Simon, *The Individual and the Political Order*, pp. 204–12.

40. *Liberal Theory of Justice*, pp. 129–30.

41. *Political Argument*, pp. 12–15.

42. Even Hobbes, after distinguishing internal (moral) from external (practical) obligation, acknowledged that moral obligation is not affected by variations of natural or legal circumstances. *Leviathan*, chap. 15.

43. For some provocative remarks on these and related questions, see Robert W. Tucker, *The Inequality of Nations*, especially chap. 4. I do not entirely agree with the thrust of his argument, but it must be considered carefully. For a useful survey of the current debate on the political level, see Robert W. Cox, "Ideologies and the New International Economic Order: Reflections on Some Recent Literature," *International Organization* 33, 2 (Spring 1979): 257–302.

44. See *Theory of Justice*, pp. 378–79.

45. For a more detailed examination of this question, see the essays by Raphael, Gregg, and Franck in *Nomos 9: Equality*, J. Roland Pennock and John W. Chapman, eds., pp. 277–313.

46. For a systematic attempt to extend Rawls's principles of distribution to international relations, see Charles R. Beitz, *Political Theory and International Relations*.

47. The seminal work is Peter Singer, *Animal Liberation*. Nozick's *Anarchy, State, and Utopia*, pp. 35–51, offers a provocative brief discussion. Two useful recent collections are S. and R. Godlovitch and J. Harris, eds., *Animals, Men and Morals*, and Tom Regan and Peter Singer, eds., *Animal Rights and Human Obligations*. Recent controversies include: Jan Narveson, "Animal Rights," and Tom Regan, "Narveson on Egoism and the Rights of Animals," in *Canadian Journal of Philosophy* 7, 1 (March 1977): 161–86; Lawrence Haworth, "Rights, Wrongs, and Animals"; Michael Fox, "Animal Liberation: A Critique" and "Animal Suffering and Rights"; Peter Singer, "The Fable of the Fox and the Unliberated Animals"; and Tom Regan, "Fox's Critique of Animal Liberation," all in *Ethics* 88, 2 (January 1978): 95–138; R. G. Frey, "Animal Rights," *Analysis* 37, 4 (June 1977): 186–89, and Dale Jamieson and Tom Regan, "Animal Rights: A Reply to Frey," *Analysis* 38, 1 (January 1978): 32–36. John Rodman's "The Liberation of Nature?" *Inquiry* 20, 1 (Spring 1977): 83–131, broadens the scope of the debate to include various historical and metaphysical questions, and his extensive notes

open up important avenues for research.

48. For related remarks, see Joel Feinberg, "Can Animals Have Rights?" in *Animal Rights and Human Obligations*, p. 195.

49. Consider the story of Xerxes at the Hellespont; Herodotus, *The Histories*, trans. Aubrey de Sélincourt, p. 429.

50. See Nozick, *Anarchy, State, and Utopia*, pp. 38–39, and Henry Salt's "Logic of the Larder" in Regan and Singer, eds., *Animal Rights and Human Obligations*, pp. 185–89.

51. See especially Richard Flathman, *The Practice of Rights*, pp. 71, 76.

52. "Liberalism," in Hampshire, ed., *Public and Private Morality*, p. 127.

53. *Theory of Justice*, pp. 327–29.

54. *Rights and Persons*, p. 136.

55. *Ibid.*, p. 129; also pp. 14, 168.

56. *Anarchy, State, and Utopia*, pp. 30–31.

57. *Ibid.*, pp. 32–33.

58. *Ibid.*, p. 325.

59. *Taking Rights Seriously*, p. xi.

60. *Ibid.*, pp. 313–15.

61. *Ibid.*, pp. 272–73.

62. For a persuasive argument that rights have no point without this teleological component, see Flathman, *The Practice of Rights*, passim, and especially pp. 234–35.

63. *Taking Rights Seriously*, p. 275.

64. *Ibid.*, p. 276.

65. *Ibid.*, p. 277.

66. Jules Coleman, *California Law Review* 66, 4 (1978): 917–18.

67. *Social Philosophy*, pp. 86–88.

68. The foregoing arguments also tell against some of the claims of Bernard Williams in J. J. C. Smart and Bernard Williams, *Utilitarianism: For and Against*, pp. 93–118, and Nozick, *Anarchy, State, and Utopia*, pp. 28–35.

69. Miller, *Social Justice*, p. 56.

70. *Ibid.*, p. 56.

71. *Ibid.*, pp. 57–58.

72. *Ibid.*, p. 85.

73. Feinberg, *Social Philosophy*, p. 67.

74. "Rights, Goals, and Fairness," in Hampshire, ed., *Public and Private Morality*, pp. 99–100. This section as a whole is heavily indebted to Scanlon's formulation of the problem. For an early, thorough, and highly engaging defense of ideal utilitarianism, see Hastings Rashdall, *The Theory of Good and Evil*, 1: chaps. 7, 8. Rashdall carefully considered, but eventually rejected, a version of Scanlon's suggestion that morally desirable states of affairs be included in the maximand. He argued, rather, that including individual virtues will accomplish the same purpose with much less philosophical arbitrariness (pp. 264–69). The difficulty with this suggestion is that the key virtue—a "will to distribute justly"—cannot be defined except in relation to a just state of affairs . . . which is precisely what we are seeking to determine! The risk of arbitrariness has been traded in for the certainty of circularity.

Chapter Five

1. *Freedom and Reason*, p. 11.

2. *Ibid.*, pp. 15, 21. Sen points out that if this is taken as a logical necessity, then states of affairs can lead directly to moral judgments, violating Hare's Humean commitments. See *Collective Choice and Social Welfare*, pp. 131–34.

3. See Joel Feinberg, *Social Philosophy*, p. 99; Isaiah Berlin, "Equality as an Ideal," in Frederick Olafson, ed., *Justice and Social Policy*, p. 129; John Rawls, *A Theory of Justice*, pp. 58–59.

4. See Richard Flathman, "Equality and Generalization: A Formal Analysis," in J. Roland Pennock and John W. Chapman, eds., *Nomos 9: Equality*, pp. 38–60.

5. *Social Principles and the Democratic State*, pp. 110–11.

6. *Social Philosophy*, pp. 100–102; see also Nozick's remarks, *Anarchy, State, and Utopia*, pp. 222–24. I do not endorse his conclusion.

7. *Freedom and Reason*, p. 118.

8. *Freedom and Reason*, p. 119. Hare seems to have renounced this move in his more recent "Justice and Equality," in John Arthur and William Shaw, eds., *Justice and Economic Distribution*, pp. 116–31.

9. *Freedom and Reason*, p. 123.

10. *Ibid.*, pp. 171–72.

11. *Ibid.*, p. 174; my emphasis.

12. Hare contradicts himself here. In a passage we have just discussed (*Freedom and Reason*, p. 123), he implicitly equates desires and interests. On p. 147 he goes so far as to state that in situations in which "everybody gets what he or she wants, nobody's interests are harmed."

13. *The Concept of Justice*, p. 17. I have translated Nathan's terms into my own without, I hope, seriously distorting his assertion.

14. *Ibid.*, p. 15.

15. For other suggestions, see Nicholas Rescher, *Distributive Justice*, pp. 108–12.

16. I am under no illusions that these brief remarks can do justice either to this topic or to the vast literature it has generated. In addition to the works I discuss and cite, an adequate treatment would at the very least have to take into account the important essays by Bedau, Benn, and Plamenatz in Pennock and Chapman, eds., *Nomos 9: Equality*; by Tawney and Lucas in Flathman, ed., *Concepts in Social and Political Philosophy*; by Frankena in Richard Brandt, ed., *Social Justice*; by McCloskey in *The Australasian Journal of Philosophy* 44, 1 (May 1966): 50–69, and *Canadian Journal of Philosophy* 6, 4 (December 1976): 625–42.

17. "Justice and Equality," in Brandt, ed., *Social Justice*, p. 43. Bernard Williams's well-known essay, "The Idea of Equality," rests in part on a similar distinction. See Peter Laslett and W. G. Runciman, eds., *Philosophy, Politics, and Society: Second Series*, pp. 116–19.

18. "Justice and Equality," pp. 43–44.

19. *Ibid.*, pp. 44–45.

20. See *Ethics* 8. 12. 1161b17 and 9. 7. 1167b28.

21. Vlastos admits that stratified citizenship is at least logically consistent, given meritarian premises. See "Justice and Equality," p. 46.

22. *Ibid.*, p. 47.

23. For a further examination of many of these points, especially the last, see Gregory Vlastos, "The Individual as an Object of Love in Plato," in *Platonic Studies*. He begins, quite properly, with Aristotle's claim that full or genuine love involves wishing another person good for that person's sake. But he goes on to insist that the "good" of that person is bound up with what he himself

thinks, feels, and wants, and is violated by the imposition of an external standard of excellence (p. 32). This move seems worse than arbitrary. It does not follow from the fact that we must treat each individual we care for differently and delicately, that we do solely in furtherance of that person's own subjectivity, whatever it may be. It is one of the traditional and proper offices of the true friend or lover to challenge the errant acts and desires of the beloved—that is, to embody the good and to strive to make what is good for the other and what is good without qualification converge.

24. *Theory of Justice*, p. 508.

25. *Reason and Morality*, pp. 121–22.

26. *Theory of Justice*, p. 505.

27. *Ibid.*, p. 506.

28. *Ethics* 10. 9. 1179b11–1180a5.

29. As Rawls concedes. See *Theory of Justice*, pp. 232–33.

30. *Reason and Morality*, p. 122.

31. *Ibid.*, p. 123.

32. *Ibid.*, p. 122.

33. *Ibid.*, p. 124.

34. See Joel Feinberg, "Can Animals Have Rights?" in Regan and Singer, eds., *Animals Rights and Human Obligations*, p. 195.

35. See *Republic* 487B–497A.

36. See *Social Contract* I:2.

37. *Politics* 1. 5. 1254b10–13.

38. *Politics* 1. 5. 1254a32–37.

39. For a wide-ranging, occasionally eccentric survey of the question of need, see Ross Fitzgerald, ed., *Human Needs and Politics*. The bibliography is especially valuable. The two essays Fitzgerald contributed criticize the concept of need on the ground that it cannot, as is frequently alleged, bridge the is/ought gap in any straightforward manner. I agree with Fitzgerald that when theorists try to use it in this way, their analyses invariably rest on some equivocation. But this criticism does not touch my own analysis, because I explicitly defined need in terms of an antecedent account of the good, never supposing that it would allow me to dispense with that account.

40. *Political Argument*, pp. 47–49.

41. *Social Justice*, pp. 126–28.

42. See *Republic* 372A–373E. For a discussion of "essential interests" and "subsistence needs" that rests on similar considerations, see James S. Fishkin, *Tyranny and Legitimacy: A Critique of Political Theories*, pp. 18–43. Charles Fried defends the distinctiveness and utility of needs in "Difficulties in the Economic Analysis of Rights," pp. 182–83. Guido Calabresi and Philip Bobbitt link these concerns to the economists' notion of "merit wants" and "merit goods" in *Tragic Choices*, pp. 89–92. A. K. Sen offers an interpretation of needs from the standpoint of formal social choice theory in *On Economic Inequality*, chap. 4.

43. *Social Justice*, pp. 129–36. The criterion of intelligibility is designed to steer a middle course between a moral ranking of life plans and the formal account that forces Rawls to assert that a person whose only pleasure is derived from counting blades of grass must be considered to have a life plan. See *Theory of Justice*, pp. 432–33.

44. *Social Justice*, pp. 140–41.

45. This has the consequence of allowing the numbers of individuals affected by a policy to make a difference. To return to our earlier example: If by allowing

one child to starve a million could be educated, it is not at all clear that one should choose to feed the one. Of course this is empirically ridiculous; resources required to feed one child could not educate even one other, let alone a million. But other examples embodying the same principle are not only not ridiculous but are beginning to occur regularly. The expense of technologically complex medical life-maintenance procedures raises the issue of the value of a human life very starkly. Is a community obligated to provide, at a cost of $100,000 a unit, artificial hearts to all who cannot remain alive without them?

46. For a related, though somewhat narrower, conclusion focused on past actions as desert-bases, see James Rachels, "What People Deserve," in John Arthur and William Shaw, eds., *Justice and Economic Distribution*, pp. 154–59.

47. The most significant contemporary contribution is Joel Feinberg, *Doing and Deserving*. David Miller's discussion in *Social Justice* offers a number of significant assertions, debated later. The dimensions of the controversy between Rawls and Nozick on this point are now well known. In addition to the article by Rachels already cited, see Michael Slote, "Desert, Consent, and Justice," *Philosophy and Public Affairs* 2, 4 (Summer 1973): 323–47; James Dick, "How to Justify a Distribution of Earnings," *Philosophy and Public Affairs* 4, 3 (Spring 1975): 248–72; Alan Zaitchik, "On Deserving to Deserve," *Philosophy and Public Affairs* 6, 4 (Summer 1977): 371–88; George Sher, "Effort, Ability, and Personal Desert," *Philosophy and Public Affairs* 8, 4 (Summer 1979): 361–76.

48. *Doing and Deserving*, pp. 55–56, 85–87; *Social Justice*, pp. 90–92.

49. *Doing and Deserving*, pp. 58–59.

50. *Ibid.*, p. 61; *Social Justice*, pp. 117–18.

51. See *Theory of Justice*, sec. 48, where he speaks indiscriminately of "desert," "moral desert," and "virtue."

52. *Ibid.*, p. 15.

53. *Anarchy, State, and Utopia*, pp. 213–15.

54. *Theory of Justice*, p. 311.

55. *Ibid.*, p. 311.

56. *Ibid.*, pp. 312–13.

57. *Ibid.*, p. 315.

58. *Doing and Deserving*, p. 90.

59. See *ibid.*, p. 91n.

60. See *Anarchy, State, and Utopia*, pp. 225–27; *Social Justice*, p. 87n8.

61. *Social Justice*, pp. 95–100.

62. *Political Argument*, p. 106.

63. *Ibid.*, p. 108.

64. *Social Justice*, p. 86.

65. *Ibid.*, p. 96.

66. *Ibid.*, p. 85.

67. *Doing and Deserving*, p. 61.

68. *Social Justice*, p. 86.

69. *Ibid.*, p. 93; see also *Political Argument*, p. 111, *Doing and Deserving*, p. 81.

70. *Doing and Deserving*, pp. 88–94.

71. *Ibid.*, pp. 78–80.

72. *Political Argument*, p. 106.

73. See *Social Justice*, pp. 114–17.

74. After I had completed writing this section, I obtained Norman Daniels's essay "Meritocracy," in Arthur and Shaw, *Justice and Economic Distribution*, pp. 164–78. Daniels and I are in complete agreement on virtually every important

point and in particular on the interpretation of meritocracy as a principle of efficiency; on the distinction between ability and other senses of "desert"; and on the logical gap between principles governing task assignments and those governing what Daniels calls the reward schedules with which they are correlated. Daniels makes one perspicuous point that I shall presuppose for the remainder of this book. He distinguishes between microproductivity—the principle of efficiency applied to a particular task, and macroproductivity—efficiency applied to the full range of tasks within a community. He observes that meritocracy ought to be interpreted as a macroproductive principle; individual claims based on ability must be considered in light of the task allocations that will be maximally efficient in the aggregate. The fact that A can do x better than B can does not mean that A has a valid claim to do x, if it is also the case that A can do y better than B can, by a factor greater than A's superiority in the performance of x. Throughout the discussion of task assignment in Chapter 6 I shall assume that all background conditions for the application of the macroproductivity principle are in fact satisfied.

75. New York: Random House, 1959.

76. *Rise of the Meritocracy*, p. 24.

77. *Ibid.*, pp. 124–26.

78. See *Leviathan*, chap. 15, and Marvin Zetterbaum, "Equality and Human Need," *American Political Science Review* 71, 3 (September 1977): 984.

79. John Schaar, "Equality of Opportunity, and Beyond," in J. Roland Pennock and John W. Chapman, eds., *Nomos 9: Equality*, pp. 228–49.

80. It is not accidental that Schaar is much more critical of the substance of American life than most "liberal" defenders of EO. See "Equality of Opportunity, and Beyond," p. 231, for a clear if intemperate presentation of his view.

81. "Equality of Opportunity, and Beyond," pp. 243–44.

82. Schaar never attempts to specify at what point economic inequality becomes incompatible with democracy. Thus, the familiar figures he cites do not prove anything. In addition, many theorists have contended that democracy is most likely to be maximized and preserved in circumstances conducive to the emergence of a dominant middle class. Historically, EO has performed this task with considerable efficiency.

83. See *Ethics* 1. 1. 1094a9–17. Of course, the architect may design better if in command of the rudiments of the subsidiary arts, and the various artisans may participate from time to time in the process of designing, at least to the extent of advising the architect that a particular proposal will be expensive and technically complex. But these considerations do not rebut the general point.

84. For some additional remarks on Schaar's argument, see John Stanley, "Equality of Opportunity as Philosophy and Ideology," *Political Theory* 5, 1 (February 1977): 61–74.

85. *Anarchy, State, and Utopia*, pp. 309–12.

86. *Ibid.*, pp. 329–31.

87. *Ibid.*, p. 30n.

88. *Ibid.*, pp. 179n, 238.

89. *Ibid.*, p. 181.

90. *Ibid.*, pp. 38–39.

91. Leo Strauss, *Natural Right and History*, p. 235; see also pp. 235n, and 242.

Chapter Six

1. A thorough consideration of these questions would take into account the considerations raised by such works as: Robert A. Dahl and Charles E. Lindblom, *Politics, Economics, and Welfare;* Charles E. Lindblom, *Politics and Markets: The World's Political Economic Systems;* Jude Wanniski, *The Way the World Works: How Economies Fail—and Succeed;* J. E. Meade, *The Just Economy;* Guido Calabresi and Philip Bobbit, *Tragic Choices;* Amartya K. Sen, *Collective Choice and Social Welfare;* Jürgen Habermas, *Legitimation Crisis.*

2. David Hume, *A Treatise of Human Nature,* p. 502.

3. For a discussion, see Norman Frohlich and Joe Oppenheimer, *Modern Political Economy,* especially chaps. 2 and 3.

4. *Social Principles and the Democratic State,* pp. 146–47.

5. For further discussion of functional needs, see C. B. Macpherson, *Democratic Theory,* pp. 60, 63–70.

6. This is not to say that rewarding certain virtues with money is unjustified *simpliciter,* although, as Feinberg points out, such a practice runs the risk of perverting virtue at its core. See Joel Feinberg, *Doing and Deserving,* pp. 90–92.

7. See *ibid.,* p. 93; David Miller, *Social Justice,* pp. 110–13.

8. *New York Times,* 9 July 1978, p. 29.

9. Aristotle's theory of corrective justice encounters similar difficulties. The general idea is that when *A* wrongs *B, A* reaps an unjustified gain while *B* incurs an unjustified loss. Justice requires that the status quo ante, a kind of moral equality, be restored by transferring *A*'s ill-gotten gain to *B*. But consider the case, to which Aristotle himself alluded, in which *A* physically injures *B*. First, it may well be the case that although *B* has incurred a loss, *A* has gained nothing. Second, it is not clear what transfer to *B* would make up for his loss. Some components of the transfer are straightforward: payment of medical costs and compensation for lost earnings. But what is required to equalize pain and suffering, or loss of function? (See *Ethics* 5. 4. 1131b25–1132b20.)

This problem of commensurability gives the ancient doctrine of "an eye for an eye" a superficial appeal: at least *A* is made to undergo roughly the same privation he has inflicted on *B*. The problem, of course, is that *A*'s loss is not transferred to *B*, so that no compensation takes place. This raises an intriguing possibility. Suppose that *A* assaults *B* in such a way that one of *B*'s kidneys is irreparably damaged. If it were medically possible for *A* to serve as a kidney donor for *B*, would it be unjust to require that he do so?

10. *Social Justice,* p. 109.

11. For the most influential recent statement of this position, see John Rawls, *A Theory of Justice,* pp. 104, 312.

12. Robert Nozick, *Anarchy, State, and Utopia,* p. 214.

13. *Theory of Justice,* p. 312.

14. *Ibid.,* p. 104.

15. See pp. 172–73.

16. See *Social Justice,* pp. 106–7.

17. *Ibid.,* pp. 105–6.

18. *Ibid.,* pp. 107–8.

19. For further reflections on the problem of indeterminacy, see Nicholas Rescher, *Distributive Justice,* pp. 108–12. I am indebted to Harrison Wagner for the suggestion that it might be sensible to view *A*'s marginal contribution as 13 $(21 - 8)$ and *B*'s as 15 $(21 - 6)$ and to distribute the benefits of cooperation in

proportion to the marginal contribution of each. This would give A a total of 9.3 and B, 11.7.

20. See *Social Justice*, pp. 119, 128–30.

21. Thomas Hobbes, *Leviathan*, chap. 10.

22. L. T. Hobhouse, *The Elements of Social Justice*, pp. 140–41.

23. *Social Philosophy*, p. 116.

24. For this, see Hobhouse's analysis in *The Elements of Social Justice*, pp. 164–66.

25. *The Accumulation of Capital*, p. 394. See also John Stuart Mill, *Principles of Political Economy*, in C. B. Macpherson, ed., *Property: Mainstream and Critical Positions*, pp. 85–94.

26. *Income Distribution: Facts, Theories, Policies*, p. 114.

27. *Accumulation of Capital*, pp. 393–94.

28. *Ibid.*, p. 395.

29. See *Risk, Uncertainty, and Profit*, pp. 233–34.

30. For some consequences of this, see *Accumulation of Capital*, pp. 85–87.

31. For discussions of this phenomenon from various standpoints, see Brian Barry, *The Liberal Theory of Justice*, p. 159; Hobhouse, *The Elements of Social Justice*, pp. 141–43; Pen, *Income Distribution*, p. 128.

32. Something like this assumption provides the context within which Barry's discussion in *Political Argument* makes sense. See especially p. xviii.

33. *Elements of Social Justice*, p. 152.

34. See Hannah Arendt, *The Human Condition*, chap. 4, especially pp. 136–38.

35. See *Politics* 1. 4.

36. See *Anarchy, State, and Utopia*, p. 180.

37. John Locke, *The Second Treatise of Government*, sec. 36.

38. *Ibid.*, sec. 41.

39. Nozick's term—see *Anarchy, State, and Utopia*, pp. 177–78.

40. *Ibid.*, p. 181.

41. *Distributive Justice*, pp. 29–31.

42. *The Second Treatise of Government*, sec. 28.

43. See Jean-Jacques Rousseau, *Social Contract*, 1:9.

44. See Miller, *Social Justice*, pp. 164–65.

45. Though adequate for the purposes of this book, the foregoing is hardly a complete treatment of the philosophic dimensions of property relations. In a future study I hope to do better. For those who wish to pursue the subject, Richard Schlatter's *Private Property: The History of an Idea* is a comprehensive introductory survey. Lawrence C. Becker's *Property Rights: Philosophic Foundations* is a crisp and lucid analysis of the different kinds of arguments that have or can be offered in defense of property holdings. Other significant recent discussions include Bruce Ackerman, *Private Property and the Constitution*, and C. B. Macpherson, ed., *Property: Mainstream and Critical Positions*. George O'Brien, *An Essay on Mediaeval Economic Teaching*, summarizes the Thomistic position. J. Vernon Bartlet, ed., *Property: Its Duties and Rights*, offers a group of provocative essays by authors representing idealistic, ideal–utilitarian, and liberal Christian positions. L. T. Hobhouse's *Elements of Social Justice* should also be consulted.

46. See *Theory of Justice*, p. 290.

47. See *New York Times*, 26 July 1978, p. A13.

48. Some have disputed this point. Booker T. Washington argued that the sacrifices that slaves had been forced to endure constituted a kind of moral education. Recently, Alexander Solzhenitsyn has advanced similar claims about

the tyrannical oppression Russians have undergone. It seems to me that these claims result from the projection of self-awareness onto the external world. Only extraordinary individuals can profit from involuntary sacrifice.

49. See *Laws* 626 B–E.

50. On these points see Peter Singer, "Famine, Affluence, and Morality"; Onora Nell, "Lifeboat Earth," *Philosophy and Public Affairs* 4, 3 (Spring 1975): 273–92; Thomas Nagel, "Poverty and Food: Why Charity Is Not Enough," in Peter G. Brown and Henry Shue, eds., *Food Policy: The Responsibility of the United States in the Life and Death Choices*, pp. 54–62.

51. For one method of arriving at this estimate, see A. B. Atkinson, *The Economics of Inequality*, p. 252.

52. *New York Times*, 30 July 1978, p. E3.

53. Beitz, *Political Theory and International Relations*, pp. 136–43; Barry, "Circumstances of Justice and Future Generations," in R. I. Sikora and Brian Barry, eds., *Obligations to Future Generations*, pp. 242–44.

54. This gives rise to the well-known gibe that foreign aid is poor people in rich countries giving money to rich people in poor countries. For evidence that income distribution in poor countries is significantly more skewed than in richer ones, see *The Economics of Inequality*, pp. 247–48.

55. See Thomas Schwartz, "Welfare Judgments and Future Generations," *Theory and Decision* 11 (1979): 181–94, and "Obligations to Posterity," in Sikora and Barry, eds., *Obligations to Future Generations*, pp. 3–13. Readers interested in this question may profitably consult all the essays in this volume.

56. See *Theory of Justice*, p. 286.

57. See *Distributive Justice*, p. 120.

58. See "Welfare Judgments and Future Generations," pp. 188–91.

59. To avoid misunderstanding, I should make it clear that I also reject the universal application of Pareto optimality as a criterion for alternatives involving identical reference-groups. My strongest reason is that neither subjective individual preferences, nor objectively defined individual interests, nor any combination of the two, exhausts the full range of relevant moral considerations. For example, if *A* has committed a morally wrong act, then depriving *A* of some good may be the correct social choice even if *A* is made worse off and no one is made better off. The moral worth of states of affairs is sensitive to but is not determined by the preferences or interests of their constituent individuals. Pareto optimality ignores what I have called "relational goods." See pp. 83–85, 102–5. For some important additional considerations, see Sen, *Collective Choice and Social Welfare*, pp. 83–85, 196–98.

60. "On the Common Saying: 'This may be True in Theory, but it does not Apply in Practice'," in *Kant's Political Writings*, Hans Reiss, ed., p. 88.

61. I can hardly claim to have resolved this extraordinarily complex question. For an approach to which I am particularly sympathetic, see Martin P. Golding, "Obligations to Future Generations," *The Monist* 56, 1 (January 1972): 85–99. See also Brian Barry, "Justice Between Generations," in P. M. S. Hacker and J. Raz, eds., *Law, Morality, and Society: Essays in Honour of H. L. A. Hart*; Robert L. Cunningham, "Ethics, Ecology, and the Rights of Future Generations," *Modern Age* 19, 3 (Summer 1975): 260–71; Richard T. De George, "Do We Owe the Future Anything?" in Eugene Dais, ed., *Law and the Ecological Challenge*, pp. 180–90, and "The Environment, Rights, and Future Generations," in Kenneth E. Goodpastor and Kenneth M. Sayre, eds., *Ethics and Problems of the 21st Century*, pp. 93–105; Robert L. Heilbroner, "What Has Posterity Ever Done for

Me?" in *An Inquiry into the Human Prospect*, pp. 169–76.

62. *Politics* 1. 5. 1254b10–13.

63. See *Politics* 1. 8. 1256b15–22.

64. See *Theory of Justice*, pp. 101, 107, 326–32.

65. See *Anarchy, State, and Utopia*, p. 167n.

66. See *Doing and Deserving*, p. 57.

67. See *Social Contract*, 2:11.

68. See *Kant's Political Writings*, p. 78.

69. See especially Norman Daniels, "Equal Liberty and Unequal Worth of Liberty," in Daniels, ed., *Reading Rawls*, pp. 253–81.

70. See *Ethics* 9. 6.

71. On preference for one's own, see *Ethics* 8. 9. 1159b35–1160a8; Dworkin, "Liberalism," in Hampshire, ed., *Public and Private Morality*, p. 125.

72. For some intriguing reflections on these and related problems, see Albert Hirschman, *Exit, Voice, and Loyalty*, especially chaps. 3, 4, and 7.

73. *Ethics* 1. 5. 1095b27–30.

74. For another discussion of some of these issues, coupled with a spirited defense of the compatibility of the unequal distribution of honor and equality of human worth, see Gregory Vlastos, "Justice and Equality," in Richard Brandt, ed., *Social Justice*, pp. 63–72. For the most comprehensive treatment of the phenomenon of public honor, see William J. Goode, *The Celebration of Heroes: Prestige as a Control System*.

Chapter Seven

1. See *Politics* 3. 1. 1275b5–7.

2. On the points raised in the preceding three paragraphs, see Frohlich and Oppenheimer, *Modern Political Economy*, chap. 6.

3. See *Theory of Justice*, p. 360.

4. *Politics* 7. 9. 1328b37–1329a2.

5. *Politics* 7. 8. 1328a37–40.

6. *Politics* 7. 10. 1330a31–33.

7. *Politics* 7. 9. 1329a15–16.

8. *Ethics* 8. 1. 1155a26–27.

Bibliography

Ackerman, Bruce. *Private Property and the Constitution*. New Haven: Yale University Press, 1977.

Adorno, Theodor W., et al. *The Positivist Dispute in German Sociology*. Translated by Glyn Adey and David Frisby. New York: Harper & Row, 1976.

Anscombe, G. E. M. "Modern Moral Philosophy." In *The Is–Ought Question*, edited by W. D. Hudson. London: Macmillan, 1969.

Aquinas, Thomas. *The Disputed Questions on Truth*. Translated by R. W. Mulligan. Chicago: Regnery, 1964.

Arendt, Hannah. *The Human Condition*. Chicago: University of Chicago Press, 1958.

Aristotle. *Nicomachean Ethics*. Translated by Martin Ostwald. Indianapolis: Bobbs-Merrill, 1962.

———. *On Interpretation*. Translated by E. M. Edghill. Edited by W. D. Ross. *The Works of Aristotle*, vol. 1. Oxford: Clarendon Press, 1928.

———. *On the Soul*. Translated by W. S. Hett. Loeb Classical Library. London: William Heinemann, 1935.

———. *Physics*. Translated by Richard Hope. Lincoln: University of Nebraska Press, 1961.

———. *Politics*. Translated by Ernest Barker. New York: Oxford University Press, 1958.

Arthur, John, and Shaw, William, eds. *Justice and Economic Distribution*. Englewood Cliffs: Prentice-Hall, 1978.

Atkinson, A. B. *The Economics of Inequality*. Oxford: Clarendon Press, 1975.

Atwell, John. "Objective Ends in Kant's Ethics." *Archiv für Geschichte der Philosophie* (Berlin) 56, 2 (1974): 156–71.

Barry, Brian. "Circumstances of Justice and Future Generations." In *Obligations to Future Generations*, edited by R. I. Sikora and Brian Barry. Philadelphia: Temple University Press, 1978.

———. "Justice Between Generations." In *Law, Morality, and Society: Essays in Honour of H. L. A. Hart*, edited by P. M. S. Hacker and J. Raz. Oxford: Clarendon Press, 1977.

————. *The Liberal Theory of Justice*. Oxford: Clarendon Press, 1973.

————. *Political Argument*. London: Routledge & Kegan Paul, 1965.

Bartlet, J. Vernon, ed. *Property: Its Duties and Rights*. 2d ed. London: Macmillan, 1915.

Bartley, W. W., III. *The Retreat to Commitment*. New York: Alfred A. Knopf, 1962.

Beardsmore, R. W. *Moral Reasoning*. London: Routledge & Kegan Paul, 1969.

Beauvoir, Simone de. *Force of Circumstance*. Translated by Richard Howard. New York: Putnam, 1965.

Becker, Lawrence C. *Property Rights: Philosophic Foundations*. London: Routledge & Kegan Paul, 1977.

Beitz, Charles R. *Political Theory and International Relations*. Princeton: Princeton University Press, 1979.

Benn, S. I., and Peters, R. S. *Social Principles and the Democratic State*. London: George Allen & Unwin, 1959.

Benthall, Jonathan, ed. *The Limits of Human Nature*. New York: Dutton, 1974.

Bergmann, Frithjof. *On Being Free*. Notre Dame: University of Notre Dame Press, 1977.

Berlin, Isaiah. "Equality as an Ideal." In *Justice and Social Policy*, edited by Frederick Olafson. Englewood Cliffs: Prentice-Hall, 1961.

————. *Four Essays on Liberty*. London: Oxford University Press, 1969.

Bowie, Norman, and Simon, Robert. *The Individual and the Political Order*. Englewood Cliffs: Prentice-Hall, 1977.

Boyle, Joseph M., Jr.; Grisez, Germain; and Tollefsen, Olaf. *Free Choice: A Self-Referential Argument*. Notre Dame: University of Notre Dame Press, 1976.

Brandt, Richard, ed. *Social Justice*. Englewood Cliffs: Prentice-Hall, 1962.

Calabresi, Guido, and Bobbitt, Philip. *Tragic Choices*. New York: W. W. Norton, 1978.

Casey, John. "Human Virtue and Human Nature." In *The Limits of Human Nature*, edited by Jonathan Benthall. New York: Dutton, 1974.

Coleman, Jules. Review of Ronald Dworkin, *Taking Rights Seriously*. *California Law Review* 66, 4 (1978): 885–919.

Cooper, John M. *Reason and Human Good in Aristotle*. Cambridge: Harvard University Press, 1975.

Cox, Robert W. "Ideologies and the New International Economic Order: Reflections on Some Recent Literature." *International Organization* 33, 2 (Spring 1979): 257–302.

Cunningham, Robert L. "Ethics, Ecology, and the Rights of Future Generations." *Modern Age* 19, 3 (Summer 1975): 260–71.

Dahl, Robert A., and Lindblom, Charles E. *Politics, Economics, and Welfare.* 2d ed. Chicago: University of Chicago Press, 1976.

Daniels, Norman. "Equal Liberty and Unequal Worth of Liberty." In *Reading Rawls,* edited by Norman Daniels. New York: Basic Books, 1974.

———. "Meritocracy." In *Justice and Economic Distribution,* edited by John Arthur and William Shaw. Englewood Cliffs: Prentice-Hall, 1978.

———. "Wide Reflective Equilibrium and Theory Acceptance in Ethics." *Journal of Philosophy* 76, 5 (May 1979): 256–82.

———, ed. *Reading Rawls.* New York: Basic Books, 1974.

De George, Richard T. "Do We Owe the Future Anything?" In *Law and the Ecological Challenge,* edited by Eugene Dais. Buffalo: William S. Hein, 1978.

———. "The Environment, Rights, and Future Generations." In *Ethics and Problems of the 21st Century,* edited by Kenneth E. Goodpastor and Kenneth M. Sayre. Notre Dame: University of Notre Dame Press, 1978.

del Vecchio, Giorgio. *Justice.* New York: Philosophical Library, 1953.

Derrida, Jacques. *Of Grammatology.* Translated by Gayatri Chakravorty Spivak. Baltimore: Johns Hopkins University Press, 1976.

Desan, Wilfred. *The Tragic Finale.* New York: Harper & Row, 1960.

Descartes, René. *Discourse on Method.* Translated by Arthur Wollaston. London: Penguin Books, 1960.

Dick, James. "How to Justify a Distribution of Earnings." *Philosophy and Public Affairs* 4, 3 (Spring 1975): 248–72.

Dworkin, Ronald. "Liberalism." In *Public and Private Morality,* edited by Stuart Hampshire. Cambridge: Cambridge University Press, 1978.

———. "The Original Position." In *Reading Rawls,* edited by Norman Daniels. New York: Basic Books, 1974.

———. *Taking Rights Seriously.* Cambridge: Harvard University Press, 1978.

Edwards, Paul. "Life, Meaning and Value of." In *The Encyclopedia of Philosophy,* edited by Paul Edwards. New York: Macmillan, 1967.

Feinberg, Joel. "Can Animals Have Rights?" In *Animal Rights and Human Obligations,* edited by Tom Regan and Peter Singer. Englewood Cliffs: Prentice-Hall, 1976.

———. *Doing and Deserving.* Princeton: Princeton University Press, 1970.

———. *Social Philosophy.* Englewood Cliffs: Prentice-Hall, 1973.

Fishkin, James S. *Tyranny and Legitimacy: A Critique of Political Theories.* Baltimore: Johns Hopkins University Press, 1979.

Fitzgerald, Ross, ed. *Human Needs and Politics.* Rushcutters Bay, Australia: Pergamon Press, 1977.

Flathman, Richard. "Equality and Generalization: A Formal Analysis." In *Nomos 9: Equality,* edited by J. Roland Pennock and John W. Chapman. New York: Atherton, 1967.

———. *The Practice of Rights.* Cambridge: Cambridge University Press, 1976.

———, ed. *Concepts in Social and Political Philosophy.* New York: Macmillan, 1973.

Foot, Philippa. *Virtues and Vices and Other Essays in Moral Philosophy.* Berkeley: University of California Press, 1978.

Fox, Michael. "Animal Liberation: A Critique." *Ethics* 88, 2 (January 1978): 106–18.

———. "Animal Suffering and Rights." *Ethics* 88, 2 (January 1978): 134–38.

Frankena, William. *Ethics.* Englewood Cliffs: Prentice-Hall, 1963.

Frey, R. G. "Animal Rights." *Analysis* 37, 4 (June 1977): 186–89.

Fried, Charles. "Difficulties in the Economic Analysis of Rights." In *Markets and Morals,* edited by Gerald Dworkin, Gordon Bermant, and Peter G. Brown. New York: John Wiley, 1977.

Frohlich, Norman, and Oppenheimer, Joe. *Modern Political Economy.* Englewood Cliffs: Prentice-Hall, 1978.

Galston, William. *Kant and the Problem of History.* Chicago: University of Chicago Press, 1975.

Gauthier, David, ed. *Morality and Rational Self-Interest.* Englewood Cliffs: Prentice-Hall, 1970.

Gewirth, Alan. *Reason and Morality.* Chicago: University of Chicago Press, 1978.

Godlovitch, S. and R., and Harris, J., eds. *Animals, Men, and Morals.* New York: Taplinger, 1972.

Golding, Martin P. "Obligations to Future Generations." *The Monist* 56, 1 (January 1972): 85–99.

Goode, William J. *The Celebration of Heroes: Prestige as a Control System.* Berkeley: University of California Press, 1978.

Gregor, Mary. *The Laws of Freedom.* New York: Barnes & Noble, 1963.

Habermas, Jürgen. *Communication and the Evolution of Society.* Boston: Beacon Press, 1979.

———. *Knowledge and Human Interests.* Boston: Beacon Press, 1972.

———. *Legitimation Crisis.* Boston: Beacon Press, 1975.

———. *Theory and Practice.* Boston: Beacon Press, 1973.

———. "Towards a Theory of Communicative Competence." *Inquiry* 13, 4 (Winter 1970): 360–75.

Hampshire, Stuart, ed. *Public and Private Morality.* Cambridge: Cambridge University Press, 1978.

Hare, R. M. "Descriptivism." In *The Is–Ought Question*, edited by W. D. Hudson. London: Macmillan, 1969.

———. *Freedom and Reason*. Oxford: Oxford University Press, 1963.

———. "Justice and Equality." In *Justice and Economic Distribution*, edited by John Arthur and William Shaw. Englewood Cliffs: Prentice-Hall, 1978.

Haworth, Lawrence. "Rights, Wrongs, and Animals." *Ethics* 88, 2 (January 1978): 95–105.

Hegel, Georg W. F. *The Encyclopedia of the Philosophical Sciences*. Vol. 1: *Logic*. Translated by William Wallace. Oxford: Clarendon Press, 1892. Vol. 2: *Philosophy of Nature*. Translated by A. V. Miller. Oxford: Clarendon Press, 1970. Vol. 3: *Philosophy of Mind*. Translated by A. V. Miller and William Wallace. Oxford: Clarendon Press, 1971.

———. *The Phenomenology of Mind*. Translated by J. B. Baillie. New York: Harper & Row, 1967.

Heilbroner, Robert L. "What Has Posterity Ever Done for Me?" In *An Inquiry into the Human Prospect*. New York: W. W. Norton, 1975.

Held, Virginia. "Rationality and Reasonable Cooperation." *Social Research* 44, 4 (Winter 1977): 708–44.

———, Nielsen, Kai, and Parsons, Charles, eds. *Philosophy and Political Action*. New York: Oxford University Press, 1972.

Heller, Agnes. "Towards a Marxist Theory of Value." *Kinesis* 5, 1 (Fall 1972).

Herman, Barbara. "Morality as Rationality: A Study of Kant's Ethics." Ph.D. dissertation, Harvard University, 1976.

Herodotus. *The Histories*. Translated by Aubrey de Sélincourt. Baltimore: Penguin Books, 1954.

Hirschman, Albert. *Exit, Voice, and Loyalty*. Cambridge: Harvard University Press, 1970.

Hobbes, Thomas. *Leviathan*. Edited by Michael Oakeshott. New York: Crowell-Collier, 1962.

Hobhouse, L. T. *The Elements of Social Justice*. London: George Allen & Unwin, 1922.

Hudson, W. D. *Modern Moral Philosophy*. Garden City: Doubleday, 1970.

———, ed. *The Is–Ought Question*. London: Macmillan, 1969.

Hull, David L. *Philosophy of Biological Science*. Englewood Cliffs: Prentice-Hall, 1974.

Hume, David. *An Inquiry Concerning the Principles of Morals*. Edited by Charles Hendel. Indianapolis: Bobbs-Merrill, 1957.

———. *A Treatise of Human Nature*. Edited by L. A. Selby-Bigge. Oxford: Clarendon Press, 1888.

Jaffa, Harry. "Aristotle." In *History of Political Philosophy*, edited by Leo

Strauss and Joseph Cropsey. Chicago: Rand McNally, 1963.

Jamieson, Dale, and Regan, Tom. "Animal Rights: A Reply to Frey." *Analysis* 38, 1 (January 1978): 32–36.

Jones, Hardy. *Kant's Principle of Personality.* Madison: University of Wisconsin Press, 1971.

Kalin, Jesse. "In Defense of Egoism." In *Morality and Rational Self-Interest,* edited by David Gauthier. Englewood Cliffs: Prentice-Hall, 1970.

Kant, Immanuel. *Critique of Practical Reason.* Translated by Lewis White Beck. Indianapolis: Bobbs-Merrill, 1956.

———. *Critique of Pure Reason.* Translated by Norman Kemp Smith. London: Macmillan, 1963.

———. *Foundations of the Metaphysics of Morals.* Translated by Lewis White Beck. Indianapolis: Bobbs-Merrill, 1959.

———. "Perpetual Peace." In *Kant's Political Writings,* edited by Hans Reiss. Cambridge: Cambridge University Press, 1971.

Kateb, George. *Utopia and Its Enemies.* New York: Schocken, 1972.

Kekes, John. *A Justification of Rationality.* Albany: SUNY Press, 1976.

Knight, Frank. *Risk, Uncertainty, and Profit.* Boston: Houghton Mifflin, 1921.

Körner, Stephan, ed. *Practical Reason.* New Haven: Yale University Press, 1974.

Lindblom, Charles E. *Politics and Markets: The World's Political Economic Systems.* New York: Basic Books, 1977.

Locke, John. *Two Treatises of Government.* Edited by Peter Laslett. New York: Mentor, 1965.

Lyons, David. "Nature and Soundness of the Contract and Coherence Arguments." In *Reading Rawls,* edited by Norman Daniels. New York: Basic Books, 1974.

MacCallum, Gerald C., Jr. "Negative and Positive Freedom." In *Concepts in Social and Political Philosophy,* edited by Richard Flathman. New York: Macmillan, 1973.

McCarthy, Thomas. *The Critical Theory of Jürgen Habermas.* Cambridge: MIT Press, 1978.

———. "A Theory of Communicative Competence." *Philosophy of the Social Sciences* 3, 2 (June 1973): 135–56.

Machiavelli, Niccolò. *The "Prince" and the "Discourses."* New York: Random House, 1950.

Macpherson, C. B. *Democratic Theory.* Oxford: Clarendon Press, 1973.

———, ed. *Property: Mainstream and Critical Positions.* Toronto: University of Toronto Press, 1978.

Manuel, Frank E., and Fritzie P. *Utopian Thought in the Western World.* Cambridge: Harvard University Press, 1979.

Márkus, György. "Human Essence and History." *International Journal of Sociology* 4, 1 (Spring 1974): 82–135.

Meade, J. E. *The Just Economy*. London: George Allen & Unwin, 1976.

Medlin, Brian. "Ultimate Principles and Ethical Egoism." In *Morality and Rational Self-Interest*, edited by David Gauthier. Englewood Cliffs: Prentice-Hall, 1970.

Melden, A. I. *Rights and Persons*. Berkeley: University of California Press, 1977.

Miller, David. *Social Justice*. Oxford: Clarendon Press, 1976.

Miller, James. "Some Implications of Nietzsche's Thought for Marxism." *Telos* 37 (Fall 1978): 22–41.

Murphy, Jeffrie. *Kant: The Philosophy of Right*. London: Macmillan, 1970.

Nagel, Thomas. "Poverty and Food: Why Charity Is Not Enough." In *Food Policy: The Responsibility of the United States in the Life and Death Choices*, edited by Peter G. Brown and Henry Shue. New York: Free Press, 1977.

————. "Rawls on Justice." In *Reading Rawls*, edited by Norman Daniels. New York: Basic Books, 1974.

Narveson, Jan. "Animal Rights." *Canadian Journal of Philosophy* 7, 1 (March 1977): 161–78.

Nathan, N. M. L. *The Concept of Justice*. London: Macmillan, 1971.

Nell, Onora. "Lifeboat Earth." *Philosophy and Public Affairs* 4, 3 (Spring 1975): 273–92.

Nietzsche, Friedrich. *Birth of Tragedy*. Translated by Clifton Fadiman. In *The Philosophy of Nietzsche*. New York: Random House, 1927.

————. *Use and Abuse of History*. Translated by Adrian Collins. Indianapolis: Bobbs-Merrill, 1957.

Nozick, Robert. *Anarchy, State, and Utopia*. New York: Basic Books, 1974.

Oakeshott, Michael. *Rationalism in Politics*. London: Methuen, 1962.

O'Brien, George. *An Essay on Mediaeval Economic Teaching*. London: Longmans, Green, 1920.

Pen, Jan. *Income Distribution: Facts, Theories, Policies*. New York: Praeger, 1971.

Pennock, J. Roland, and Chapman, John W., eds. *Nomos 9: Equality*. New York: Atherton, 1967.

Peters, R. S., ed. *Nature and Conduct*. London: Macmillan, 1975.

Phillips, D. Z., and Mounce, H. O. "On Morality's Having a Point." In *The Is–Ought Question*, edited by W. D. Hudson. London: Macmillan, 1969.

Plato. *Gorgias*. Translated by W. C. Helmbold. Indianapolis: Bobbs-Merrill, 1952.

———. *Laws*. Translated by R. G. Bury. London: William Heinemann, 1926.

———. *Republic*. Translated by Allan Bloom. New York: Basic Books, 1968.

———. *Symposium*. Translated by W. H. D. Rouse. In *Great Dialogues of Plato*. New York: Mentor, 1956.

Rachels, James. "What People Deserve." In *Justice and Economic Distribution*, edited by John Arthur and William Shaw. Englewood Cliffs: Prentice-Hall, 1978.

Radnitzky, Gerard. *Contemporary Schools of Metascience*. Göteborg: Akademiförlaget, 1970.

Rashdall, Hastings. *The Theory of Good and Evil*. 2d ed. London: Oxford University Press, 1924.

Rawls, John. "Outline of a Decision Procedure for Ethics." *Philosophical Review* 60, 2 (April 1951): 177–97.

———. *A Theory of Justice*. Cambridge: Harvard University Press, 1971.

Regan, Tom. "Fox's Critique of Animal Liberation." *Ethics* 88, 2 (January 1978): 126–33.

———. "Narveson on Egoism and the Rights of Animals." *Canadian Journal of Philosophy* 7, 1 (March 1977): 179–86.

——— and Singer, Peter, eds. *Animal Rights and Human Obligations*. Englewood Cliffs: Prentice-Hall, 1976.

Rescher, Nicholas. *Distributive Justice*. Indianapolis: Bobbs-Merrill, 1966.

Riley, Patrick. "On the 'Kantian' Foundations of Robert Paul Wolff's Anarchism." In *Nomos 19: Anarchism*, edited by J. Roland Pennock and John W. Chapman. New York: New York University Press, 1978.

Robinson, Joan. *The Accumulation of Capital*. London: Macmillan, 1958.

Rodman, John. "The Liberation of Nature?" *Inquiry* 20, 1 (Spring 1977): 83–131.

Ross, W. D. *The Right and the Good*. Oxford: Clarendon Press, 1930.

Rousseau, Jean-Jacques. *The First and Second Discourses*. Translated by Roger and Judith Masters. New York: St. Martin's Press, 1964.

———. *On the Social Contract*. Translated by Judith Masters. New York: St. Martin's Press, 1978.

Ryan, John. *Distributive Justice*. New York: Macmillan, 1935.

Salt, Henry. "Logic of the Larder." In *Animal Rights and Human Obligations*, edited by Tom Regan and Peter Singer. Englewood Cliffs: Prentice-Hall, 1976.

Sartre, Jean-Paul. *Being and Nothingness*. Translated by Hazel Barnes. New York: Citadel, 1965.

Scanlon, T. M. "Preference and Urgency." *Journal of Philosophy* 72, 19 (6 November 1975): 655–69.

————. "Rights, Goals, and Fairness." In *Public and Private Morality*, edited by Stuart Hampshire. Cambridge: Cambridge University Press, 1978.

Schaar, John. "Equality of Opportunity, and Beyond." In *Nomos 9: Equality*, edited by J. Roland Pennock and John W. Chapman. New York: Atherton, 1967.

Schlatter, Richard. *Private Property: The History of an Idea*. New Brunswick: Rutgers University Press, 1951.

Schwartz, Thomas. "Obligations to Posterity." In *Obligations to Future Generations*, edited by R. I. Sikora and Brian Barry. Philadelphia: Temple University Press, 1978.

————. "Welfare Judgments and Future Generations." *Theory and Decision* 11, 2 (June 1979): 181–94.

Sen, Amartya K. *Collective Choice and Social Welfare*. San Francisco: Holden-Day, 1970.

————. *On Economic Inequality*. Oxford: Clarendon Press, 1973.

Sher, George. "Effort, Ability, and Personal Desert." *Philosophy and Public Affairs* 8, 4 (Summer 1979): 361–76.

Sikora, R. I., and Barry, Brian, eds. *Obligations to Future Generations*. Philadelphia: Temple University Press, 1978.

Singer, Peter. *Animal Liberation*. New York: New York Review Press, 1975.

————. "The Fable of the Fox and the Unliberated Animals." *Ethics* 88, 2 (January 1978): 119–25.

————. "Famine, Affluence, and Morality." *Philosophy and Public Affairs* 1, 3 (Spring 1972): 229–43.

Slote, Michael. "Desert, Consent, and Justice." *Philosophy and Public Affairs* 2, 4 (Summer 1973): 323–47.

Smart, J. J. C., and Williams, Bernard. *Utilitarianism: For and Against*. Cambridge: Cambridge University Press, 1973.

Stanley, John. "Equality of Opportunity as Philosophy and Ideology." *Political Theory* 5, 1 (February 1977): 61–74.

Strauss, Leo. *Natural Right and History*. Chicago: University of Chicago Press, 1953.

Tucker, Robert W. *The Inequality of Nations*. New York: Basic Books, 1977.

Vlastos, Gregory. "Justice and Equality." In *Social Justice*, edited by Richard Brandt. Englewood Cliffs: Prentice-Hall, 1962.

————. *Platonic Studies*. Princeton: Princeton University Press, 1973.

Wallace, James D. *Virtues and Vices*. Ithaca: Cornell University Press, 1978.

Walzer, Michael. *Just and Unjust Wars*. New York: Basic Books, 1977.

Wanniski, Jude. *The Way the World Works: How Economies Fail—and*

Succeed. New York: Basic Books, 1978.

Ward, Keith. "Kant's Teleological Ethics." *Philosophical Quarterly* 21, 85 (October 1971): 337–51.

Watkins, J. W. N. "Comprehensively Critical Rationalism." *Philosophy* 44, 167 (January 1969): 57–62.

Williams, Bernard. "The Idea of Equality." In *Philosophy, Politics, and Society: Second Series,* edited by Peter Laslett and W. G. Runciman. New York: Barnes and Noble, 1962.

Winch, Peter. *Ethics and Action.* London: Routledge & Kegan Paul, 1972.

Wittgenstein, Ludwig. *Philosophical Investigations.* Translated by G. E. M. Anscombe. 3d ed. New York: Macmillan, 1962.

Wolff, Robert Paul. *Understanding Rawls.* Princeton: Princeton University Press, 1977.

Young, Michael. *The Rise of the Meritocracy.* New York: Random House, 1959.

Zaitchik, Alan. "On Deserving to Deserve." *Philosophy and Public Affairs* 6, 4 (Summer 1977): 371–88.

Zetterbaum, Marvin. "Equality and Human Need." *American Political Science Review* 71, 3 (September 1977): 983–99.

Index

Ability: as criterion for citizenship, 266; intrinsic satisfaction of, 179; and material rewards, 179; military, 62; technical, and political authority, 179, 184–85; undesirable, 62; and worth, 179

Abolitionists, 23

Absolute prohibitions, 29

Action: as basis for equality, 158; and character, 204–5; and claims, 201; and concept of agency, 99; consequences of, 137–38; and contradiction, 88; distinguished from animal behavior, 158; formal features of, 8, 14, 49–50; intrinsic characteristics of, 137–38; moral, 86; and moral philosophy, 14; political, 27–28, 30; and possibility, 31; and production, 27; and propositions, 88; and rational expectations, 201; and truth claims, 89

Agathon, 76–77

Analytical separation, 84, 103

Animality, 43, 89–90

Animals: and equal treatment, 157; good of, 161–62; interests of, 8, 125–26; killing of, 95; use of, in research, 21–22

Antigone, 284

Appropriateness, 111–12

Aquinas, Thomas, 19

Arendt, Hannah, 27–28

Aristocracy, natural, 156, 158

Aristophanes, 79

Aristotle: on advantage, 102; on animality, 91–92, 127; on animals, 162, 260–61; on citizenship, 281; on civic friendship, 267; on continuous activity, 67–68; on democracy, 277; on desire to know, 53; on *energeia*, 24; on equality, 10; on experience, 19; on friendship, 282; on habit, 26; on happiness, 82; on heterogeneity of political claims, 289 n.17; on highest good, 66–67; on honor, 274–75; as ideal utilitarian, 281; on justice, 6, 101, 102, 160, 299 n.9; on leisure, 46; on love of one's own, 152; on making and judging, 115, 272; on methods of inquiry, 26; on moral argument, 59; on pain, 58; on particularity, 26; on *physis*, 24; on Plato's *Republic*, 2, 32, 130–31; on politics, 27, 28, 30, 118; on possibility, 26, 31; on priority of the good, 78; on private property, 227–28; on production and action, 179; on property, 226; on reason as liberation, 65; on rule of the poor, 279; on self-interest, 101–2; on sense of justice, 156; on sensitivity, 290 n.25; on slavery, 281; on suicide, 58; on technical hierarchies, 183; on temporal and teleological ends, 26; on tribe and polis, 195; on virtue, 24, 54, 56–57; on worth of existence, 58; *Eudemian Ethics*, 66; *Metaphysics*, 46, 53; *Nicomachean Ethics*, 66–67; *On the Soul*, 290 n.25; *Politics*, 281

Art, 284

Assignment, 109, 111–12

Atwell, John, 39–40

Augustine, 19

Authority: in process of production, 238; and specialization, 183–84; within technical activities, 183–84

Bankruptcy, laws of, 146

Barry, Brian: on ambiguity of self-interest, 115; on desert, 172–73, 176; on equal access to natural resources, 249; on international justice, 120–21; on needs, 162–63; on primary goods, 114; on reference groups, 7

Beardsmore, R. W., 20–23

Beauvoir, Simone de, 2–3

313

Index

Beethoven, Ludwig van, 61–62
Beitz, Charles, 249
Beneficence, 10
Benn, S. I., 143–44, 197
Bentham, Jeremy, 135, 144
Bergmann, Frithjof, 98–99
Berlin, Isaiah, 289 n.3
Bradley, F. H., 21
Brentano, Franz, 53–54, 61
Burke, Edmund, 14–15

Callicles, 18, 34, 42, 71, 88–89
Capacities: as basis of claims, 160; duality of, 160–61; extraordinary, 161; higher and lower, 68–69, 160; and ideal utilitarianism, 160; individual, 161; inseparable from individuals, 160; as nonrelational goods, 160; ordering among, 67–69; principle of choice among, 69; and unity of the self, 68
Capital: and entrepreneurship, 216–17; and inheritance, 212; interest on, 214–15; productivity of, 213–14; and propensity to consume, 215; and property, 212; requirement for, 213; return on, 216; and savings, 212–13
Catholic church, 253, 277
Certainty, quest for, 19, 59
Character, 103, 204–5
Children: birth defects in, 61, 254–55; development of senses in, 61; love of, for parents, 268; love of parents for, 151–52; malnutrition in, 61; obligation to have, 253–54; obligations of, 99, 268–69; sacrifice of parents for, 240; training of, 166; treatment of least talented, 263
Chomsky, Noam, 35
Christian view of politics, 19, 28
Cicero, 63
Citizenship, 265; as accident of birth, 121; and cultural understanding, 267–68; and democracy, 277–78; equality of, 172, 265–66; European, and Christianity, 268; and independence, 266; and intellectual ability, 266; Jewish, 268; and judgment of policy, 271; and just economy, 266; and loyalty, 268–69; and mental normality, 266–67; and merit, 153; and production, 281; and self-preference, 267; sufficient conditions of, 269–70; unequal aptitudes for, 156–57; valid claims to, 265–70

Civil rights movement, 23
Claim-rights, 139–41; and democratic decisionmaking, 139–40; and desert, 140; as prima facie, 139; and promises, 139; as social institutions, 139; teleological understanding of, 139
Claims, 2, 5, 105; absolute, 146; of actual existence, 253; based on voluntary transactions, 198; as basis of rights, 134; as constraints on maximizing principles, 259; and criteria, 146; and harm to others, 106; and individuals, 140; of potential existence, 253–54; possible satisfaction of, 146; relative, 146
Coleman, Jules, 135–36
Colonialism, 251
Competition: and cooperation, 182; ineradicable, 181; promotes community, 181–82; range of, 182–83; and scarcity, 182; and self-esteem, 182
Consciousness, 75–82
Consent, 179
Conservatism, 30, 34
Contemplation, 71, 79–80
Contradiction, 23, 89
Contribution: and capital, 210–17 (*see also* Capital; Savings); as claim on production, 201; and duration, 203–4; and effort, 204–6 (*see also* Effort); and entrepreneurship, 217–18 (*see also* Entrepreneurship); general criterion of, 210–11; and incentives, 224–25; and invention, 218–21 (*see also* Invention); and moral education, 223–24; and moral sentiments, 223–24; opportunities for, 201, 204; personal, 211–12; as principle of income distribution, 223; and productivity, 206–8 (*see also* Productivity); and proportionality, 203; and quality, 208–9; and relative worth of tasks, 209–11; and sacrifice, 201–3 (*see also* Sacrifice); social, 211–12
Cooperation, 1–2; and intellectual development, 64; not natural, 63; origination of, 208; in production, 207–8
Courage, 65, 105
Cowardice, 101
Creon, 284
Cyrus, 232

Daniels, Norman, 297 n.74
Da Vinci, Leonardo, 68

314

property, 229–30, 232; and requirements of justice, 101; and risk, 241–42; seriousness of, 241

Hedonism, 18

Hegel, Georg W. F.: on actuality, 23–24; on animal desire, 290 n.25; existentialist critique of, 2–3; on Kantian morality, 38; on Kant's utopianism, 15; on the moral life, 21; on realm of absolute spirit, 284

History, 24–25

Hitler, Adolf, 15

Hobbes, Thomas: on abuses of speech, 47–48; on equality and consent, 179; on happiness, 73–74; on justice, 2, 20, 54, 120–21, 280; on morality as social, 48–49, 293 n.42; on reasoning, 64; on self-interest, 2; on worth of tasks, 211

Hobhouse, L. T., 211–12, 225

Human good: and access to resources, 249; as basis for teleological theory, 141; and complex communities, 195; contributions to, 209–11; and economic production, 195; as ends rather than means, 6; no absolute right to, 94; not equivalent to preferences, 56; not purely instrumental, 56; not a single developed capacity, 67; role of a theory of, 6; social influences on, 113–14; and tasks, 234

—elements of, 7; independent of one another, 93; intrinsic rather than instrumental, 93; priority among, 58, 95; trade-offs among, 7, 94. *See also* Development; Existence; Rational Action, Principle of; Subjective satisfaction

—principles of: and belief, 57; and fundamental features of human existence, 57–58; and moral sphere, 57; and practical reasoning, 57; and theories of justice, 56; ultimate, 57

Human nature, 32–35

Hume, David: on forced transfers, 232–33; on individual characteristics and justice, 194; on priority of self-interest over justice, 117; on scarcity, 6, 116–17; on scope of justice, 102, 112–13; on social modification of distributive patterns, 114

Immanent: critique, 23

—arguments, 41–51; strengths and weaknesses of, 51–52

Immigration: and collective selfishness, 245–46; and conditions for citizenship, 269–70; and domestic policy, 245; and income distribution, 245; and injustice, 270; and international distribution, 250; Jewish, 245; legitimate limits on, 244–45; Mexican, 245

Impartiality, 248

Incentives: as basis of income distribution, 221–22; competitive determination of, 222; constraints on, 224–25, 242; and desert-claims, 200; distinguished from compensation, 221; and education, 221; and intrinsic worth of tasks, 179, 221–22; within just system, 222; material, 33; purpose of, 225; surplus from, 225

Income, distribution of. *See* Contribution; Incentives; Need

Individuality: compatible with abstract qualities, 153–54; and contingency, 154; and equality of development, 159–60; and personal qualities, 151; personal qualities inseparable from, 154; and private property, 227; and temporality, 154

Individuals: as benchmark of justice, 7, 106–8; benefit to, 92; equal worth of development of, 159–62

Industrial Revolution, 229

Injustice, collective, 107

Instruments, 124–25

Integrity, 48–49

Interests, 158; as basis for equality, 158–59; distinguished from preferences, 129–30, 145; not confined to human beings, 159; not of equal weight, 159; relation of, to moral reflection, 159; universalizability of, 145

International distribution: and collective selfishness, 248; economic requirements of, 248; and equal access to natural resources, 249–50; and immigration policy, 250; and independence, 251; and intervention, 250; and justice between generations, 251; and man-made disasters, 248–49; and need, 248, 251; practical difficulties of, 250; and production, 247–48; as regressive, 301 n.54; and reparations, 246; and self-preference, 248; strategies of, 251. *See also* Justice, international

Intuitionism, 3–4

Index

Invention, 218; and competitive economies, 219; and entrepreneurship, 218–19; and imperfect benevolence, 218; joint, 220; net contribution of, 219–20; and pace of innovation, 220; as personal property, 218–21; and public benefit, 220; socialized system of, 220–21

Jefferson, Thomas, 172, 185
Jesus, 68, 114
Julius Caesar, 68
Just war, 121–22
Justice: and appropriateness, 55, 101, 104–5; and claims, 259; and the common good, 1–2; comparative, 101; and comparative needs, 167–68; as component of political excellence, 272; and democracy, 277–79; and deontology, 3; distinguished from legality, 26; and distribution, 109–16; divine, 110; domain of, 85, 110–16, 193; effects of, on recipients, 103–4; elements of theory of, 92; epistemological status of, 5; and exclusive possession, 92–93; and extreme situations, 119; and false consciousness, 111; and friendship, 282; and the good, 55; and grading, 111; individual, 101; and individuals, 3, 55, 93, 104, 106–8; and initial holdings of resources, 249–50; and institutions, 276–77, 283; interest in, 1; internal definition of, 100, 280; and intrinsic goods, 105; limits of, 147, 282–84; and love, 282; and loyalty, 269; and maximization, 258–59; as maximizing satisfaction of valid claims, 142; and moral harm, 292 n.10; as natural duty, 4–5; and natural facts, 110; as negative principle, 147; in nonideal circumstances, 13; and opportunities for development (*see* Opportunities for development); oriented toward the present, 104; partial indeterminacy of, 149–50, 208, 225; as personal advantage, 280–81; and political practice, 283; and possessive relations, 5, 102–4; as prima facie requirement, 108–9; problematic character of, 1–2, 279–80; and property, 226; and public honor, 274 (*see also* Public honor); and rationality, 55, 90, 92, 280; as relation among relations, 101, 107; and sacrifice, 281; and scarcity, 116–20; and self-love, 282; sense of, 156; as social

virtue, 101; and states of affairs, 5, 100, 104–5; and tasks, 234 (*see also* Tasks, organization and allocation of); theoretical character of, 105–6; and voluntary transactions, 195, 233; as way of life for community, 115
—in allocation and organization of tasks. *See* Tasks, allocation and organization of
—toward animals, 7, 124–26; and development, 260–61; and domestication, 260–61; and existence, 260; and interests, 260; reasons for renewed interest in, 124. *See also* Animals
—economic, 195–96. *See also* Income, distribution of; Justice toward animals; Justice between generations; Justice, international; Property; Tasks, allocation and organization of
—Formal Principle of, 143, 149; and substantive principles, 143–45; violation of, 147
—between generations, 6–7; aggregate component of, 255; asymmetry of, 255; and different populations, 252–55; as equal opportunity, 258; and eternity of the human species, 256; and future possibilities, 254; and the human good, 256; and impartiality, 252; and international justice, 251; moral significance of, 259–60; and obligation to reproduce, 253–54; and physical need, 255–56; and potential beneficiaries, 253–55; and present needs, 224; and production, 259; and progress, 256, 259–60; sacrifice entailed by, 253; and savings, 213; and states of the world, 252–53; supererogatory, 256
—international, 6, 120–24, 244–51; and community self-preference, 121; and differences among regimes, 123–24; and economic questions, 123; general views of, 246; and legal relations, 121; and political divisions, 121–22; and principle of nonintervention, 123; and principle of sovereign equality, 123; and scarcity, 123; universalistic view of, 120–21. *See also* Exploitation; Immigration; International distribution
—political. *See* Citizenship; Political leadership
—principles of: constraints on, 193; and individual characteristics, 194; and the

modern world, 194–95; and political institutions, 193–94
—substantive: Aristotelian Principle of, 149–50 (*see also* Proportionality); Determination Principle of, 148–49; Linearity Principle of, 148–49; Nonviolation Principle of, 146–47, 149; Ordinal Principle of, 146–48; Supply Principle of, 146–47, 149

Kant: on basis of equality, 155; on freedom, 97, 99; on human nature, 32–33; on impossible ideals, 80; on persons as ends-in-themselves, 38–41; on politics, 28; on possibility, 31–32; on progress, 259; on radical evil, 127; on rationality in morality, 40; and realism, 19; on the relation between virtue and happiness, 82–85; on relational goods, 84–85; on respect for persons, 174; on servile occupations, 266; on teleology, 12; on virtue as entitlement, 101; *Critique of Judgment*, 160
Kennedy, John, 273
Knight, Frank, 215–16
Knowledge, 80–81

Lack, 75–78
Laing, R. D., 267
Law, 106–7
Liberalism, 128, 233–34
Life. *See* Existence
Lincoln, Abraham, 278
Locke, John: on moral animality, 90; on property, 228–31; on rights, 188
Love: cannot be coerced, 187; and justice, 282; no entitlement to, 187; not directed to all equally, 152–53; outside public sphere, 187; relation of, to personal qualities, 151–53; and subjectivity, 295 n.23
Loyalty, 268; to basic principles of community, 269; distinguished from love, 269; to individuals, 269; and justice, 269; and political opposition, 269
Luxury, 164
Lying, 62. *See also* Truth-telling
Lyons, David, 5
Lysenko, Trofim, 284

MacCallum, Gerald, 98
McCarthy, Thomas, 41, 45, 46
Machiavelli, 23, 28

Majority rule, 107
Marcus Aurelius, 63
Marx, Karl: on human nature, 33; and labor-process, 234; on social harmony, 281; and utopian thought, 15
Marxism: and moral theory, 35; orthodox, 2, 15, 23
Maximin principle, 128; as basis for equal citizenship, 153; and democracy, 277; and political institutions, 194
Means: and ends, 29–31; limits on, in extreme situations, 117; temporality of, 286 n.31
Melden, A. I., 129
Mental: illness, 266–67
—retardation, 95; and citizenship, 266; and equal treatment, 157; neglect of, 159
Merit, 151; controversial, 190; multidimensional, 190; and purposes, 190. *See also* Moral worth
Meritocracy, 176; and ability, 297 n.74; and efficiency, 297 n.74; and liberalism, 176–77; and social institutions, 176. *See also* Equality of opportunity
Mill, John Stuart, 135; on Kantian morality, 38–39; on moral equality, 144; on plural voting, 157; on rights, 136; urgency and intrinsic worth in, 96
Miller, David: on claim-rights, 139–41; on desert, 172–76; on effort, 204; on needs, 162–63, 166; on plans of life, 166–68; on productivity, 207–8; on the subject matter of justice, 100
Moderation, 100–102
Moral: propositions, 143; purity, 137; rebellion, 21; sincerity, 21
justification: involves general reasons, 89; may be abandoned, 89–92; requires more than internal rationality, 90–91; tendency toward, widely shared, 91
—reasons, 20–23, 105–6; individual benefit not sufficient as, 85–86; may be egoistic, 87; need not satisfy publicity criterion, 86–87; and sincerity, 86; tautologies not sufficient as, 86
—reflection: discrete v. continuous, 109; role of interests in, 159; and utopian thought, 109
—responsibility, 137; for desirable existence, 255; for human condition, 254; scope of, 204–5
—theory: as basis of utopian thought, 14;

319

philosophy, 161; *Gorgias,* 18, 42, 88; *Republic,* 1, 2, 14, 22, 32, 45, 54, 100, 176, 180, 227, 280; *Symposium,* 17, 76, 79, 82

Pleasure. *See* Subjective satisfaction

Political: change, 30–31; divisions, 122; harmony, 23; power, 113

—community: and collective goods, 196; as collective property, 249; good, 192; hyperindividualistic view of, 3; hyperorganic view of, 2; influence of size on, 122; just, 192; limits of, 283–84; as means to individual well-being, 3, 124; as natural, 4–5; need for moral education in, 192–93, 276; not based on friendship, 63; as organic unity, 130–31; and public services, 196; relation of individual to, 2–5, 99; requires political excellence, 185; as shared experience, 267–68; as shared fate, 141; unjust, 10; as way of life, 122

—institutions: aristocratic, 277; as barriers to injustice, 277; coercive, 276; democratic, 277–79; as imperfect procedures, 194; within just community, 276; and maximin principle, 194; as means, 8, 283; and political education, 276; and political leadership, 273; variability of, 193–94

—leadership, 172; activities of, 278; functions of, 271–72; and individual development, 273; and majority rule, 278; need for theory of, 115; rotation of, 272–73; selection of, 273; structural need for, 272; unequal capacity for, 272. *See also* Excellence, political

Politics: concerned with more than justice, 117; limits of, 284; role of tradition in, 44–45; significance of, 19

Popper, Karl, 15, 291 n.51

Possession, 30, 167

Possessive relations, 102; as formal feature of justice, 102–5; rest on concept of personal identity, 103

Possibility: categorial, 32; logical, 31; nomological, 32; practical, 32; and utopian thought, 31–32

Preferences, 56; distinction between personal and external, 135–36; and formal justice, 145; inadequate basis for moral theory, 141

Primary goods, 113–15. *See also* Need

Priority: among claims to productive tasks, 242; of equality of opportunity over property rights, 188; of internal dimension of tasks, 239–40; of need, 168, 199–200, 248, 251; among needs, 164, 168–69, 198, 224

Private resources, 196

Prizes, 150, 175

Production, systems of, 119

Productivity, 206; context of, 206–7; joint, 207–8; as partial distributive criterion, 207; and private property, 228; and worker control, 238

Promises, 108–9, 139

Property, 226; collective, 226; and control, 225–26; forced transfers of, 232–33; and harm, 229–30, 232; as institution, 233; and justice, 113, 226; and labor, 228–30; and money, 229; and need, 229–30, 232; and occupation, 231; political community as, 249; private, 227–28; and productivity, 228; and public authority, 233; rights to, not inviolable, 187–88; and scarcity, 226, 228–30; as self-expression, 33; and temporality, 226–27; and use, 228, 232; valid claims to, 228–33; and voluntary transactions, 230–31, 233

Proportionality, 6, 8; and ideal utilitarianism, 281–82; and task definitions, 190–91

Public honor, 6, 8, 274; as incentive, 274; as replacement for material incentives, 274–75; as reward, 274; and self-knowledge, 275; system of, 176; valid claims to, 274; and virtue, 274

Publicity criterion, 86–87

Punishment, 299 n.9; and desert, 173; and distribution, 109, 171–72; effects of, on criminals, 104; ignored in utopian theory, 193; justice of, 146–47; retributivist view of, 142; unjust, 101

Quality of work, 208–9

Rashdall, Hastings, 294 n.74

Rational action, principle of, 85; as basis for moral explanation, 91; as basis for self-mastery, 91; compared to theoretical rationality, 91; as force for moral coherence, 91; as moral choice, 88; as source of moral community, 91

Rawls, John: as balancing equality and inequality, 9–10; on citizenship, 115; concept of ideal theory in, 13; connection between politics and economics in, 266;